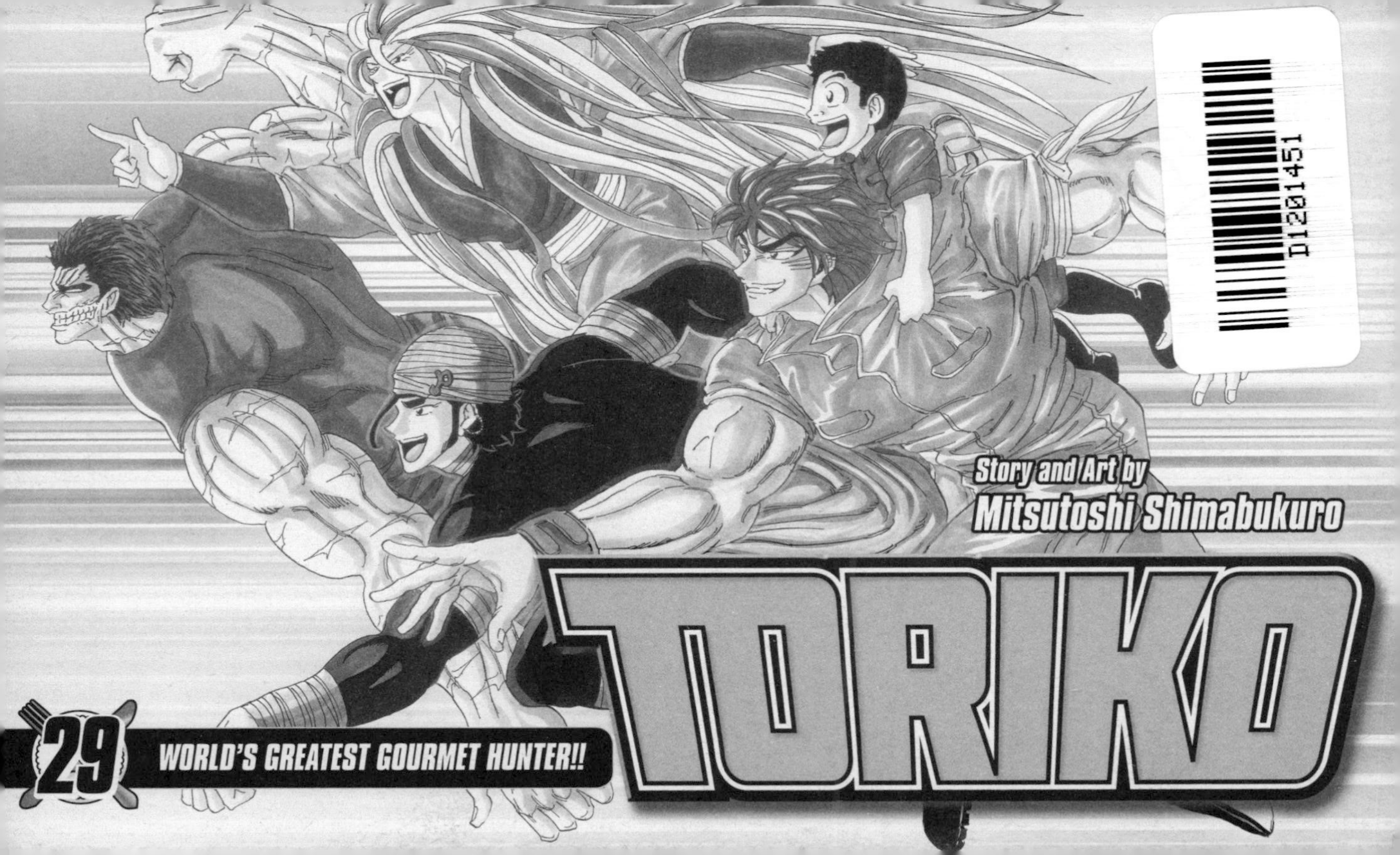

Story and Art by
Mitsutoshi Shimabukuro
TORIKO
29
WORLD'S GREATEST GOURMET HUNTER!!

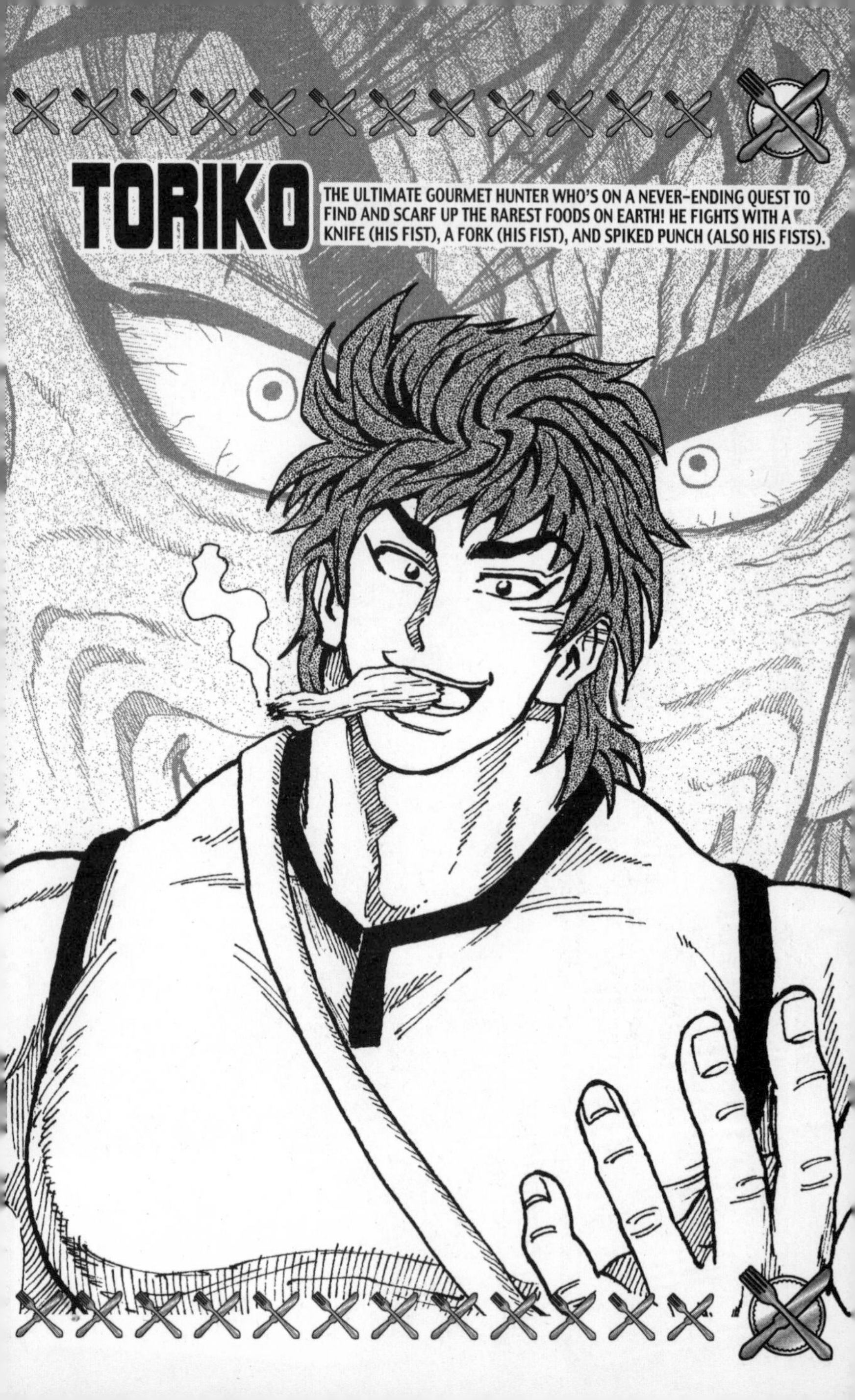
TORIKO
THE ULTIMATE GOURMET HUNTER WHO'S ON A NEVER-ENDING QUEST TO FIND AND SCARF UP THE RAREST FOODS ON EARTH! HE FIGHTS WITH A KNIFE (HIS FIST), A FORK (HIS FIST), AND SPIKED PUNCH (ALSO HIS FISTS).

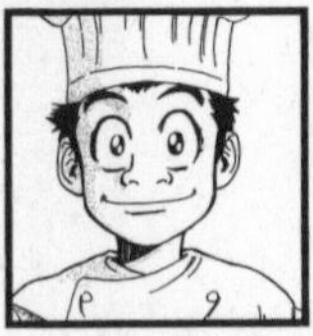

●KOMATSU
TALENTED IGO HOTEL CHEF AND TORIKO'S #1 FAN.

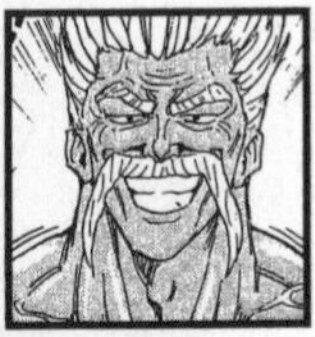

●ICHIRYU
HARDY IGO PRESIDENT AND DISCIPLE OF THE LATE GOURMET GOD ACACIA.

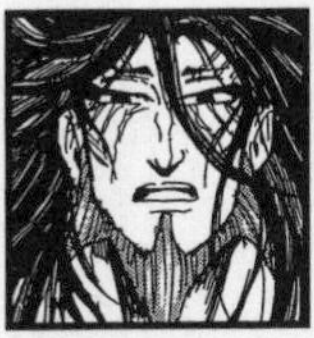

●MIDORA
BOSS OF GOURMET CORP. AND DISCIPLE OF ACACIA. LOOKING FOR GOD.

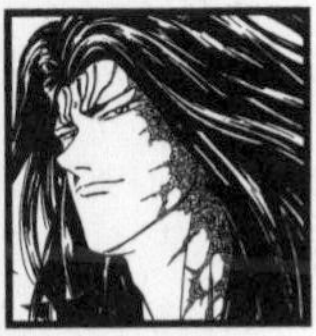

●STARJUN
ONE OF GOURMET CORP.'S THREE VICE-CHEFS. WANTS KOMATSU FOR HIS SKILLS.

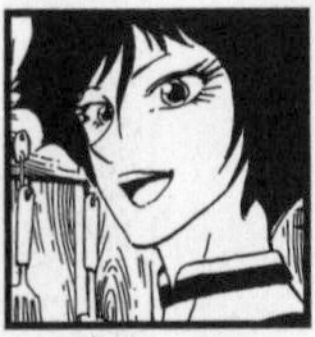

●FROESE
GOURMET GOD ACACIA'S CHEF PARTNER. SACRIFICED HER LIFE TO SAVE MIDORA.

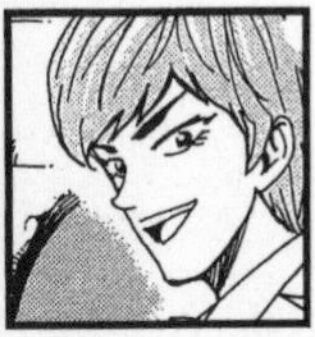

●OTAKE
KOMATSU'S BEST FRIEND. JOINED GOURMET CORP. AFTER RISING TO #99 ON THE WORLD CHEF RANKING.

WHAT'S FOR DINNER

IT'S THE AGE OF GOURMET! KOMATSU, THE HEAD CHEF AT THE HOTEL OWNED BY THE IGO (INTERNATIONAL GOURMET ORGANIZATION), BECAME FAST FRIENDS WITH THE LEGENDARY GOURMET HUNTER TORIKO WHILE GATOR HUNTING. THROUGH THEIR TRAINING AND ADVENTURES, THEY FIND THEMSELVES ENTANGLED IN THE IGO'S RIVALRY WITH THE NEFARIOUS GOURMET CORP.

AT THE COOKING FESTIVAL, WAR BREAKS OUT BETWEEN TWO RIVAL ORGANIZATIONS. WHILE THE BATTLE RAGES, BOTH SIDES ALSO CHASE AFTER GOURMET GOD ACACIA'S FULL-COURSE MEAL. AS FOR TORIKO, HIS LONG-AWAITED SHOWDOWN WITH STARJUN ENDS IN DEFEAT AND KOMATSU FALLS INTO STARJUN'S HANDS. MEANWHILE, IGO PRESIDENT ICHIRYU FACES OFF AGAINST THE BOSS OF GOURMET CORP., MIDORA. ONCE DISCIPLES OF ACACIA TOGETHER, NOW THEY ARE SWORN ENEMIES!

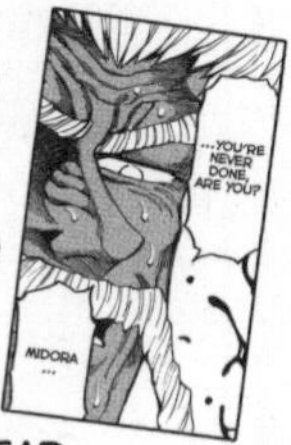
...YOU'RE NEVER DONE, ARE YOU?
MIDORA...

WHILE THE TWO SIDES TANGLE, A THIRD ORGANIZATION CALLED "NEO" EMERGES FROM THE SHADOWS, REVEALING DOUBLE AGENTS ON BOTH SIDES. SETSUNO IS CONVINCED THAT DARK CHEF JOIE IS BEHIND NEO, BUT WHEN SHE AND JIRO FIGHT HIM, JOIE'S BLACK CLOAK FALLS AWAY, REVEALING THE SUPPOSEDLY DEAD GOD CHEF FROESE!

AT THE END OF ALL THESE TORTUROUS BATTLES, THE HUMAN WORLD IS BOMBARDED WITH DEADLY "METEOR SPICE"! BETRAYALS ARE UNCOVERED, NEW RIDDLES COME TO LIGHT AND ICHIRYU CONTINUES TO BATTLE MIDORA. HOW WILL THE FINAL BATTLE REACH ITS TERRIBLE CONCLUSION?

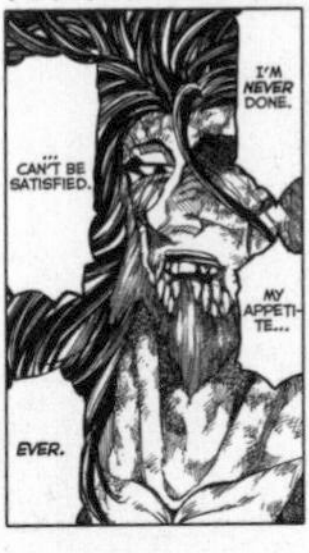
I'M NEVER DONE.
...CAN'T BE SATISFIED.
MY APPETITE...
EVER.

Contents

TORIKO

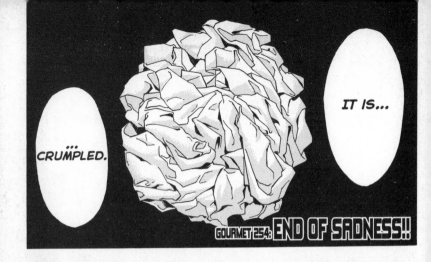

IT IS...

...CRUMPLED.

GOURMET 254: END OF SADNESS!!

EVER SINCE...

...THAT DAY...

SLIRRR

CH

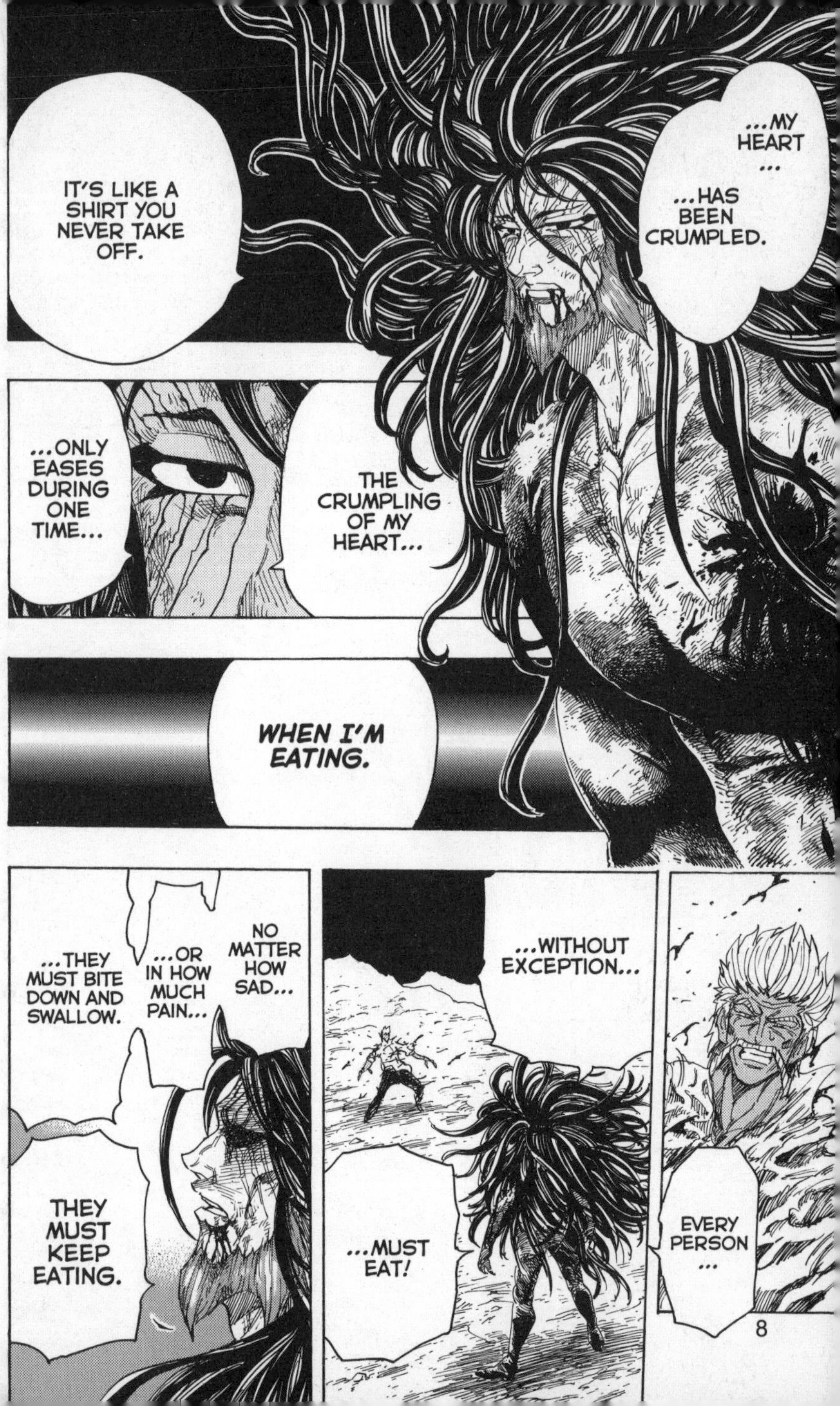
...MY HEART ... ...HAS BEEN CRUMPLED.
IT'S LIKE A SHIRT YOU NEVER TAKE OFF.
THE CRUMPLING OF MY HEART...
...ONLY EASES DURING ONE TIME...
WHEN I'M EATING.
EVERY PERSON ...
...WITHOUT EXCEPTION...
...MUST EAT!
NO MATTER HOW SAD...
...OR IN HOW MUCH PAIN...
...THEY MUST BITE DOWN AND SWALLOW.
THEY MUST KEEP EATING.

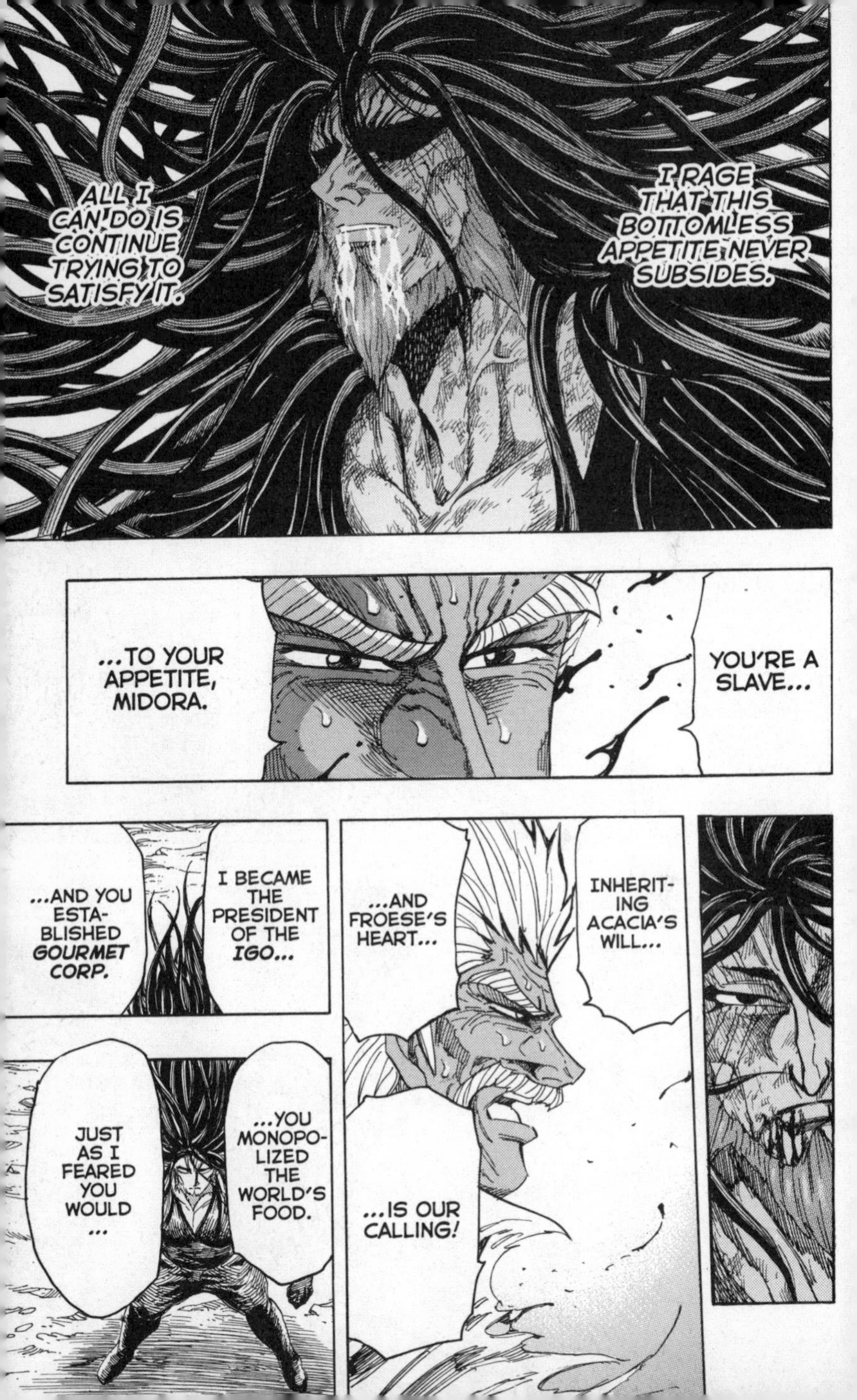
I RAGE THAT THIS BOTTOMLESS APPETITE NEVER SUBSIDES.
ALL I CAN DO IS CONTINUE TRYING TO SATISFY IT.
YOU'RE A SLAVE...
...TO YOUR APPETITE, MIDORA.
INHERIT-ING ACACIA'S WILL...
...AND FROESE'S HEART...
...IS OUR CALLING!
I BECAME THE PRESIDENT OF THE *IGO*...
...AND YOU ESTA-BLISHED *GOURMET CORP.*
...YOU MONOPO-LIZED THE WORLD'S FOOD.
JUST AS I FEARED YOU WOULD...

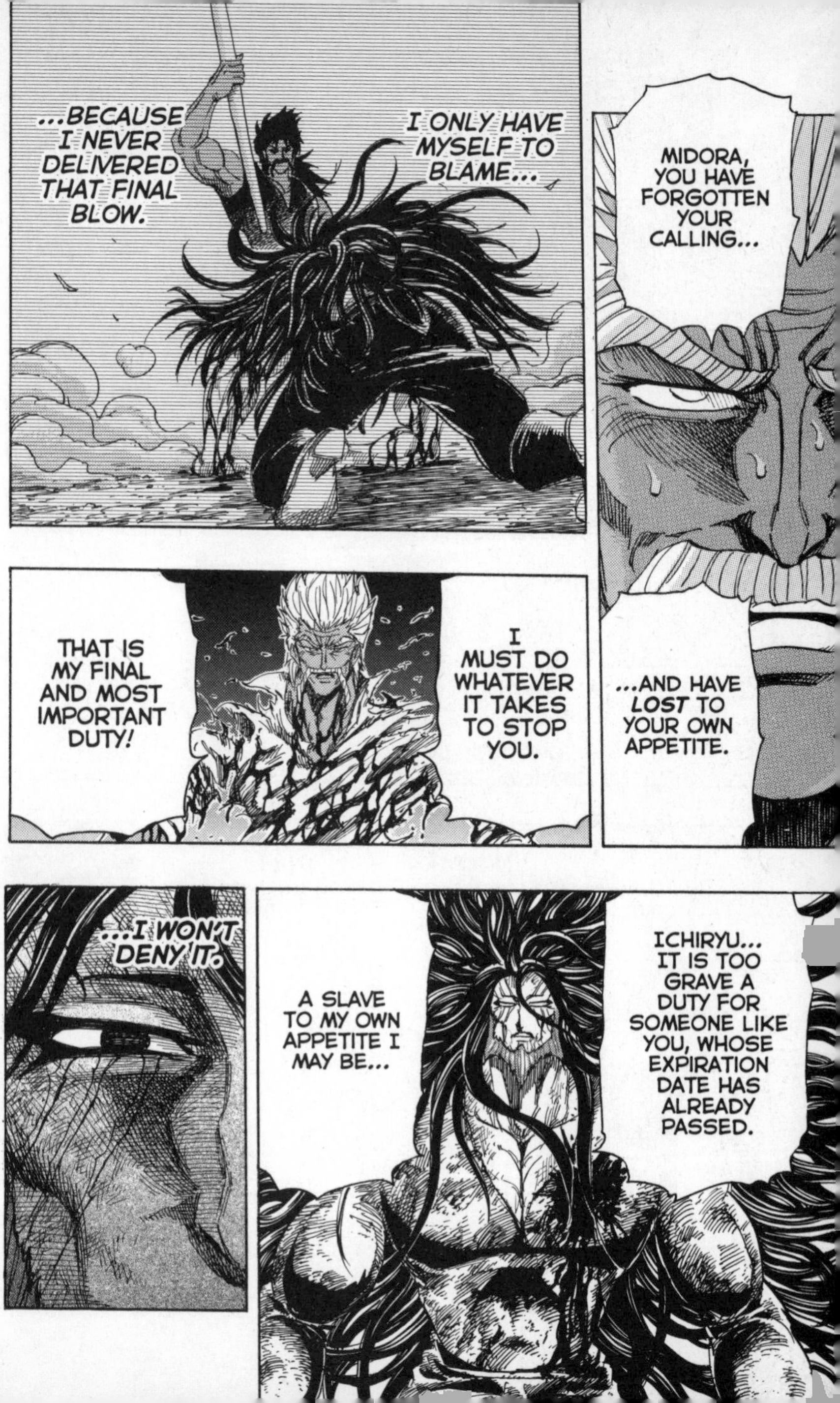
MIDORA, YOU HAVE FORGOTTEN YOUR CALLING...
...AND HAVE *LOST* TO YOUR OWN APPETITE.
I ONLY HAVE MYSELF TO BLAME...
...BECAUSE I NEVER DELIVERED THAT FINAL BLOW.
I MUST DO WHATEVER IT TAKES TO STOP YOU.
THAT IS MY FINAL AND MOST IMPORTANT DUTY!
ICHIRYU... IT IS TOO GRAVE A DUTY FOR SOMEONE LIKE YOU, WHOSE EXPIRATION DATE HAS ALREADY PASSED.
A SLAVE TO MY OWN APPETITE I MAY BE...
...I WON'T DENY IT.

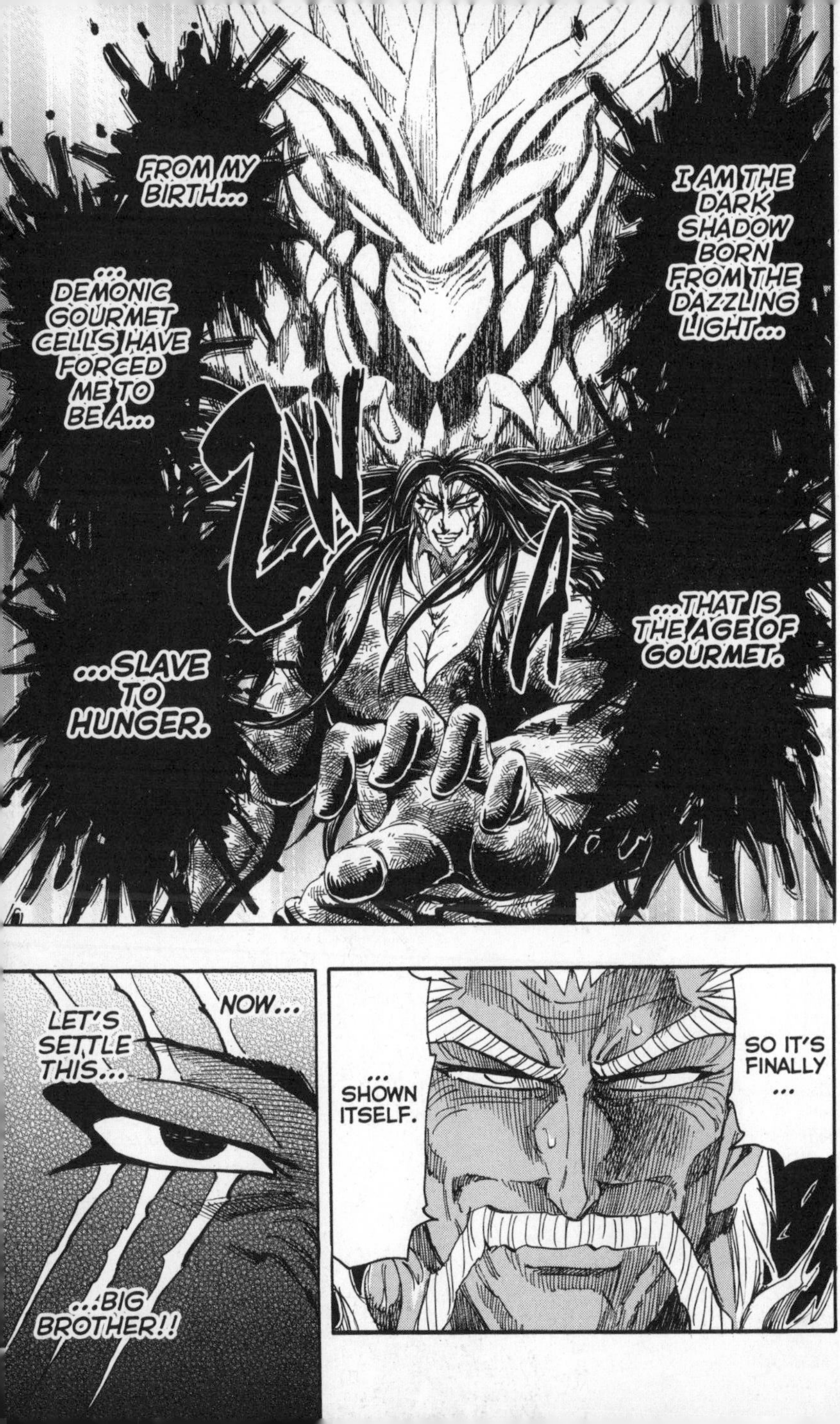
I AM THE DARK SHADOW BORN FROM THE DAZZLING LIGHT...
...THAT IS THE AGE OF GOURMET.
FROM MY BIRTH...
...DEMONIC GOURMET CELLS HAVE FORCED ME TO BE A...
...SLAVE TO HUNGER.
SO IT'S FINALLY...
...SHOWN ITSELF.
NOW...
LET'S SETTLE THIS...
...BIG BROTHER!!

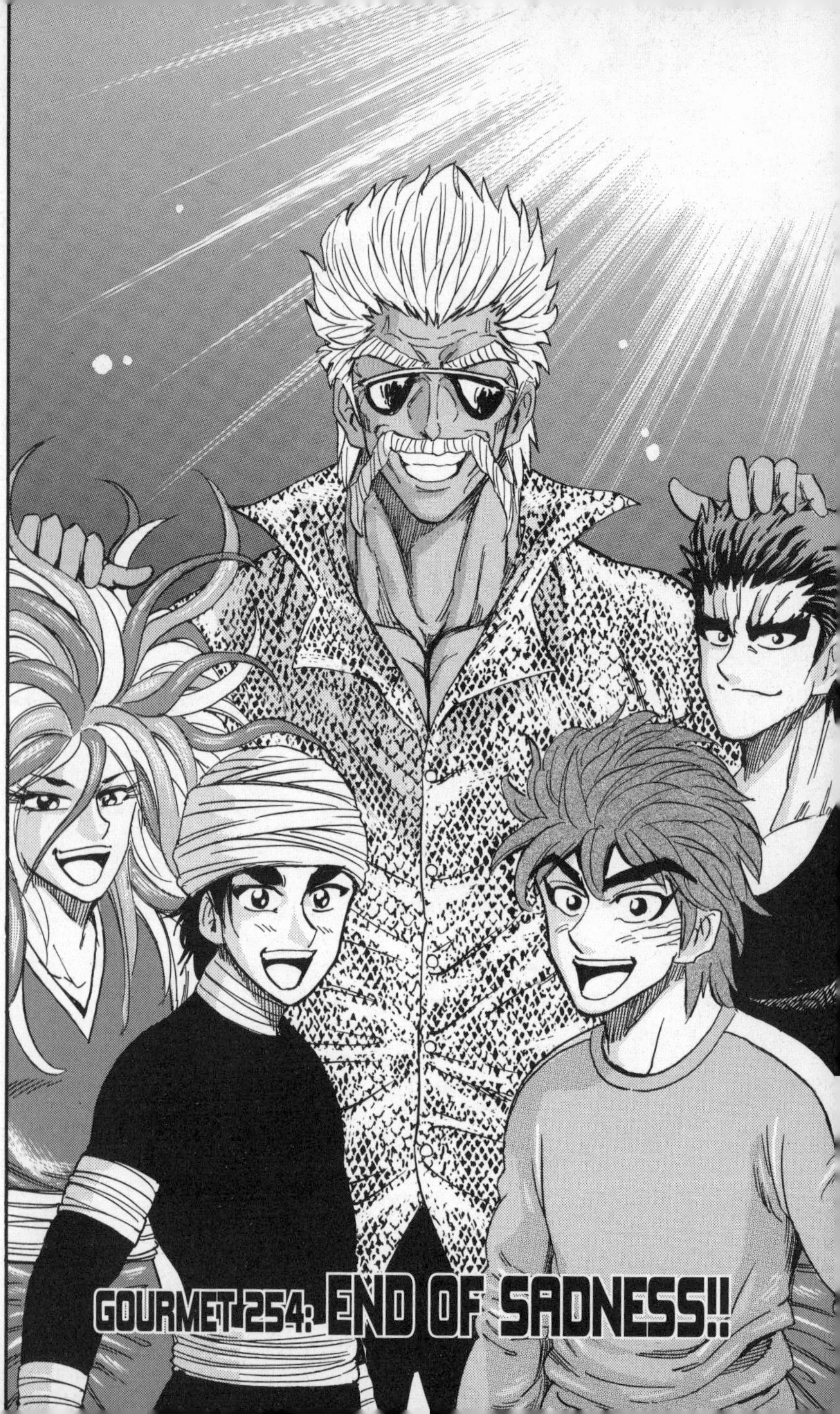
GOURMET 254: END OF SADNESS!!

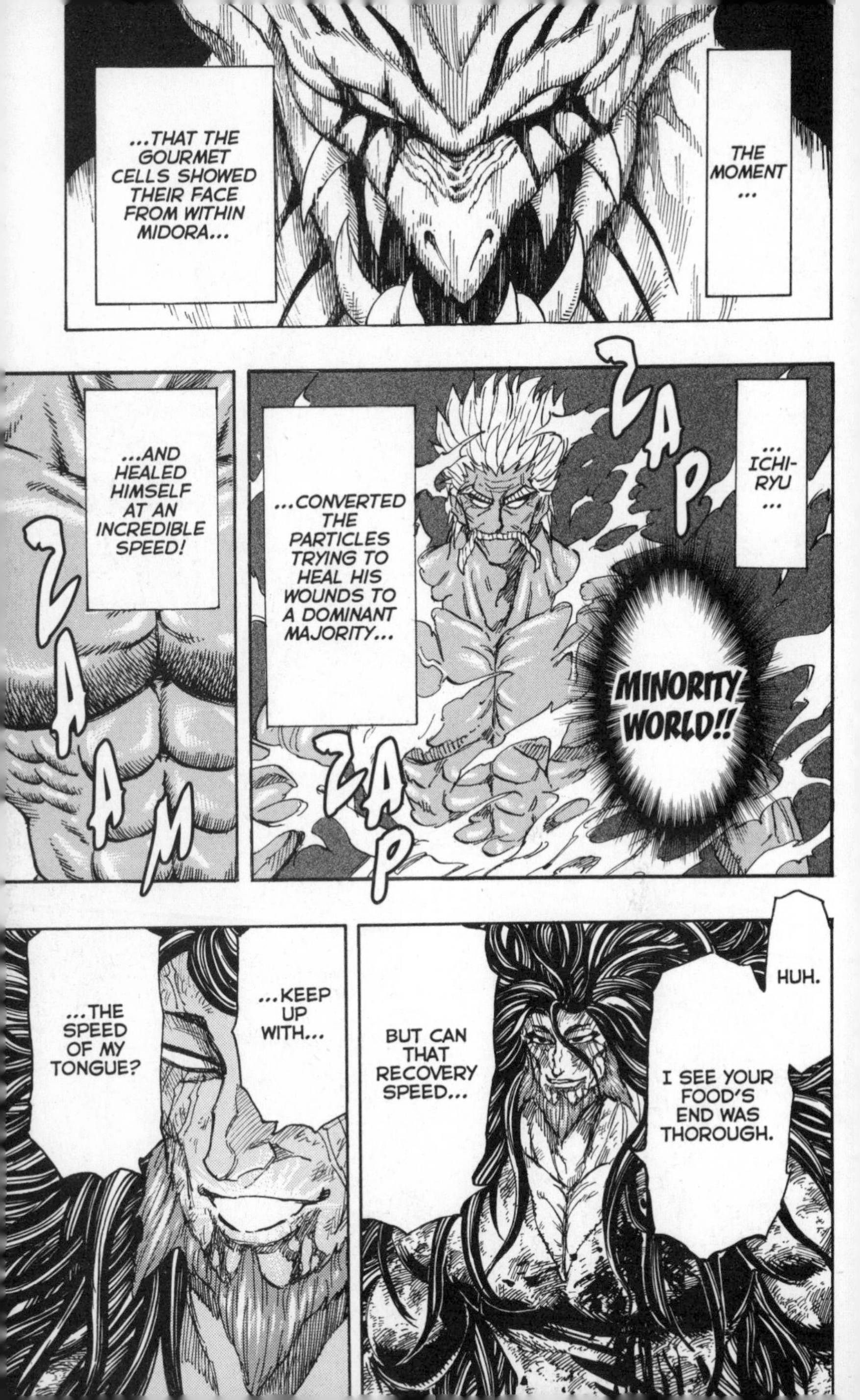
THE MOMENT...
...THAT THE GOURMET CELLS SHOWED THEIR FACE FROM WITHIN MIDORA...
...ICHIRYU...
ZAP
MINORITY WORLD!!
...CONVERTED THE PARTICLES TRYING TO HEAL HIS WOUNDS TO A DOMINANT MAJORITY...
ZAP
...AND HEALED HIMSELF AT AN INCREDIBLE SPEED!
ZAAAM
HUH.
I SEE YOUR FOOD'S END WAS THOROUGH.
BUT CAN THAT RECOVERY SPEED...
...KEEP UP WITH...
...THE SPEED OF MY TONGUE?

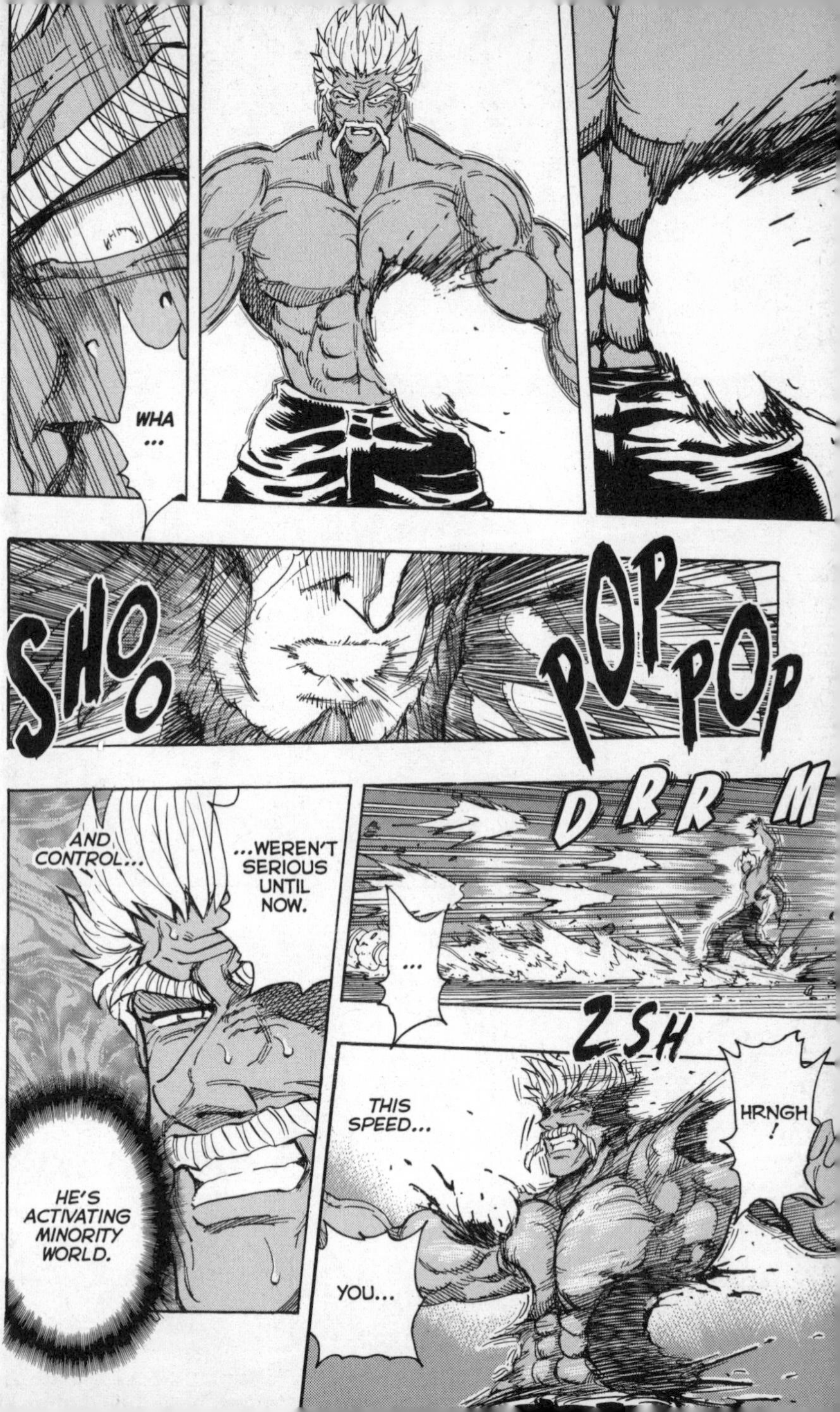
WHA...
POP POP
SHOO
DRRRM
...
ZSH
HRNGH!
THIS SPEED...
YOU...
...WEREN'T SERIOUS UNTIL NOW.
AND CONTROL...
HE'S ACTIVATING MINORITY WORLD.

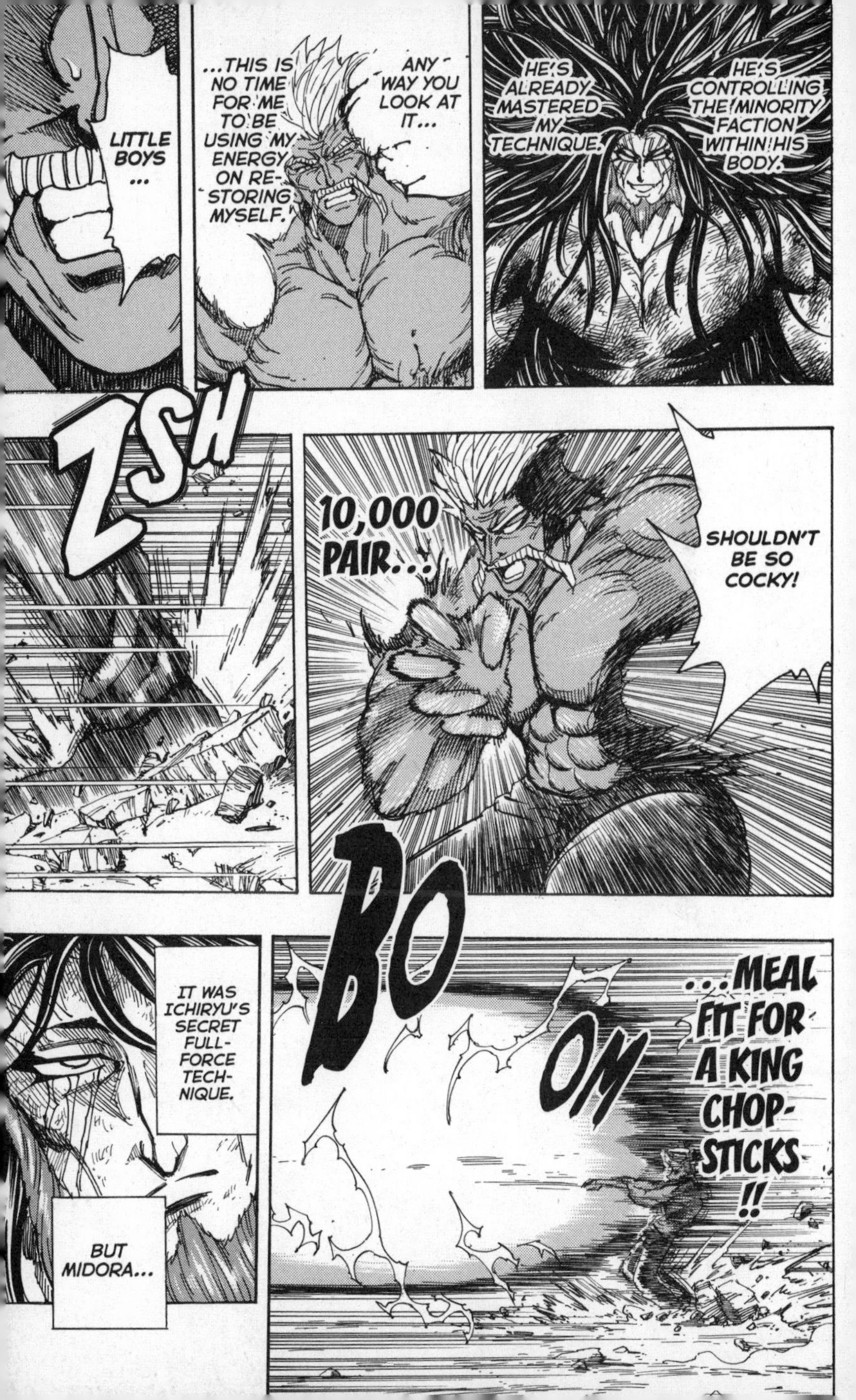
HE'S CONTROLLING THE MINORITY FACTION WITHIN HIS BODY.
HE'S ALREADY MASTERED MY TECHNIQUE.
ANY WAY YOU LOOK AT IT...
...THIS IS NO TIME FOR ME TO BE USING MY ENERGY ON RE-STORING MYSELF.
LITTLE BOYS ...
SHOULDN'T BE SO COCKY!
10,000 PAIR...
ZSH
BOOM
...MEAL FIT FOR A KING CHOP-STICKS!!
IT WAS ICHIRYU'S SECRET FULL-FORCE TECH-NIQUE.
BUT MIDORA...

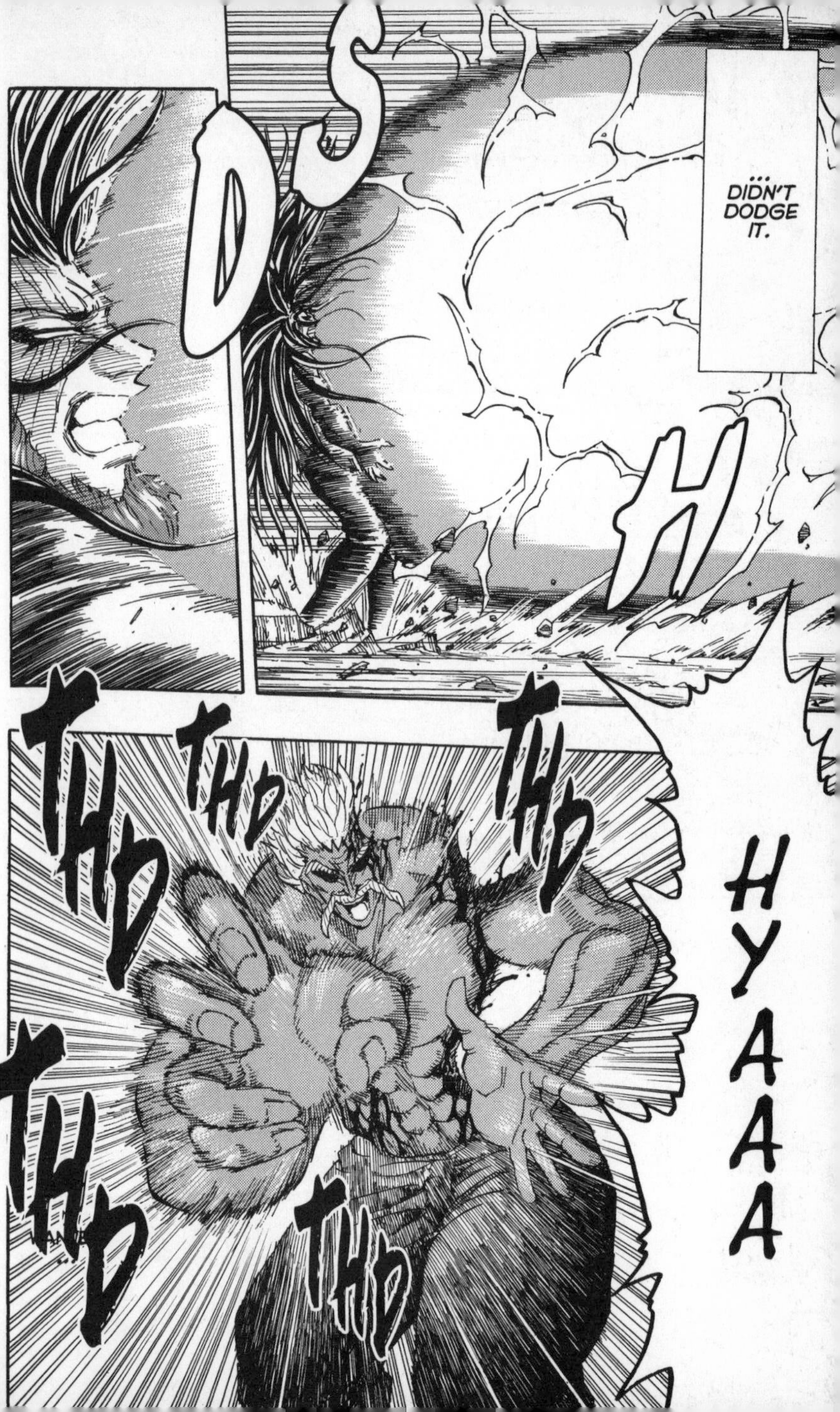
...
DIDN'T
DODGE
IT.
H
D
S
HYAAA
THD
THD
THD
THD
THD
THD

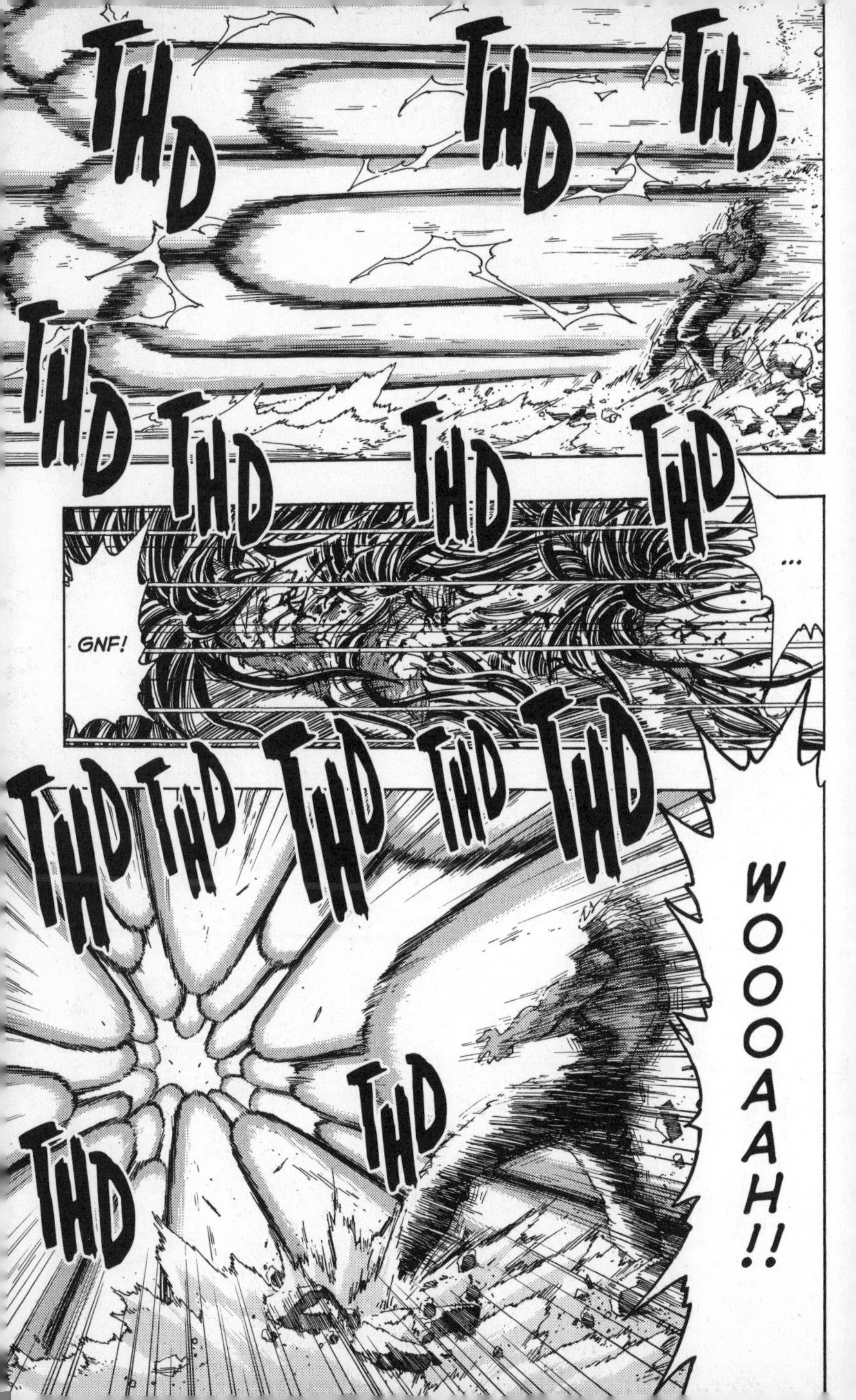
THD
THD
THD
THD
THD
THD
THD
...
GNF!
WOOOOAAH!!
THD
THD
THD
THD
THD
THD
THD

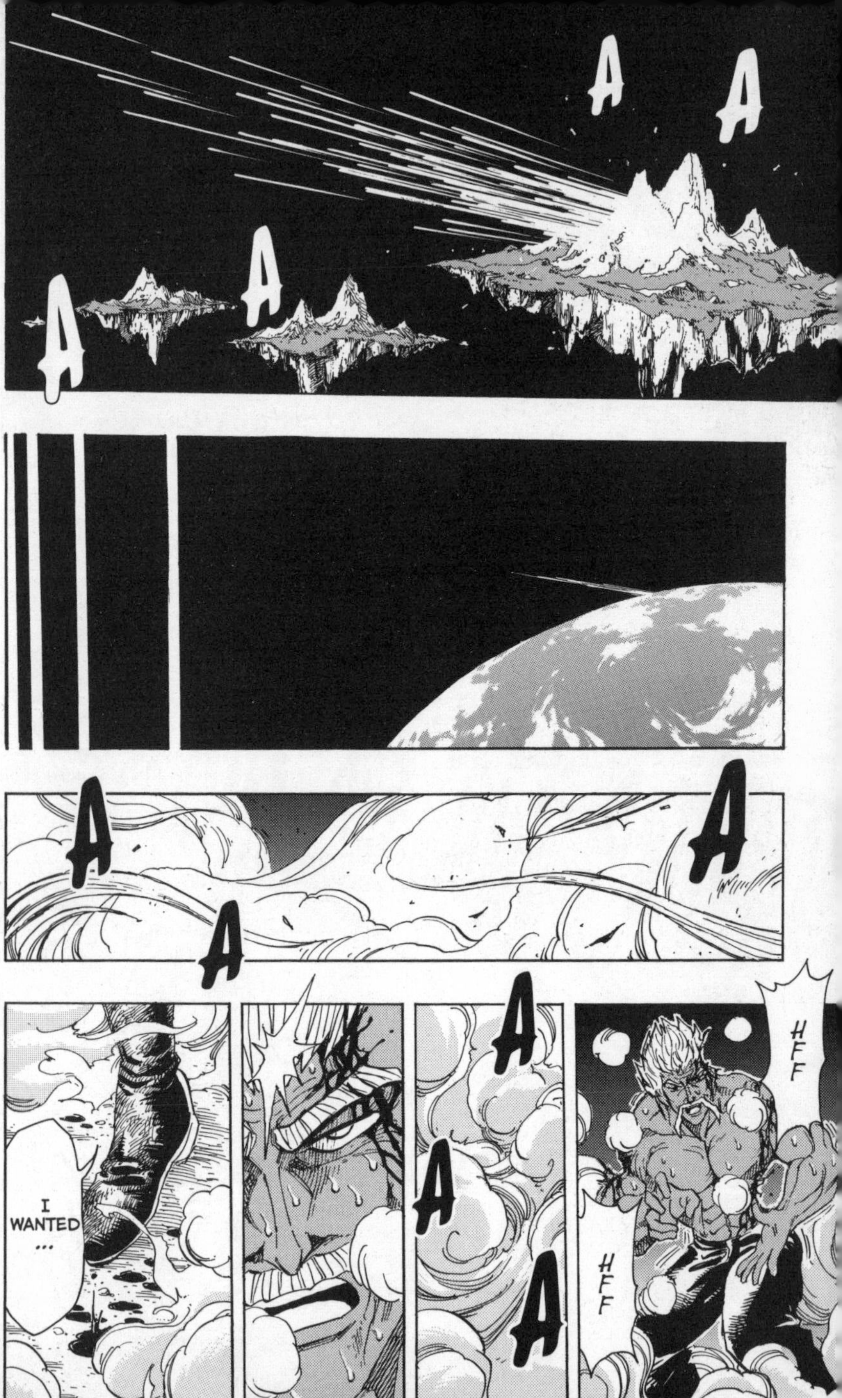
A
A
A
A
A
A
A
HFF
HFF
A
A
A
A
I WANTED ...

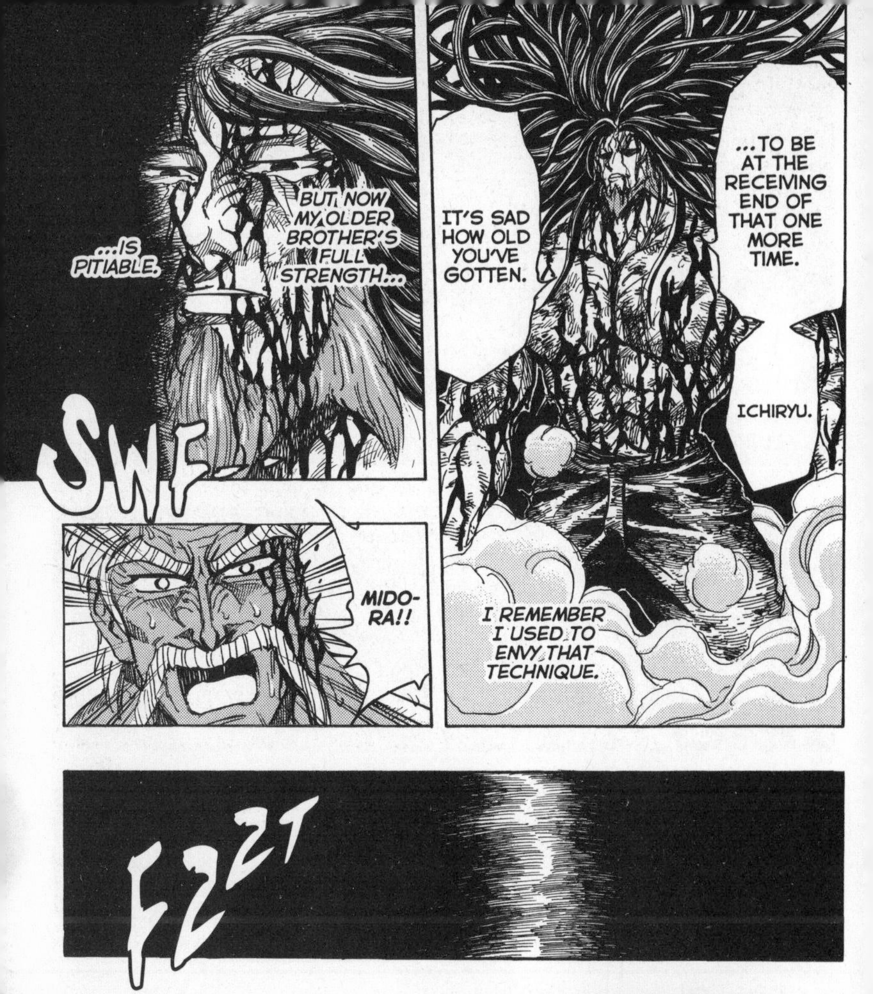
...TO BE AT THE RECEIVING END OF THAT ONE MORE TIME.
IT'S SAD HOW OLD YOU'VE GOTTEN.
ICHIRYU.
I REMEMBER I USED TO ENVY THAT TECHNIQUE.
BUT NOW MY OLDER BROTHER'S FULL STRENGTH...
...IS PITIABLE.
SWF
MIDO-RA!!
FZZT

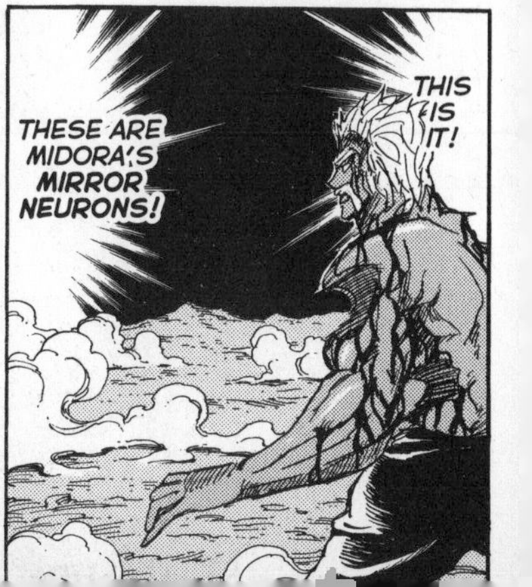
THIS IS IT!
THESE ARE MIDORA'S MIRROR NEURONS!

■MIRROR NEURONS

NEURONS THAT FIRE BOTH WHEN A CREATURE ACTS AND WHEN IT OBSERVES THE SAME ACT PERFORMED BY OTHERS.

IT IS SAID THAT OUR ABILITY TO COPY OTHERS' MOVEMENTS, ACQUIRE NEW SKILLS AND SYMPATHIZE IS THANKS TO MIRROR NEURONS.

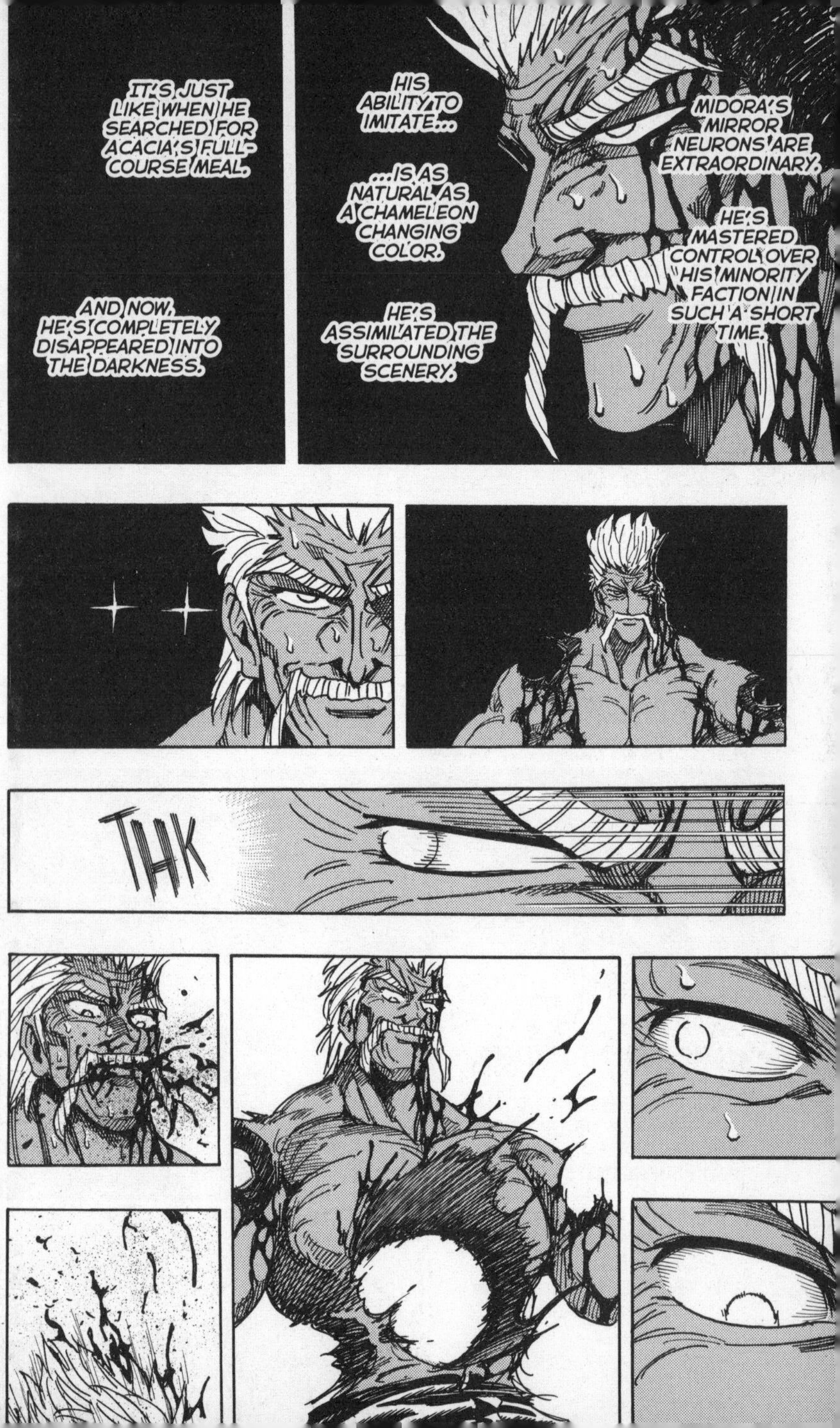

MIDORA'S MIRROR NEURONS ARE EXTRAORDINARY.
HE'S MASTERED CONTROL OVER HIS MINORITY FACTION IN SUCH A SHORT TIME.
HIS ABILITY TO IMITATE...
...IS AS NATURAL AS A CHAMELEON CHANGING COLOR.
HE'S ASSIMILATED THE SURROUNDING SCENERY.
IT'S JUST LIKE WHEN HE SEARCHED FOR ACACIA'S FULL-COURSE MEAL.
AND NOW, HE'S COMPLETELY DISAPPEARED INTO THE DARKNESS.
THK

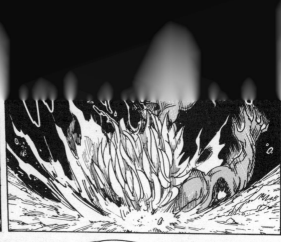

... UNH ...

SWFF

GFH ...

...

WHY ...

... CRIED ...

YOU ...

...THAT DAY TOO...

I'M HUNGRY.

WHY ARE YOU CRYING ...?

MIDORA ...

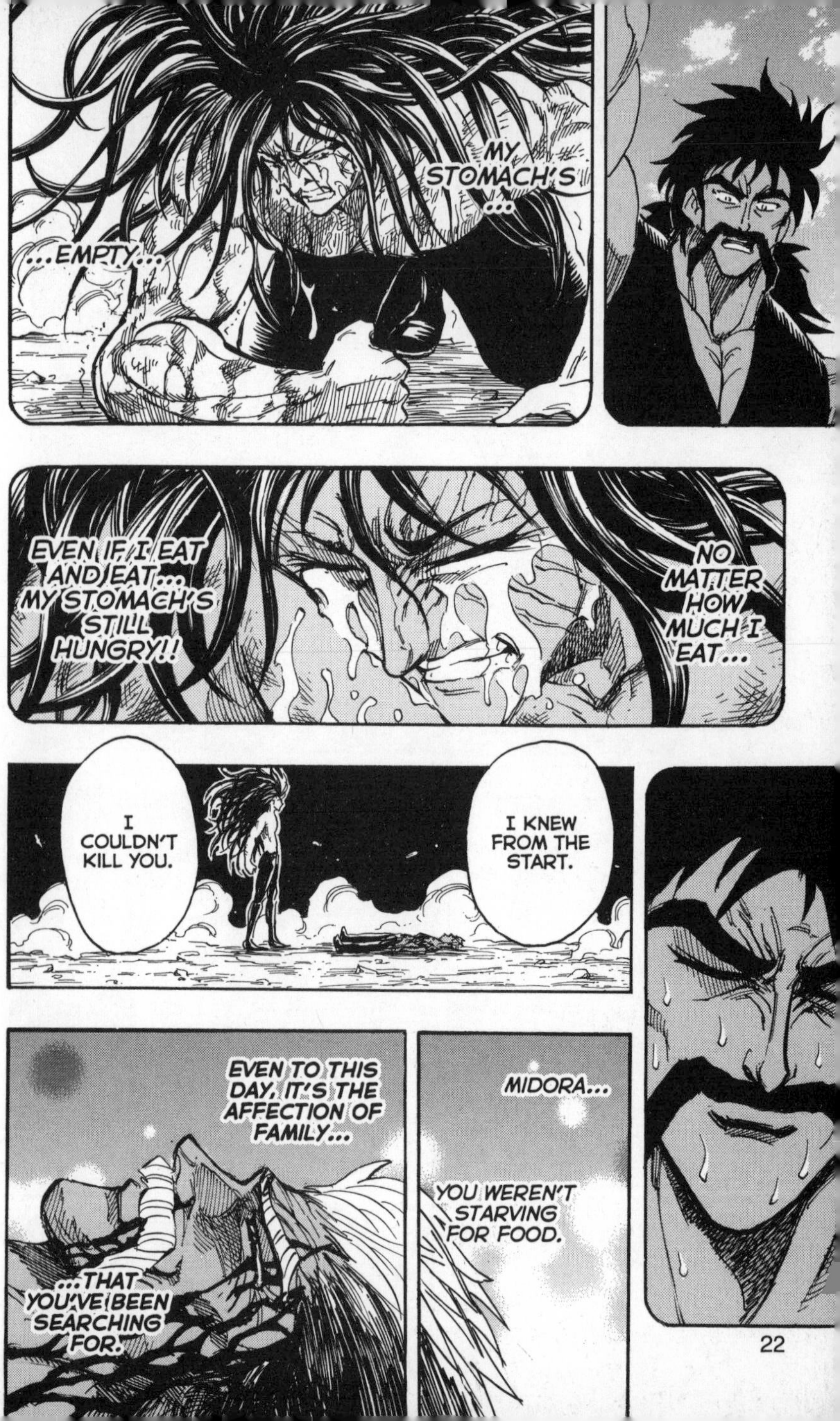
MY STOMACH'S...
...EMPTY...
NO MATTER HOW MUCH I EAT...
EVEN IF I EAT AND EAT... MY STOMACH'S STILL HUNGRY!!
I KNEW FROM THE START.
I COULDN'T KILL YOU.
MIDORA...
YOU WEREN'T STARVING FOR FOOD.
EVEN TO THIS DAY, IT'S THE AFFECTION OF FAMILY...
...THAT YOU'VE BEEN SEARCHING FOR.

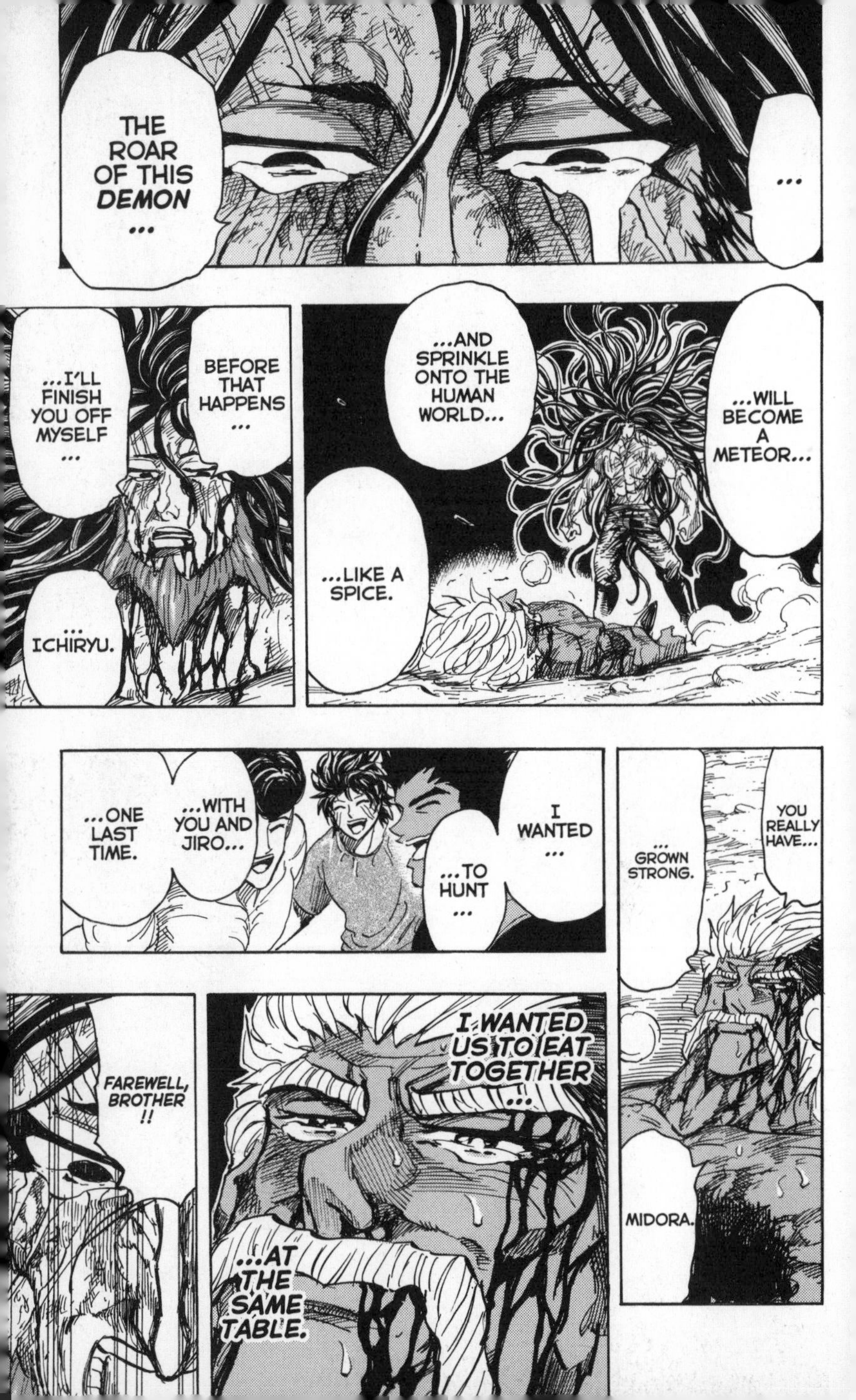
...
THE ROAR OF THIS DEMON ...
...WILL BECOME A METEOR...
...AND SPRINKLE ONTO THE HUMAN WORLD...
...LIKE A SPICE.
BEFORE THAT HAPPENS ...
...I'LL FINISH YOU OFF MYSELF ...
... ICHIRYU.
YOU REALLY HAVE...
... GROWN STRONG.
MIDORA.
I WANTED ...
...TO HUNT ...
...WITH YOU AND JIRO...
...ONE LAST TIME.
I WANTED US TO EAT TOGETHER ...
...AT THE SAME TABLE.
FAREWELL, BROTHER !!

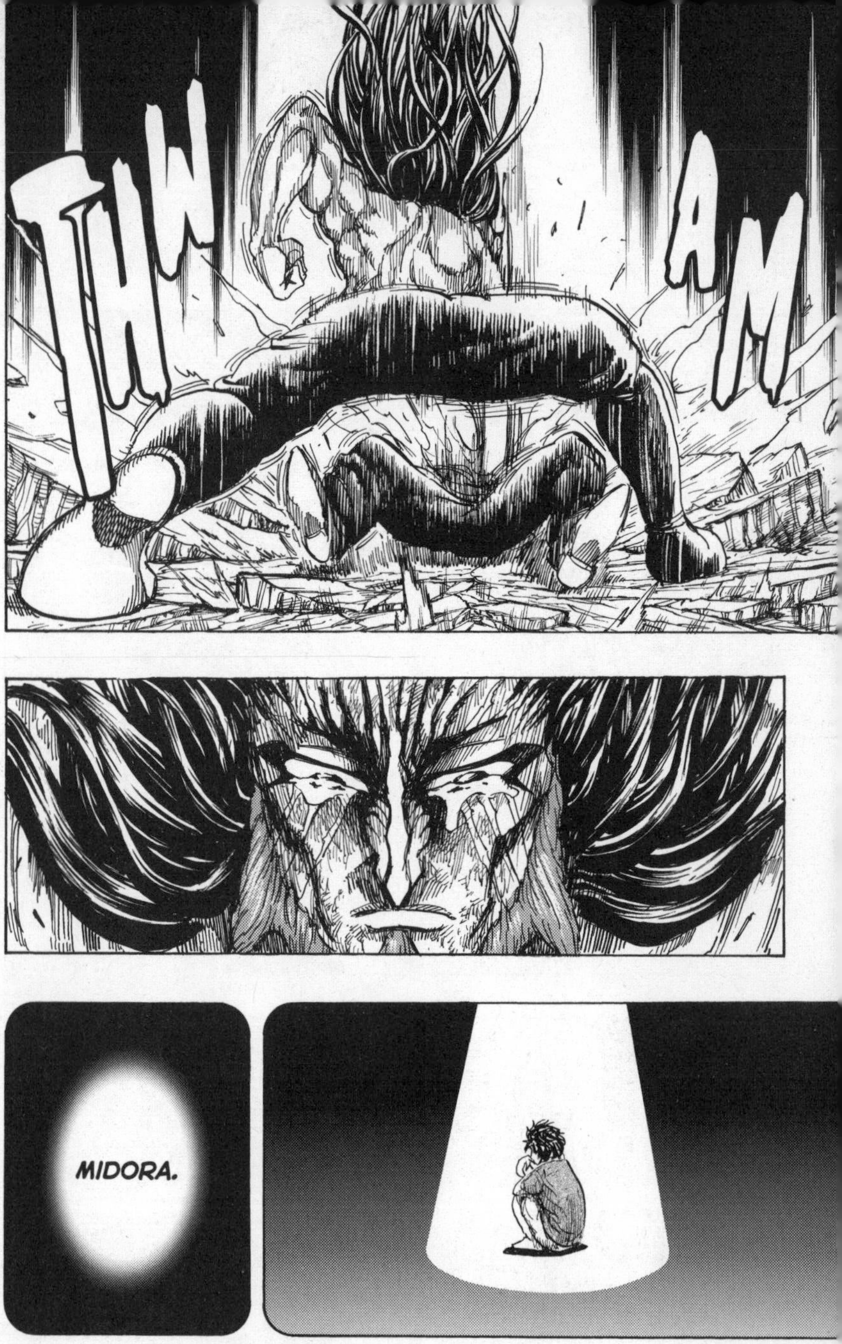
THWAM
MIDORA.

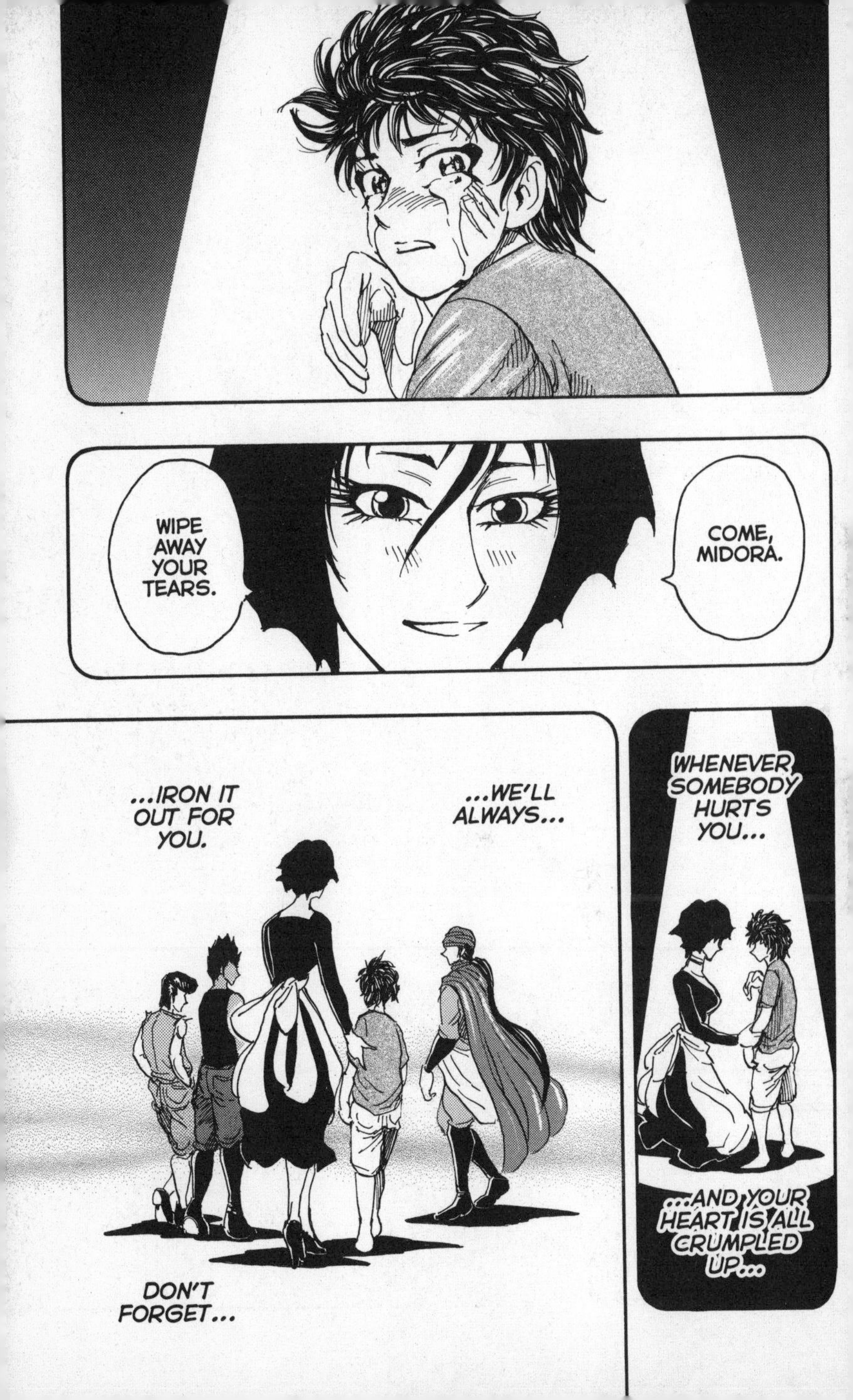
COME, MIDORA.
WIPE AWAY YOUR TEARS.
WHENEVER SOMEBODY HURTS YOU...
...AND YOUR HEART IS ALL CRUMPLED UP...
...WE'LL ALWAYS...
...IRON IT OUT FOR YOU.
DON'T FORGET...

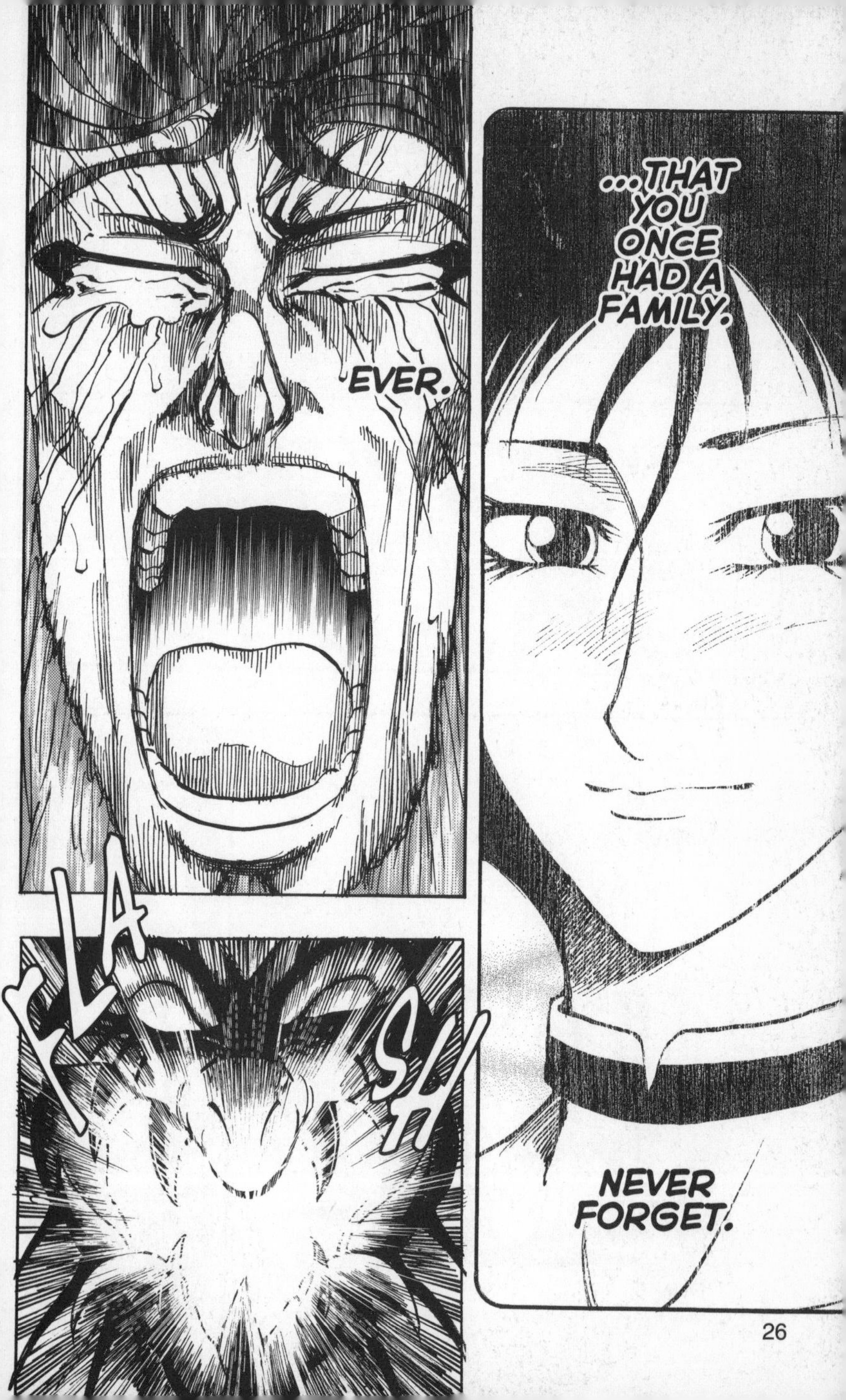
...THAT YOU ONCE HAD A FAMILY.
NEVER FORGET.
EVER.
FLASH

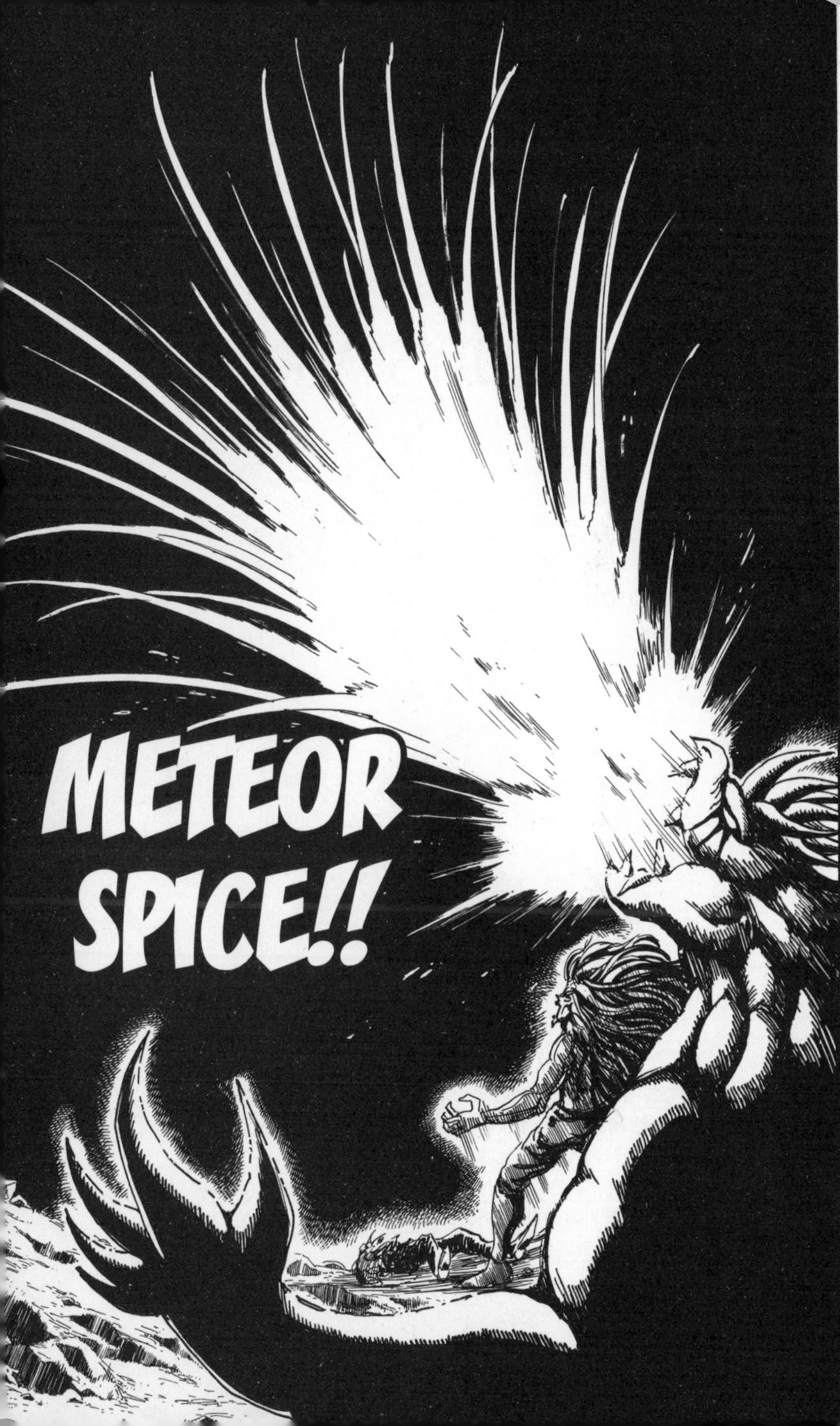
METEOR
SPICE!!

TORIKO

GOURMET CHECKLIST

Vol. 280

WOOZY SHARK
(FISH)

CAPTURE LEVEL: 23
HABITAT: SPIRITS SEA
SIZE: 25 METERS
HEIGHT: ---
WEIGHT: 18 TONS
PRICE: 100 G / 300 YEN

WAAAH! IT'S A BRIGHT RED SHARK, TORIKO!!

SCALE

A PERPETUALLY DRUNK SHARK THAT LIVES IN THE SPIRITS SEA, AN OCEAN COMPOSED OF WINE, WHISKEY, BEER, SHOCHU AND ALL MANNER OF ALCOHOL. BECAUSE IT CONSTANTLY HAS ALCOHOL COURSING THROUGH ITS BODY, THE WOOZY SHARK IS BRIGHT RED. AND BECAUSE IT IS DRUNK 24/7 IT RARELY HARMS OTHER LIVING CREATURES. IT'S TOO INEBRIATED TO BE CAPABLE OF DOING THAT. YOU COULD CALL THIS SHARK THE SYMBOL OF THE SPIRITS SEA.

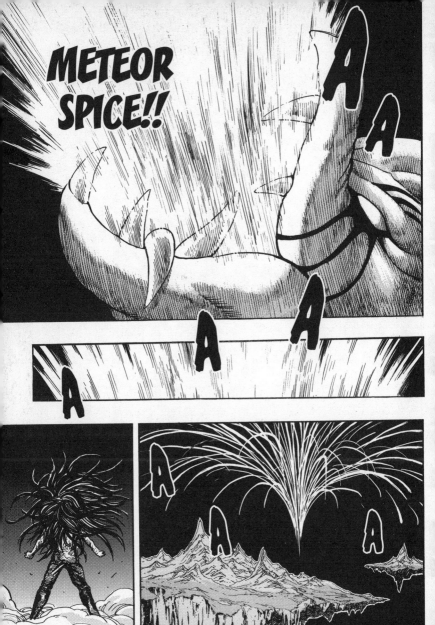

METEOR SPICE!!

GOURMET 255: WAKING!!

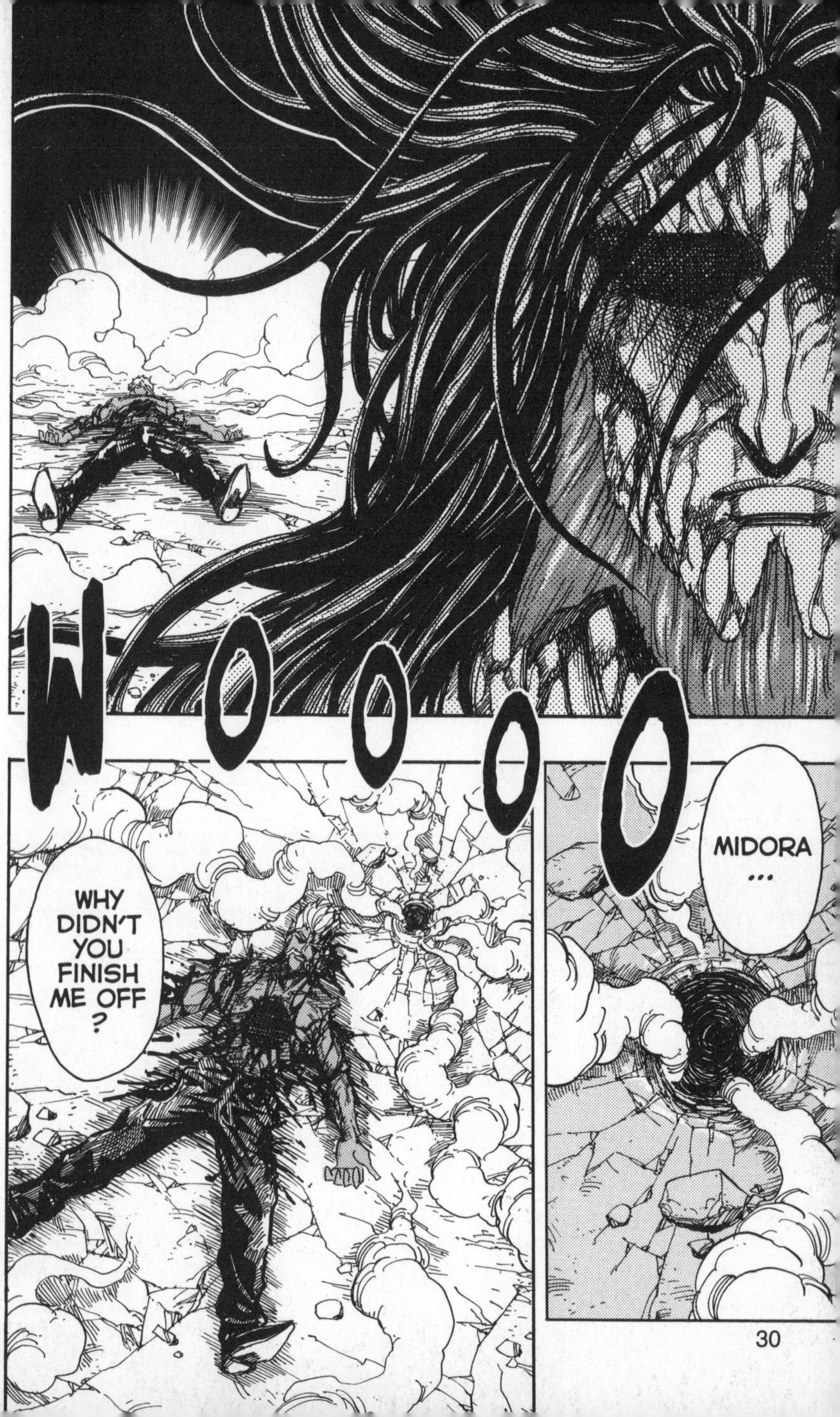
WOOOOO
MIDORA ...
WHY DIDN'T YOU FINISH ME OFF ?

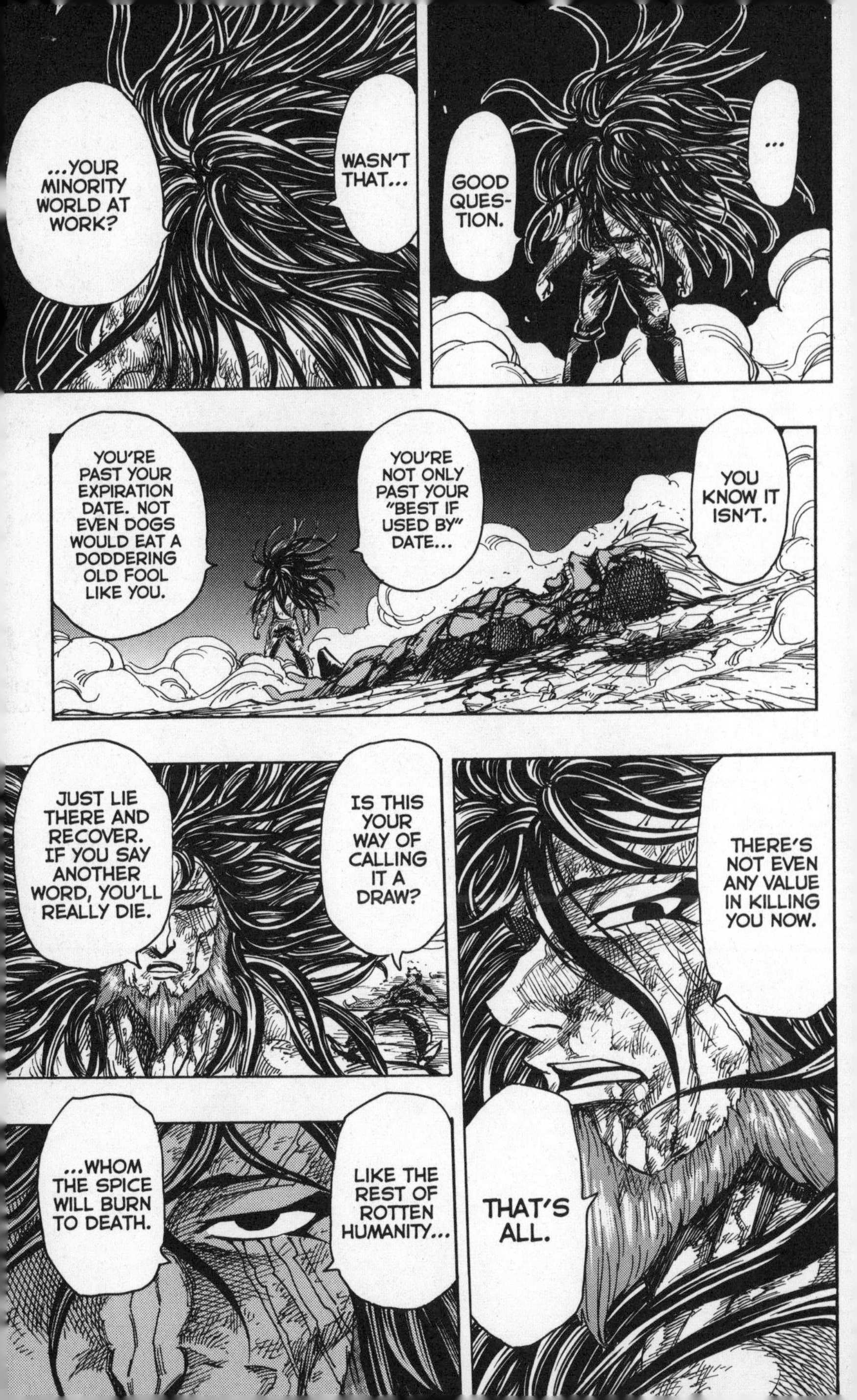
...
GOOD QUESTION.
WASN'T THAT...
...YOUR MINORITY WORLD AT WORK?
YOU KNOW IT ISN'T.
YOU'RE NOT ONLY PAST YOUR "BEST IF USED BY" DATE...
YOU'RE PAST YOUR EXPIRATION DATE. NOT EVEN DOGS WOULD EAT A DODDERING OLD FOOL LIKE YOU.
THERE'S NOT EVEN ANY VALUE IN KILLING YOU NOW.
THAT'S ALL.
IS THIS YOUR WAY OF CALLING IT A DRAW?
JUST LIE THERE AND RECOVER. IF YOU SAY ANOTHER WORD, YOU'LL REALLY DIE.
LIKE THE REST OF ROTTEN HUMANITY...
...WHOM THE SPICE WILL BURN TO DEATH.

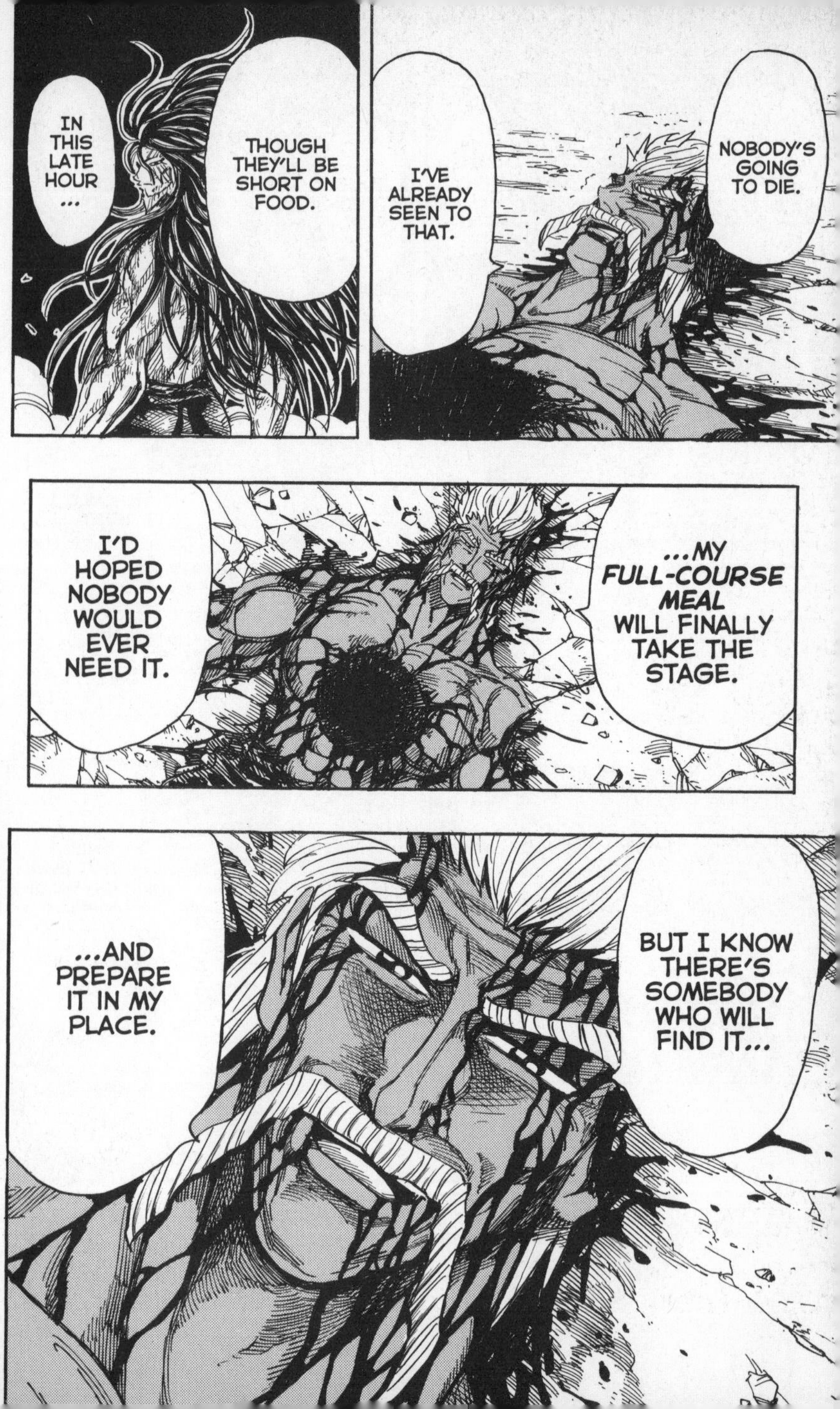
NOBODY'S GOING TO DIE.
I'VE ALREADY SEEN TO THAT.
THOUGH THEY'LL BE SHORT ON FOOD.
IN THIS LATE HOUR...
...MY FULL-COURSE MEAL WILL FINALLY TAKE THE STAGE.
I'D HOPED NOBODY WOULD EVER NEED IT.
BUT I KNOW THERE'S SOMEBODY WHO WILL FIND IT...
...AND PREPARE IT IN MY PLACE.

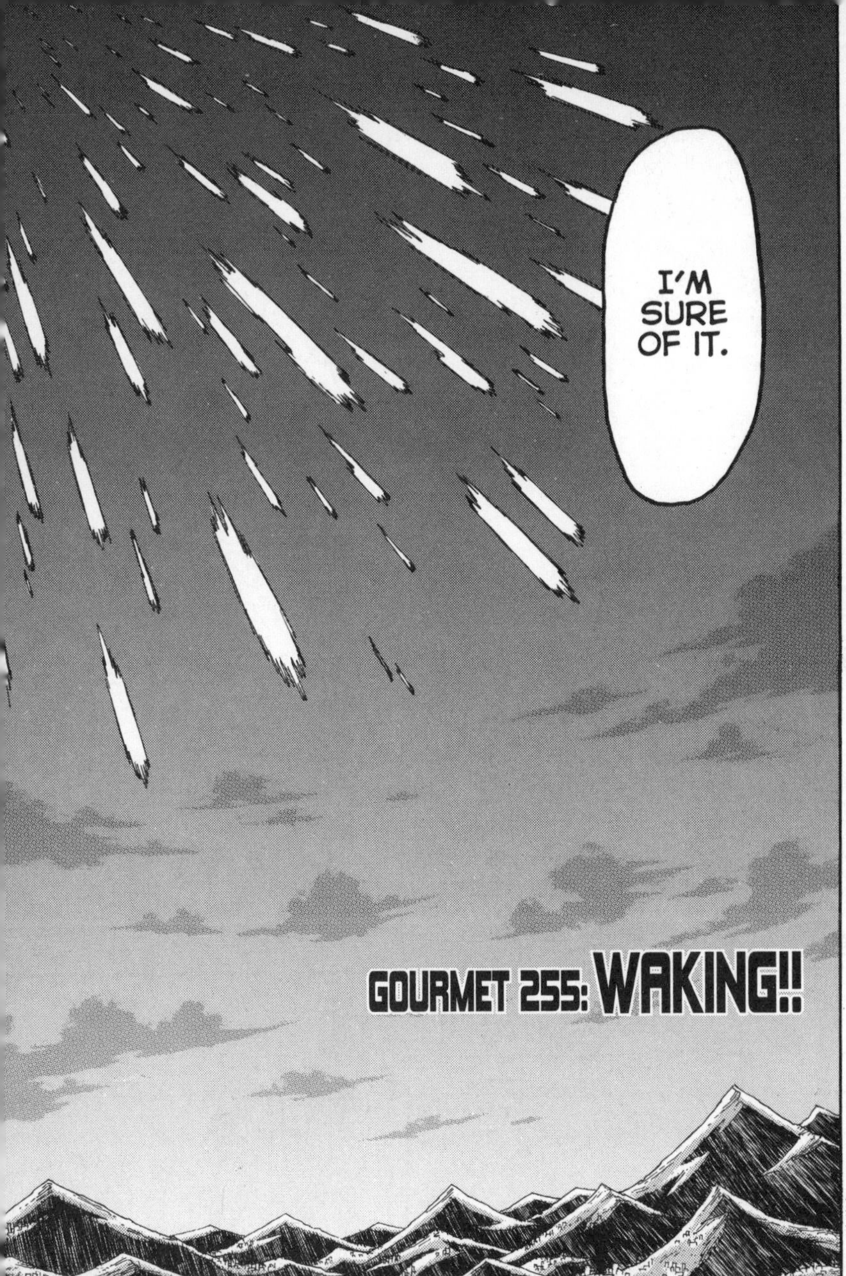
I'M SURE OF IT.
GOURMET 255: WAKING!!

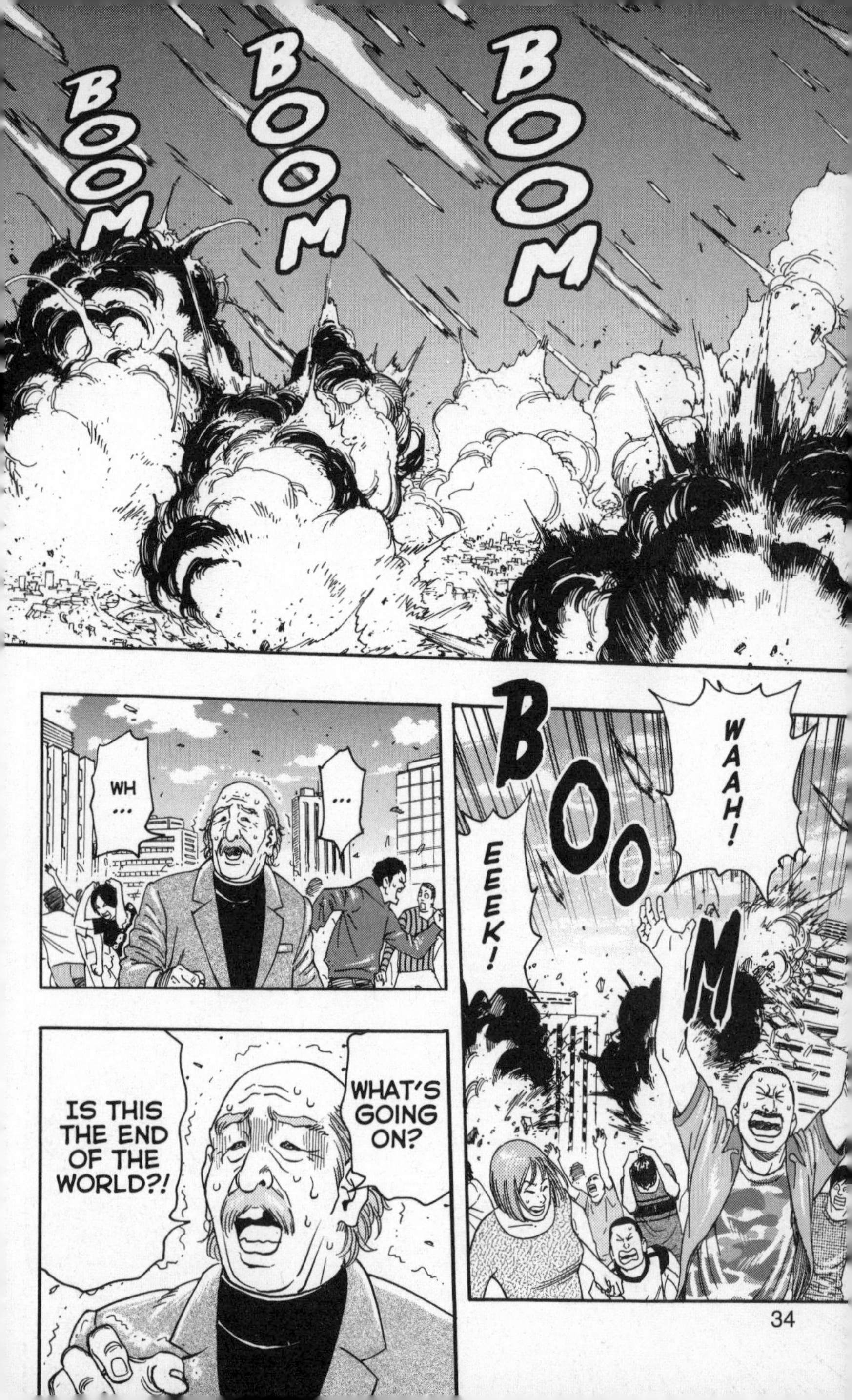
BOOM
BOOM
BOOM
BOOOM
WAAAH!
EEEK!
WH...
...
WHAT'S GOING ON?
IS THIS THE END OF THE WORLD?!

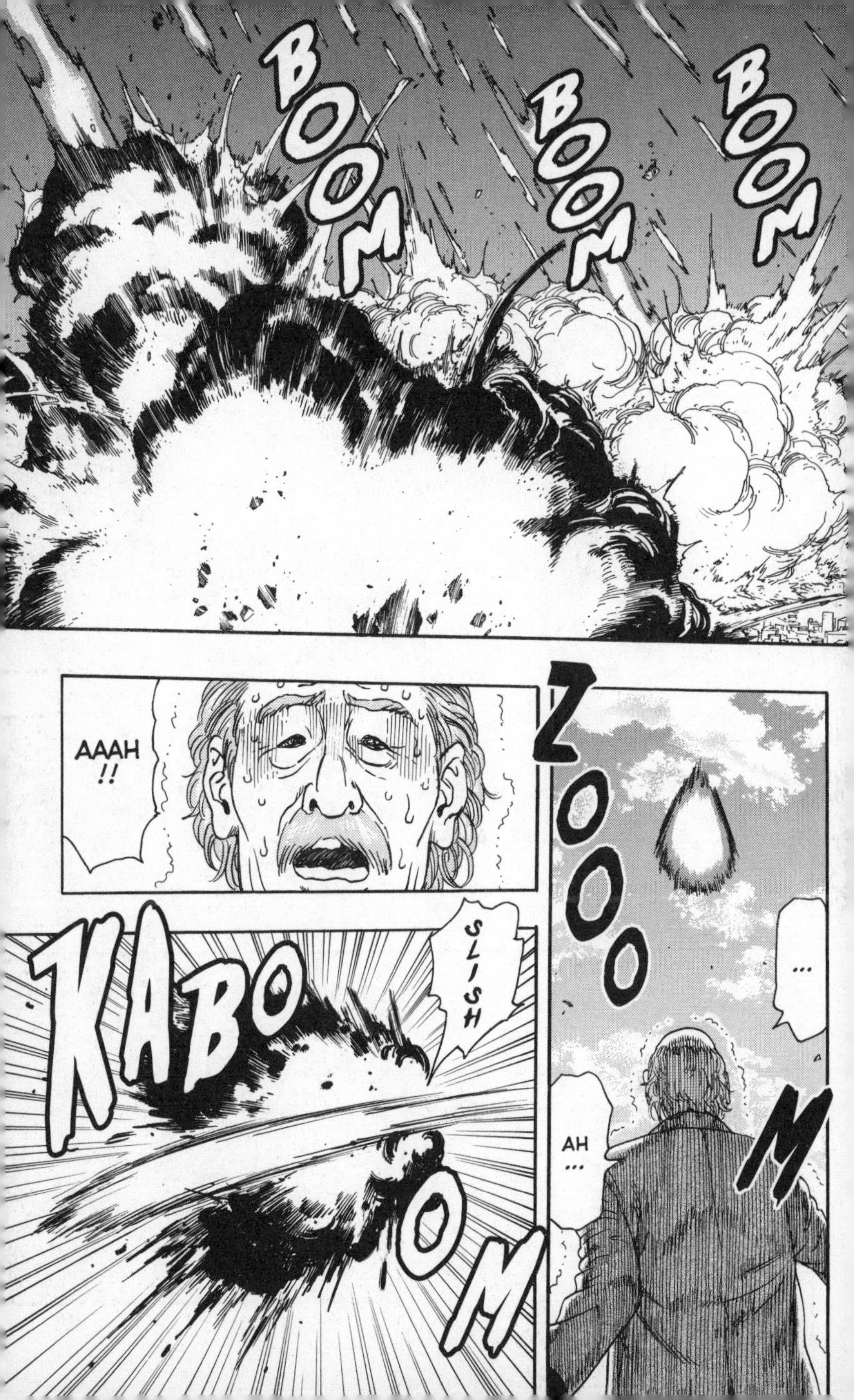
BOOM
BOOM
BOOM
ZOOOM
...
AH ...
AAAH !!
SLISH
KABOOM

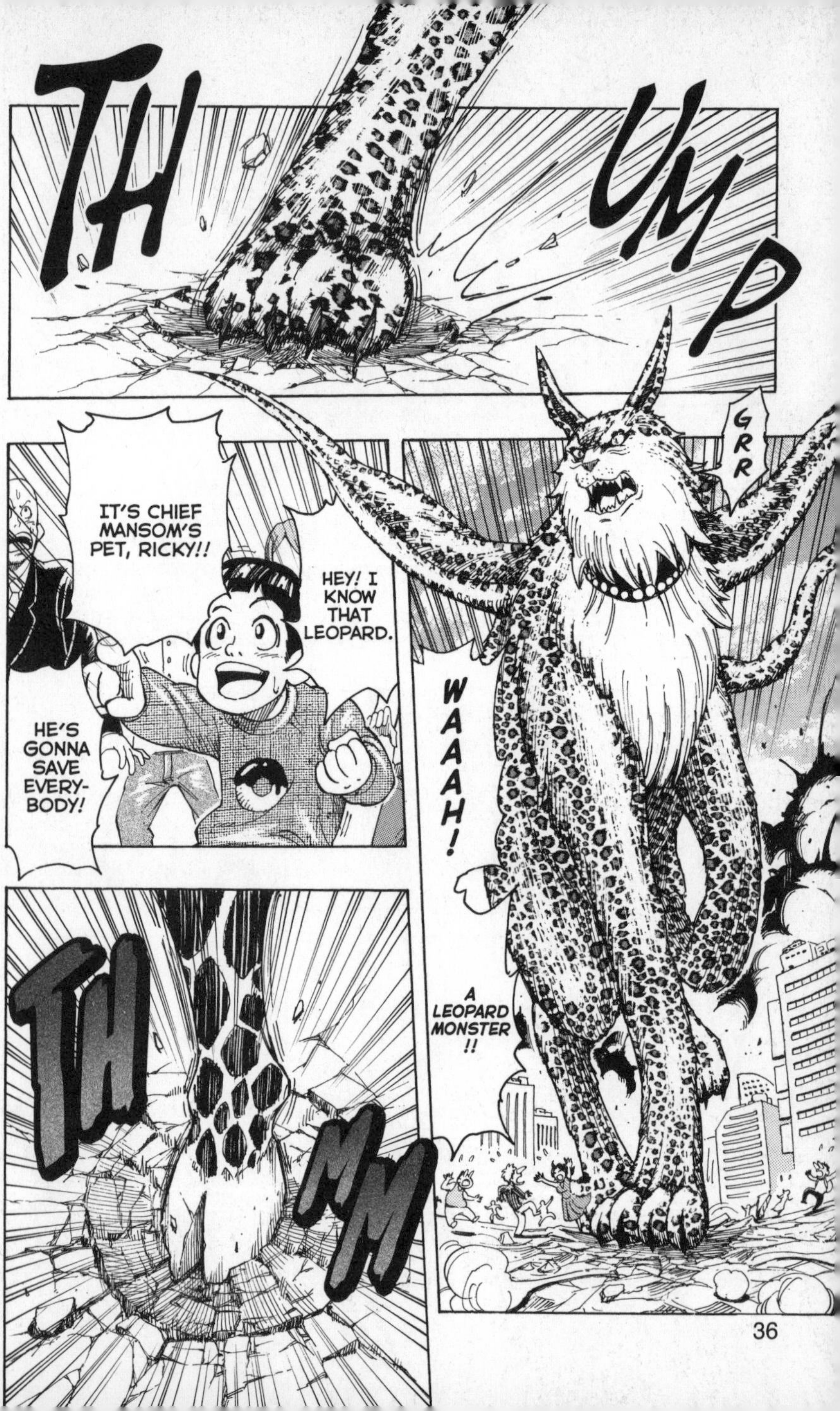

THUMP
GRR
WAAAAH!
A LEOPARD MONSTER!!
HEY! I KNOW THAT LEOPARD.
IT'S CHIEF MANSOM'S PET, RICKY!!
HE'S GONNA SAVE EVERYBODY!
THMM

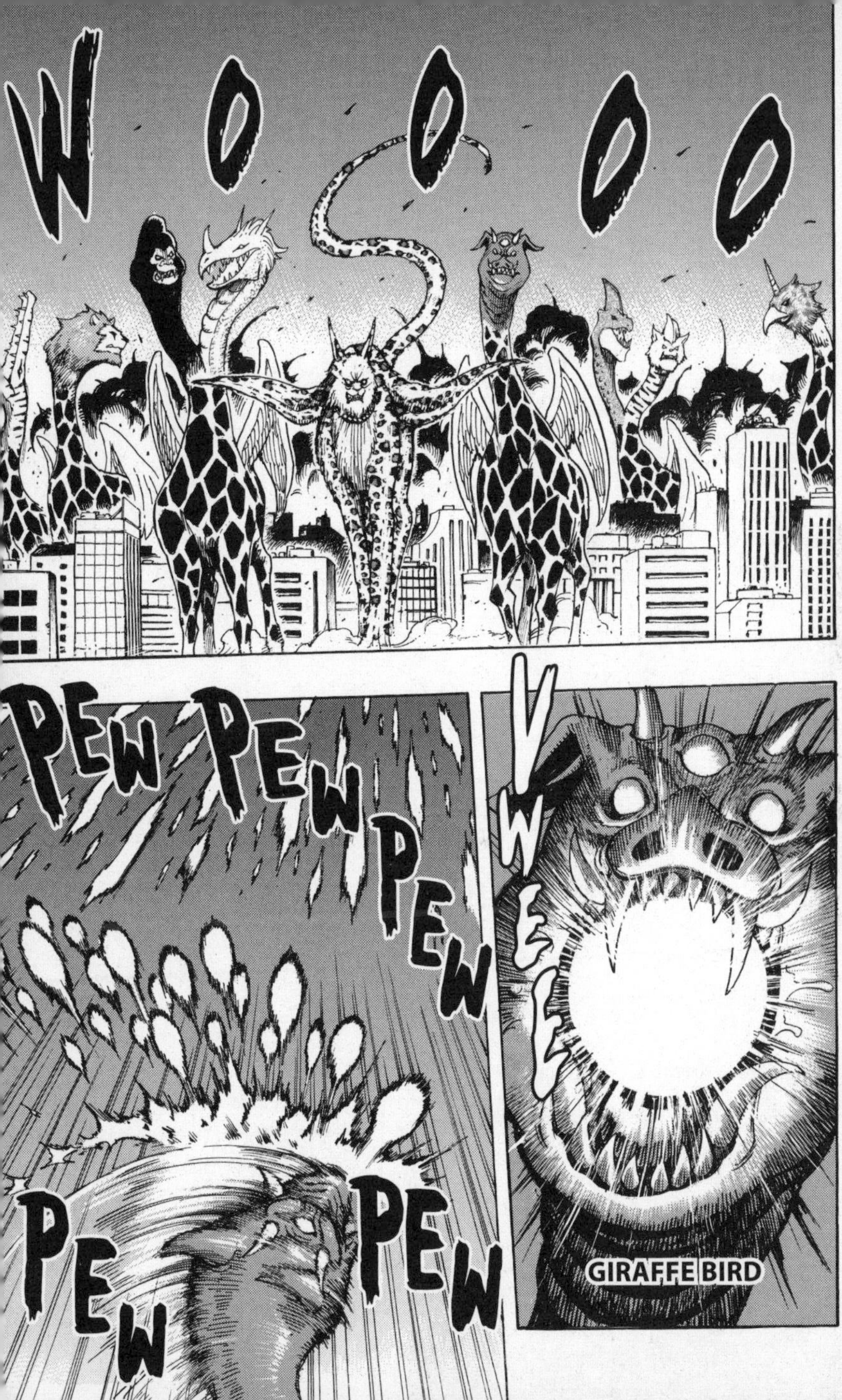
WOOOOO
VWEEE
GIRAFFE BIRD
PEW PEW
PEW PEW
PEW PEW

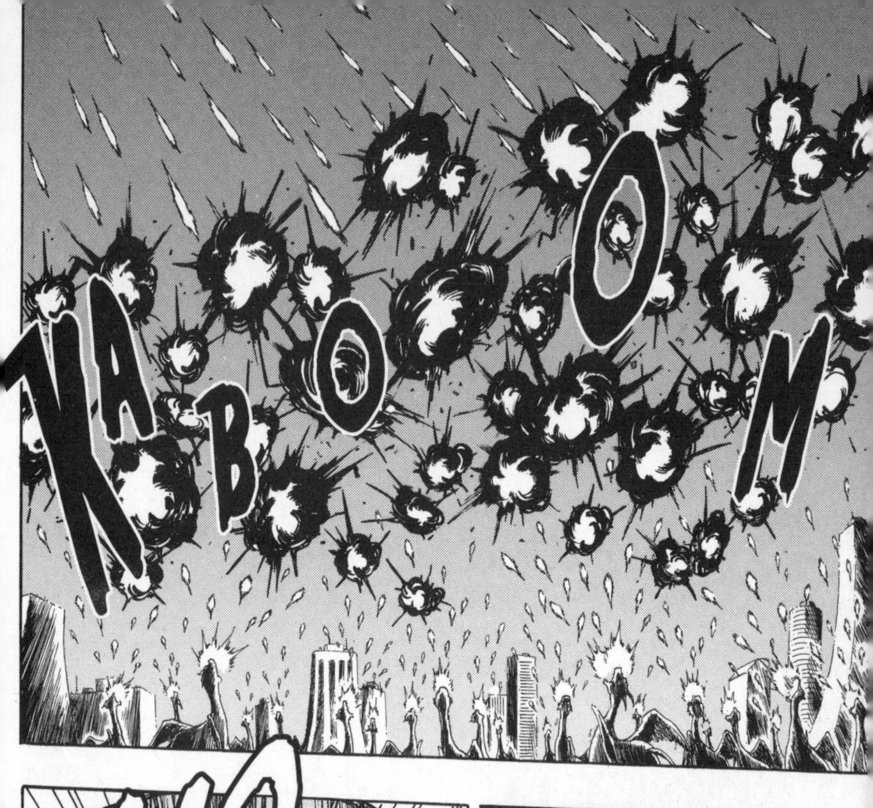
KABOOOM
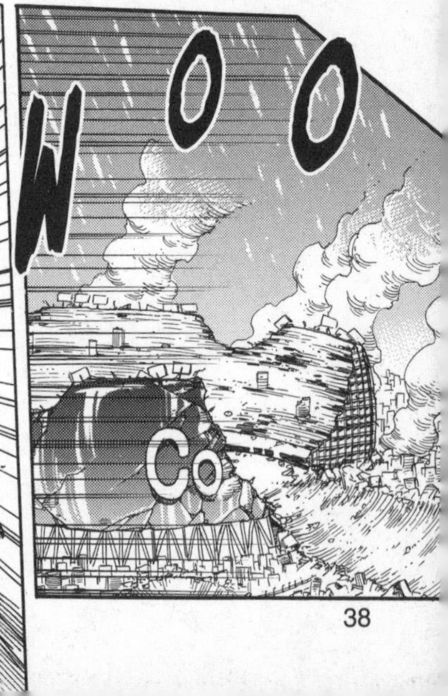
WOOO
Co
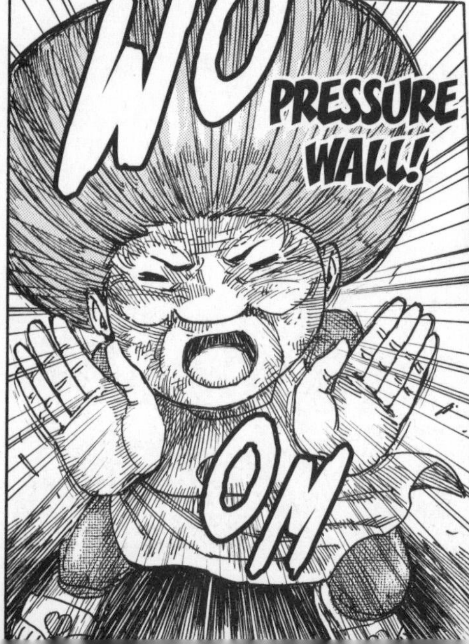
WO
PRESSURE WALL!
OM

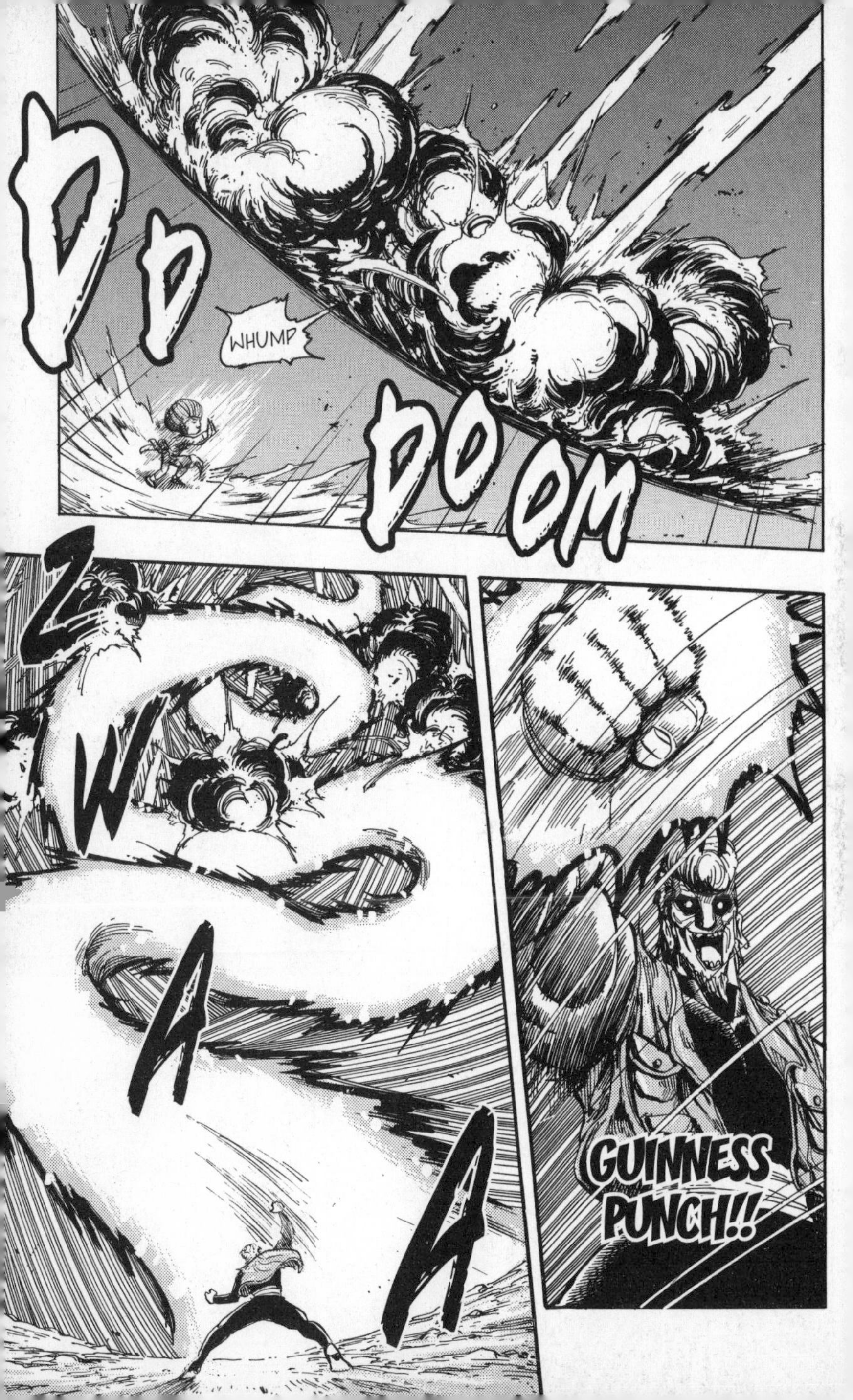
DD
WHUMP
DOOM
GUINNESS PUNCH!!
ZWAA

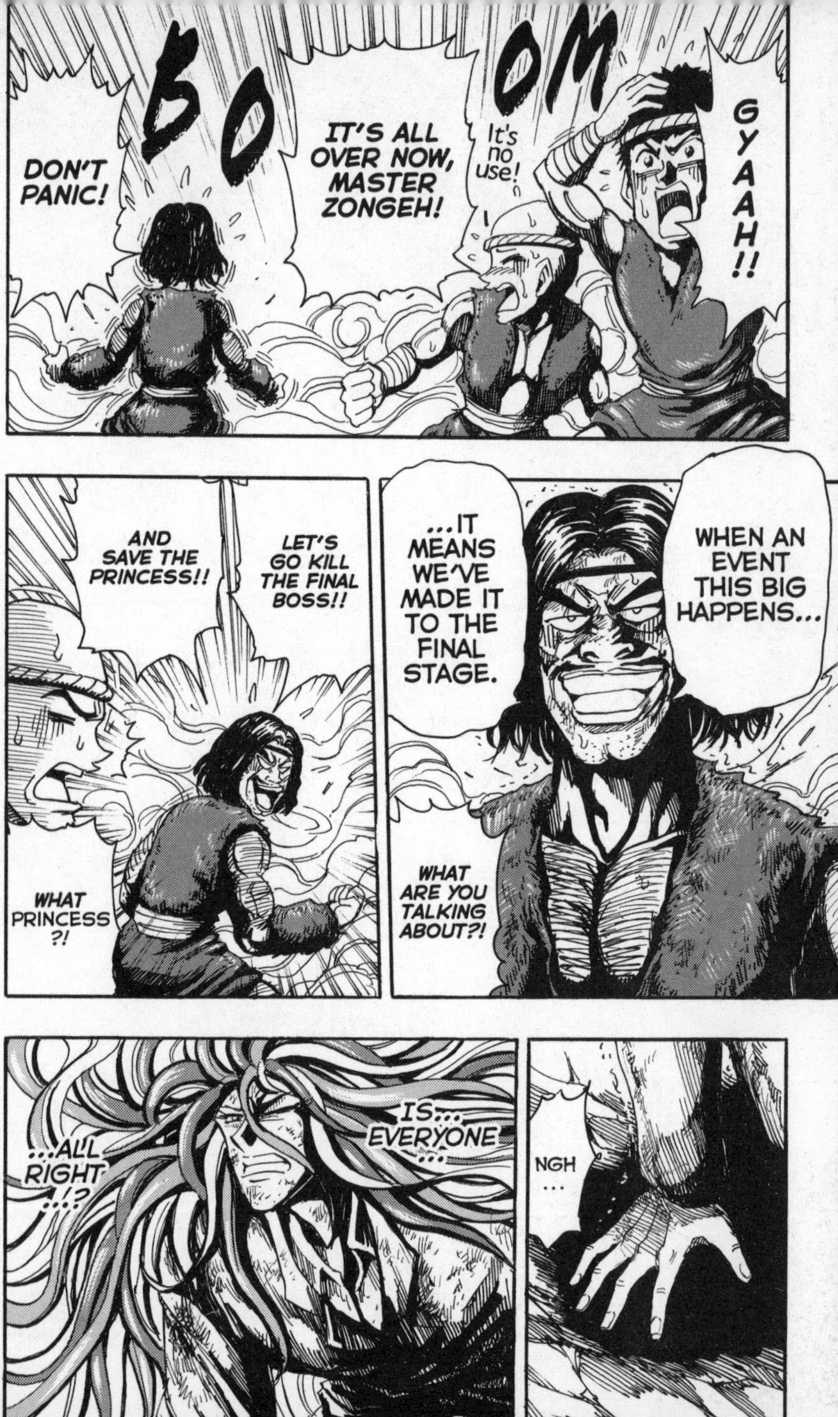
GYAAH!!
BOOM
It's no use!
IT'S ALL OVER NOW, MASTER ZONGEH!
DON'T PANIC!
WHEN AN EVENT THIS BIG HAPPENS...
...IT MEANS WE'VE MADE IT TO THE FINAL STAGE.
WHAT ARE YOU TALKING ABOUT?!
LET'S GO KILL THE FINAL BOSS!!
AND SAVE THE PRINCESS!!
WHAT PRINCESS?!
NGH...
IS... EVERYONE...
...ALL RIGHT...!?

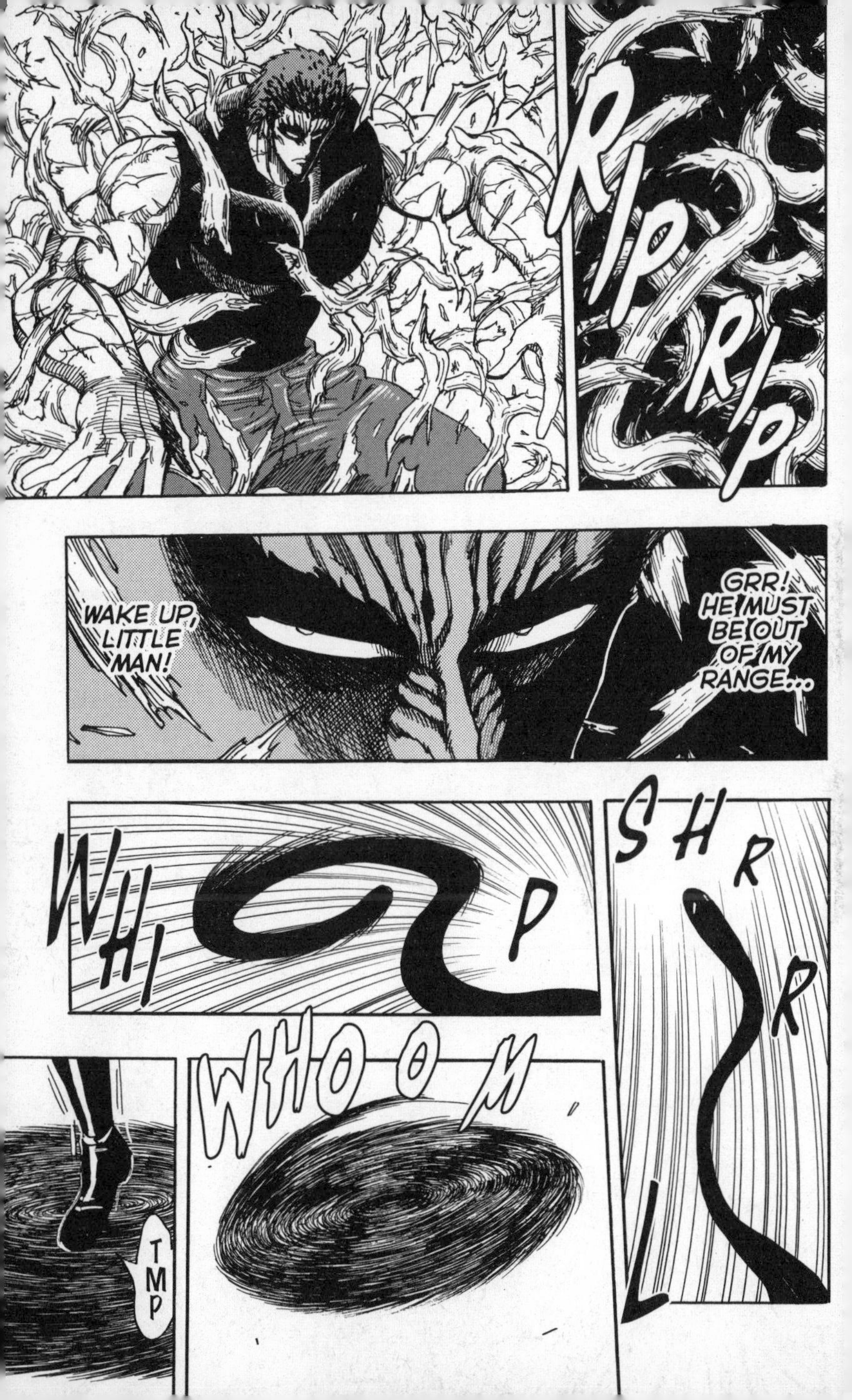
RIP RIP
GRR! HE MUST BE OUT OF MY RANGE...
WAKE UP, LITTLE MAN!
SHRRRL
WHIP
WHOOM
TMP

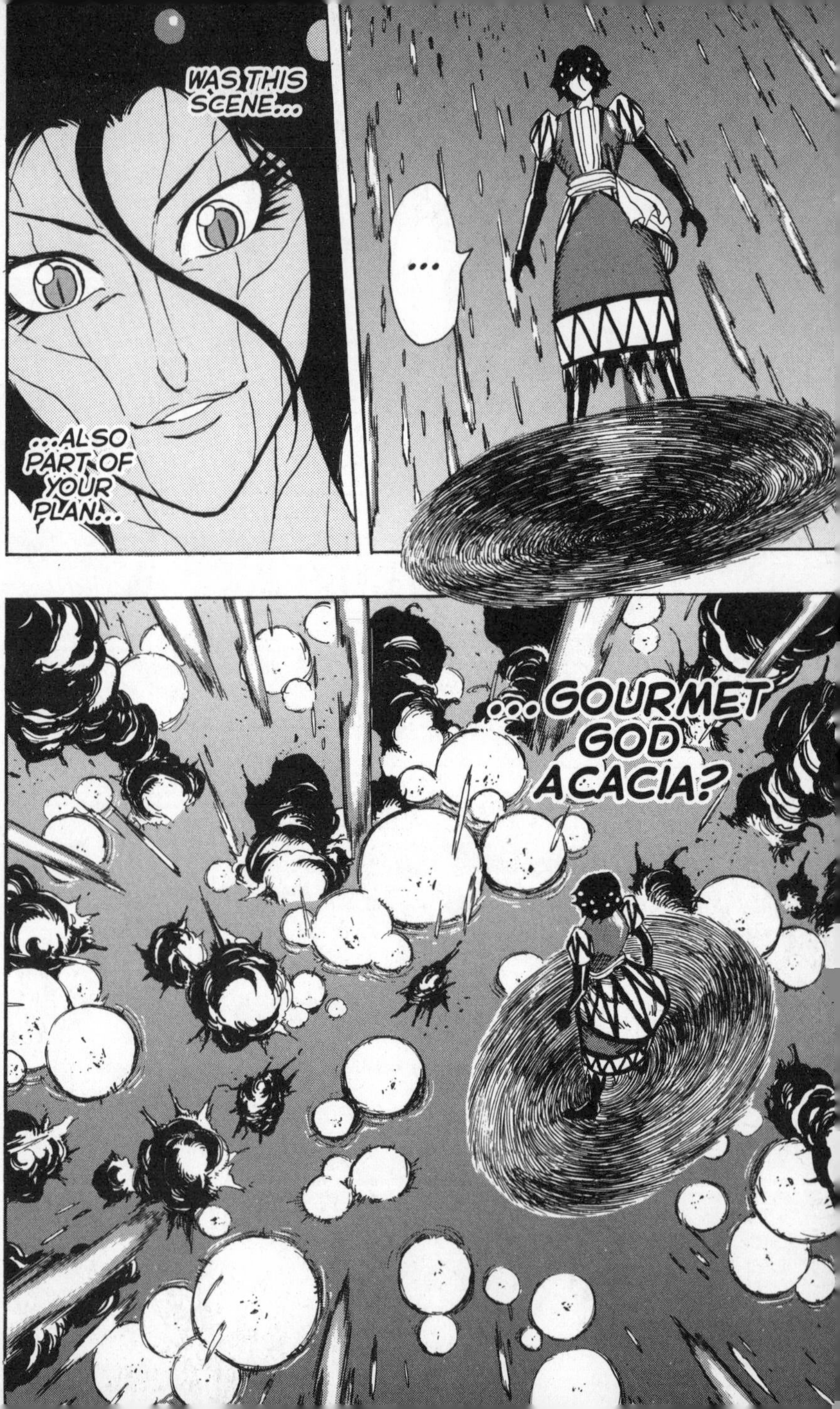
...
WAS THIS SCENE...
...ALSO PART OF YOUR PLAN...
...GOURMET GOD ACACIA?

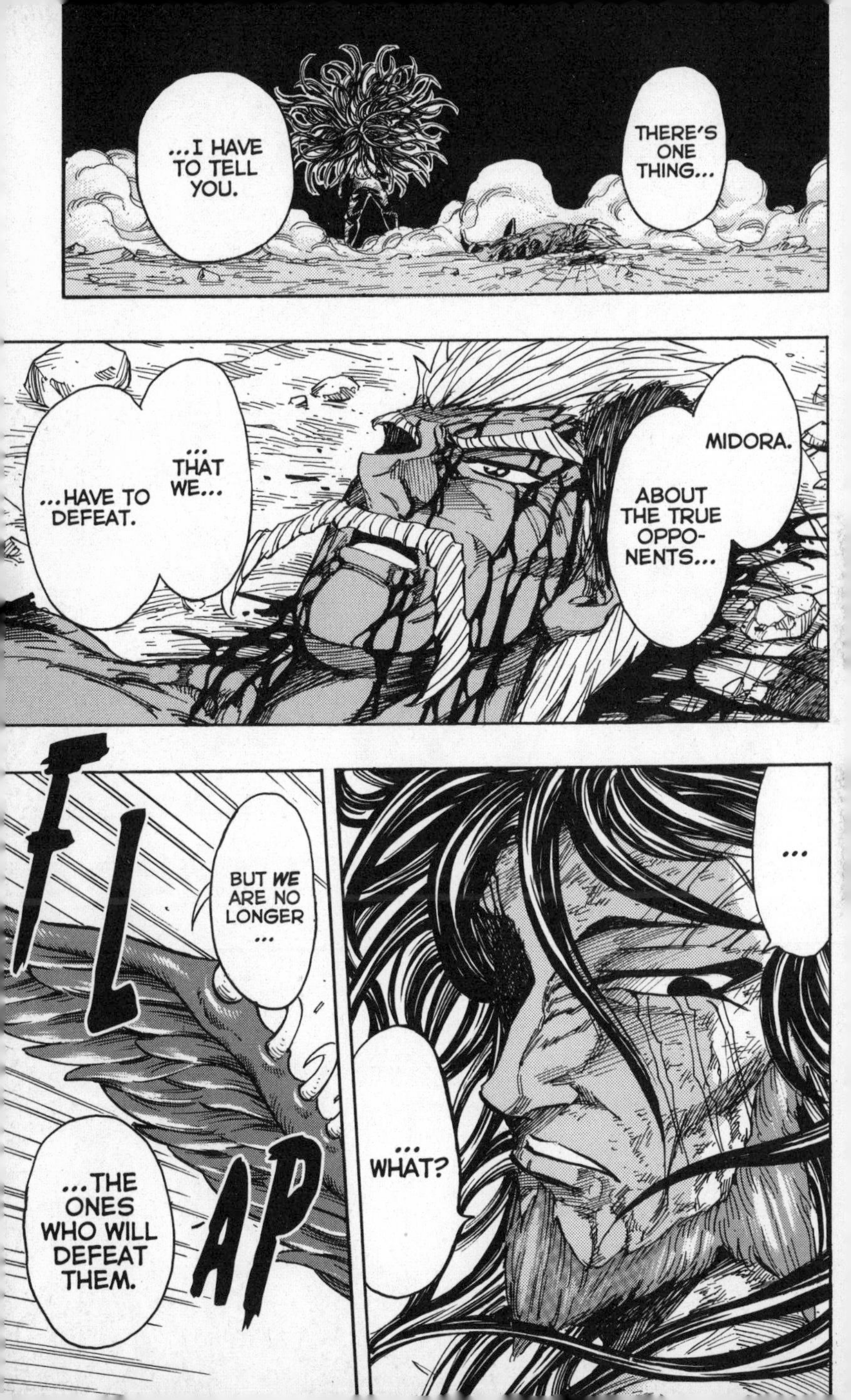
THERE'S ONE THING...
...I HAVE TO TELL YOU.
MIDORA.
ABOUT THE TRUE OPPONENTS...
...THAT WE...
...HAVE TO DEFEAT.
...
...WHAT?
BUT WE ARE NO LONGER...
...THE ONES WHO WILL DEFEAT THEM.
FLAP

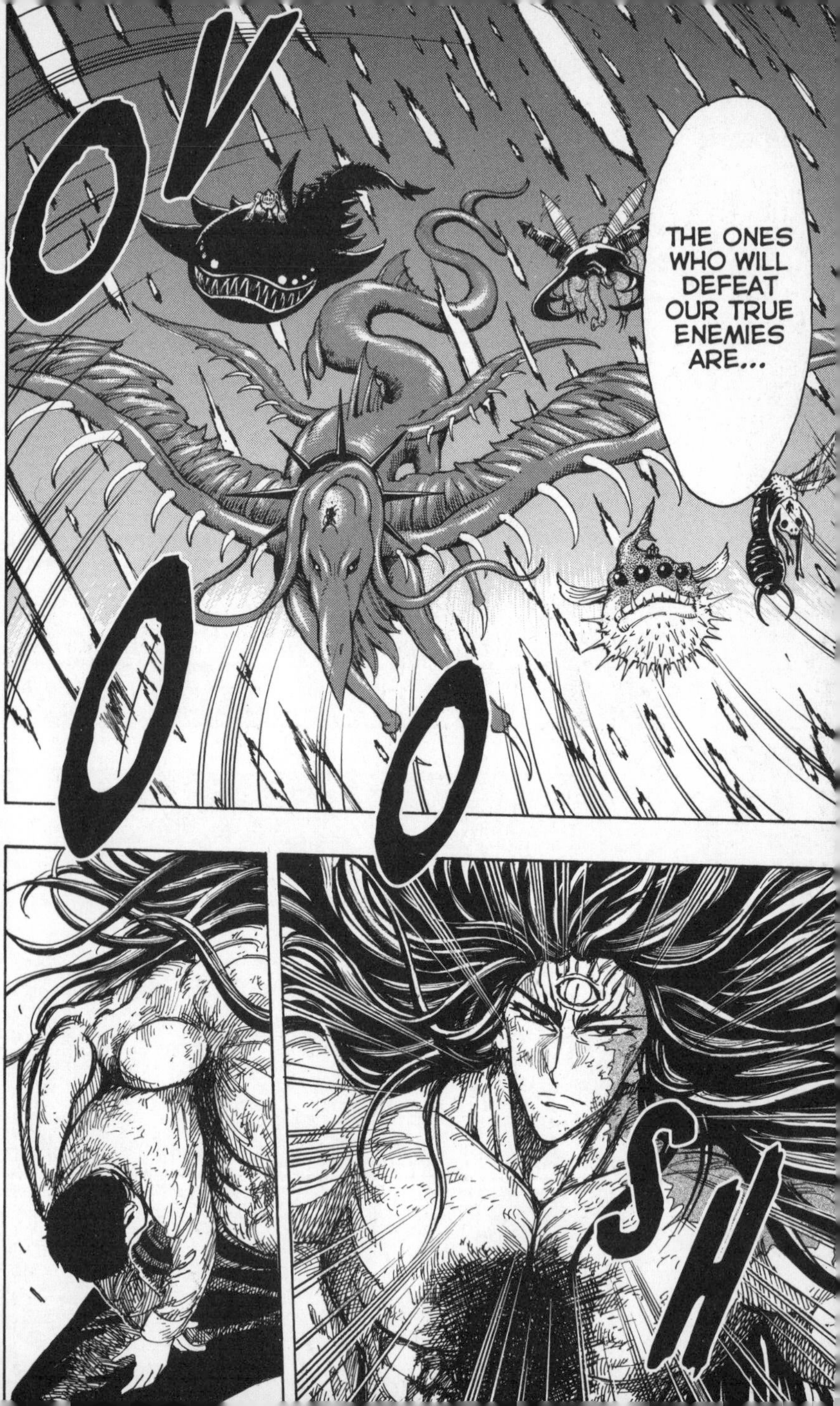
THE ONES WHO WILL DEFEAT OUR TRUE ENEMIES ARE...
VOOO
SH

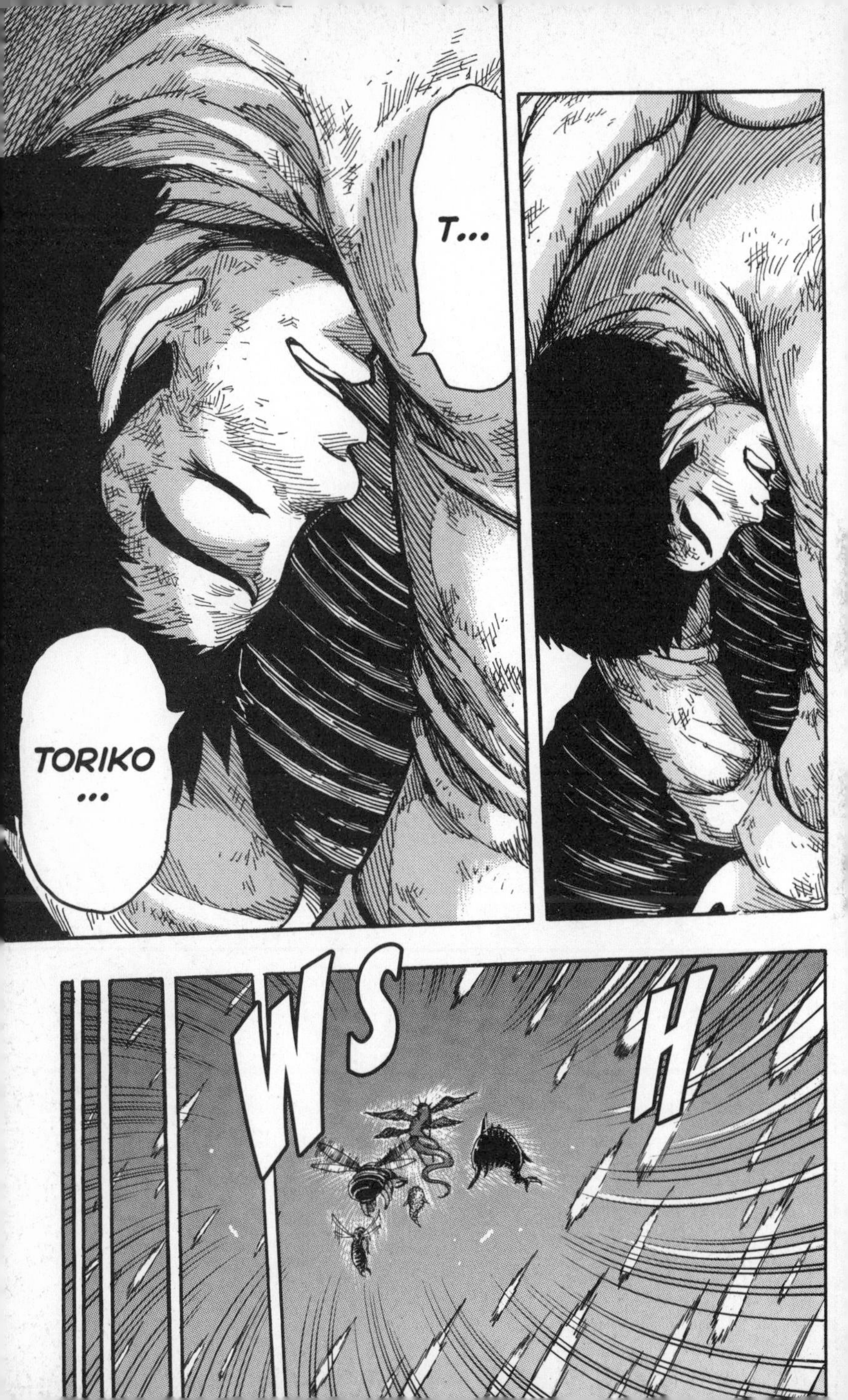
T...
TORIKO ...
WSH

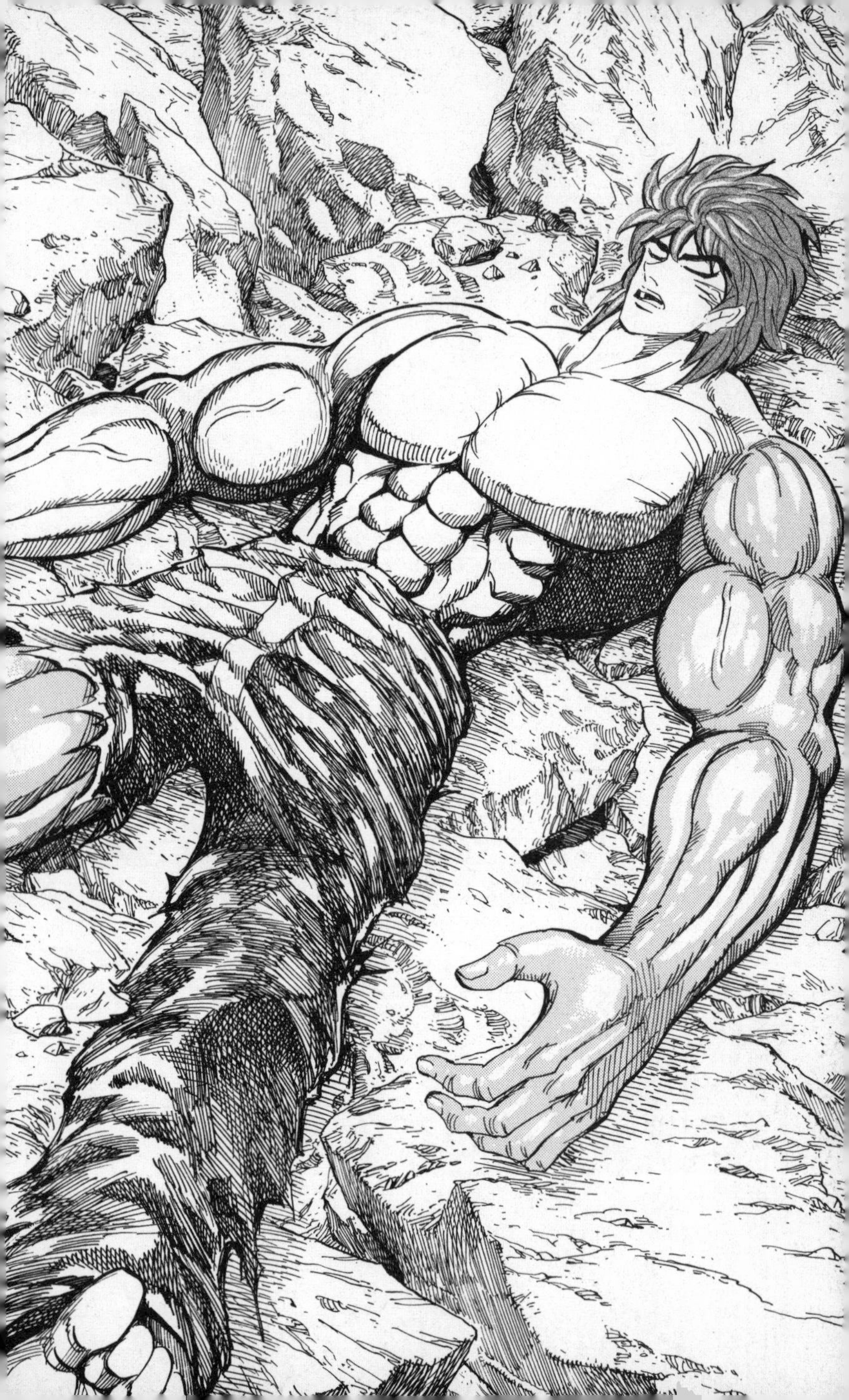

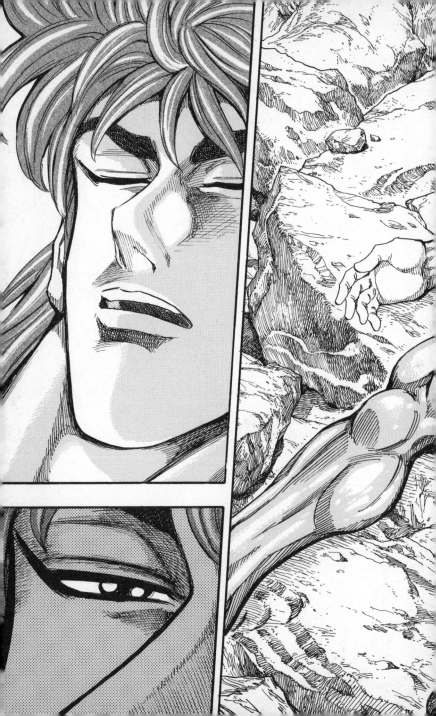

TORIKO

GOURMET CHECKLIST
Vol. 281

CHIPS TREE
(PLANT)

CAPTURE LEVEL: 2
HABITAT: SPIRITS ARCHIPELAGO
SIZE: ---
HEIGHT: 4 METERS
WEIGHT: ---
PRICE: 1 BAG (80 G) / 350 YEN

CRUNCHY!

RIP

RIP

RIP

RIP

YOU CAN PEEL THE BARK OFF AND IT TASTES LIKE POTATO CHIPS.

SCALE

THE IDEAL FOOD FOR THE SPIRITS ARCHIPELAGO! THIS PLANT'S BARK CAN BE PEELED OFF AND EATEN LIKE POTATO CHIPS. DIFFERENT TYPES HAVE DIFFERENT FLAVORS, INCLUDING CONSOMME AND CHEESE. IT'S THE PERFECT SNACK FOR ALL THE VISITORS TO THE SPIRITS ARCHIPELAGO WHO JUST CAN'T STOP DRINKING.

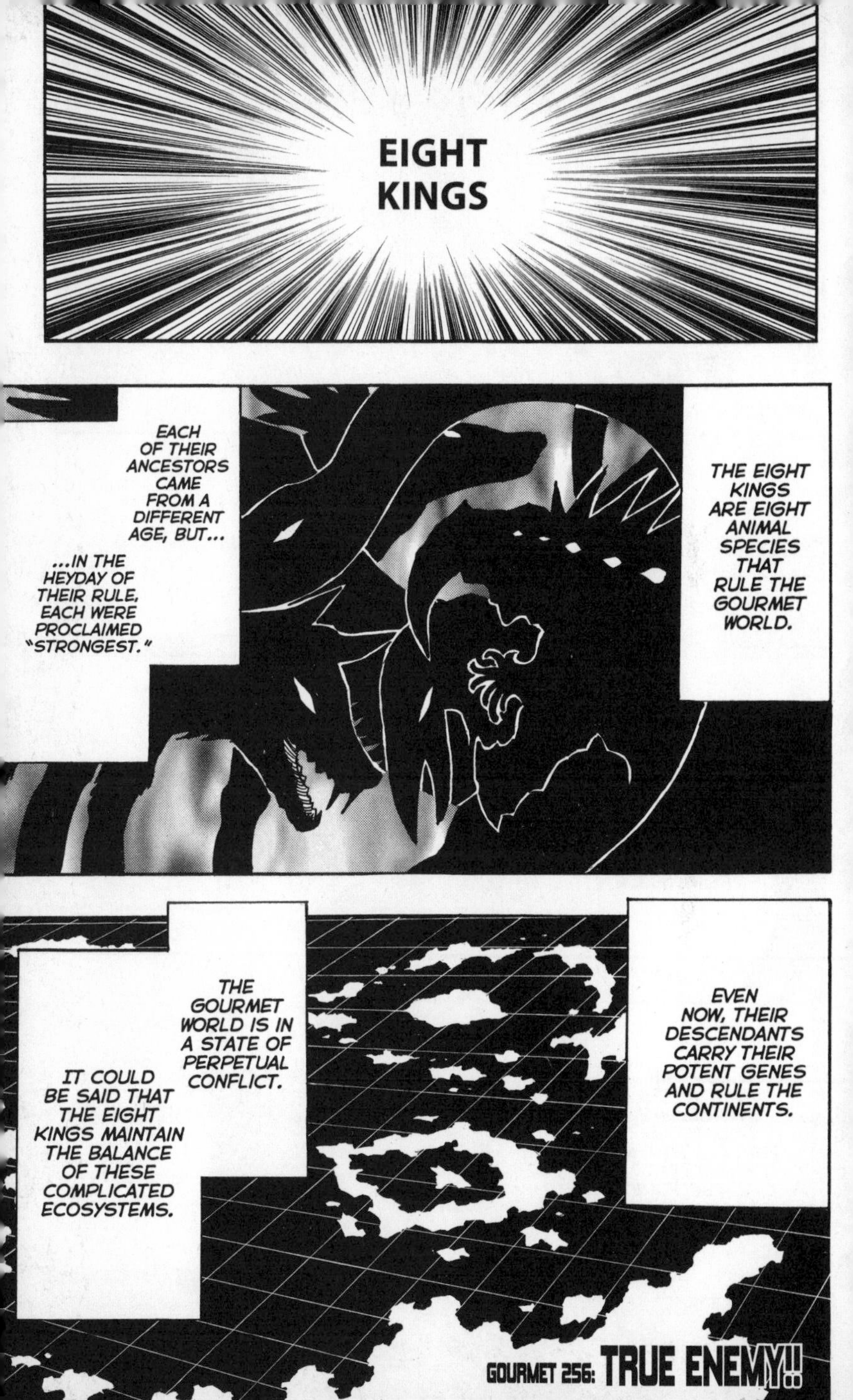
EIGHT KINGS
THE EIGHT KINGS ARE EIGHT ANIMAL SPECIES THAT RULE THE GOURMET WORLD.
EACH OF THEIR ANCESTORS CAME FROM A DIFFERENT AGE, BUT...
...IN THE HEYDAY OF THEIR RULE, EACH WERE PROCLAIMED "STRONGEST."
EVEN NOW, THEIR DESCENDANTS CARRY THEIR POTENT GENES AND RULE THE CONTINENTS.
THE GOURMET WORLD IS IN A STATE OF PERPETUAL CONFLICT.
IT COULD BE SAID THAT THE EIGHT KINGS MAINTAIN THE BALANCE OF THESE COMPLICATED ECOSYSTEMS.
GOURMET 256: TRUE ENEMY!!

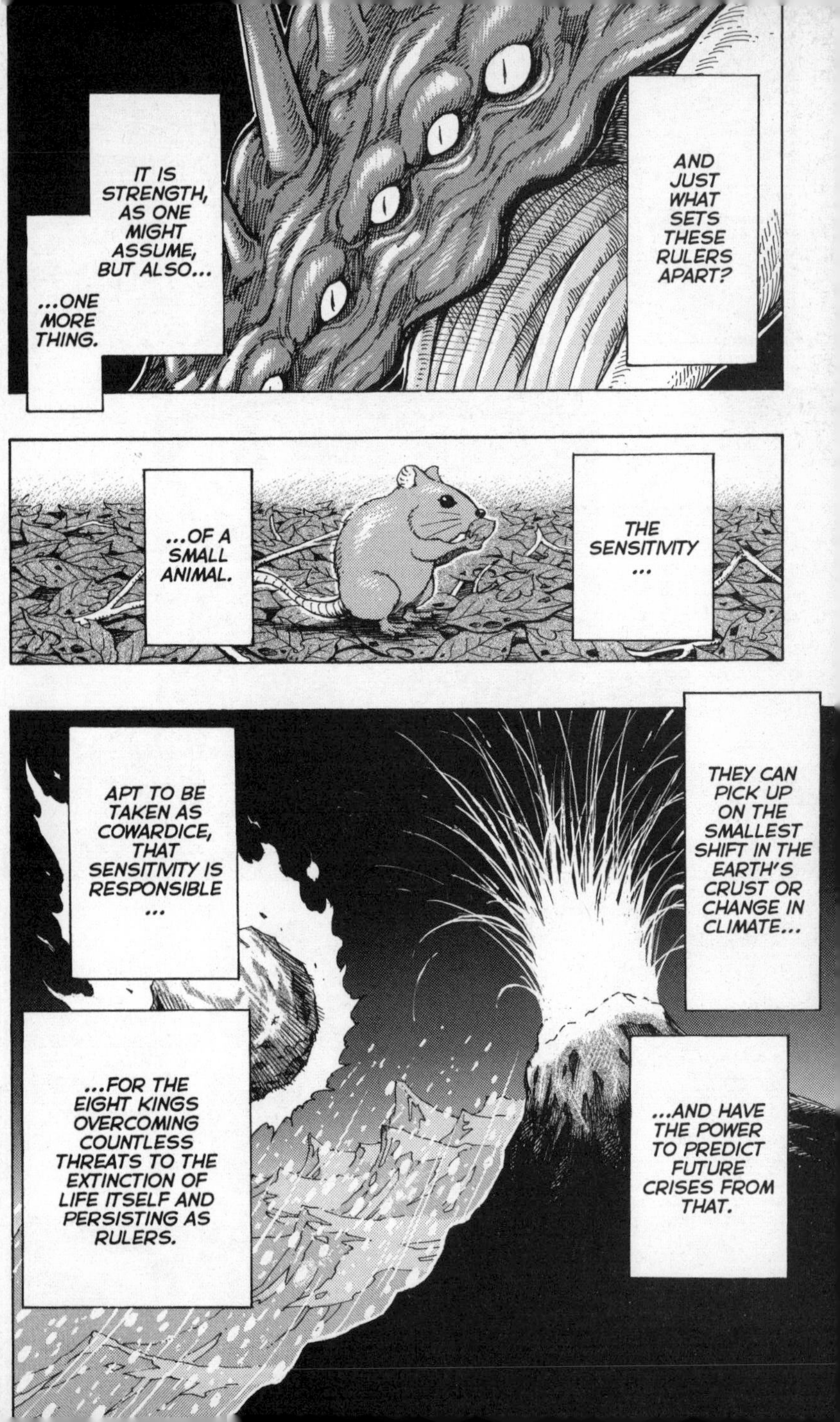
AND JUST WHAT SETS THESE RULERS APART?
IT IS STRENGTH, AS ONE MIGHT ASSUME, BUT ALSO...
...ONE MORE THING.
THE SENSITIVITY ...
...OF A SMALL ANIMAL.
THEY CAN PICK UP ON THE SMALLEST SHIFT IN THE EARTH'S CRUST OR CHANGE IN CLIMATE...
...AND HAVE THE POWER TO PREDICT FUTURE CRISES FROM THAT.
APT TO BE TAKEN AS COWARDICE, THAT SENSITIVITY IS RESPONSIBLE ...
...FOR THE EIGHT KINGS OVERCOMING COUNTLESS THREATS TO THE EXTINCTION OF LIFE ITSELF AND PERSISTING AS RULERS.

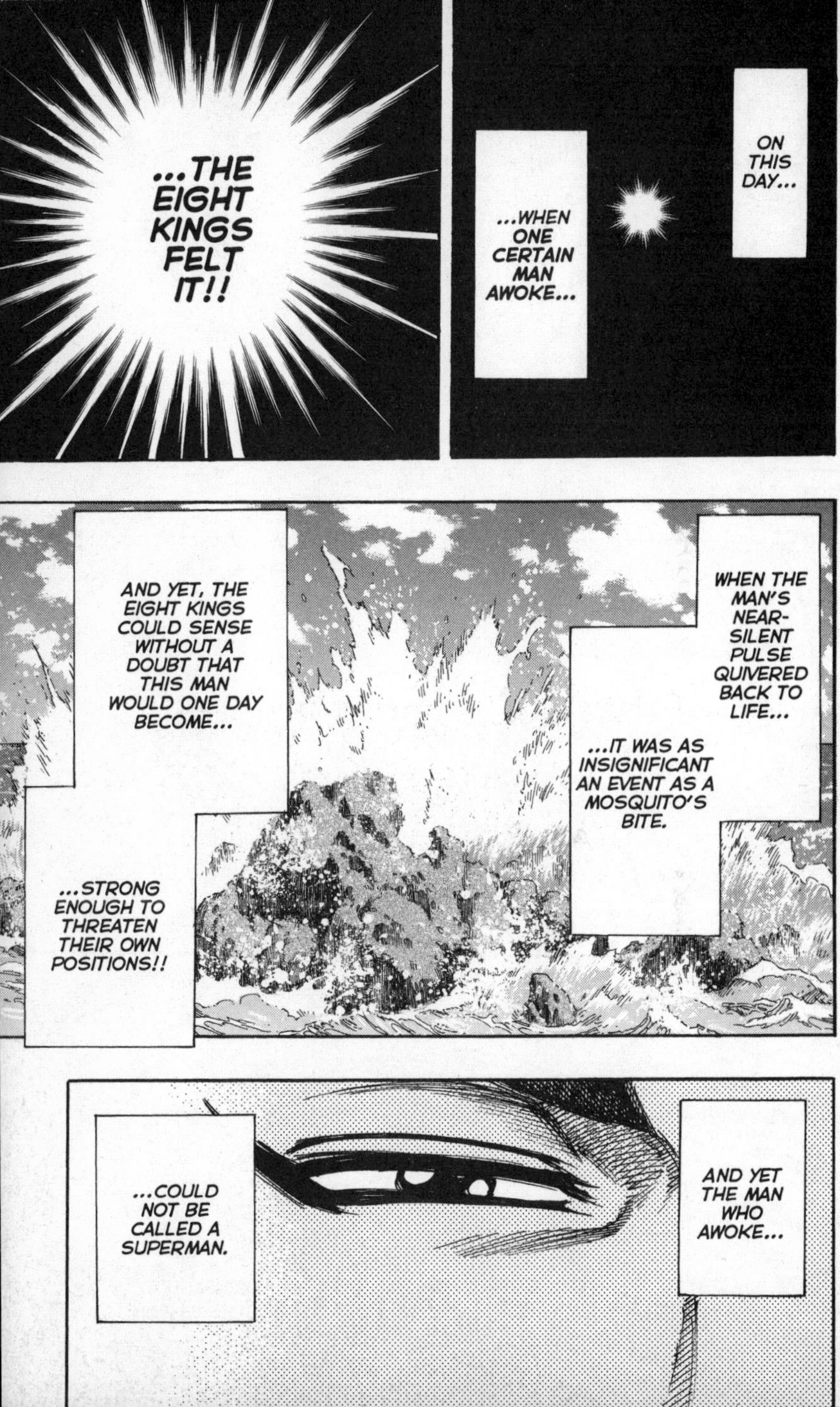
ON THIS DAY...
...WHEN ONE CERTAIN MAN AWOKE...
...THE EIGHT KINGS FELT IT!!
WHEN THE MAN'S NEAR-SILENT PULSE QUIVERED BACK TO LIFE...
...IT WAS AS INSIGNIFICANT AN EVENT AS A MOSQUITO'S BITE.
AND YET, THE EIGHT KINGS COULD SENSE WITHOUT A DOUBT THAT THIS MAN WOULD ONE DAY BECOME...
...STRONG ENOUGH TO THREATEN THEIR OWN POSITIONS!!
AND YET THE MAN WHO AWOKE...
...COULD NOT BE CALLED A SUPERMAN.

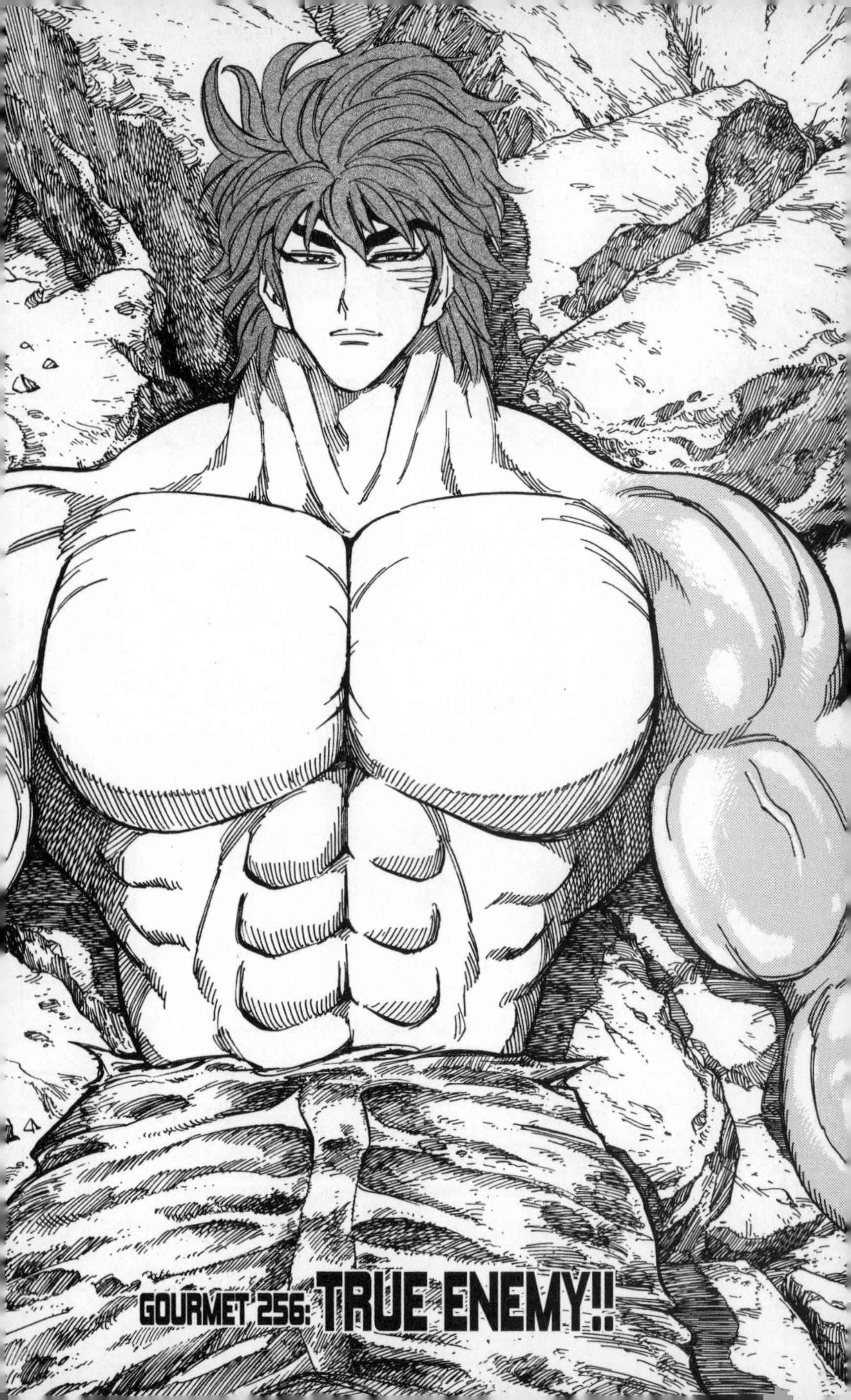
GOURMET 256: TRUE ENEMY!!

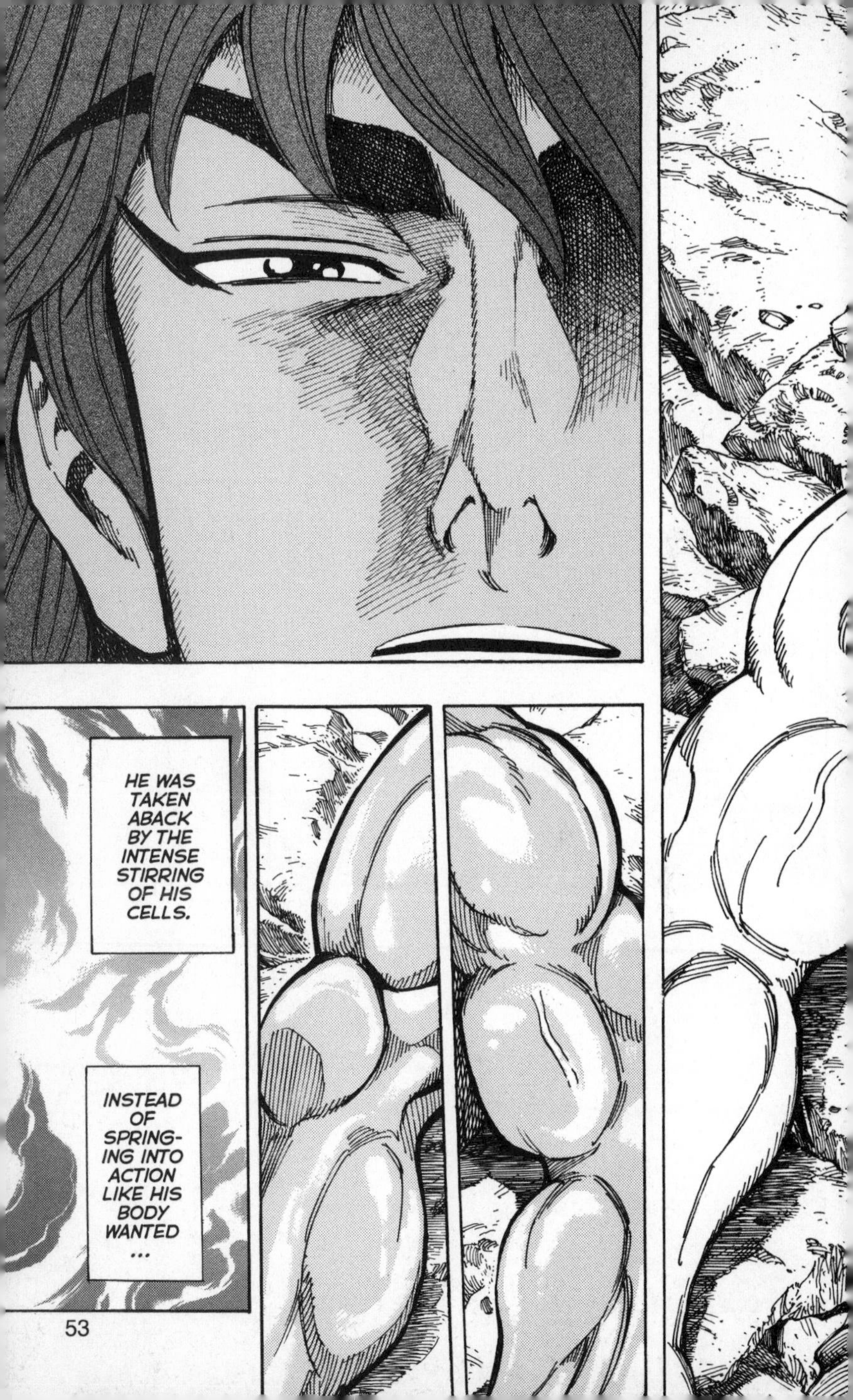
HE WAS TAKEN ABACK BY THE INTENSE STIRRING OF HIS CELLS.
INSTEAD OF SPRING-ING INTO ACTION LIKE HIS BODY WANTED ...

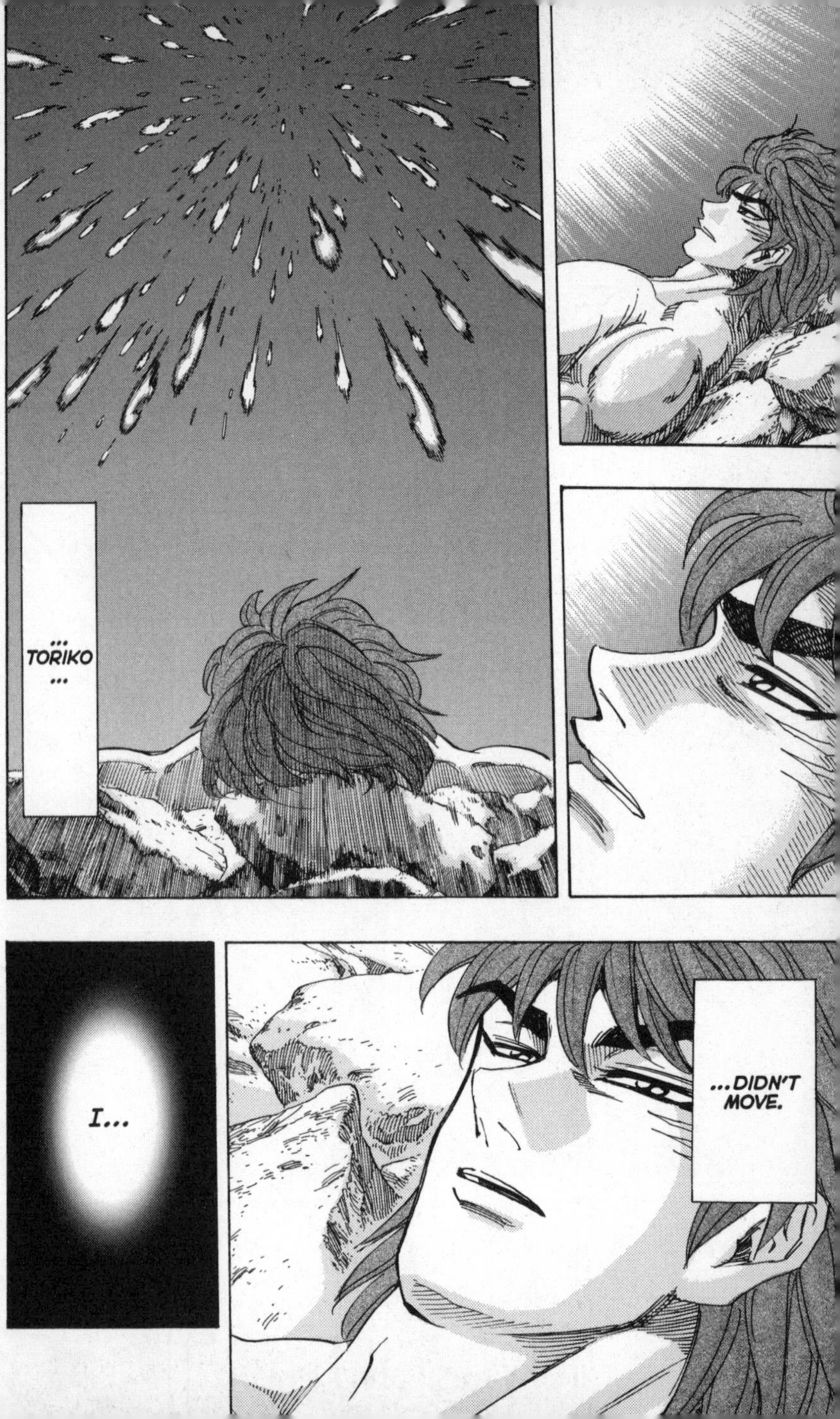
...TORIKO...
...DIDN'T MOVE.
I...

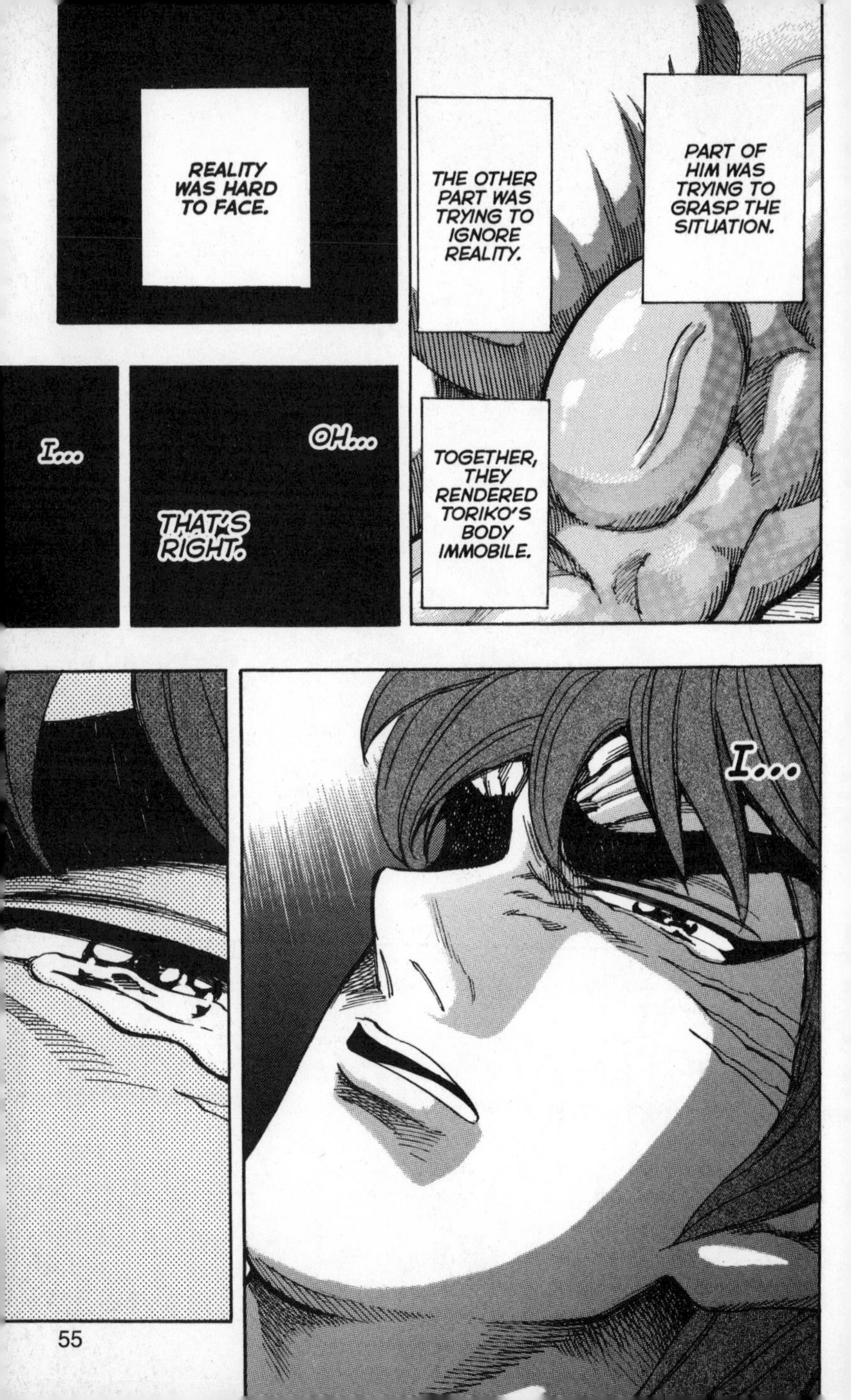
PART OF HIM WAS TRYING TO GRASP THE SITUATION.
THE OTHER PART WAS TRYING TO IGNORE REALITY.
TOGETHER, THEY RENDERED TORIKO'S BODY IMMOBILE.
REALITY WAS HARD TO FACE.
OH...
THAT'S RIGHT.
I...
I...

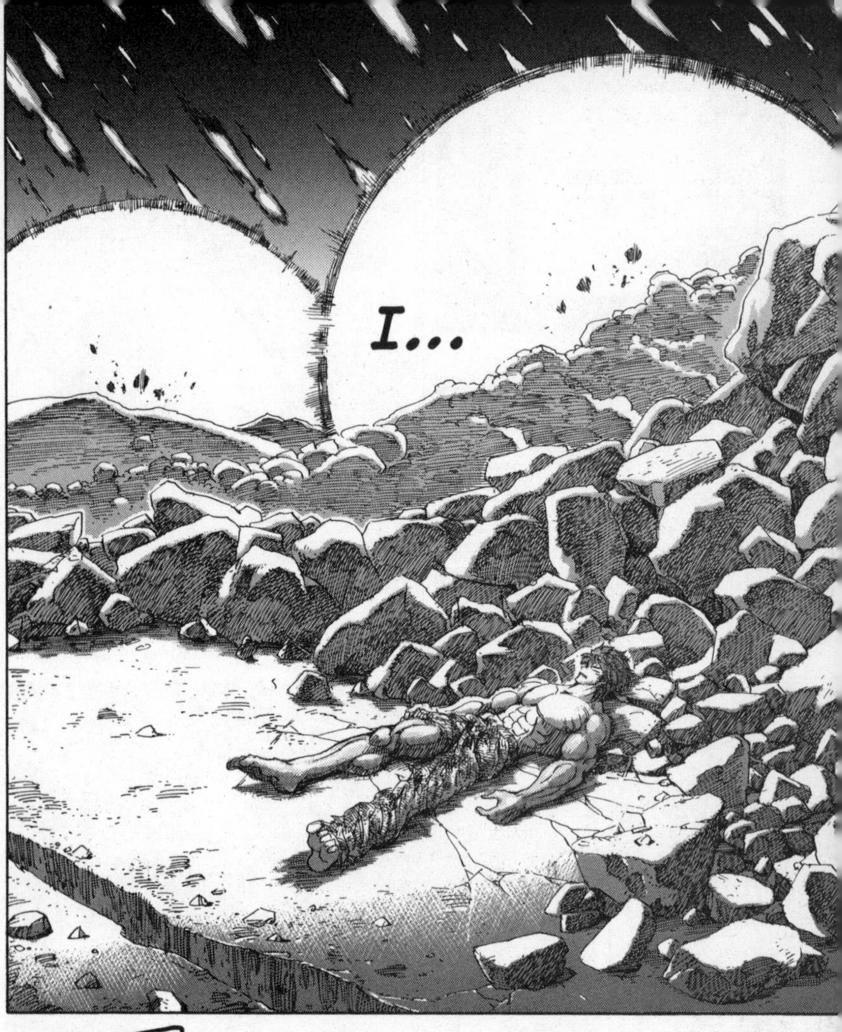
I...
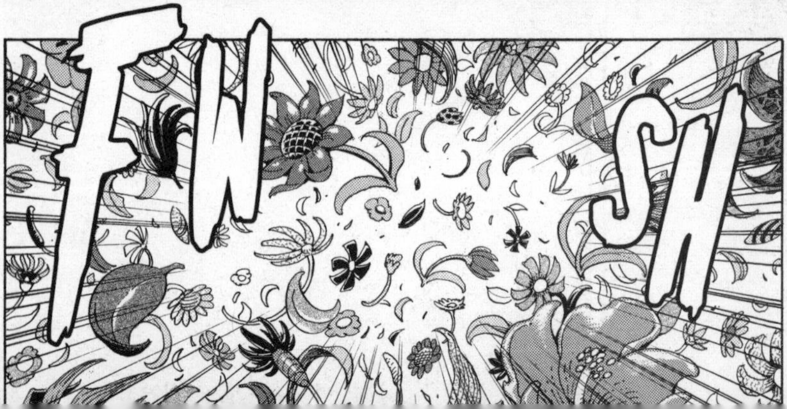
FWSH

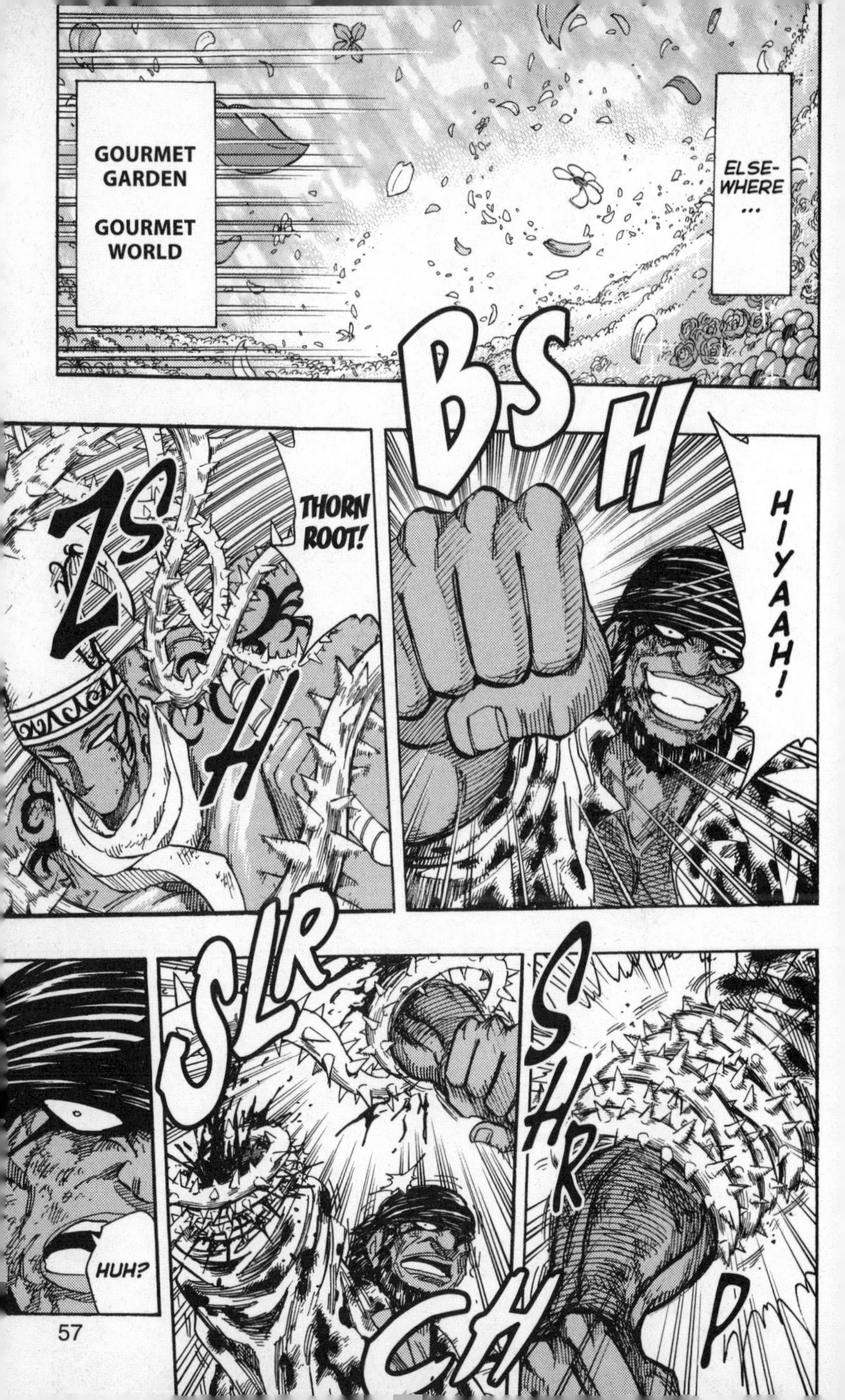
ELSE-WHERE ...
GOURMET GARDEN
GOURMET WORLD
BSH
HIYAAAH!
THORN ROOT!
ZSH
SHR
P
SLR
CH
HUH?

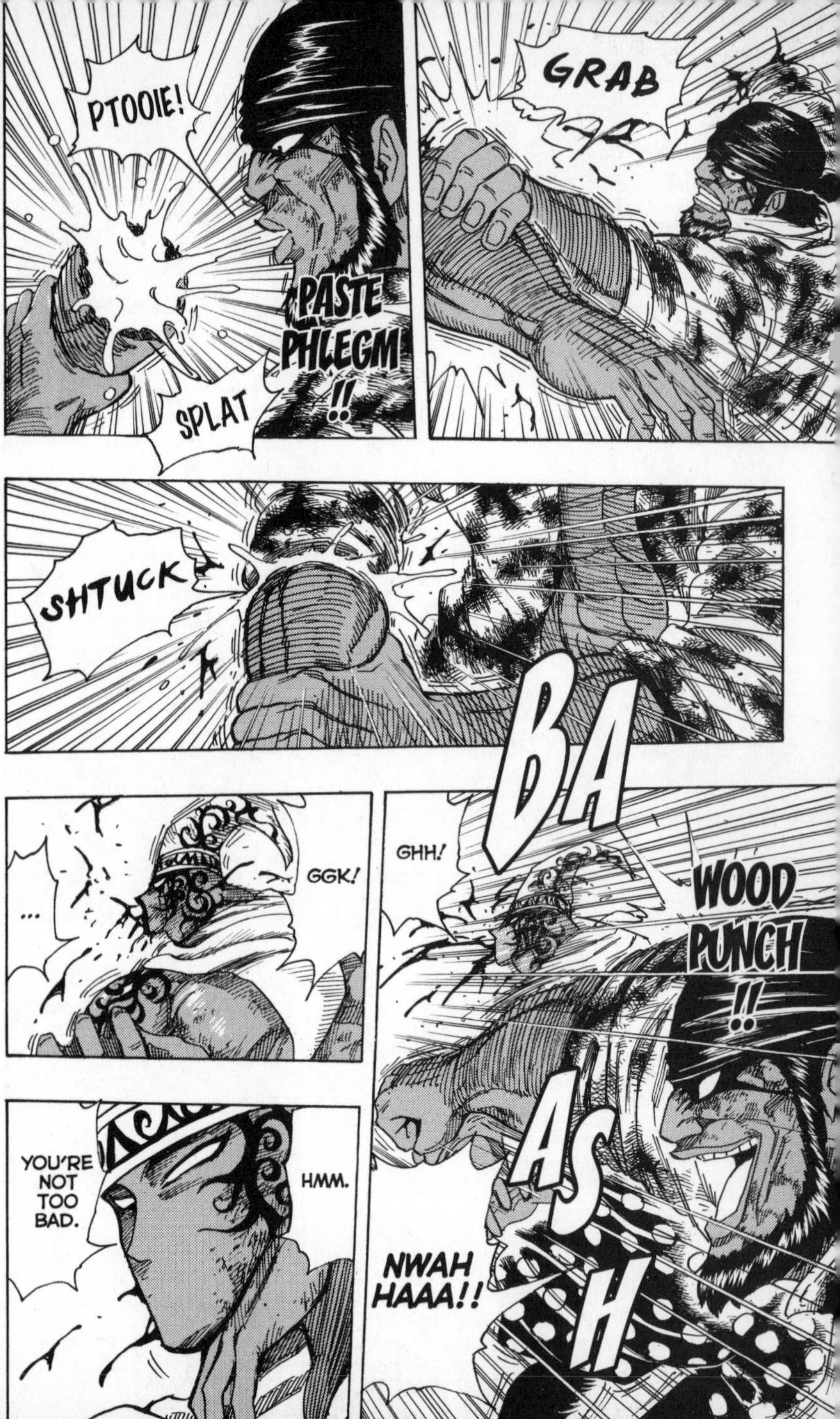
GRAB
PTOOIE!
PASTE PHLEGM!!
SPLAT
SHTUCK
BA
WOOD PUNCH!!
GHH!
ASH
NWAH HAAA!!
GGK!
...
HMM.
YOU'RE NOT TOO BAD.

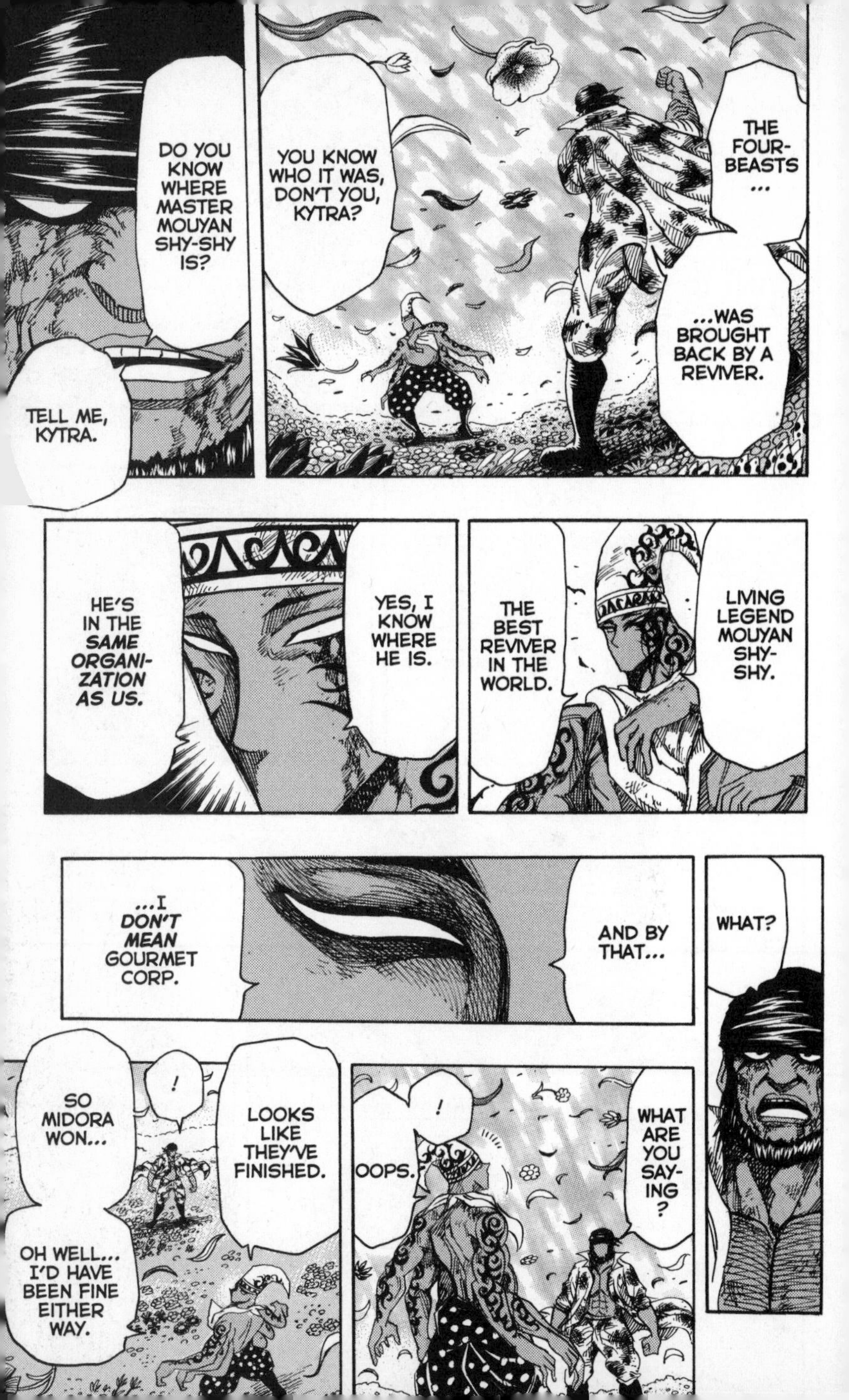
THE FOUR-BEASTS...
...WAS BROUGHT BACK BY A REVIVER.
YOU KNOW WHO IT WAS, DON'T YOU, KYTRA?
DO YOU KNOW WHERE MASTER MOUYAN SHY-SHY IS?
TELL ME, KYTRA.
LIVING LEGEND MOUYAN SHY-SHY.
THE BEST REVIVER IN THE WORLD.
YES, I KNOW WHERE HE IS.
HE'S IN THE *SAME ORGANIZATION* AS US.
WHAT?
AND BY THAT...
...I *DON'T MEAN* GOURMET CORP.
WHAT ARE YOU SAYING?
!
OOPS.
LOOKS LIKE THEY'VE FINISHED.
!
SO MIDORA WON...
OH WELL... I'D HAVE BEEN FINE EITHER WAY.

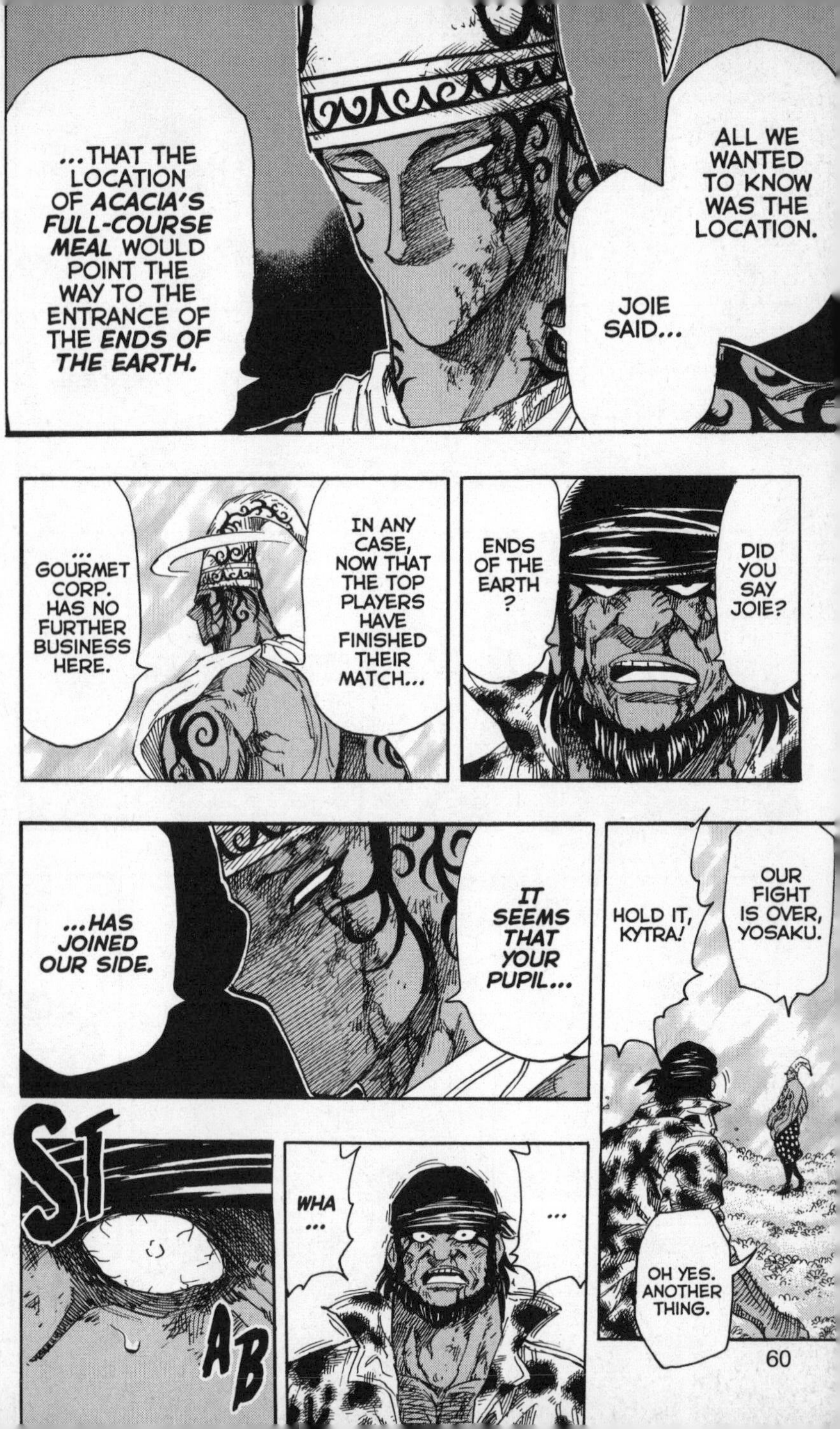
ALL WE WANTED TO KNOW WAS THE LOCATION.
JOIE SAID...
...THAT THE LOCATION OF *ACACIA'S FULL-COURSE MEAL* WOULD POINT THE WAY TO THE ENTRANCE OF THE *ENDS OF THE EARTH.*
DID YOU SAY JOIE?
ENDS OF THE EARTH ?
IN ANY CASE, NOW THAT THE TOP PLAYERS HAVE FINISHED THEIR MATCH...
... GOURMET CORP. HAS NO FURTHER BUSINESS HERE.
OUR FIGHT IS OVER, YOSAKU.
HOLD IT, KYTRA!
OH YES. ANOTHER THING.
IT SEEMS THAT YOUR PUPIL...
...HAS JOINED OUR SIDE.
WHA ...
...
ST
AB

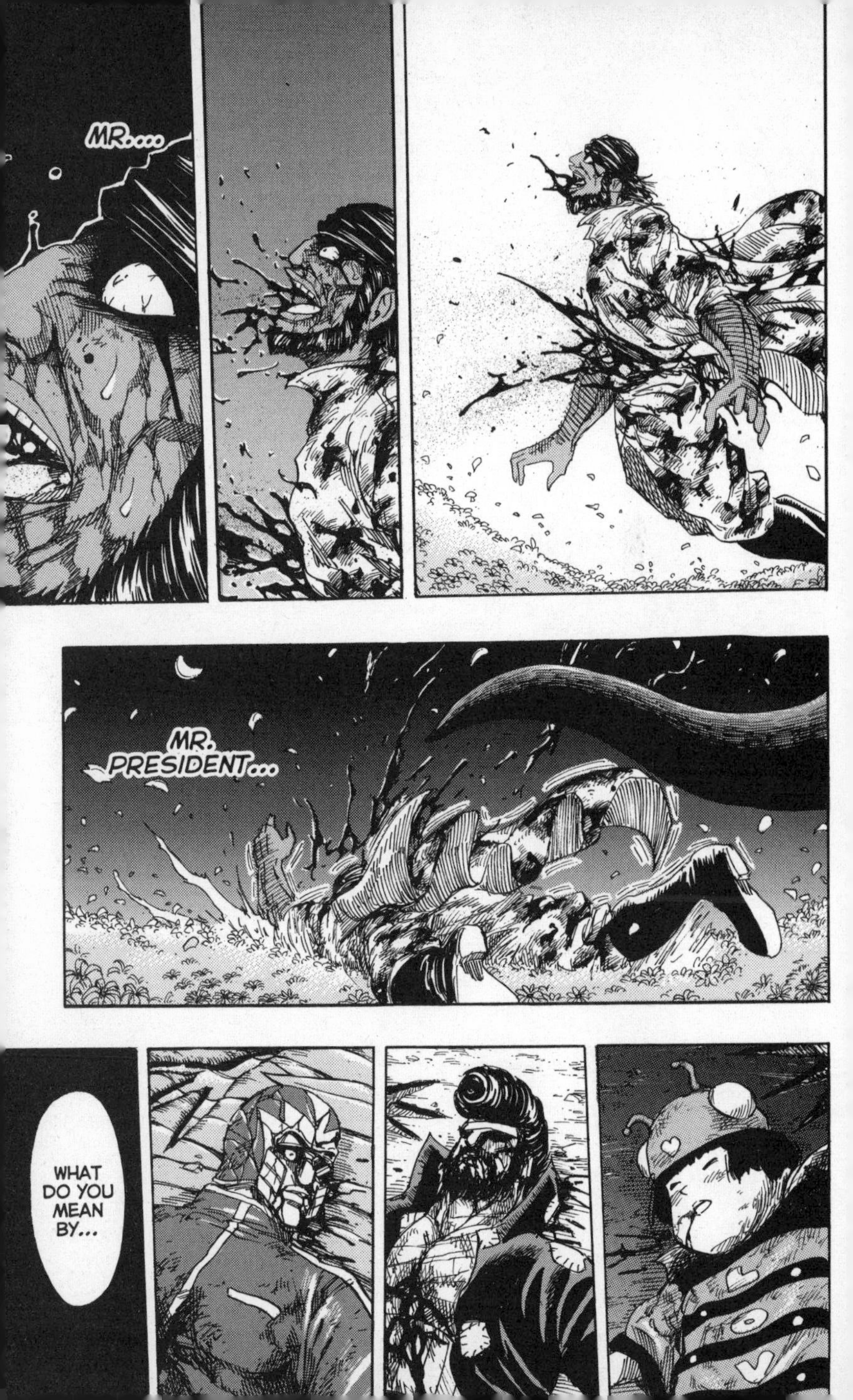
MR....
MR. PRESIDENT...
WHAT DO YOU MEAN BY...

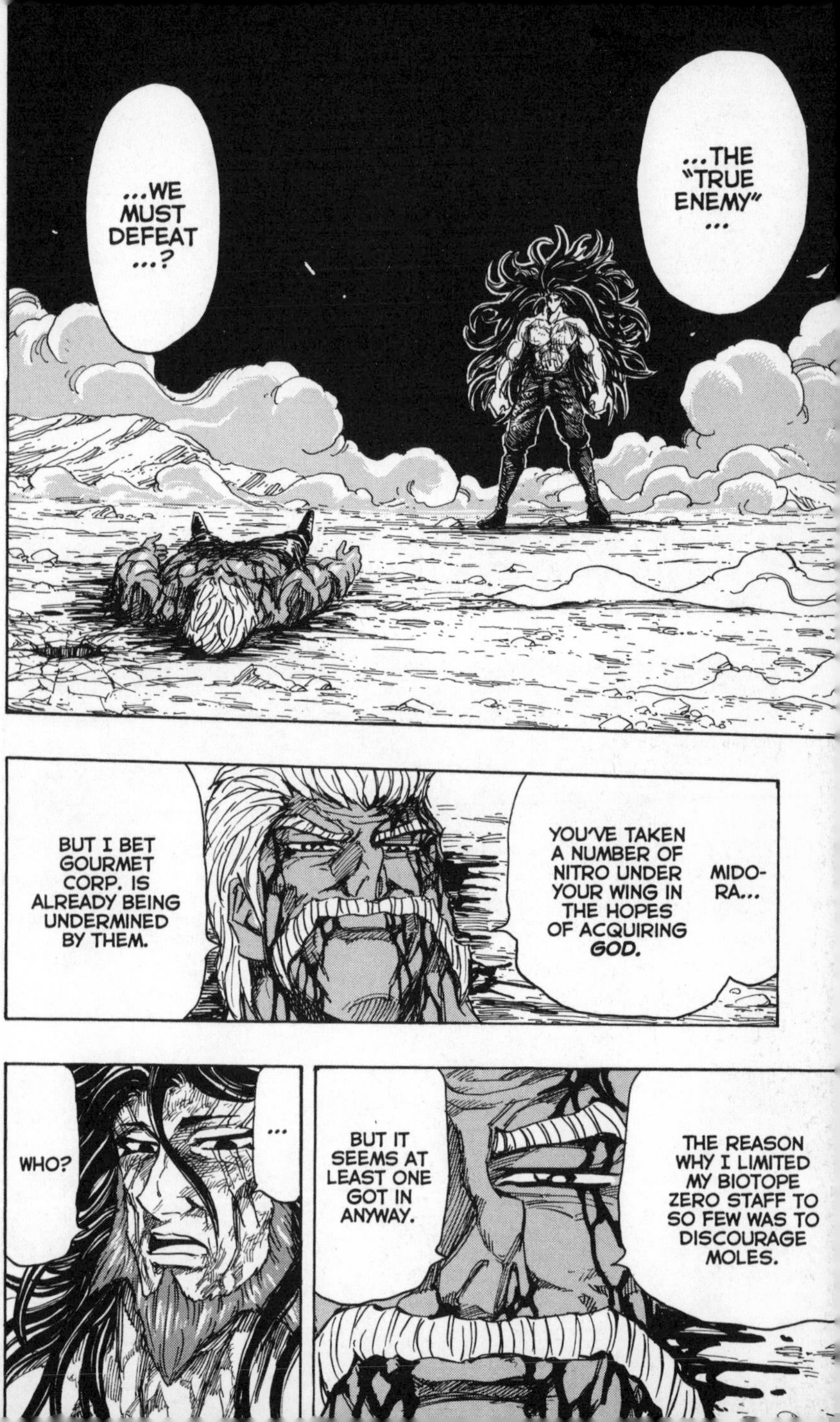
...THE "TRUE ENEMY" ...
...WE MUST DEFEAT ...?
MIDO-RA...
YOU'VE TAKEN A NUMBER OF NITRO UNDER YOUR WING IN THE HOPES OF ACQUIRING *GOD*.
BUT I BET GOURMET CORP. IS ALREADY BEING UNDERMINED BY THEM.
THE REASON WHY I LIMITED MY BIOTOPE ZERO STAFF TO SO FEW WAS TO DISCOURAGE MOLES.
BUT IT SEEMS AT LEAST ONE GOT IN ANYWAY.
...
WHO?

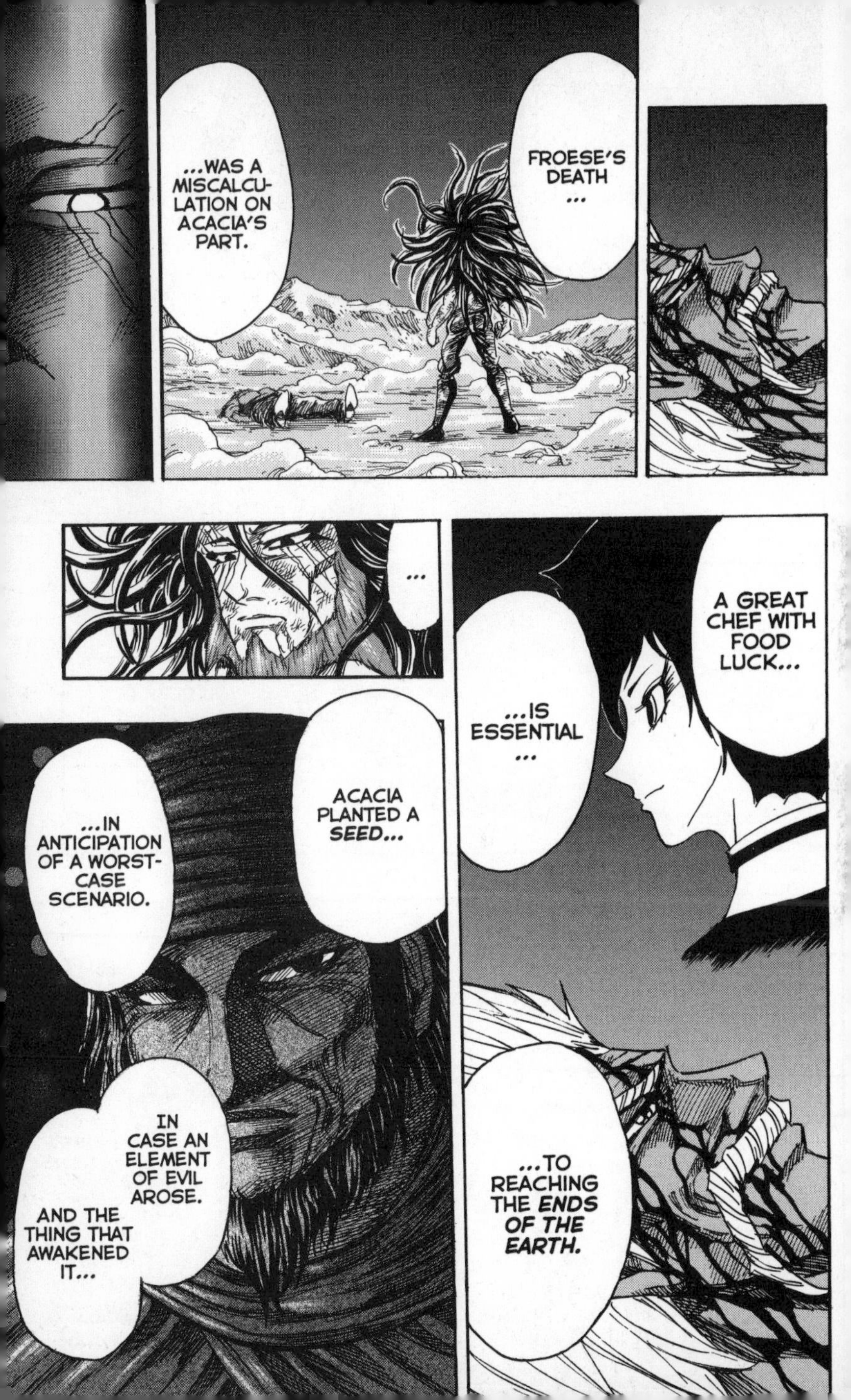
FROESE'S DEATH ...
...WAS A MISCALCU-LATION ON ACACIA'S PART.
A GREAT CHEF WITH FOOD LUCK...
...IS ESSENTIAL ...
...TO REACHING THE *ENDS OF THE EARTH.*
...
ACACIA PLANTED A *SEED...*
...IN ANTICIPATION OF A WORST-CASE SCENARIO.
IN CASE AN ELEMENT OF EVIL AROSE.
AND THE THING THAT AWAKENED IT...

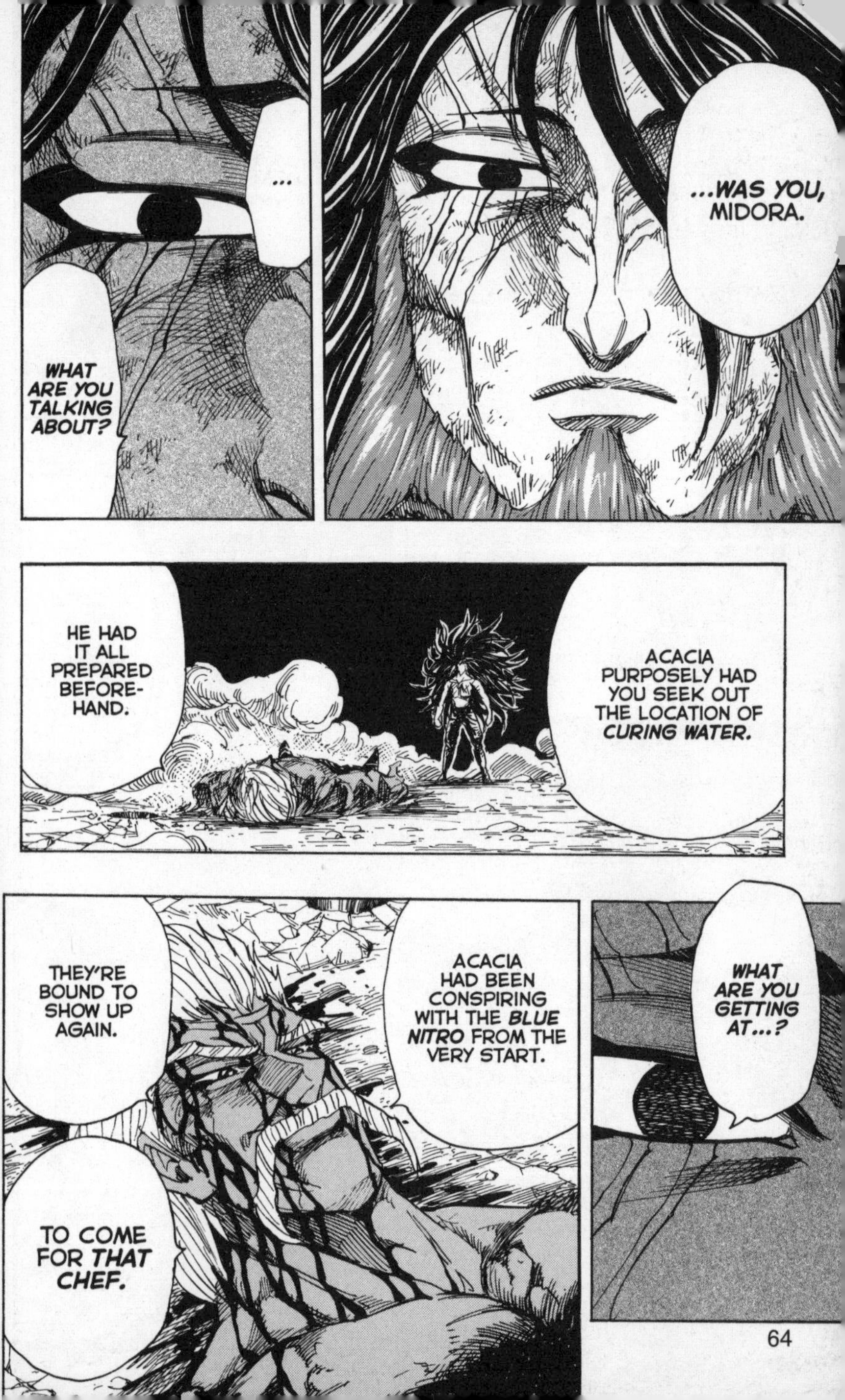

...*WAS YOU,* MIDORA.
...
WHAT ARE YOU TALKING ABOUT?
ACACIA PURPOSELY HAD YOU SEEK OUT THE LOCATION OF *CURING WATER.*
HE HAD IT ALL PREPARED BEFORE-HAND.
WHAT ARE YOU GETTING AT...?
ACACIA HAD BEEN CONSPIRING WITH THE *BLUE NITRO* FROM THE VERY START.
THEY'RE BOUND TO SHOW UP AGAIN.
TO COME FOR *THAT CHEF.*

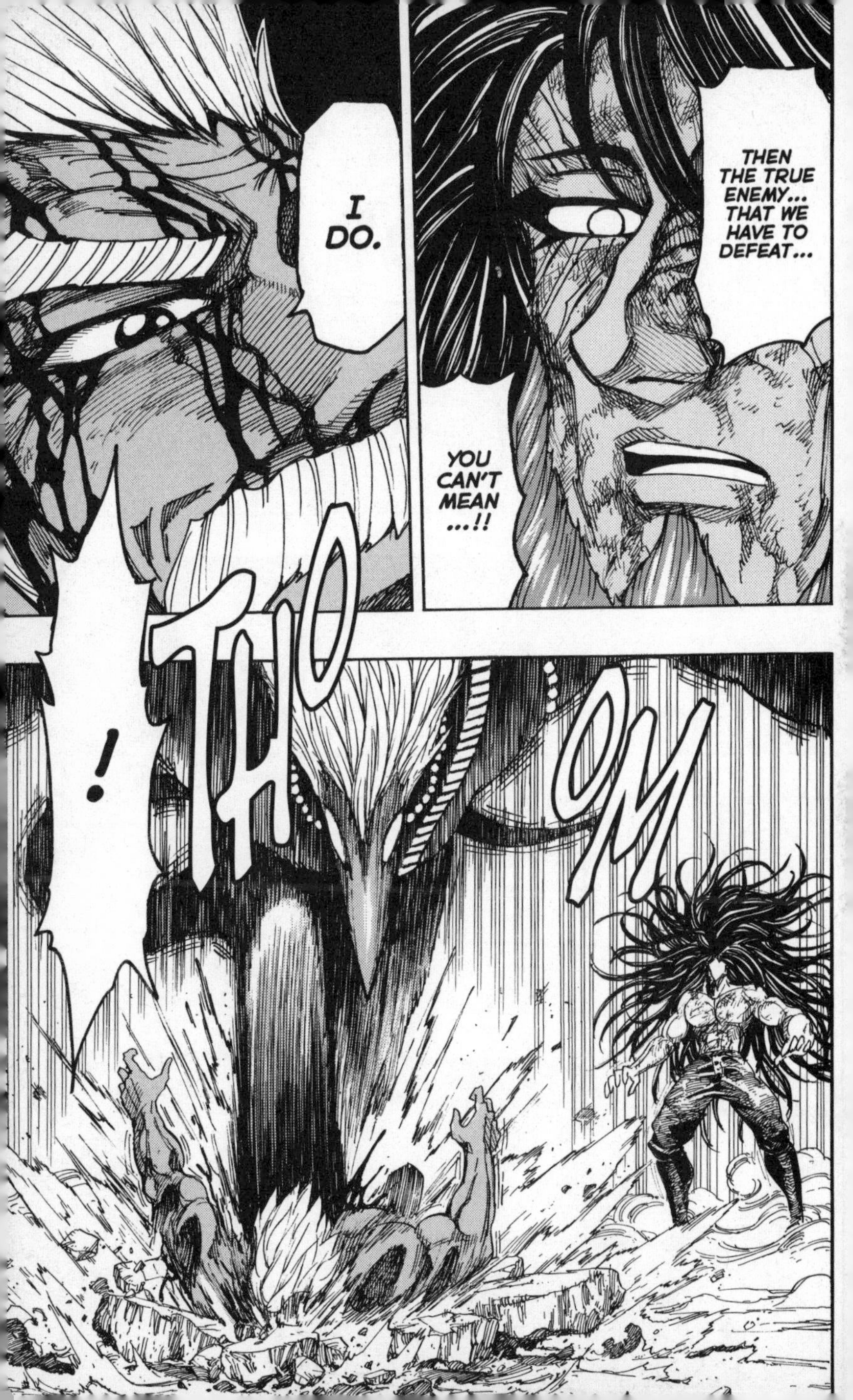
THEN THE TRUE ENEMY... THAT WE HAVE TO DEFEAT...
YOU CAN'T MEAN ...!!
I DO.
THOOM
!

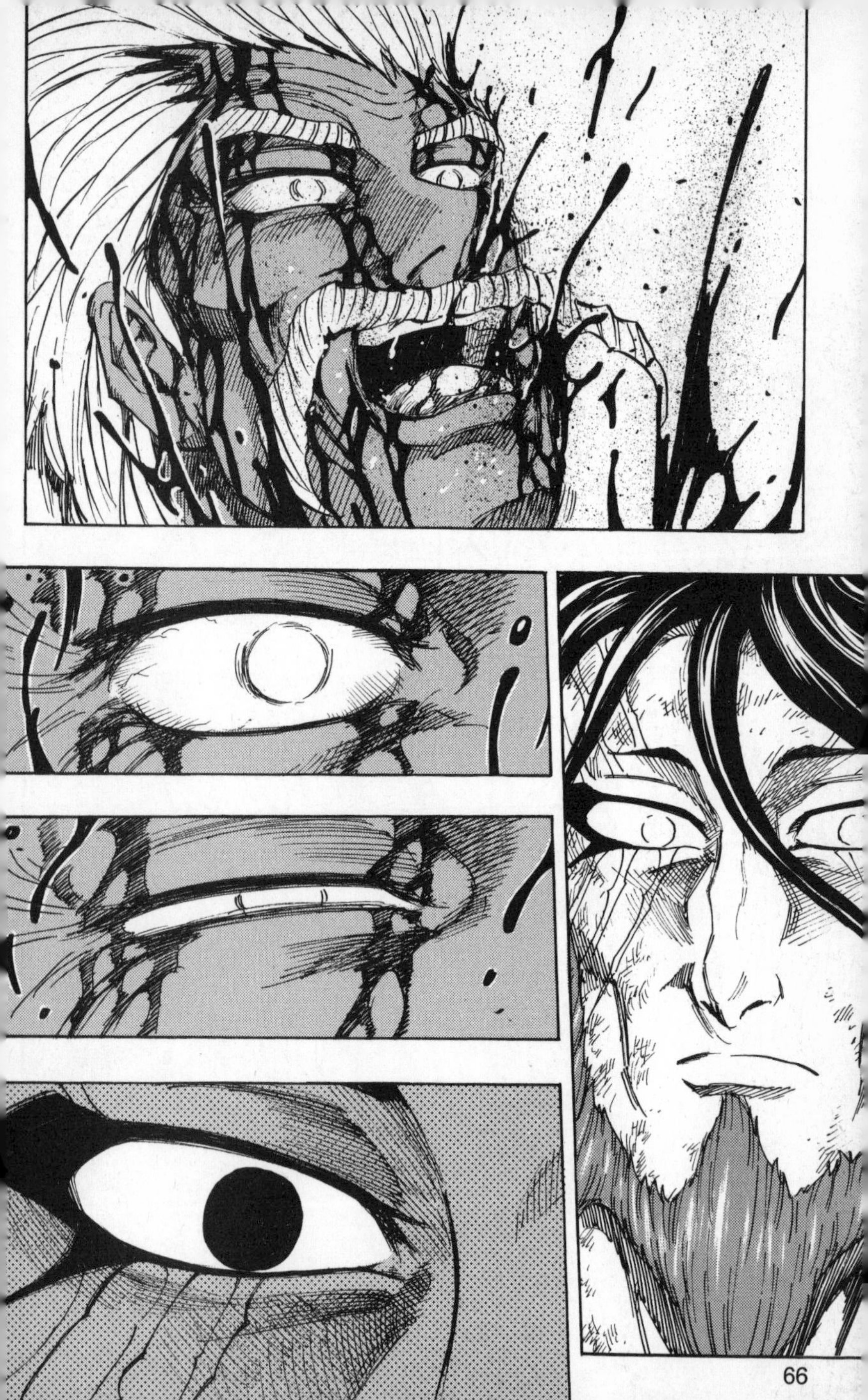

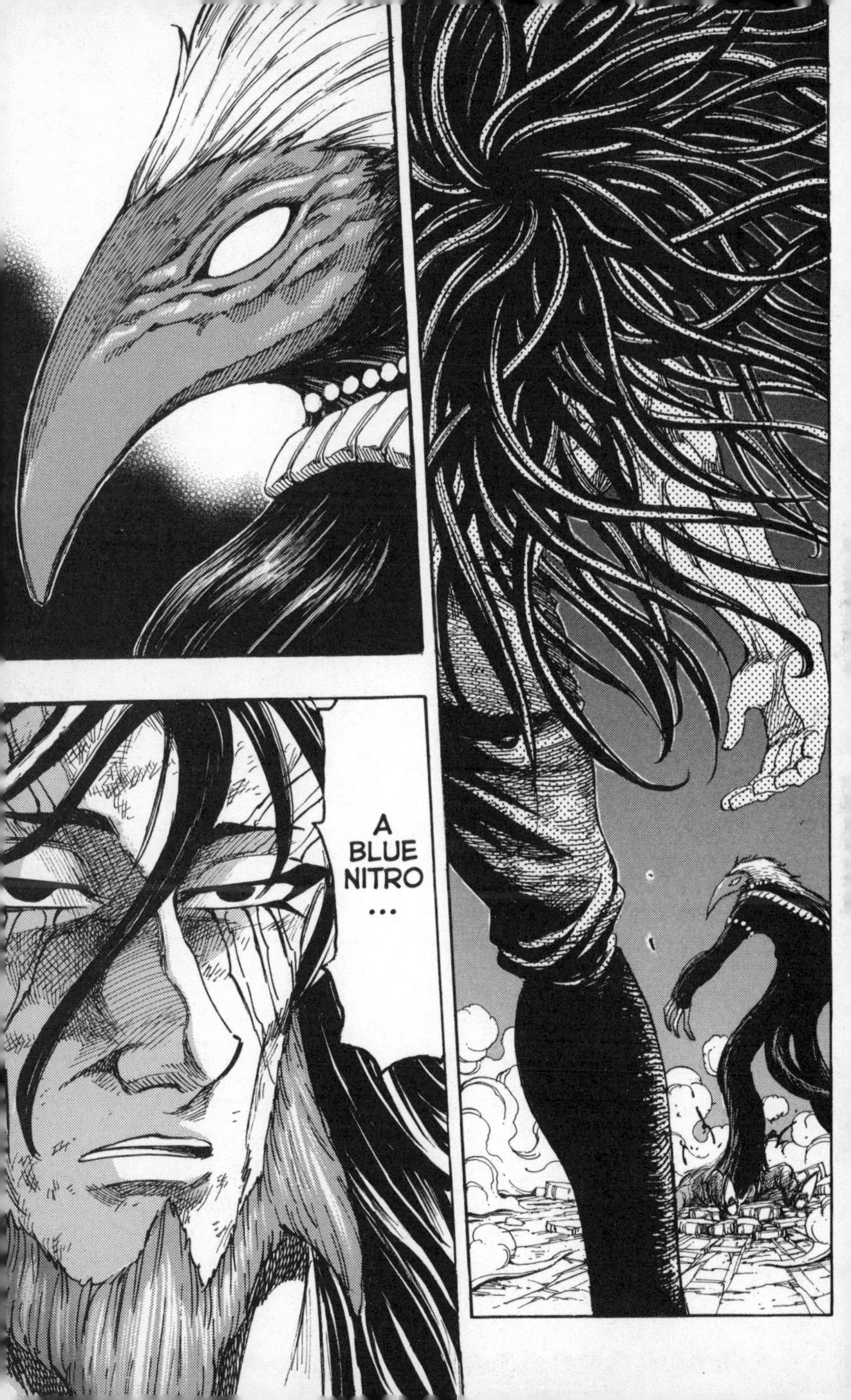
A BLUE NITRO ...

TORIKO

GOURMET CHECKLIST

Vol. 282

TURMERIC TURD
(PLANT)

CAPTURE LEVEL: LESS THAN 1
HABITAT: SPIRITS ARCHIPELAGO
SIZE: ---
HEIGHT: 15 CM
WEIGHT: 450 G
PRICE: 1,600 YEN PER TURD

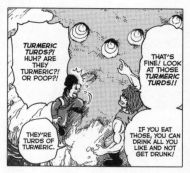

THAT'S FINE! LOOK AT THOSE TURMERIC TURDS!!
TURMERIC TURDS?! HUH? ARE THEY TURMERIC?! OR POOP?!
IF YOU EAT THOSE, YOU CAN DRINK ALL YOU LIKE AND NOT GET DRUNK!
THEY'RE TURDS OF TURMERIC.

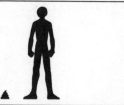

SCALE

A PERENNIAL PLANT IN THE GINGER FAMILY. YEP, IT'S SHAPED LIKE POOP. ONCE YOU GET OVER ITS APPEARANCE, YOU CAN ENJOY THE BENEFITS OF EATING TUMERIC TURD--NAMELY, DRINKING ALL YOU LIKE AND NEVER GETTING DRUNK THANKS TO ITS SUPPORT OF LIVER HEALTH. IT'S A REAL GODSEND FOR VISITORS TO THE SPIRITS ARCHIPELAGO.

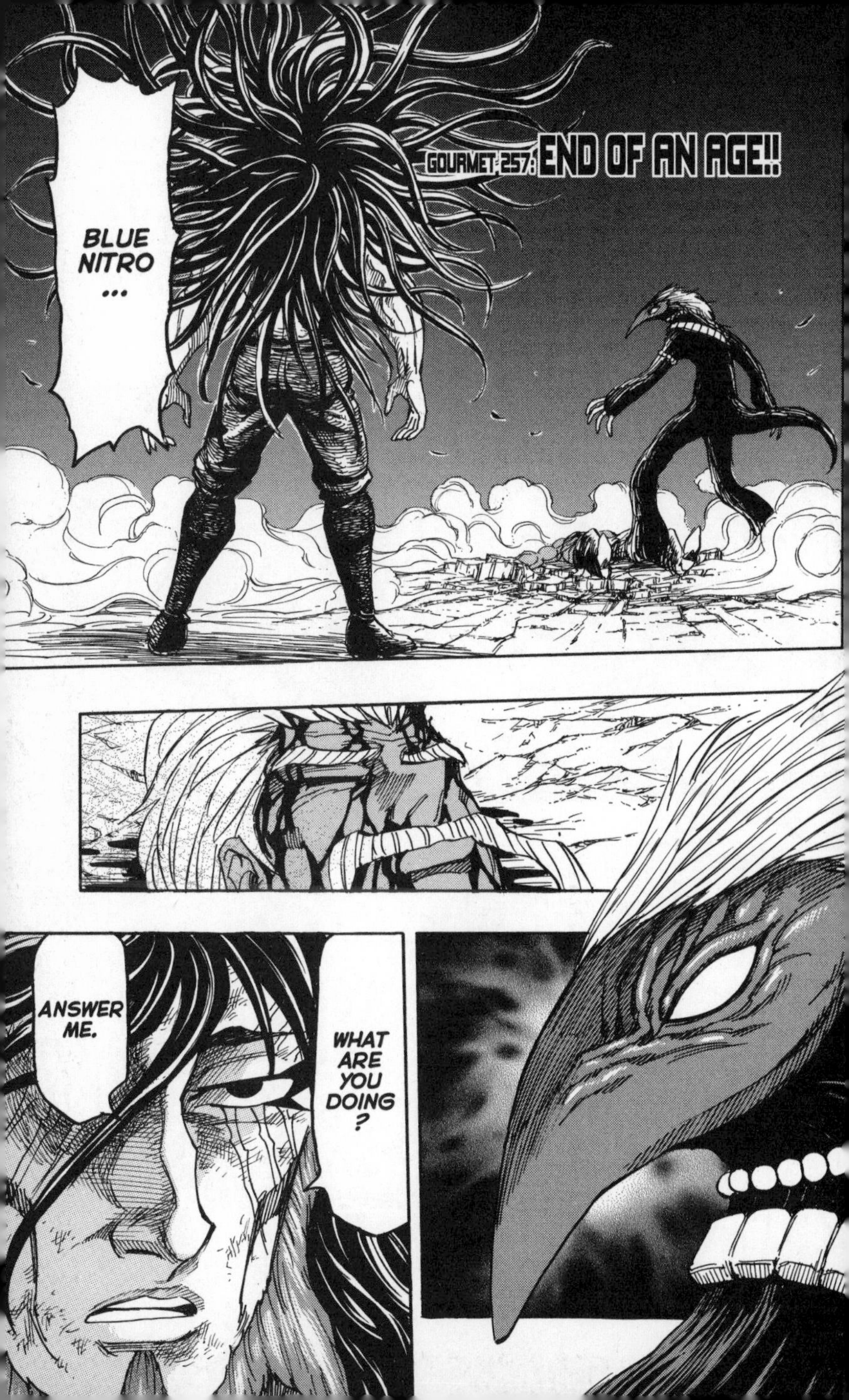
GOURMET 257: END OF AN AGE!!
BLUE NITRO...
WHAT ARE YOU DOING?
ANSWER ME.

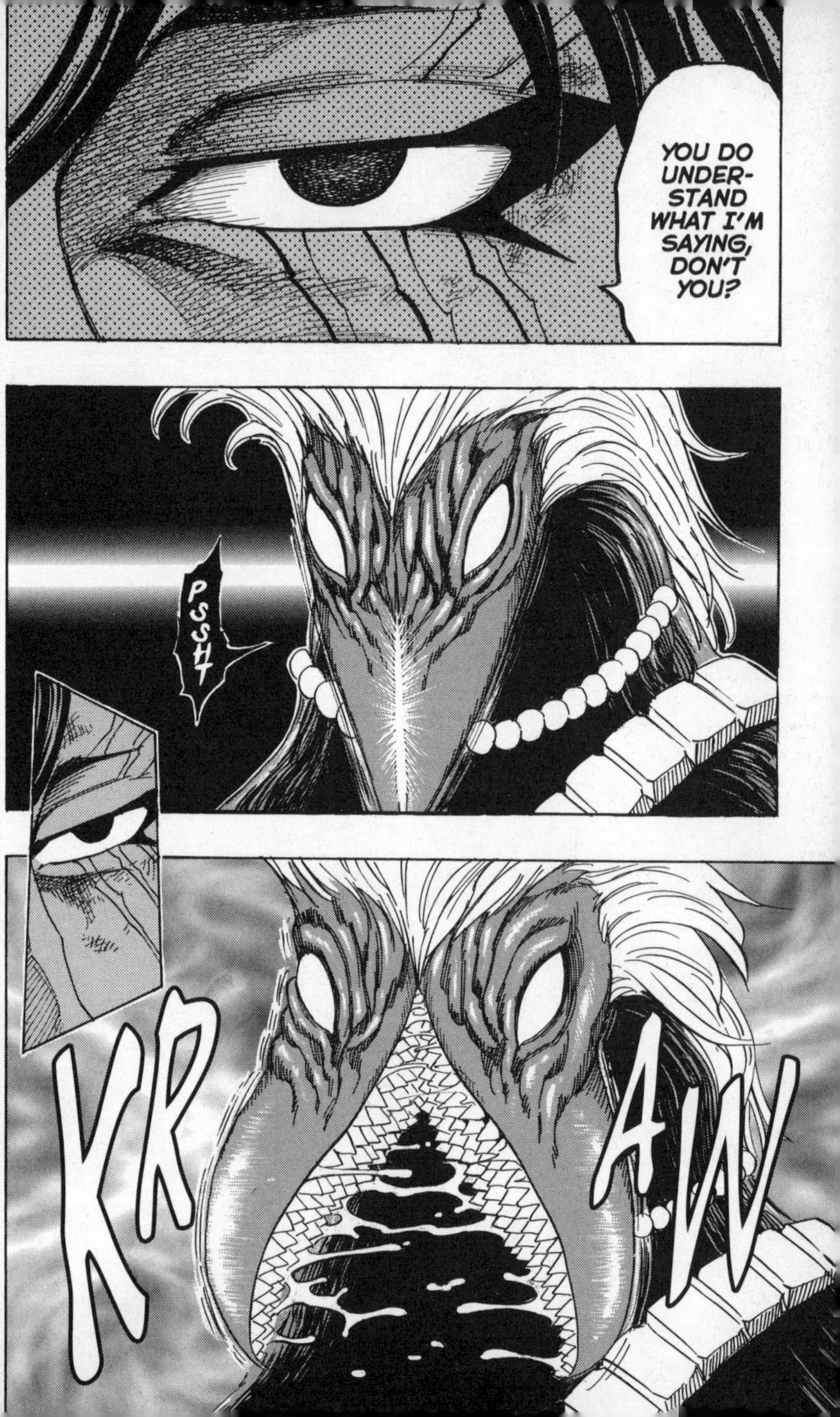
YOU DO UNDER-STAND WHAT I'M SAYING, DON'T YOU?
PSSHT
KRAAN

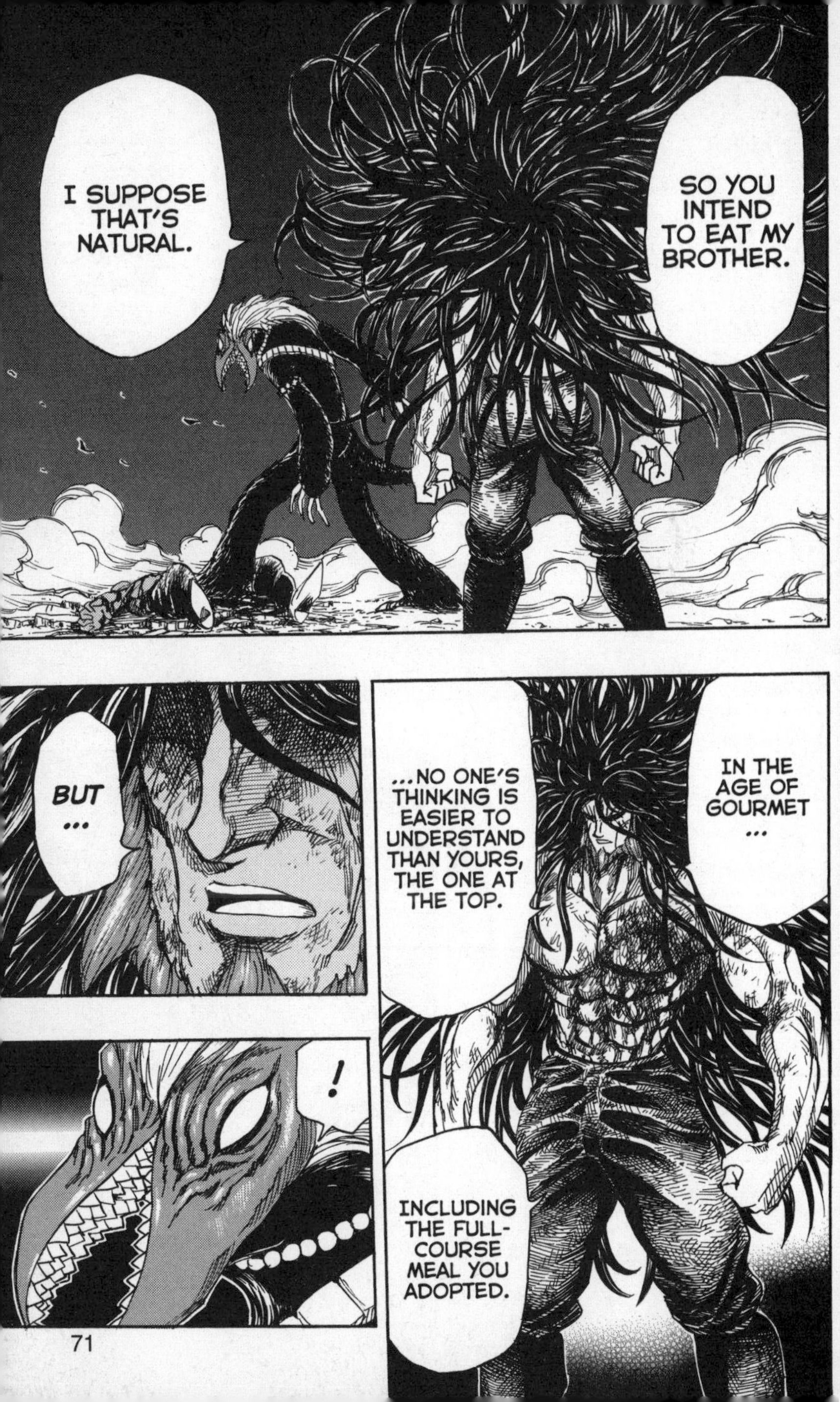
SO YOU INTEND TO EAT MY BROTHER.
I SUPPOSE THAT'S NATURAL.
IN THE AGE OF GOURMET ...
...NO ONE'S THINKING IS EASIER TO UNDERSTAND THAN YOURS, THE ONE AT THE TOP.
INCLUDING THE FULL-COURSE MEAL YOU ADOPTED.
BUT ...
!

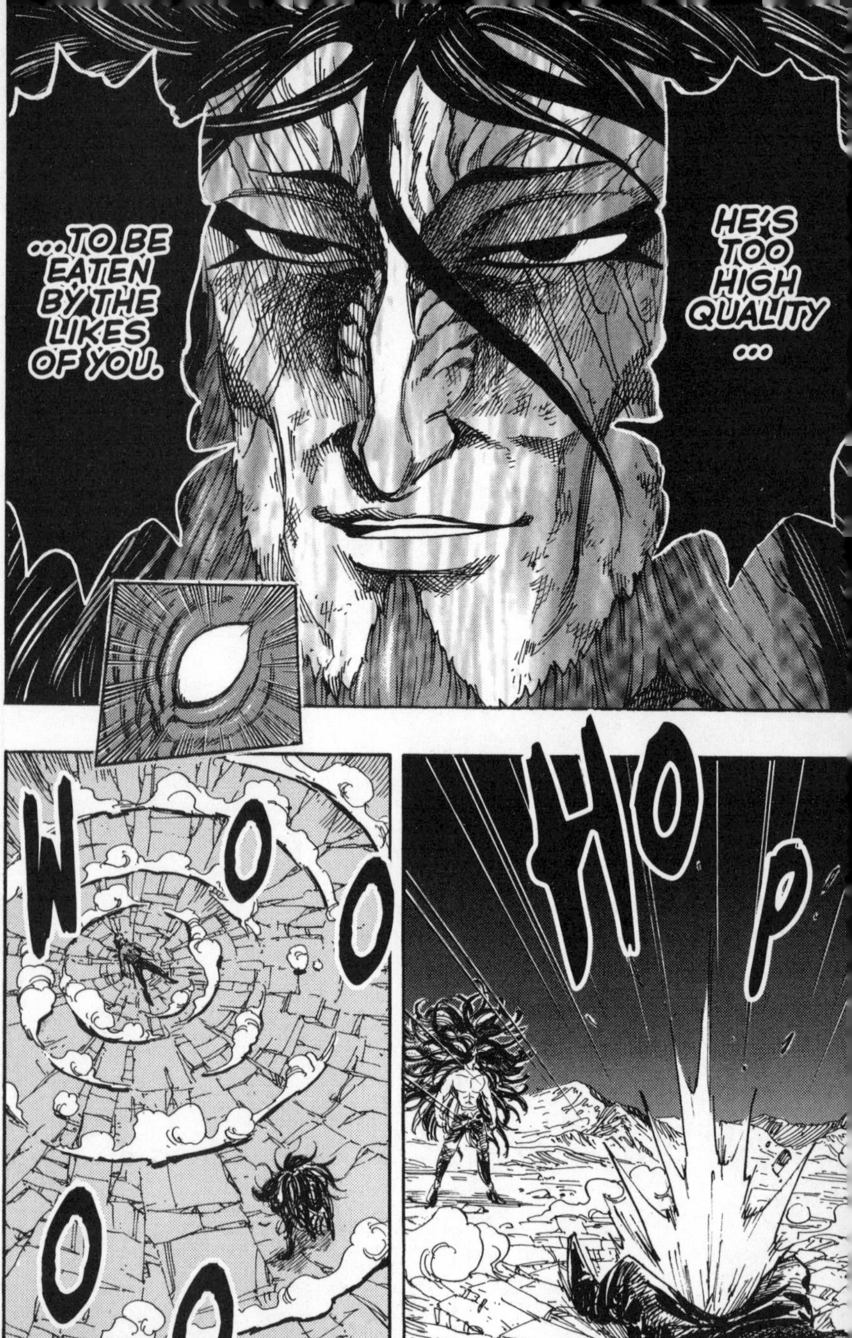
HE'S TOO HIGH QUALITY...
...TO BE EATEN BY THE LIKES OF YOU.
HOP
WOOOO

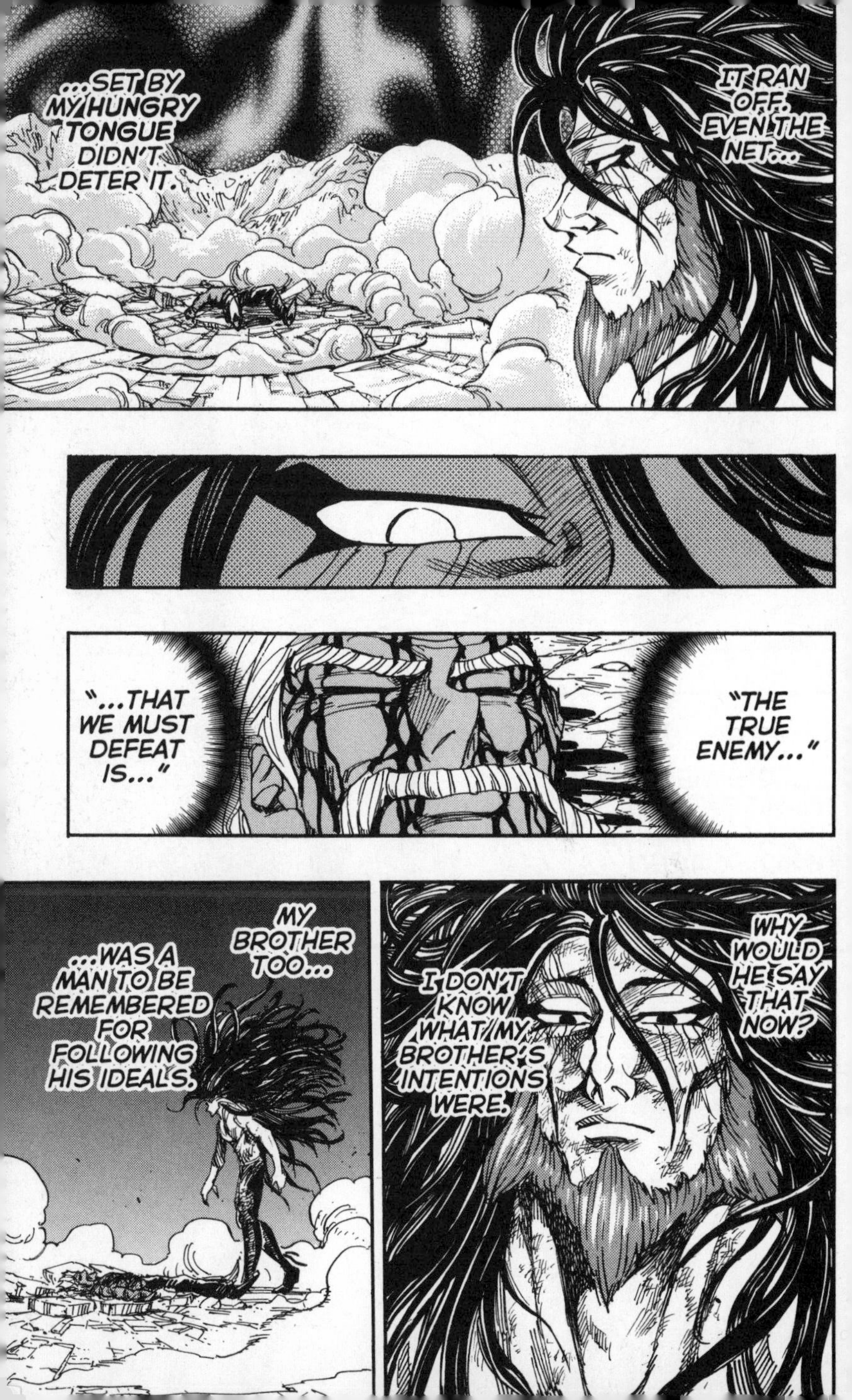
IT RAN OFF. EVEN THE NET...
...SET BY MY HUNGRY TONGUE DIDN'T DETER IT.
"THE TRUE ENEMY..."
"...THAT WE MUST DEFEAT IS..."
WHY WOULD HE SAY THAT NOW?
I DON'T KNOW WHAT MY BROTHER'S INTENTIONS WERE.
MY BROTHER TOO...
...WAS A MAN TO BE REMEMBERED FOR FOLLOWING HIS IDEALS.

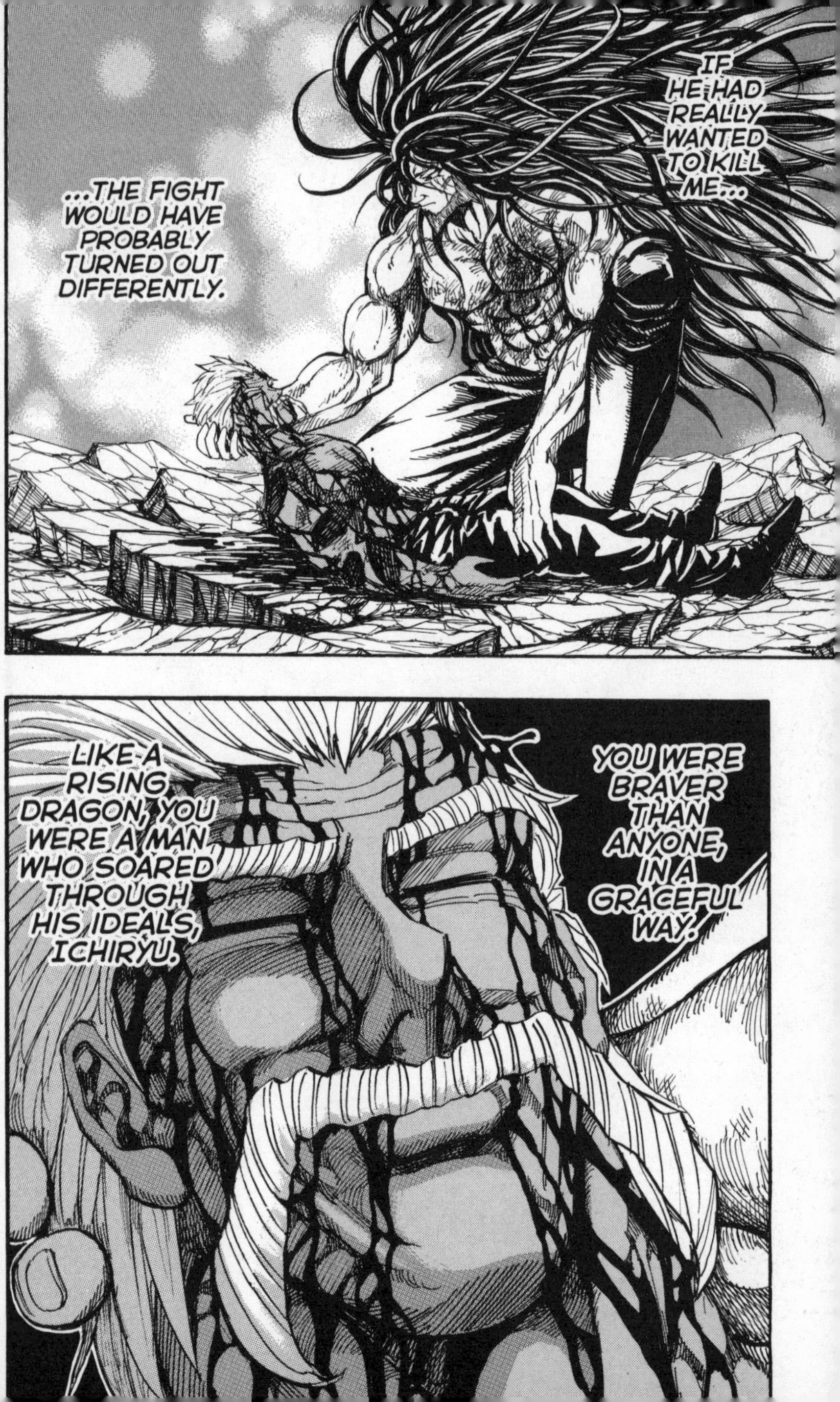
IF HE HAD REALLY WANTED TO KILL ME...
...THE FIGHT WOULD HAVE PROBABLY TURNED OUT DIFFERENTLY.
YOU WERE BRAVER THAN ANYONE, IN A GRACEFUL WAY.
LIKE A RISING DRAGON, YOU WERE A MAN WHO SOARED THROUGH HIS IDEALS, ICHIRYU.

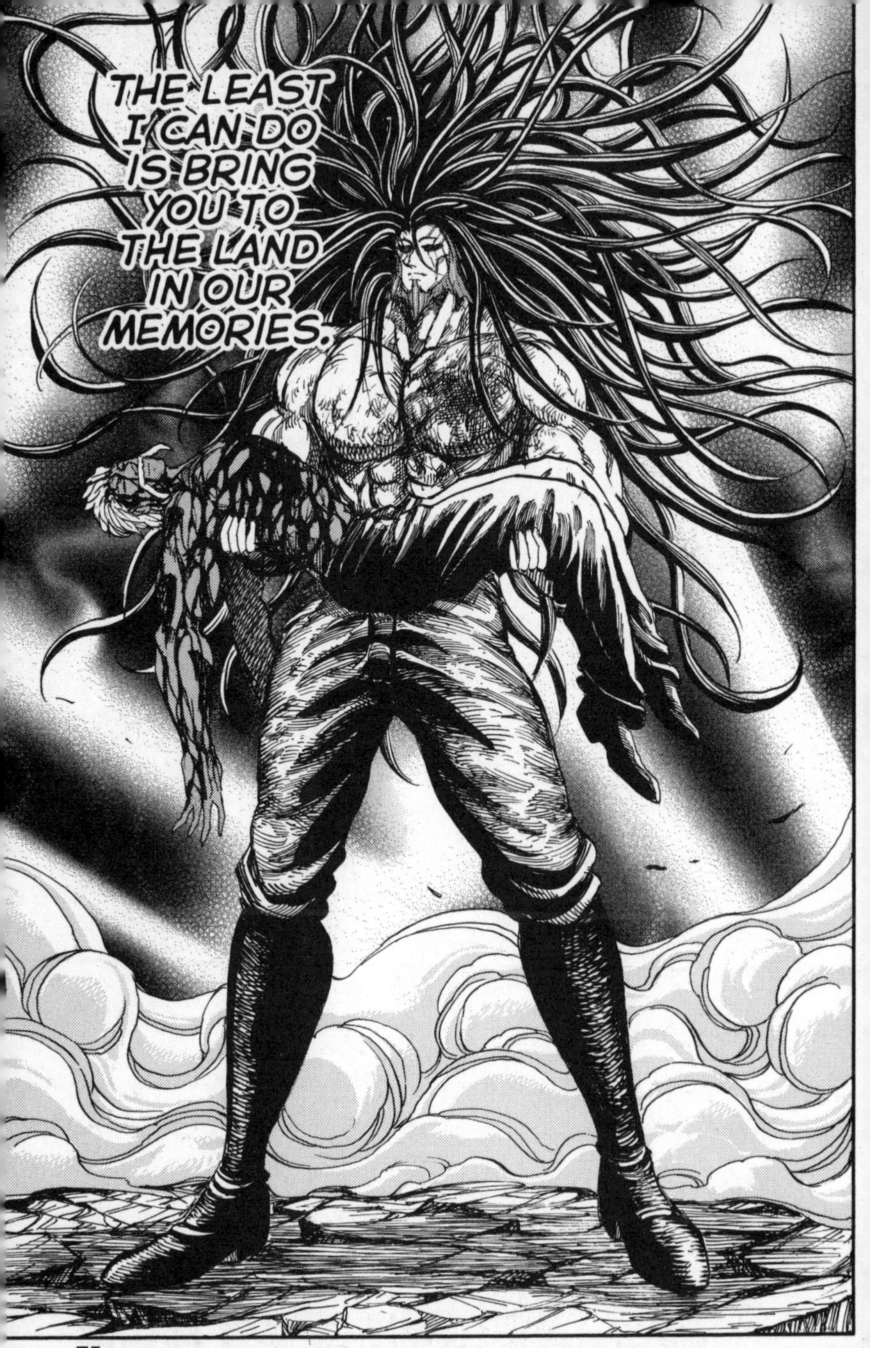
THE LEAST I CAN DO IS BRING YOU TO THE LAND IN OUR MEMORIES.

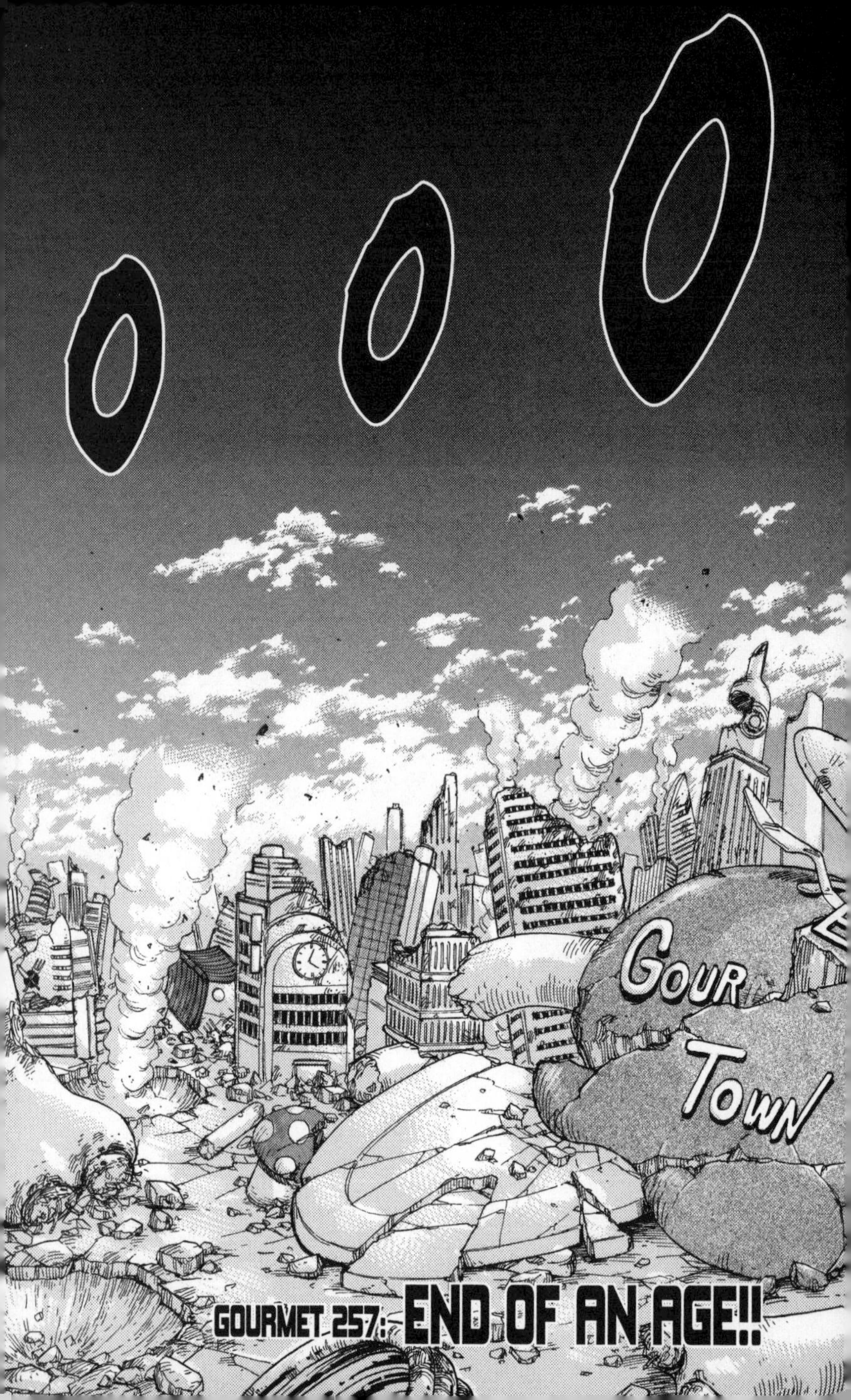
GOUR TOWN
GOURMET 257: END OF AN AGE!!

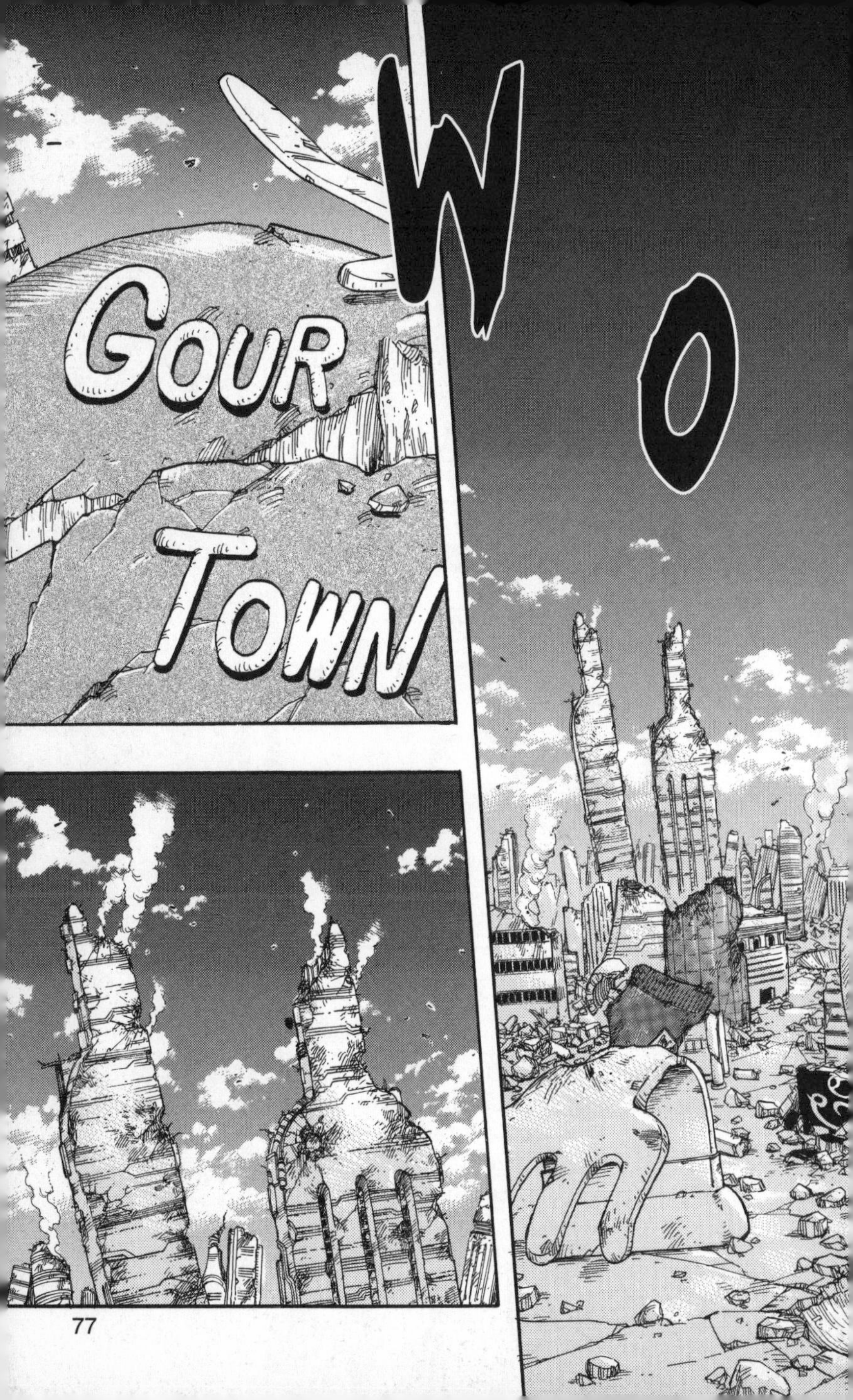
WO
GOUR TOWN

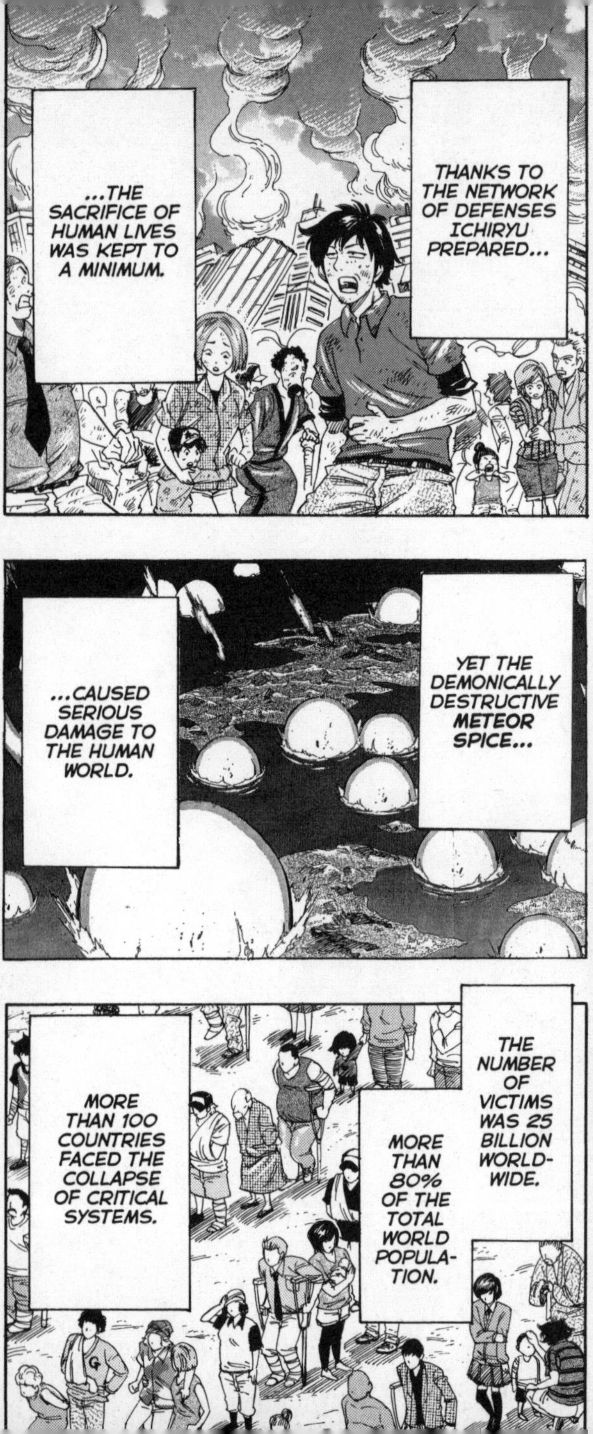
THANKS TO THE NETWORK OF DEFENSES ICHIRYU PREPARED...
...THE SACRIFICE OF HUMAN LIVES WAS KEPT TO A MINIMUM.
YET THE DEMONICALLY DESTRUCTIVE METEOR SPICE...
...CAUSED SERIOUS DAMAGE TO THE HUMAN WORLD.
THE NUMBER OF VICTIMS WAS 25 BILLION WORLD-WIDE.
MORE THAN 80% OF THE TOTAL WORLD POPULATION.
MORE THAN 100 COUNTRIES FACED THE COLLAPSE OF CRITICAL SYSTEMS.

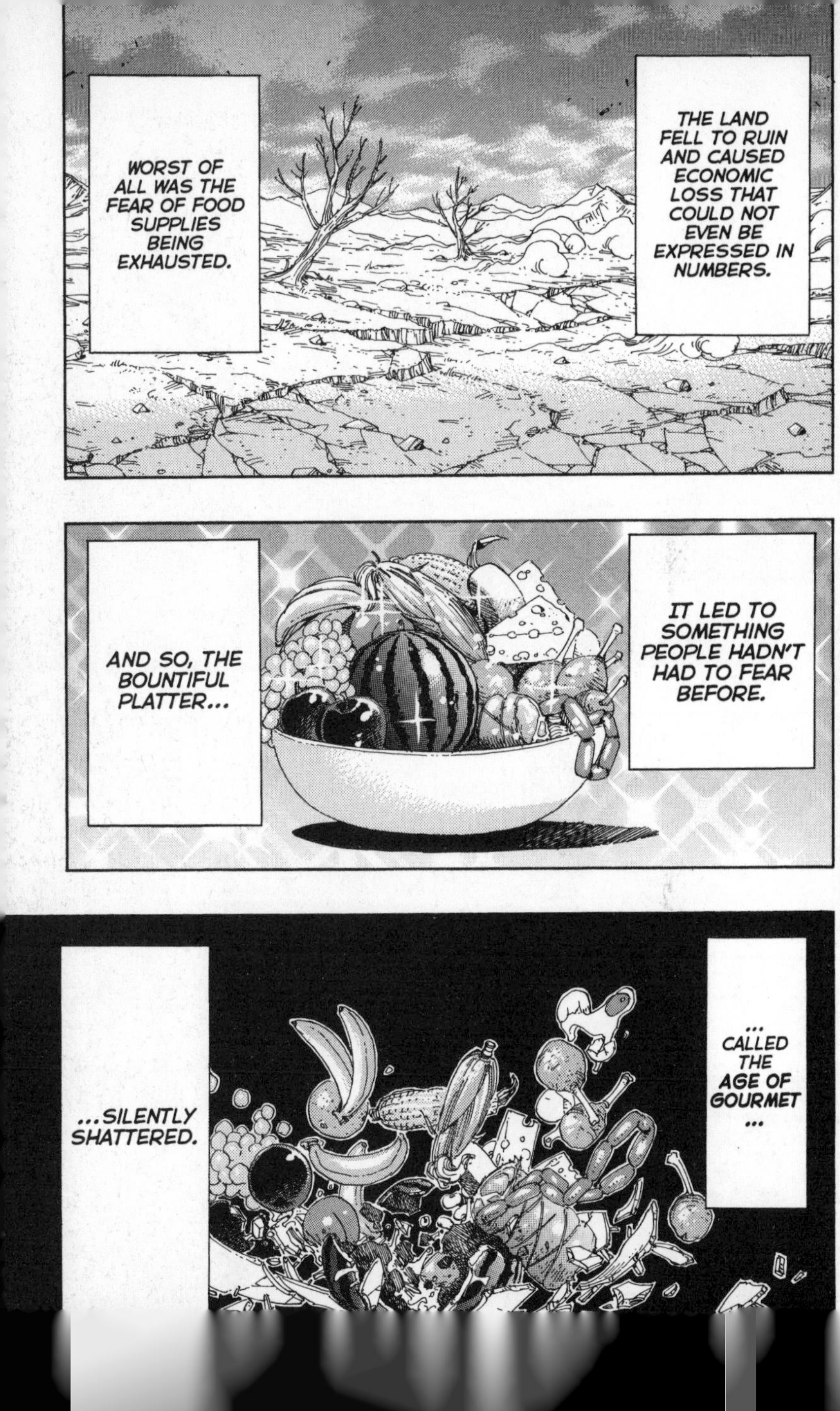
THE LAND FELL TO RUIN AND CAUSED ECONOMIC LOSS THAT COULD NOT EVEN BE EXPRESSED IN NUMBERS.
WORST OF ALL WAS THE FEAR OF FOOD SUPPLIES BEING EXHAUSTED.
IT LED TO SOMETHING PEOPLE HADN'T HAD TO FEAR BEFORE.
AND SO, THE BOUNTIFUL PLATTER...
...CALLED THE AGE OF GOURMET...
...SILENTLY SHATTERED.

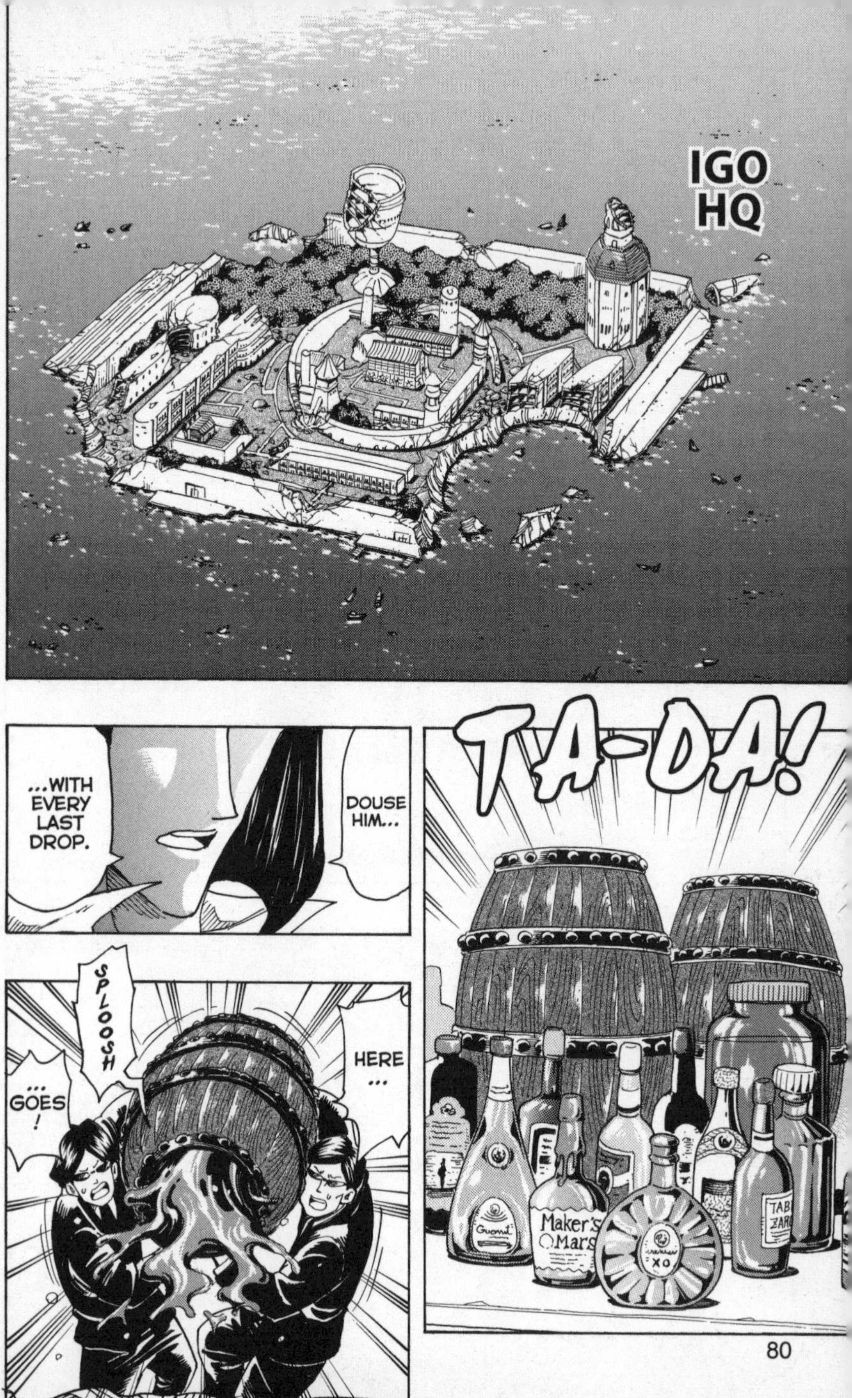
IGO HQ
T-A-D-A!
Maker's Mars
XO
DOUSE HIM...
...WITH EVERY LAST DROP.
HERE...
SPLOOSH
...GOES!

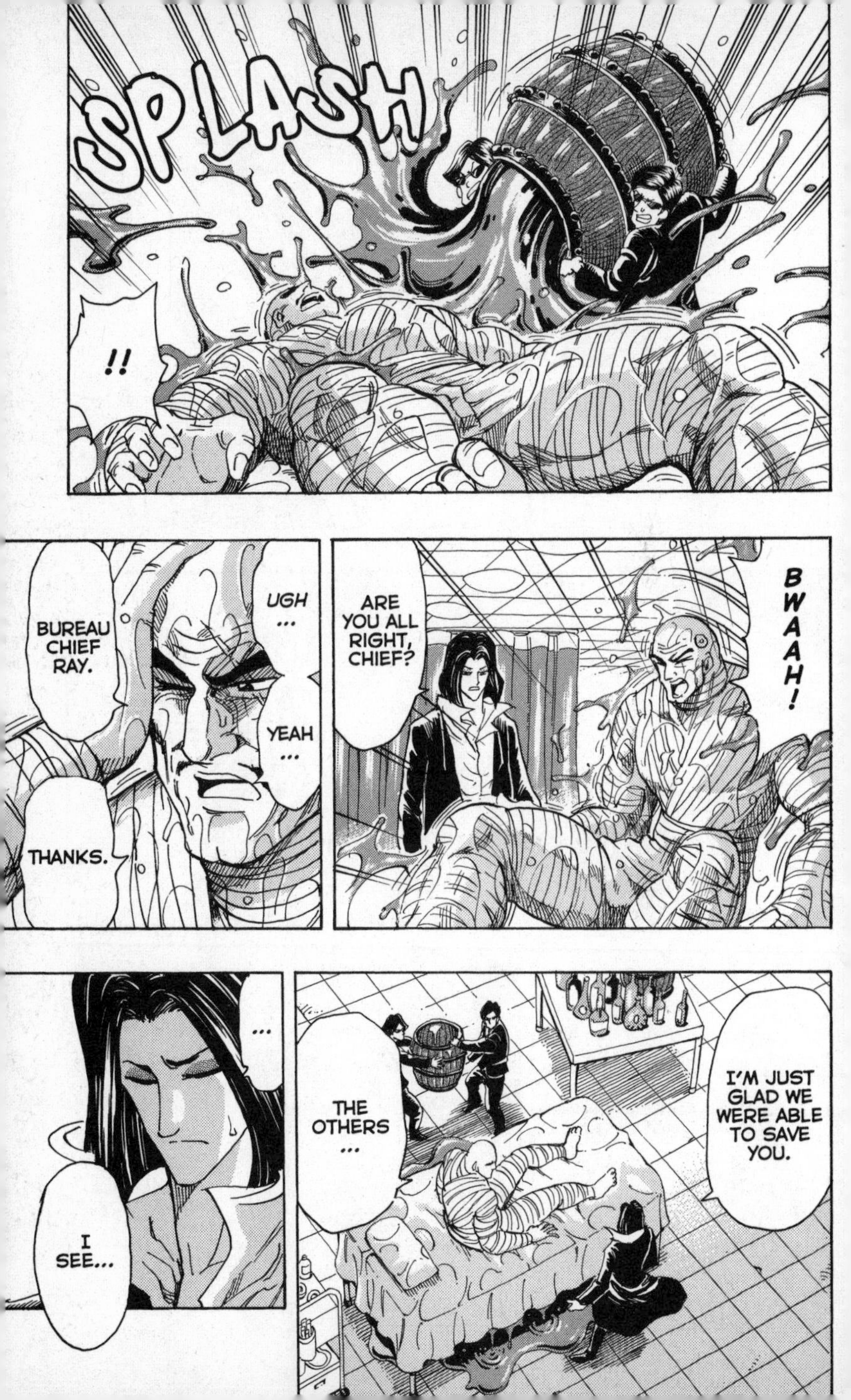
SPLASH
!!
BWAAAH!
ARE YOU ALL RIGHT, CHIEF?
UGH...
YEAH...
BUREAU CHIEF RAY.
THANKS.
I'M JUST GLAD WE WERE ABLE TO SAVE YOU.
THE OTHERS...
...
I SEE...

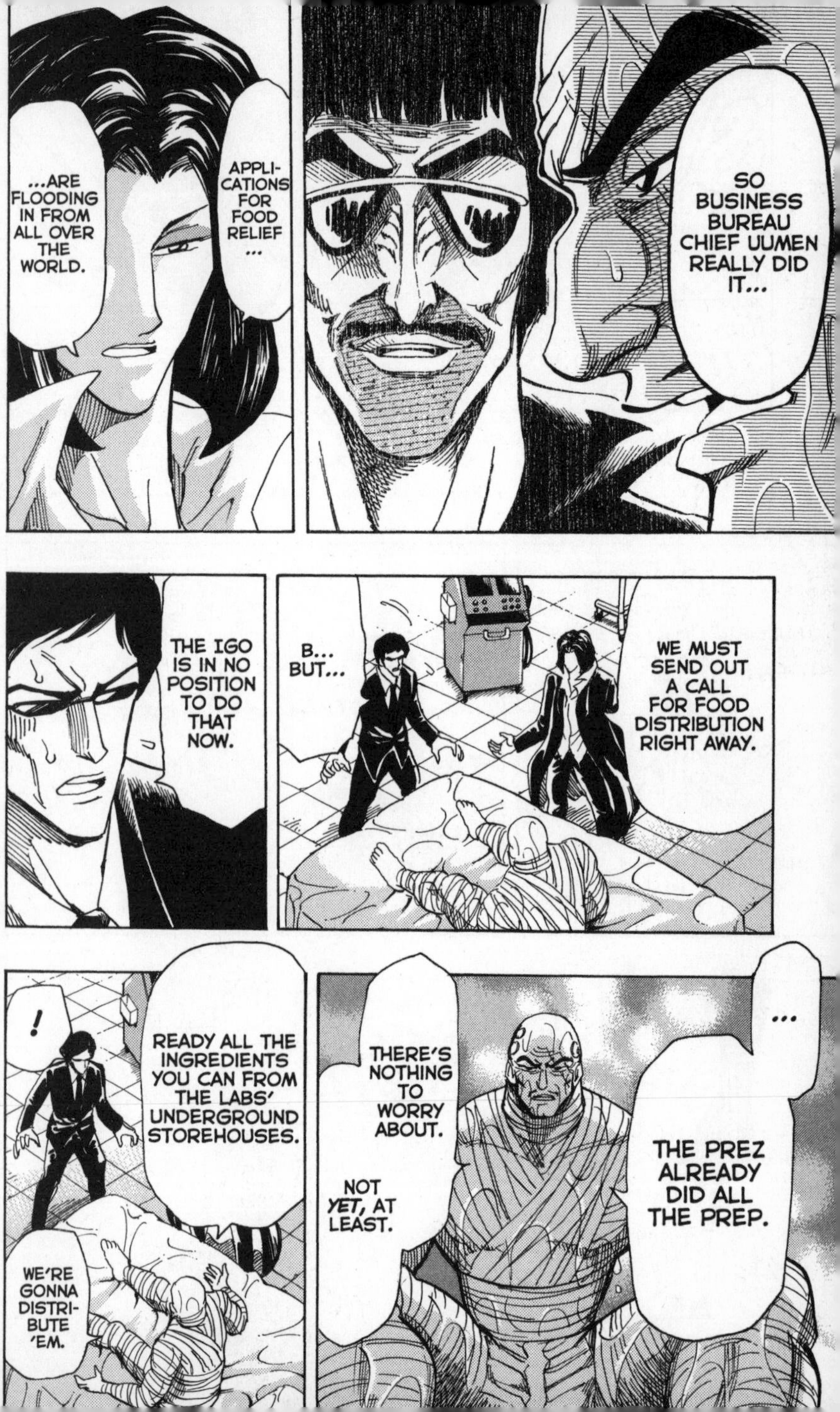
SO BUSINESS BUREAU CHIEF UUMEN REALLY DID IT...
APPLICATIONS FOR FOOD RELIEF...
...ARE FLOODING IN FROM ALL OVER THE WORLD.
WE MUST SEND OUT A CALL FOR FOOD DISTRIBUTION RIGHT AWAY.
B... BUT...
THE IGO IS IN NO POSITION TO DO THAT NOW.
...
THE PREZ ALREADY DID ALL THE PREP.
THERE'S NOTHING TO WORRY ABOUT.
NOT *YET*, AT LEAST.
READY ALL THE INGREDIENTS YOU CAN FROM THE LABS' UNDERGROUND STOREHOUSES.
!
WE'RE GONNA DISTRIBUTE 'EM.

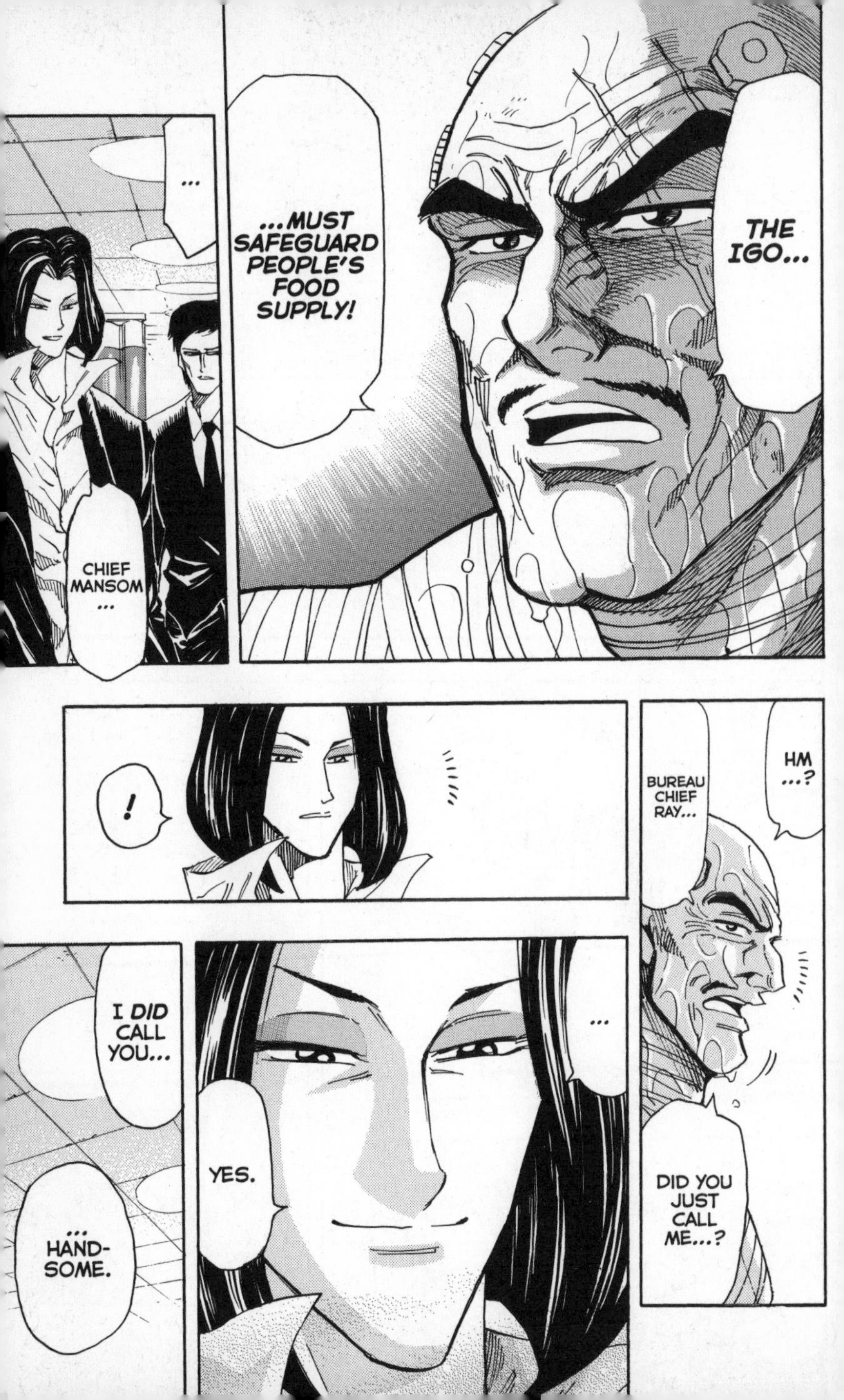
THE IGO...
...MUST SAFEGUARD PEOPLE'S FOOD SUPPLY!
...
CHIEF MANSOM ...
HM ...?
BUREAU CHIEF RAY...
DID YOU JUST CALL ME...?
!
...
YES.
I *DID* CALL YOU...
... HAND-SOME.

LIFE,
THE COUNTRY
OF HEALING

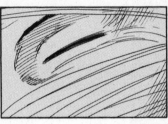

CHIN...

CH...

ARE
YOU
OKAY...

YOU CAN
KEEP
RESTING.

WHERE
AM I...?

...
CHIYO?

84

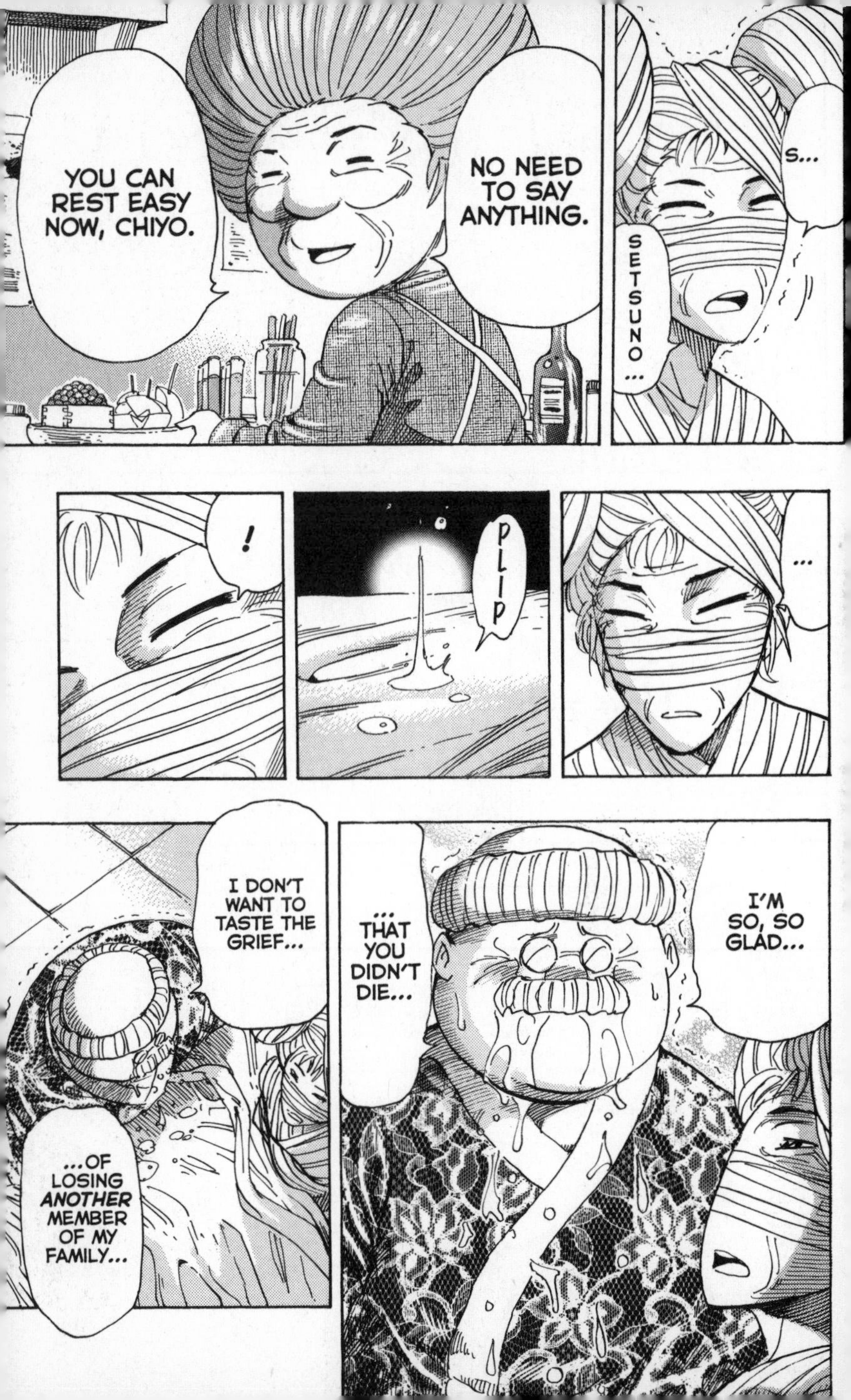
S...
SETSUNO...
NO NEED TO SAY ANYTHING.
YOU CAN REST EASY NOW, CHIYO.
...
PLIP
!
I'M SO, SO GLAD...
...THAT YOU DIDN'T DIE...
I DON'T WANT TO TASTE THE GRIEF...
...OF LOSING ANOTHER MEMBER OF MY FAMILY...

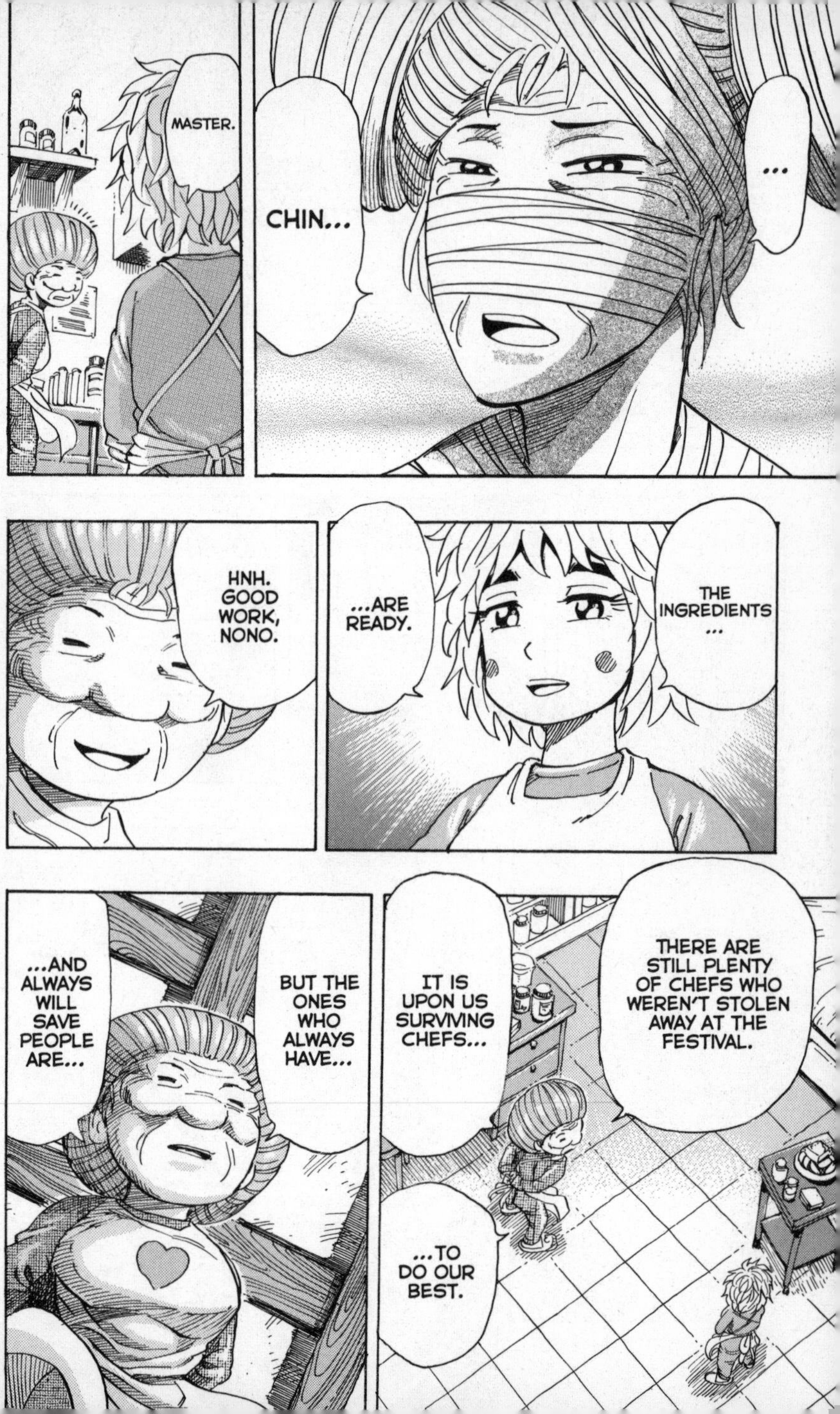
...
CHIN...
MASTER.
THE INGREDIENTS ...
...ARE READY.
HNH. GOOD WORK, NONO.
THERE ARE STILL PLENTY OF CHEFS WHO WEREN'T STOLEN AWAY AT THE FESTIVAL.
IT IS UPON US SURVIVING CHEFS...
...TO DO OUR BEST.
BUT THE ONES WHO ALWAYS HAVE...
...AND ALWAYS WILL SAVE PEOPLE ARE...

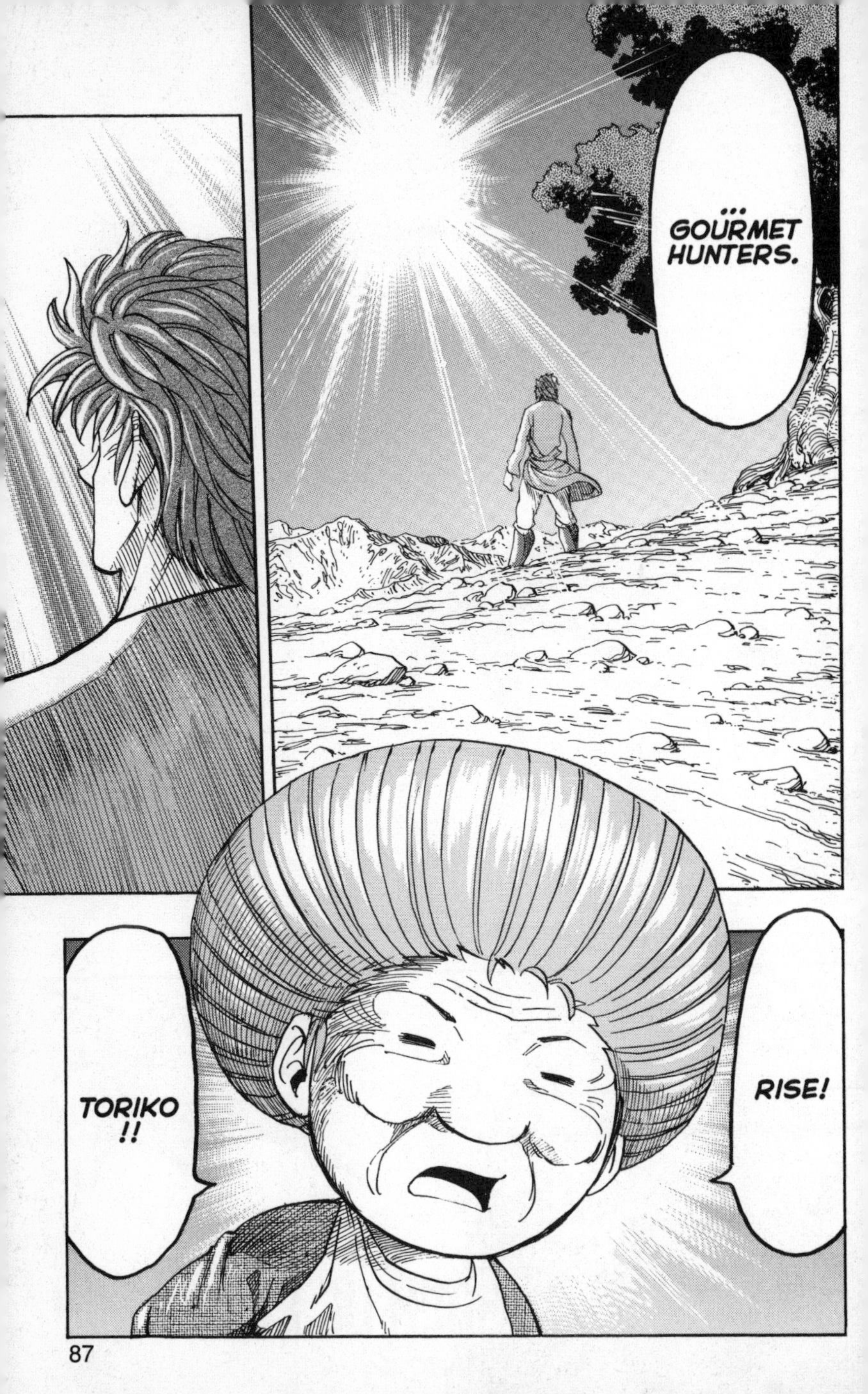
...GOURMET HUNTERS.
RISE!
TORIKO !!

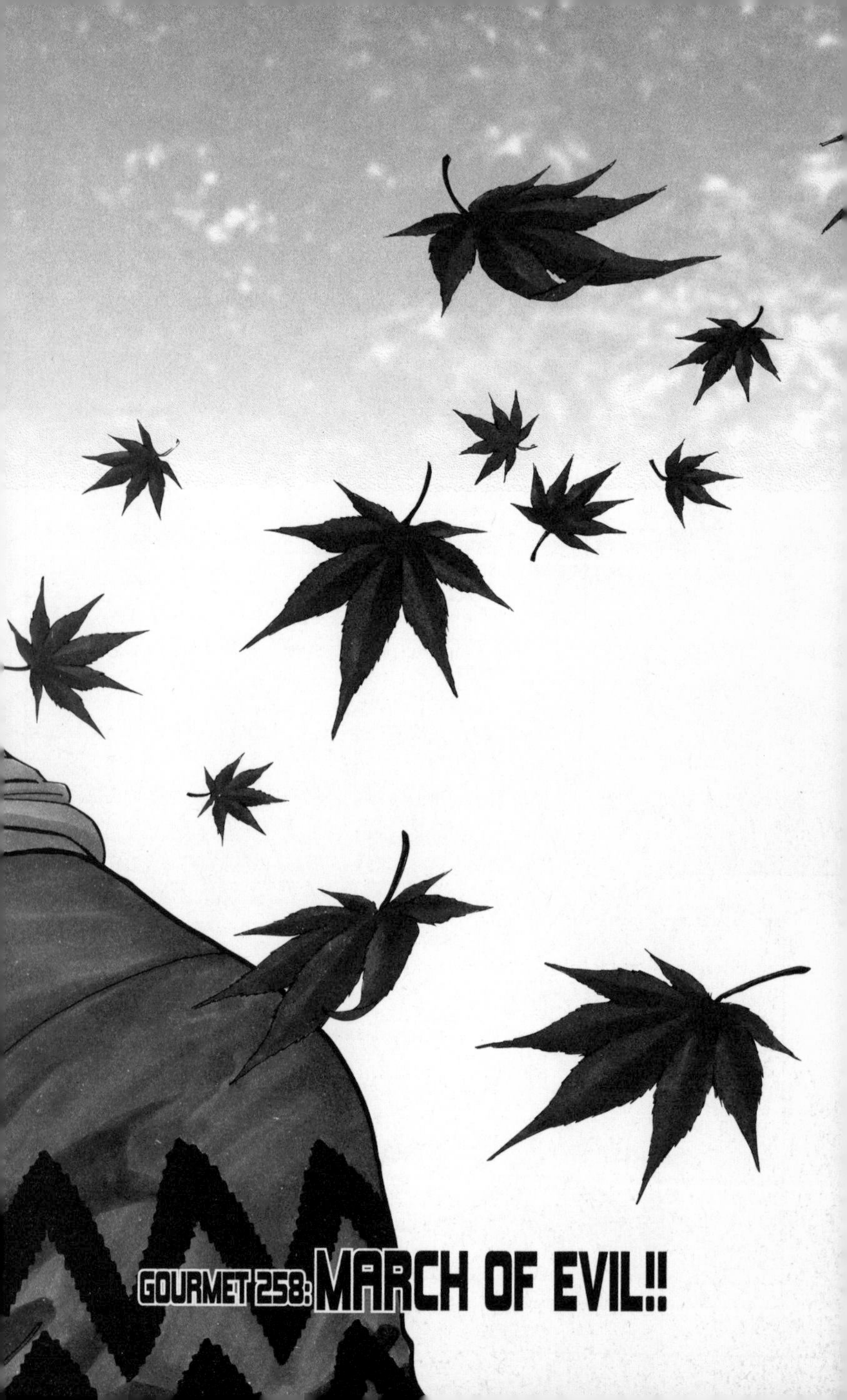
GOURMET 258: MARCH OF EVIL!!

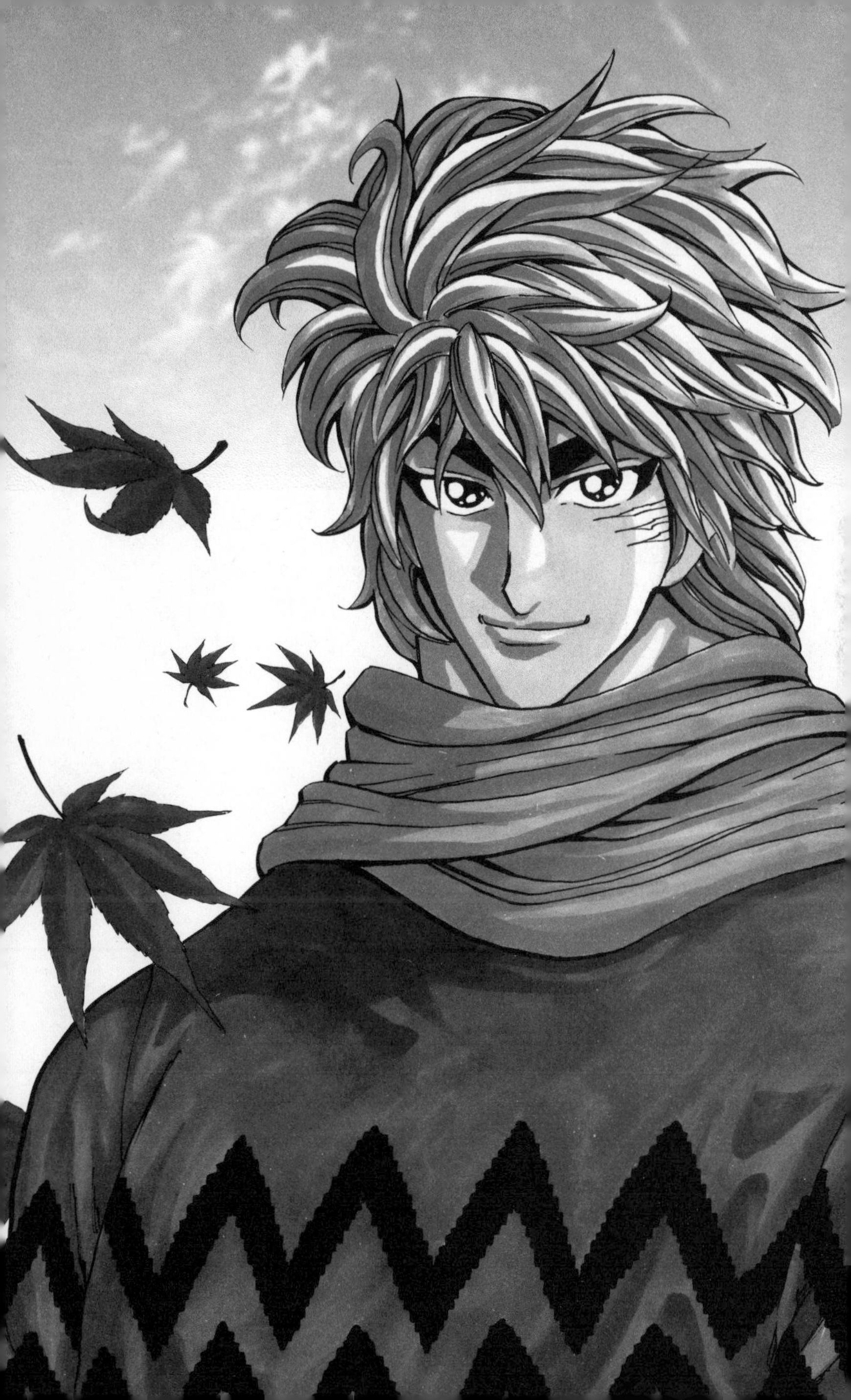

GOURMET CHECKLIST

Vol. 283

ALUMINUM CABBAGE
(PLANT)

CAPTURE LEVEL: 6

HABITAT: SPIRITS ARCHIPELAGO

SIZE: 35 CM

HEIGHT: ---

WEIGHT: 5 KG

PRICE: 2,500 YEN PER HEAD

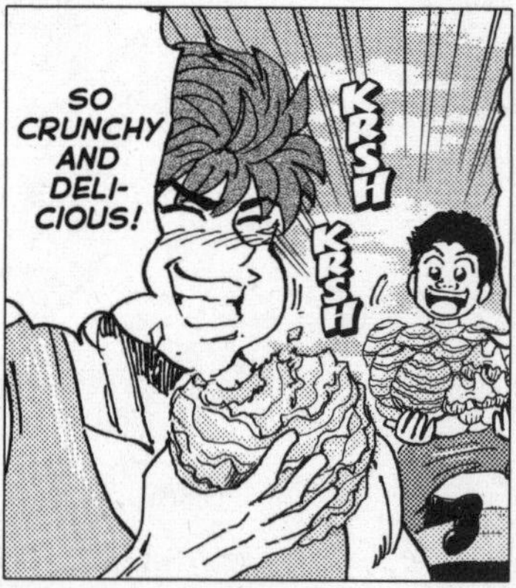
KRSH
KRSH
SO CRUNCHY AND DELI- CIOUS!

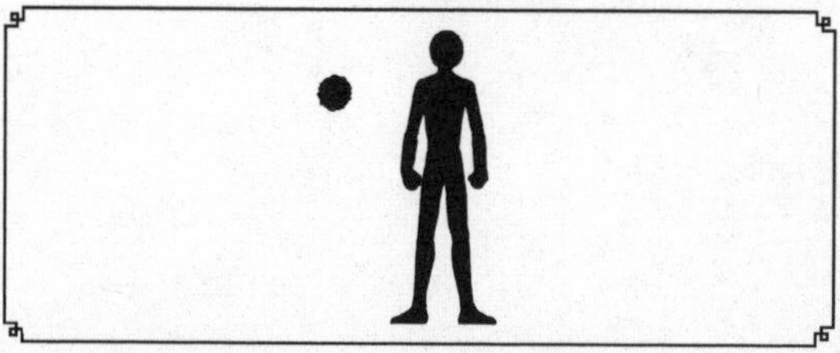

SCALE

A MYSTERIOUS CABBAGE THAT CAN GROW ABSOLUTELY ANYWHERE. IT'S THREE TIMES HEAVIER THAN A NORMAL CABBAGE AND HAS A CRUNCHY TEXTURE KIND OF LIKE ALUMINUM. IT IS NATURALLY SALTY AND MAKES A GREAT LIGHT SNACK ALL ON ITS OWN.

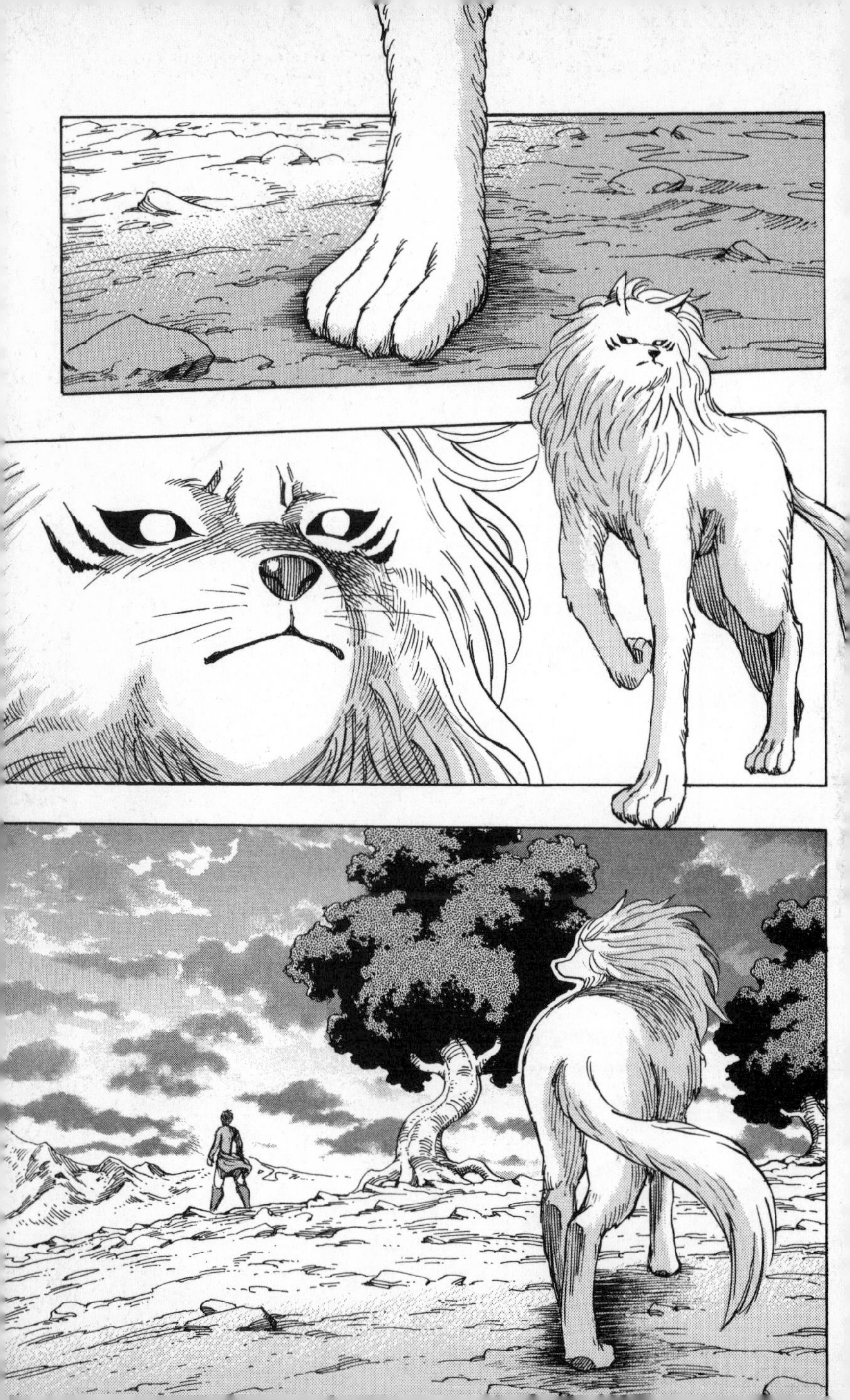

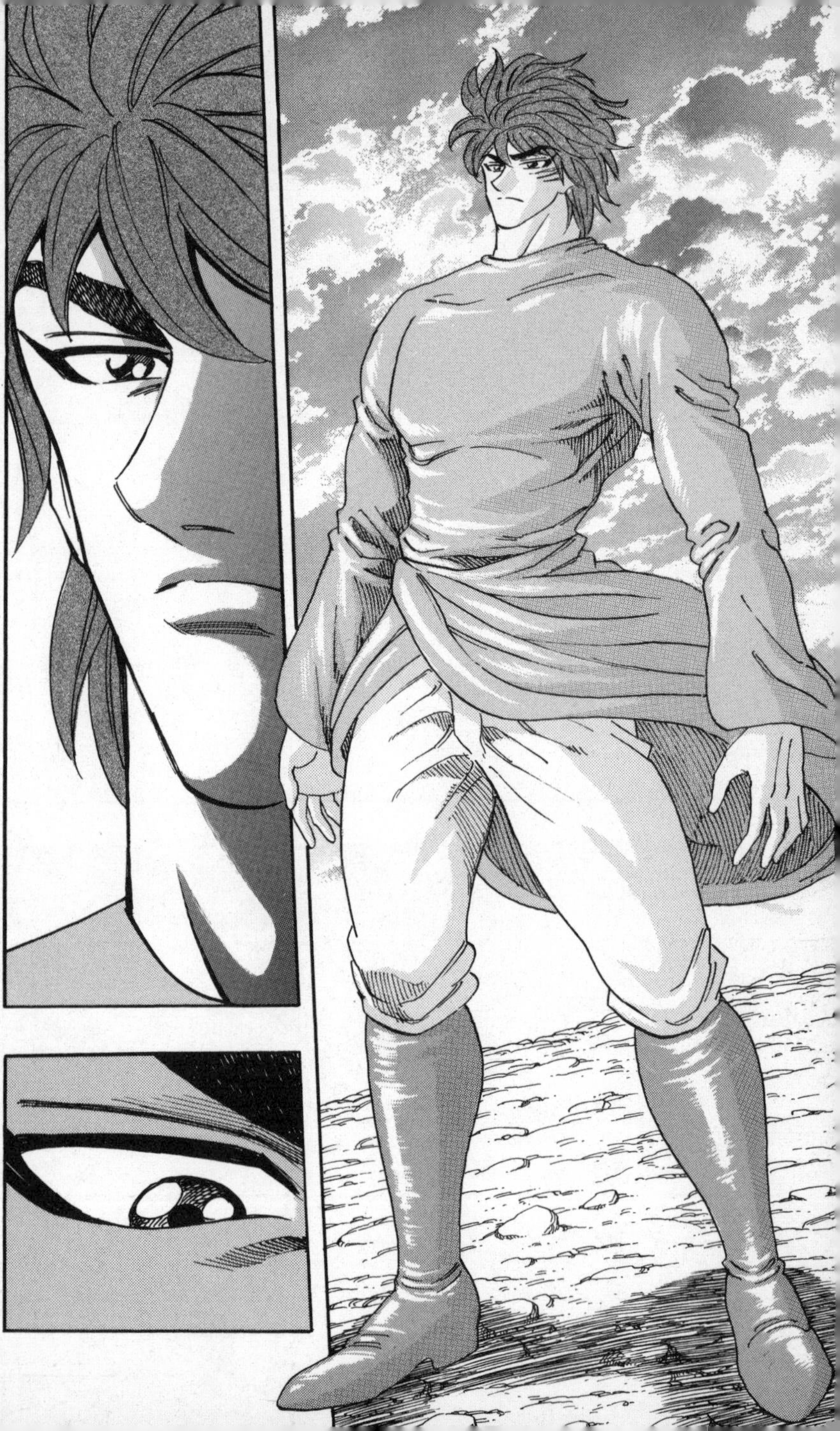

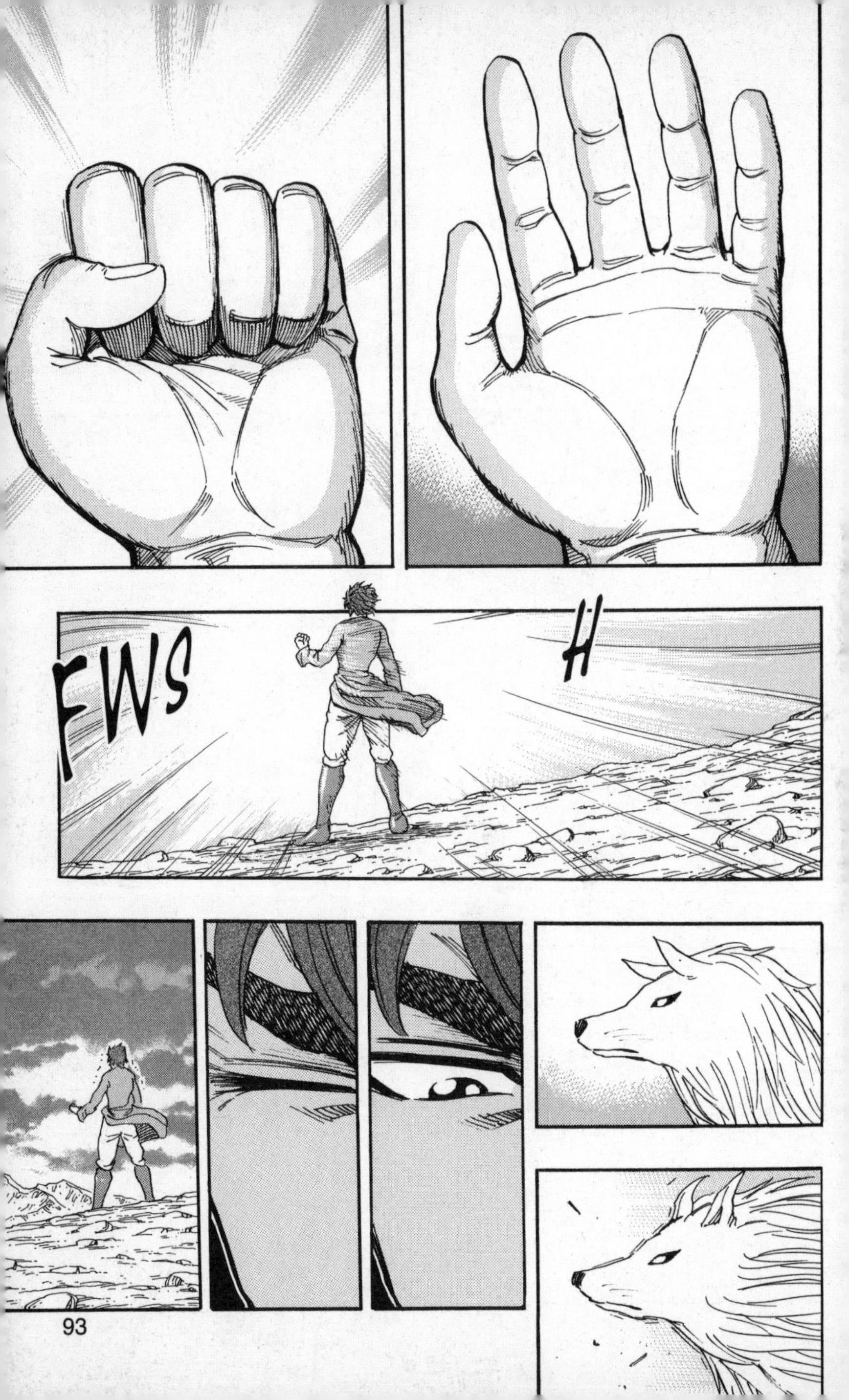
FWSH

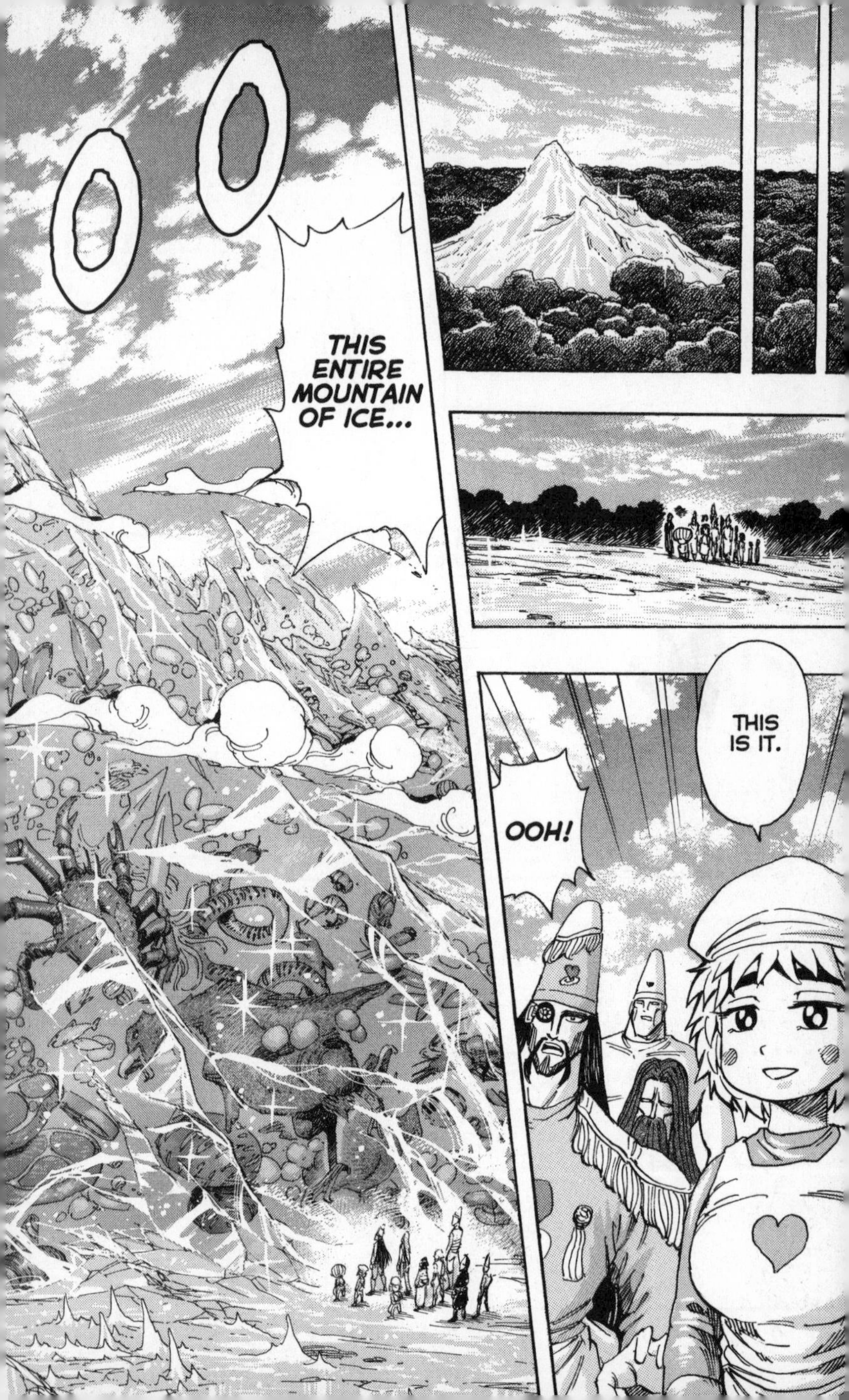
THIS IS IT.
OOH!
THIS ENTIRE MOUNTAIN OF ICE...

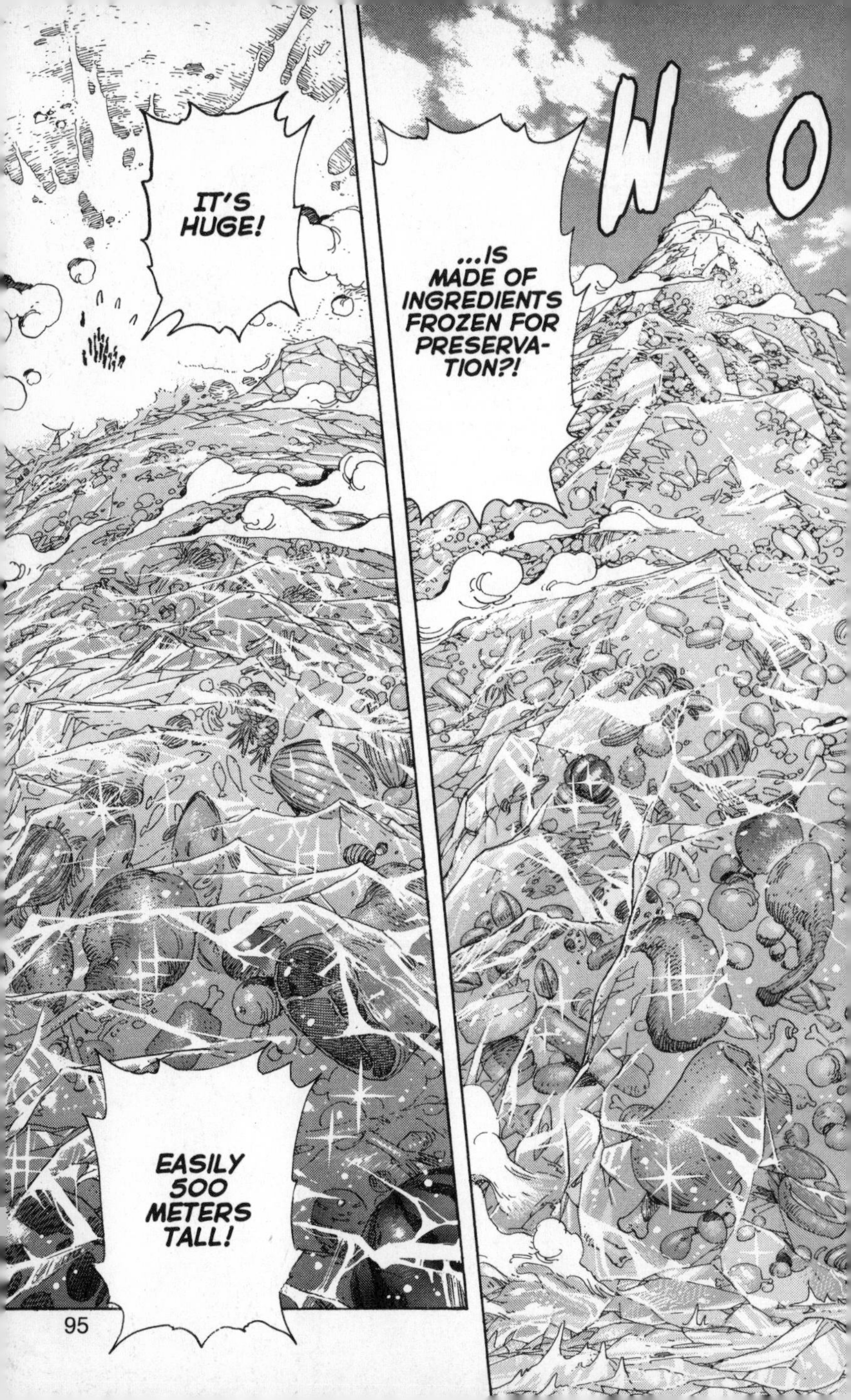
WO
...IS MADE OF INGREDIENTS FROZEN FOR PRESERVA-TION?!
IT'S HUGE!
EASILY 500 METERS TALL!

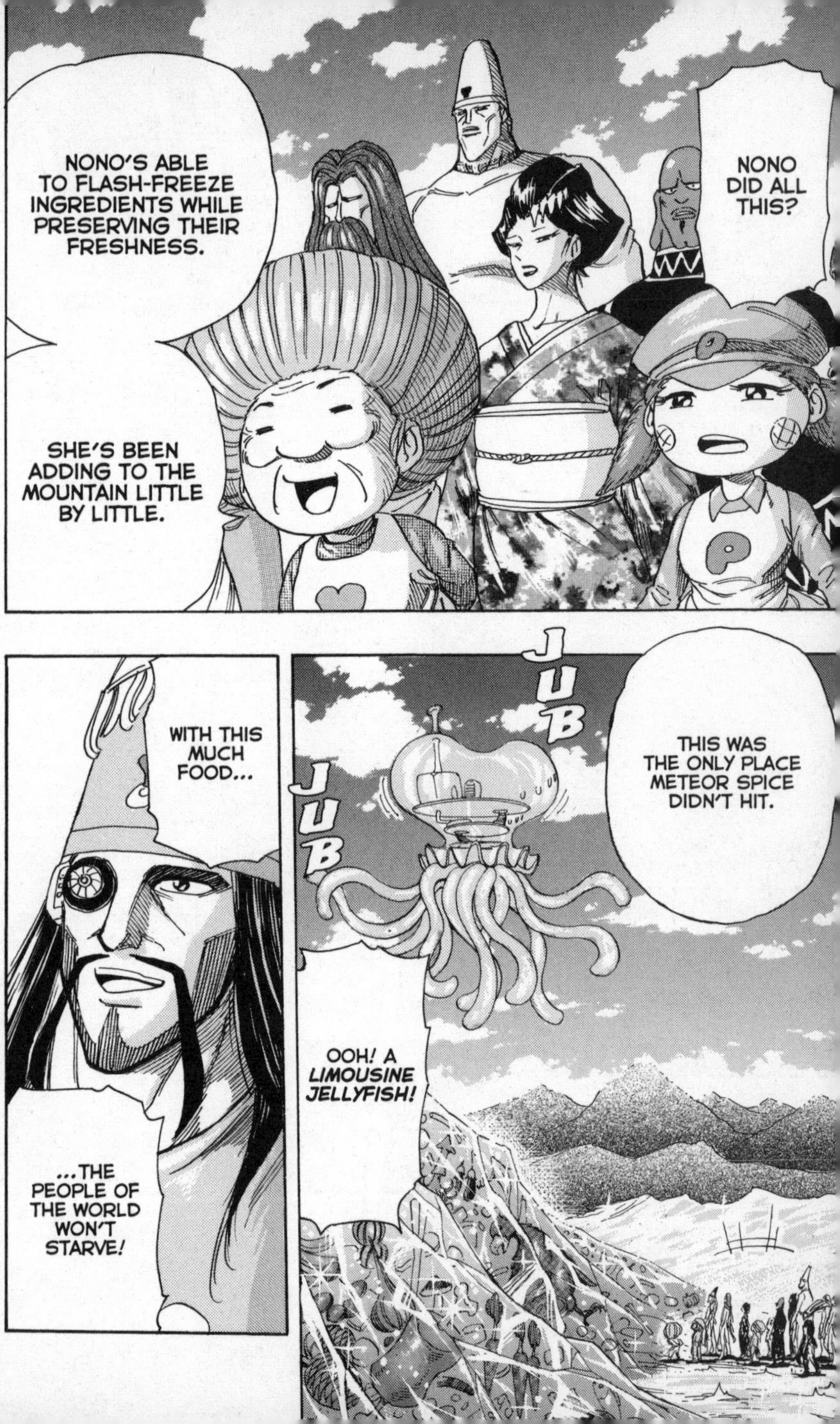
NONO DID ALL THIS?
NONO'S ABLE TO FLASH-FREEZE INGREDIENTS WHILE PRESERVING THEIR FRESHNESS.
SHE'S BEEN ADDING TO THE MOUNTAIN LITTLE BY LITTLE.
THIS WAS THE ONLY PLACE METEOR SPICE DIDN'T HIT.
JUB
JUB
JUB
JUB
OOH! A *LIMOUSINE JELLYFISH!*
WITH THIS MUCH FOOD...
...THE PEOPLE OF THE WORLD WON'T STARVE!

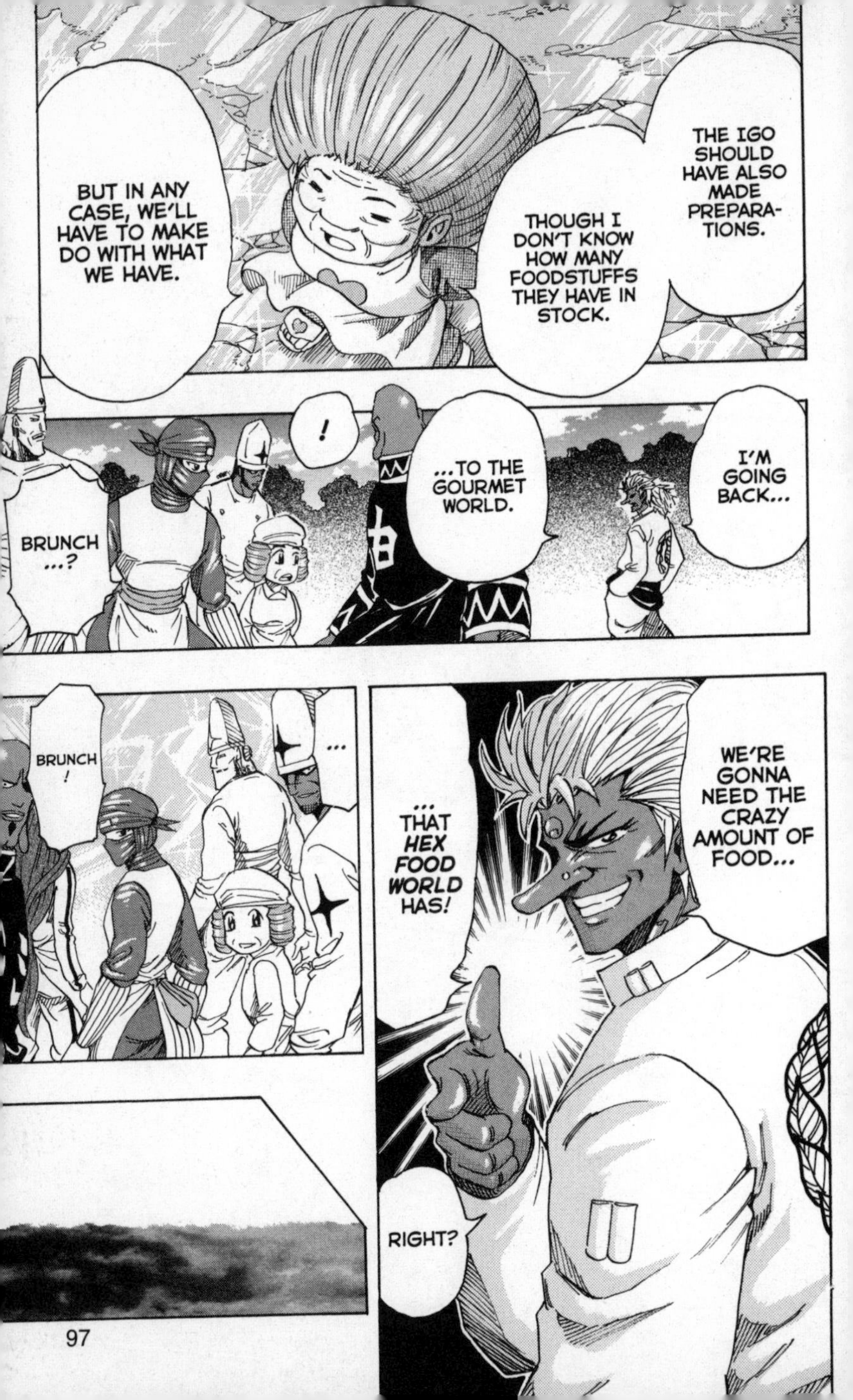
THE IGO SHOULD HAVE ALSO MADE PREPARATIONS.
THOUGH I DON'T KNOW HOW MANY FOODSTUFFS THEY HAVE IN STOCK.
BUT IN ANY CASE, WE'LL HAVE TO MAKE DO WITH WHAT WE HAVE.
I'M GOING BACK...
...TO THE GOURMET WORLD.
!
BRUNCH ...?
WE'RE GONNA NEED THE CRAZY AMOUNT OF FOOD...
...THAT *HEX FOOD WORLD* HAS!
RIGHT?
...
BRUNCH!

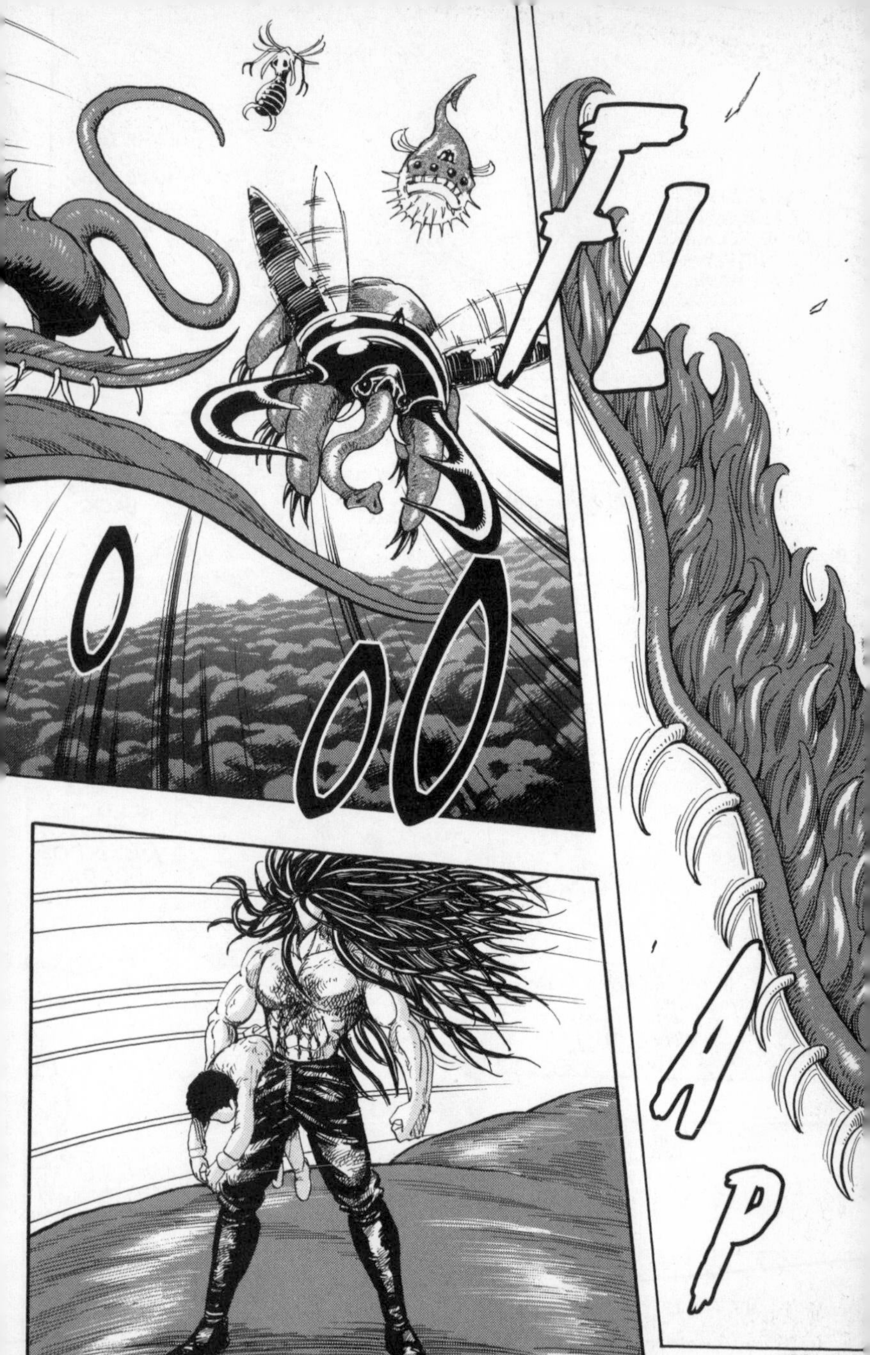
FLAP
OOOO

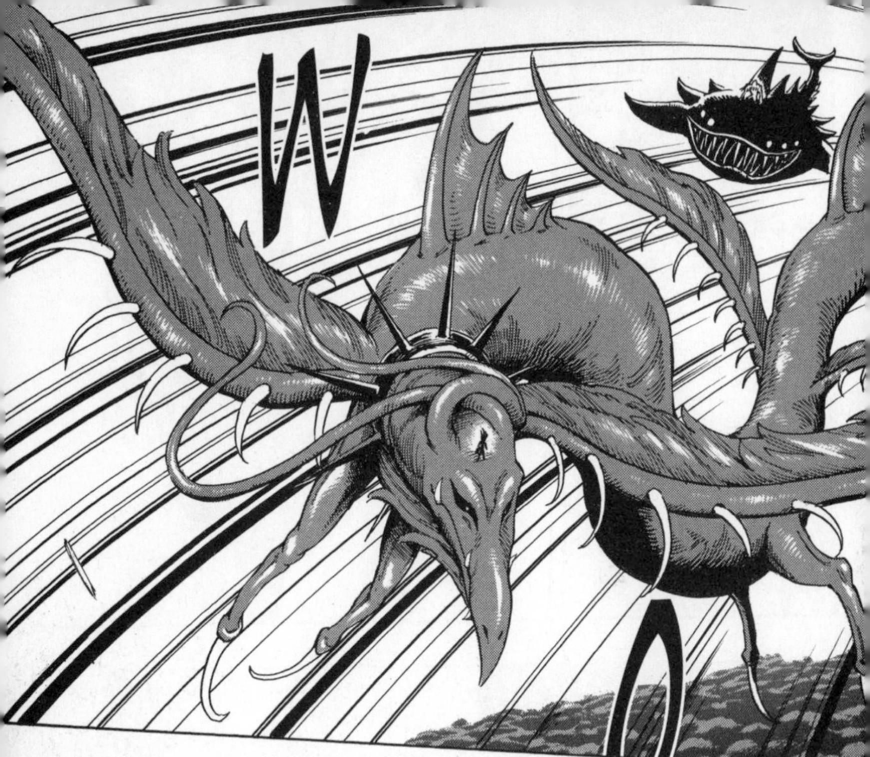
W
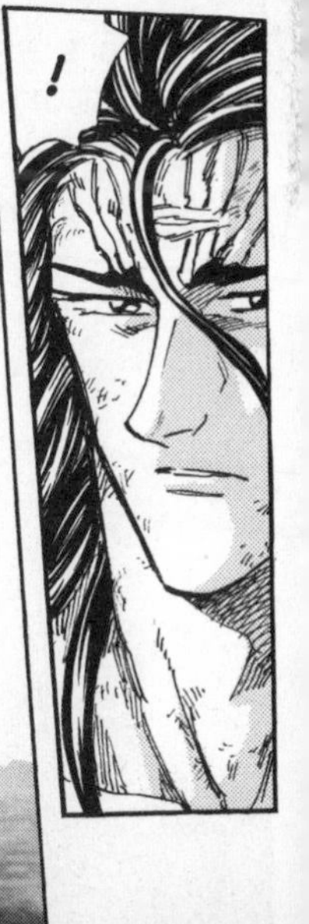
!
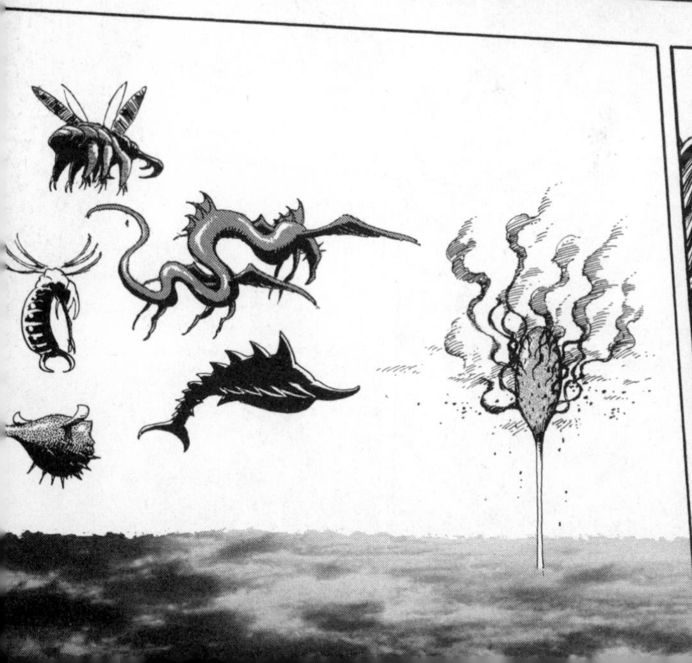

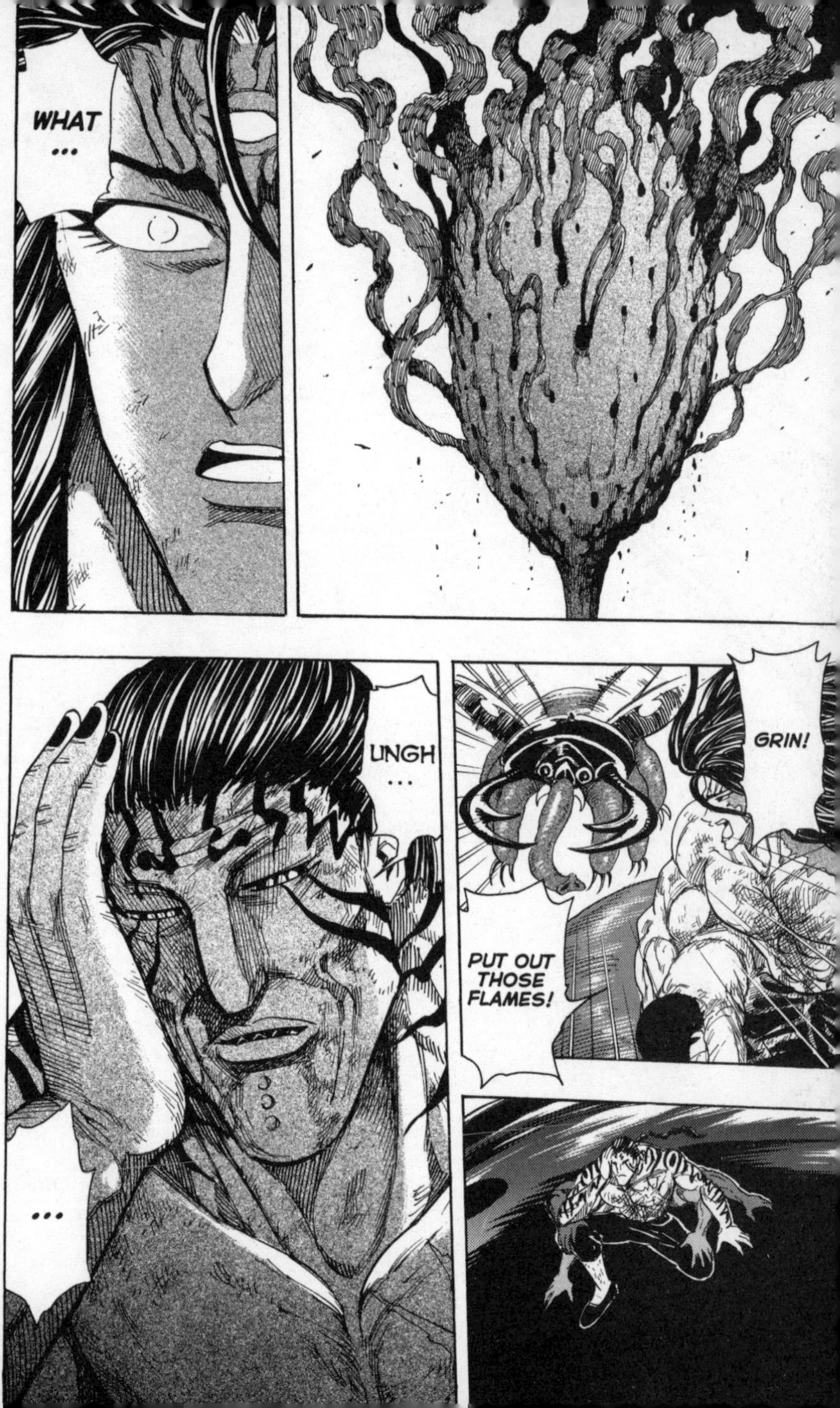
WHAT ...
GRIN!
PUT OUT THOSE FLAMES!
UNGH ...
...

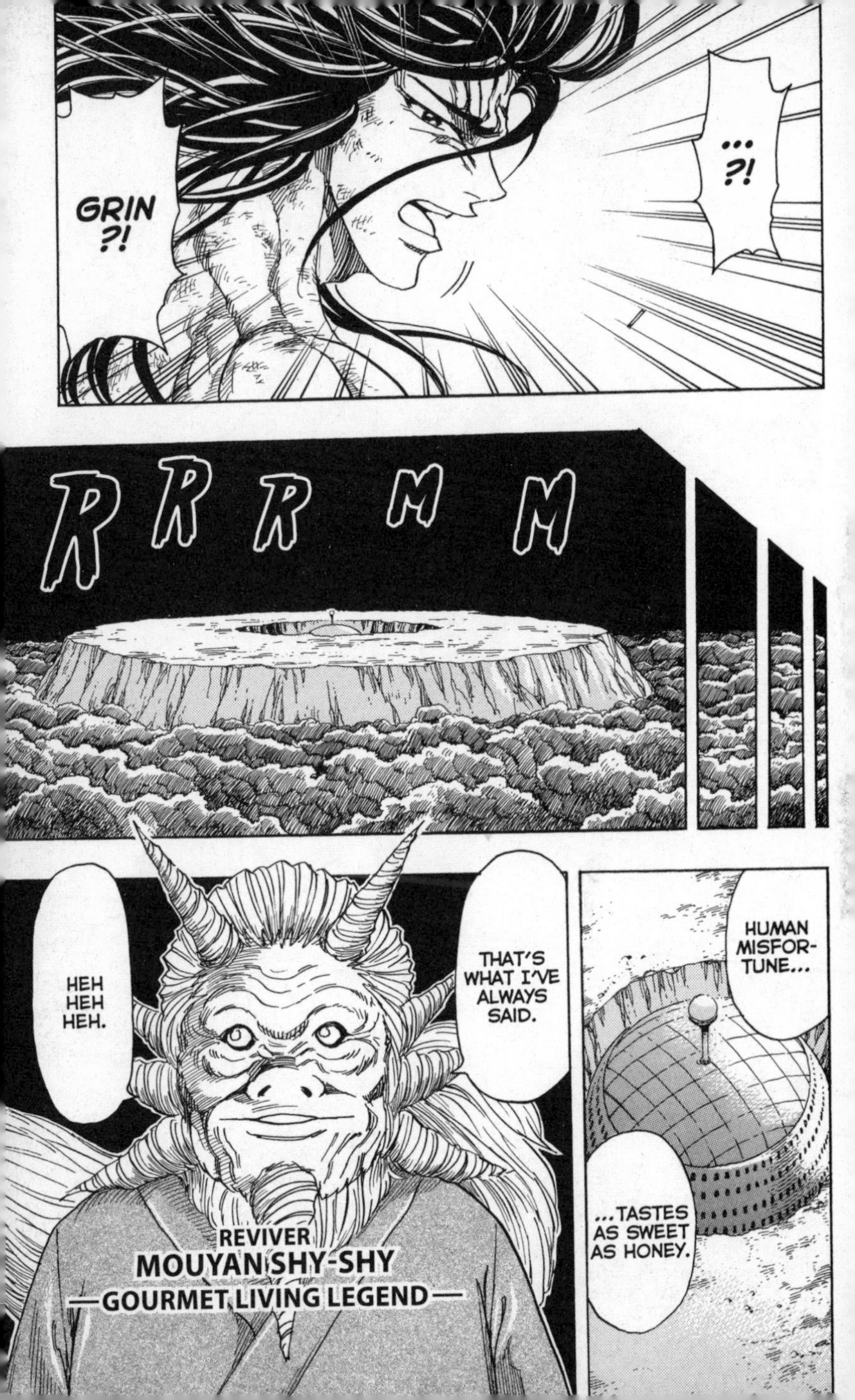
...?!
GRIN ?!
RRRMM
HUMAN MISFORTUNE...
...TASTES AS SWEET AS HONEY.
THAT'S WHAT I'VE ALWAYS SAID.
HEH HEH HEH.
REVIVER
MOUYAN SHY-SHY
—GOURMET LIVING LEGEND—

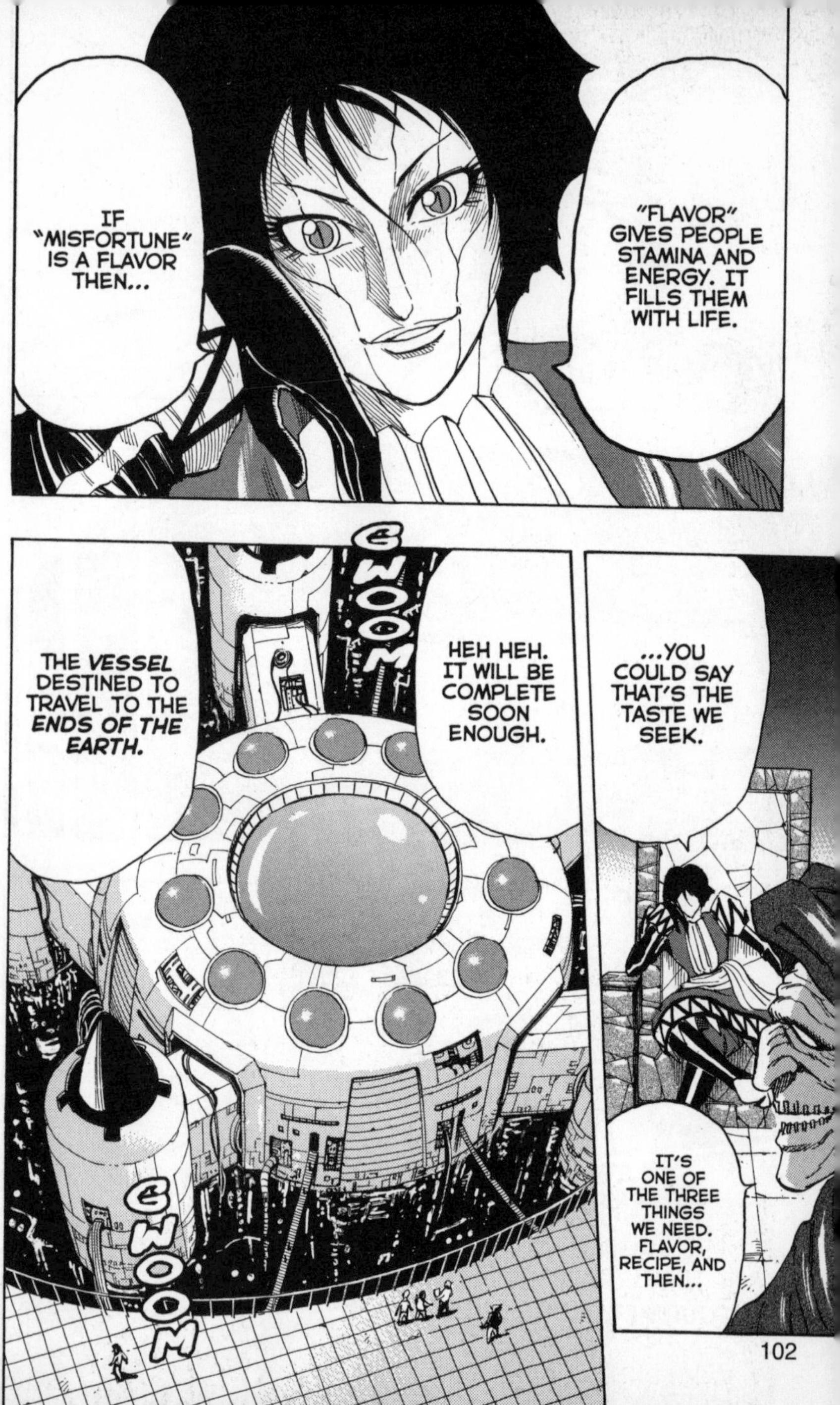
"FLAVOR" GIVES PEOPLE STAMINA AND ENERGY. IT FILLS THEM WITH LIFE.
IF "MISFORTUNE" IS A FLAVOR THEN...
...YOU COULD SAY THAT'S THE TASTE WE SEEK.
IT'S ONE OF THE THREE THINGS WE NEED. FLAVOR, RECIPE, AND THEN...
GWOOM
HEH HEH. IT WILL BE COMPLETE SOON ENOUGH.
THE *VESSEL* DESTINED TO TRAVEL TO THE *ENDS OF THE EARTH.*
GWOOM

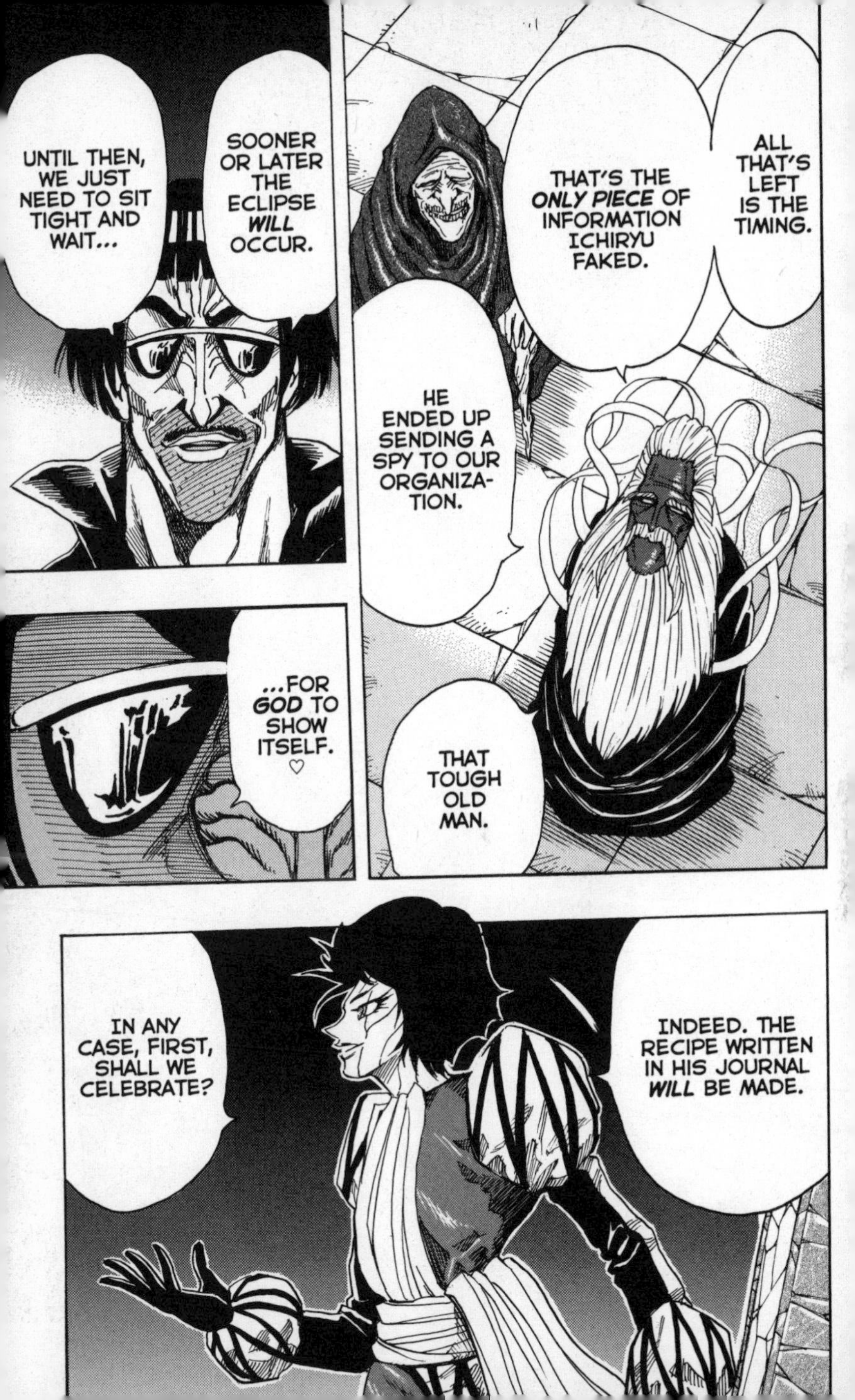
ALL THAT'S LEFT IS THE TIMING.
THAT'S THE ONLY PIECE OF INFORMATION ICHIRYU FAKED.
HE ENDED UP SENDING A SPY TO OUR ORGANIZATION.
THAT TOUGH OLD MAN.
SOONER OR LATER THE ECLIPSE WILL OCCUR.
UNTIL THEN, WE JUST NEED TO SIT TIGHT AND WAIT...
...FOR GOD TO SHOW ITSELF. ♡
INDEED. THE RECIPE WRITTEN IN HIS JOURNAL WILL BE MADE.
IN ANY CASE, FIRST, SHALL WE CELEBRATE?

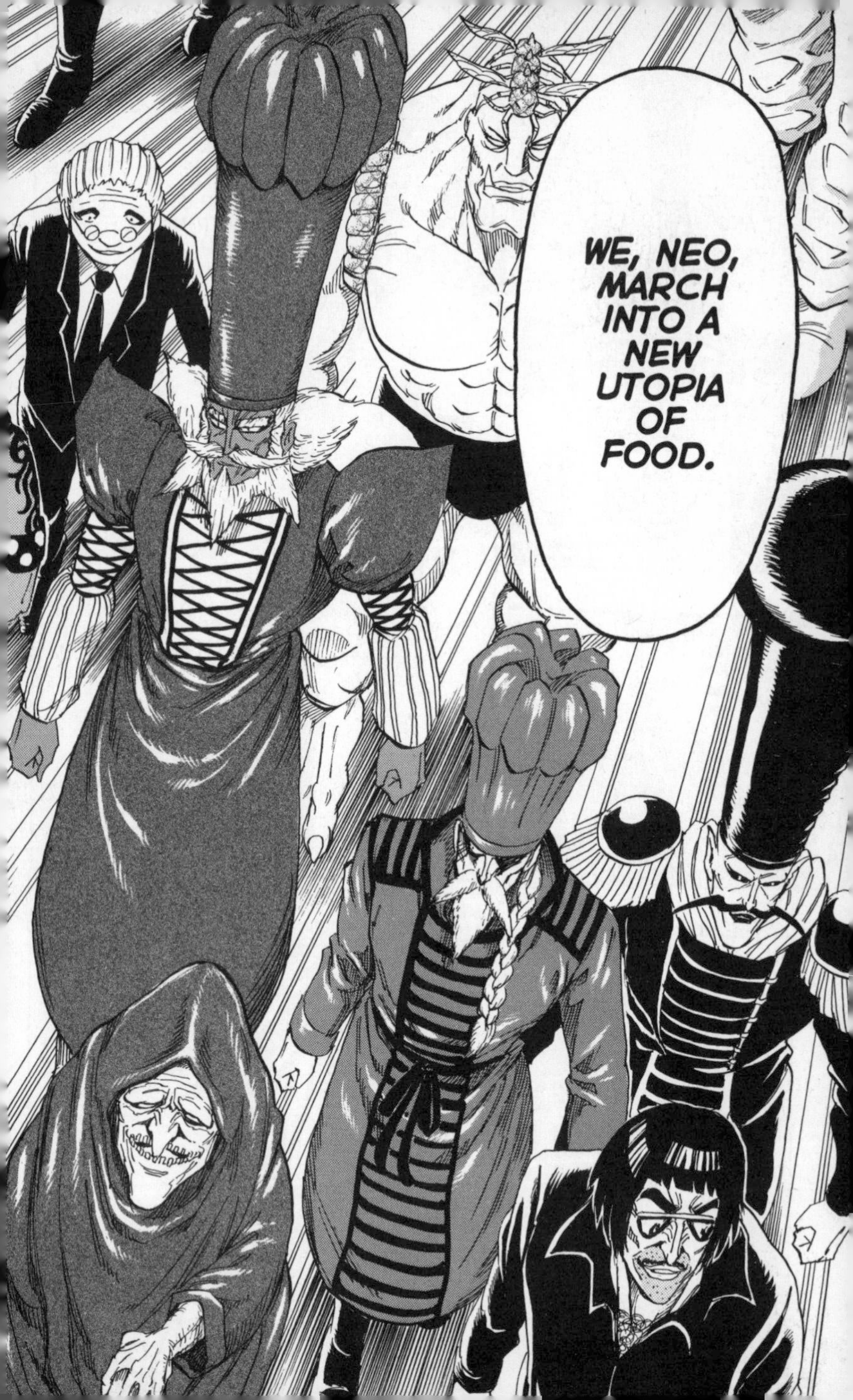
WE, NEO, MARCH INTO A NEW UTOPIA OF FOOD.

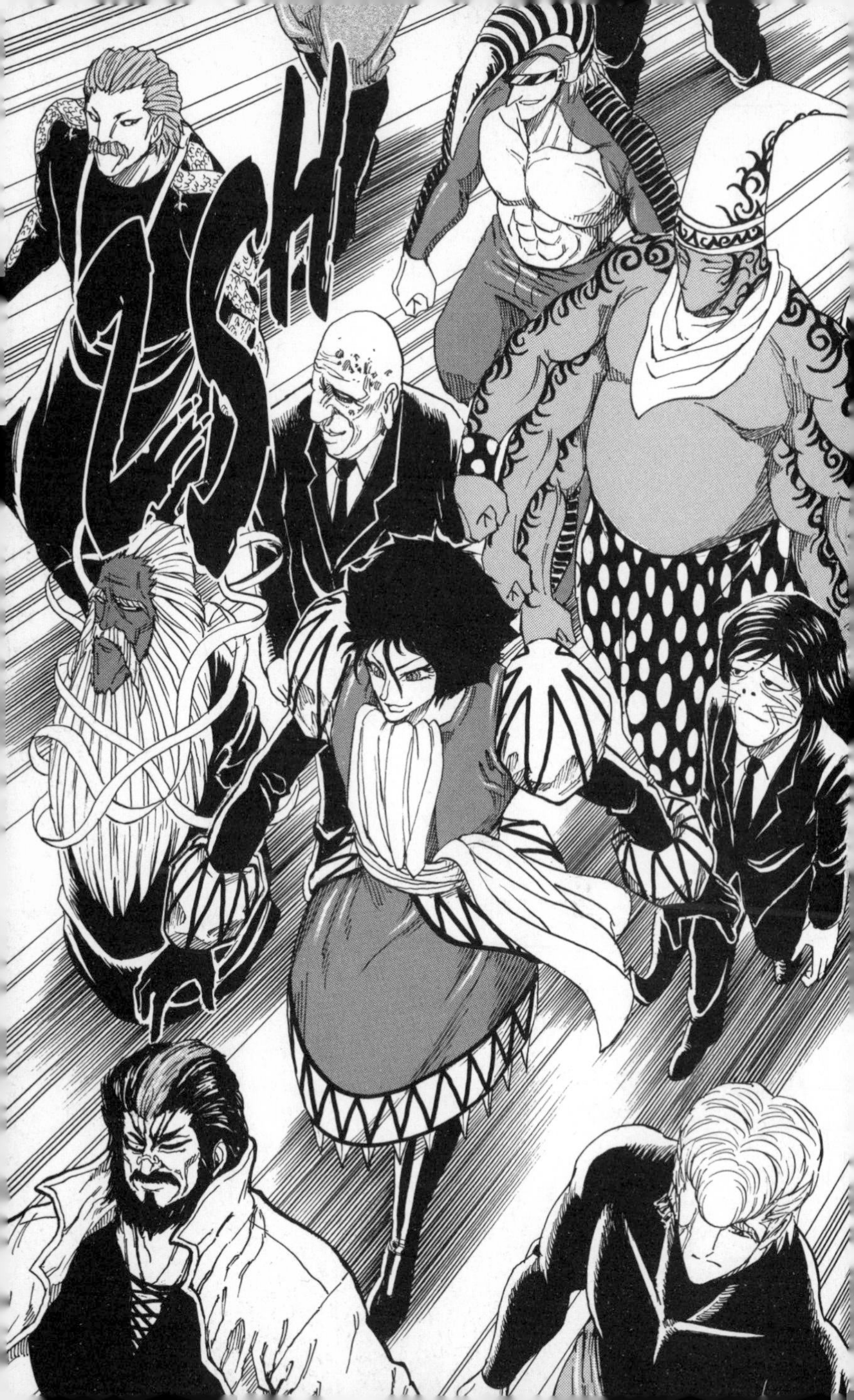
ZSCH!

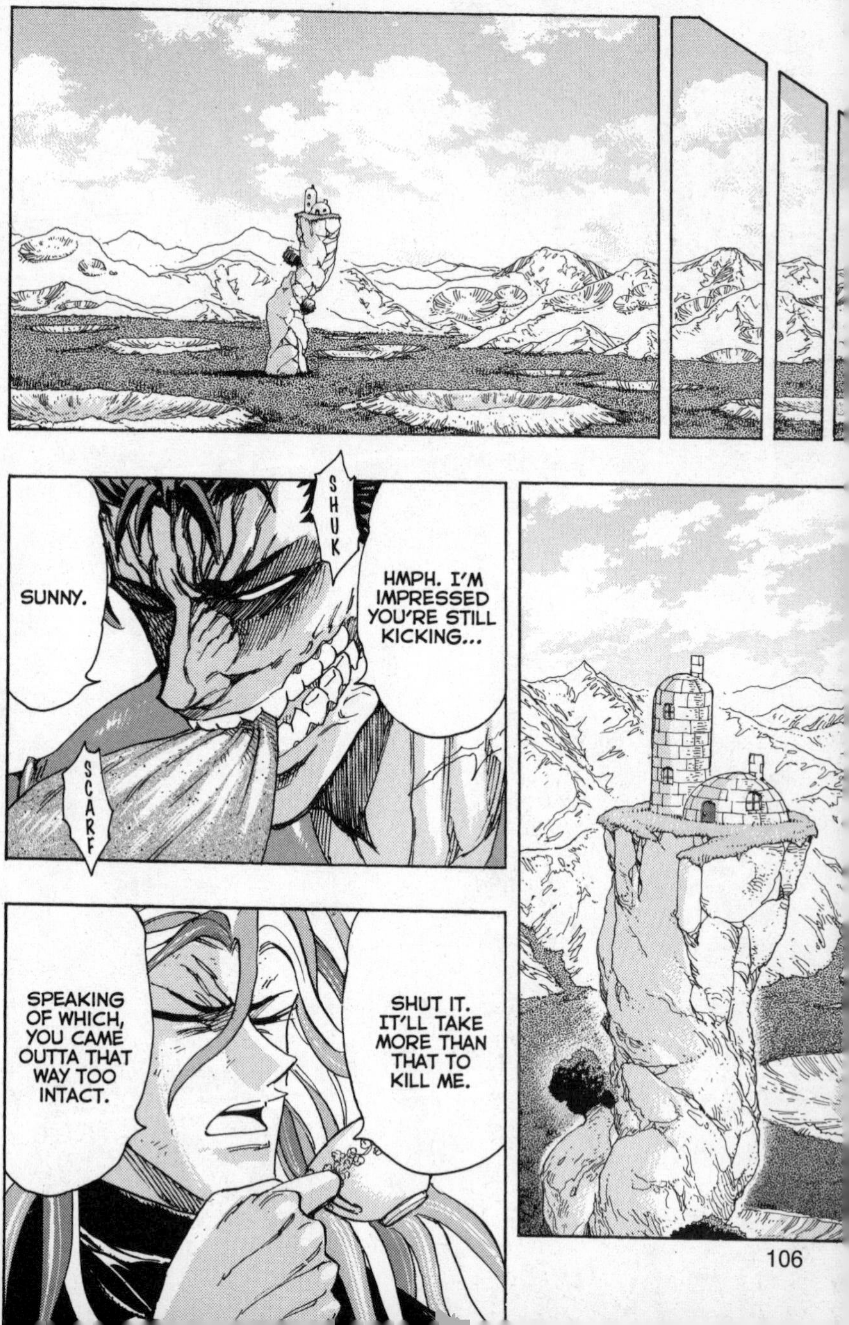
SHUK
HMPH. I'M IMPRESSED YOU'RE STILL KICKING...
SUNNY.
SCARF
SHUT IT. IT'LL TAKE MORE THAN THAT TO KILL ME.
SPEAKING OF WHICH, YOU CAME OUTTA THAT WAY TOO INTACT.

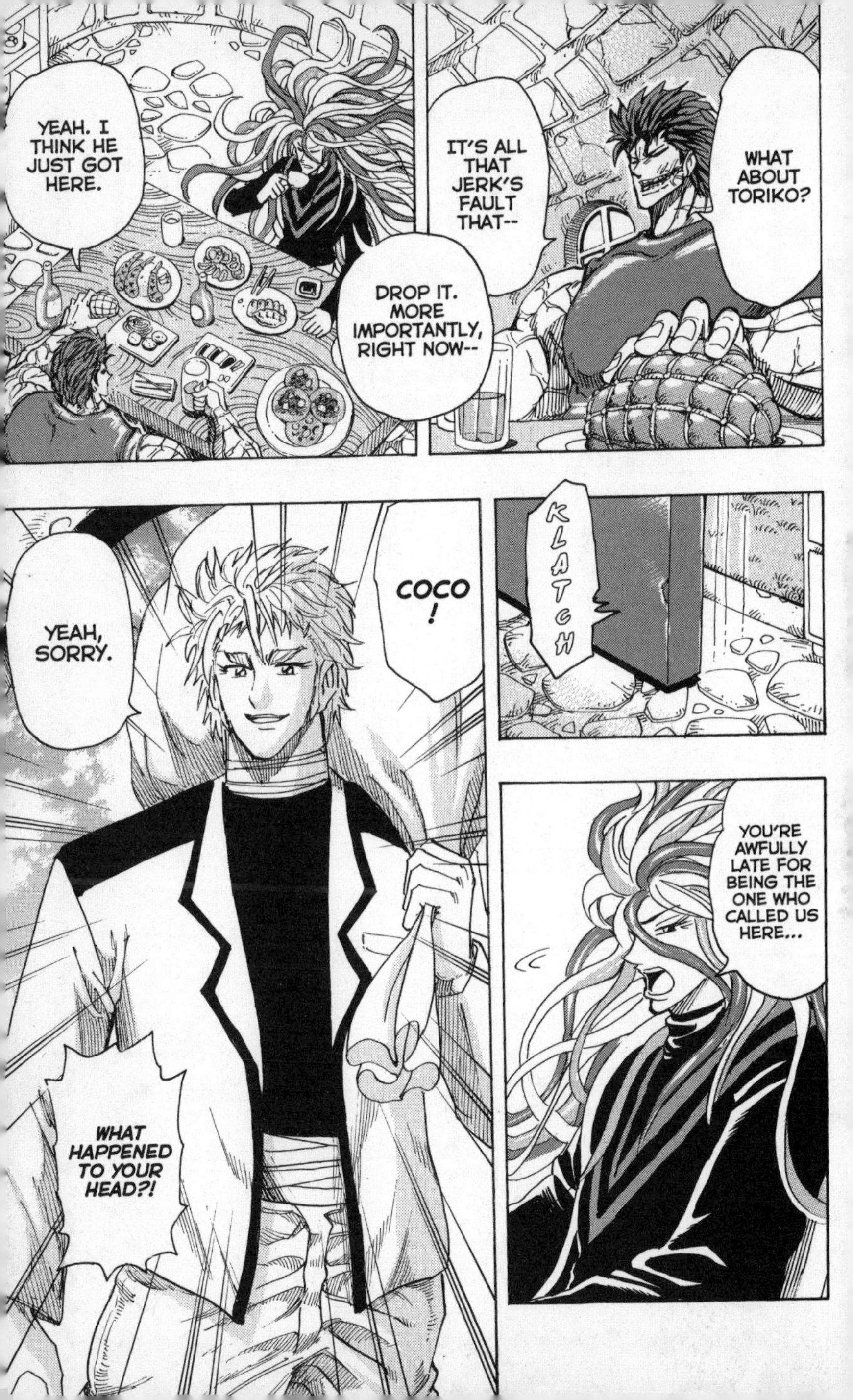
WHAT ABOUT TORIKO?
IT'S ALL THAT JERK'S FAULT THAT--
DROP IT. MORE IMPORTANTLY, RIGHT NOW--
YEAH. I THINK HE JUST GOT HERE.
KLATCH
YOU'RE AWFULLY LATE FOR BEING THE ONE WHO CALLED US HERE...
COCO!
YEAH, SORRY.
WHAT HAPPENED TO YOUR HEAD?!

TORIKO

GOURMET CHECKLIST

Vol. 284

ONION CHEESE

(PLANT)

CAPTURE LEVEL: 11

HABITAT: SPIRITS ARCHIPELAGO

SIZE: 20 CM

HEIGHT: ---

WEIGHT: 250 G

PRICE: 1,300 YEN PER PLANT

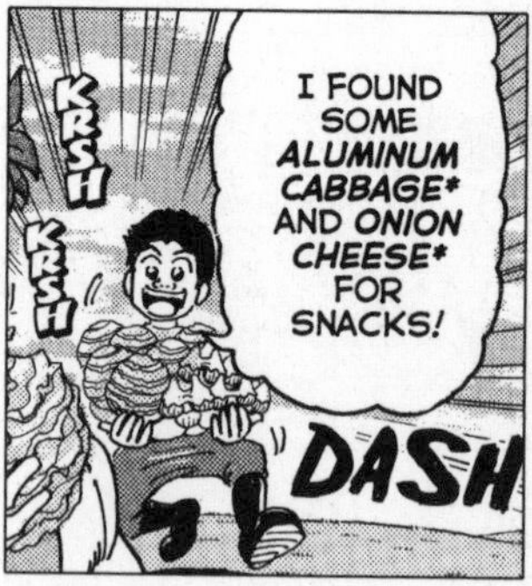
I FOUND SOME ALUMINUM CABBAGE* AND ONION CHEESE* FOR SNACKS!
KRSH KRSH
DASH

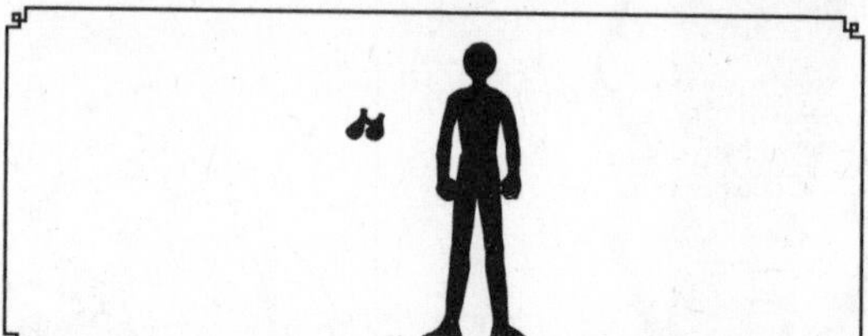

SCALE

A RARE ONION THAT ONLY GROWS IN VERY FERTILE SOIL. IT HAS THE CRUNCH OF AN ONION AND A MILD CHEESE FLAVOR. IT'S A LUXURIANT DELICACY THAT PAIRS WELL WITH RICH FLAVORS. DON'T SCARF THIS LUXURY FOOD DOWN! SAVOR IT SLOWLY WHILE SIPPING YOUR FAVORITE DRINK.

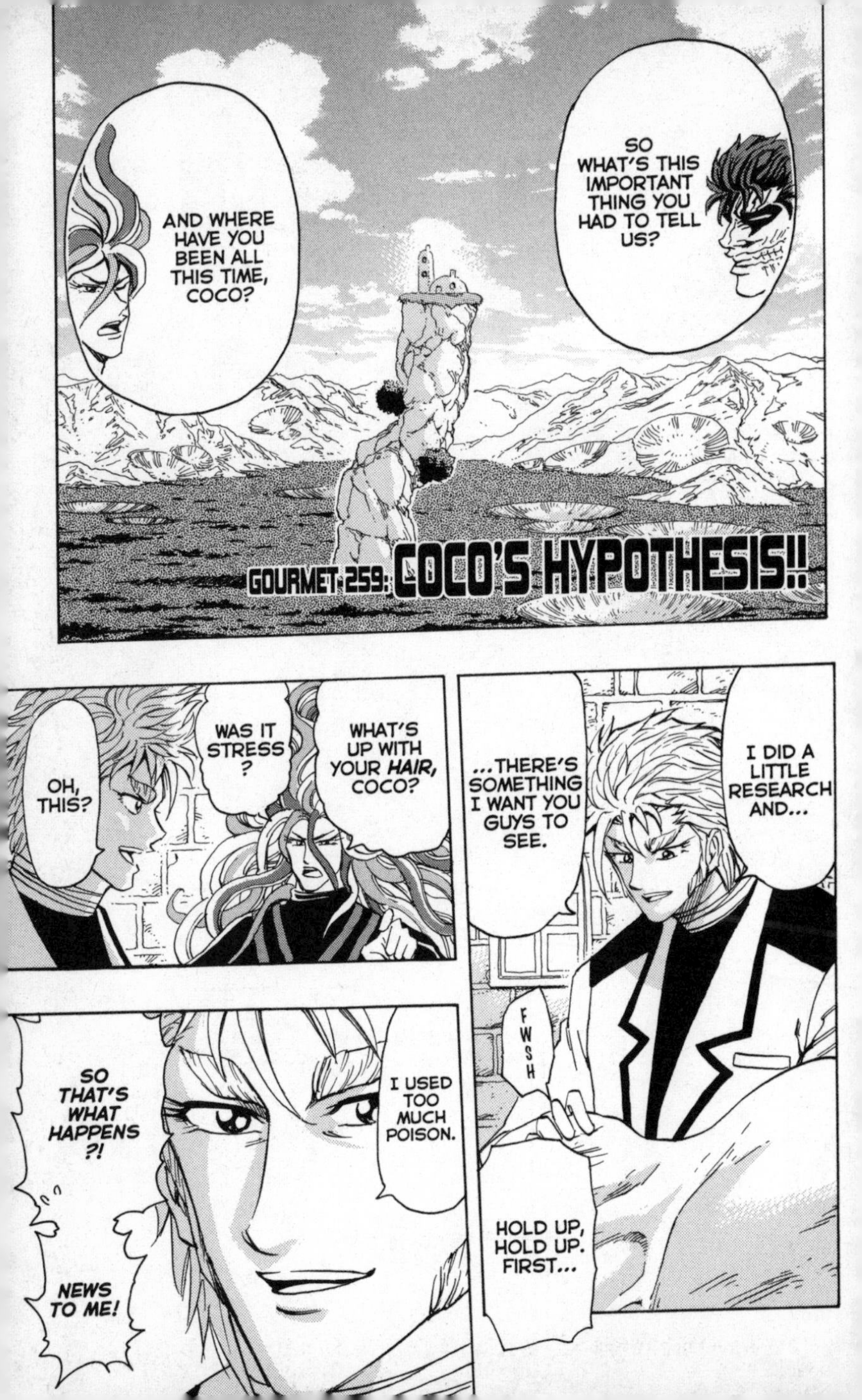

SO WHAT'S THIS IMPORTANT THING YOU HAD TO TELL US?
AND WHERE HAVE YOU BEEN ALL THIS TIME, COCO?
GOURMET 259: COCO'S HYPOTHESIS!!
I DID A LITTLE RESEARCH AND...
...THERE'S SOMETHING I WANT YOU GUYS TO SEE.
FWSH
HOLD UP, HOLD UP. FIRST...
WHAT'S UP WITH YOUR *HAIR*, COCO?
WAS IT STRESS?
OH, THIS?
I USED TOO MUCH POISON.
SO THAT'S WHAT HAPPENS?!
NEWS TO ME!

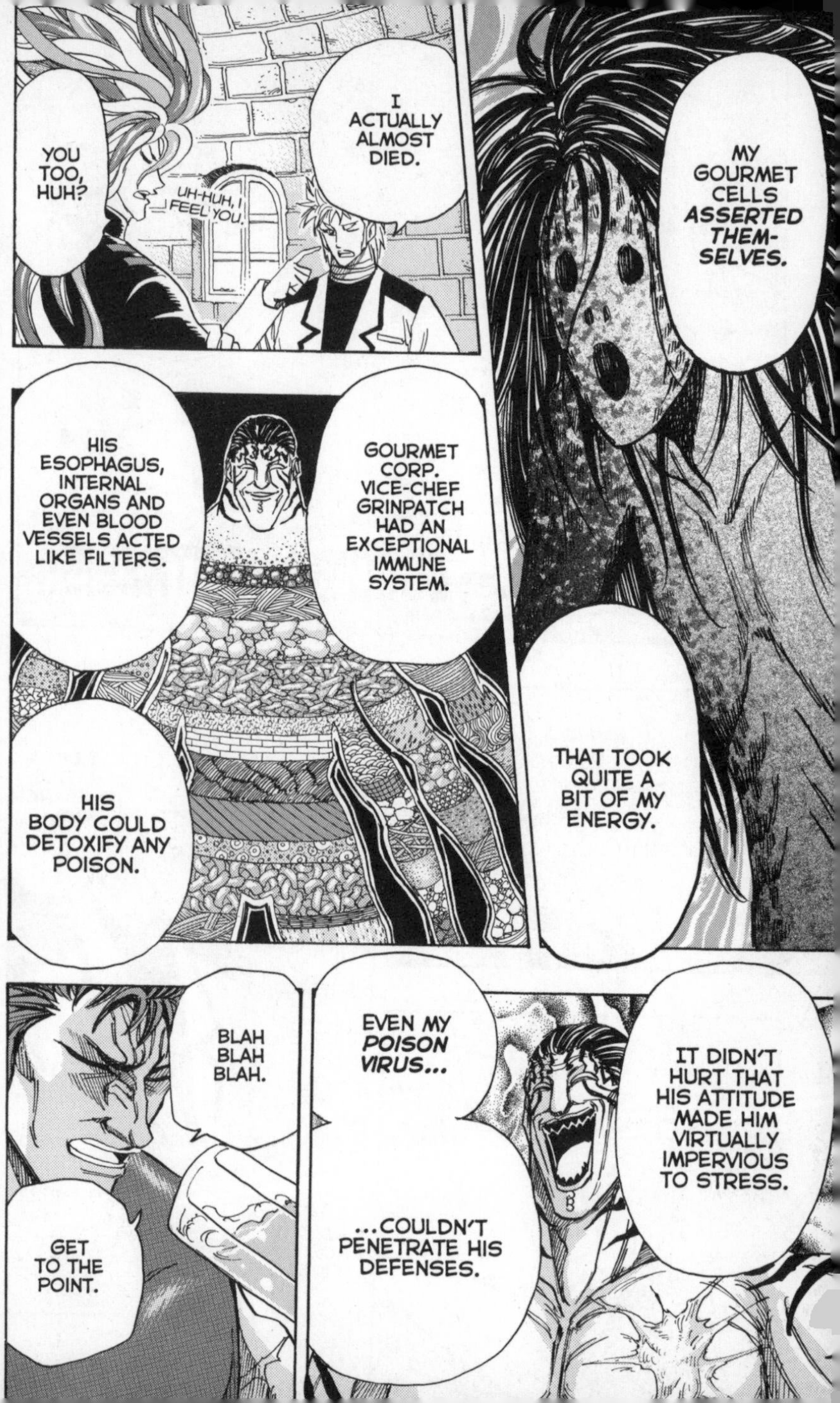
MY GOURMET CELLS ASSERTED THEM-SELVES.
THAT TOOK QUITE A BIT OF MY ENERGY.
I ACTUALLY ALMOST DIED.
UH-HUH, I FEEL YOU.
YOU TOO, HUH?
GOURMET CORP. VICE-CHEF GRINPATCH HAD AN EXCEPTIONAL IMMUNE SYSTEM.
HIS ESOPHAGUS, INTERNAL ORGANS AND EVEN BLOOD VESSELS ACTED LIKE FILTERS.
HIS BODY COULD DETOXIFY ANY POISON.
IT DIDN'T HURT THAT HIS ATTITUDE MADE HIM VIRTUALLY IMPERVIOUS TO STRESS.
EVEN MY POISON VIRUS...
...COULDN'T PENETRATE HIS DEFENSES.
BLAH BLAH BLAH.
GET TO THE POINT.

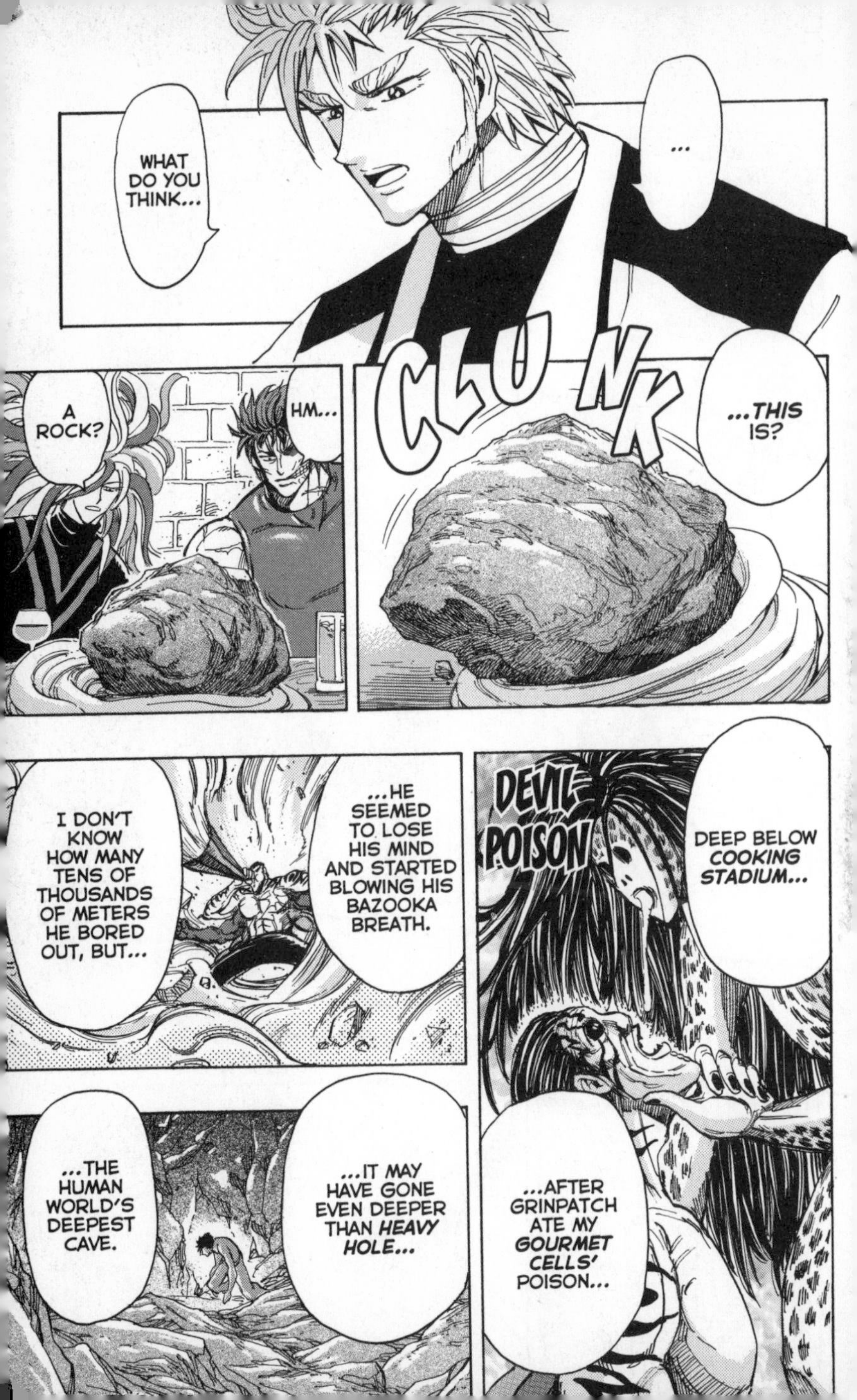
...
WHAT DO YOU THINK...
...THIS IS?
CLUNK
HM...
A ROCK?
DEEP BELOW COOKING STADIUM...
DEVIL POISON
...AFTER GRINPATCH ATE MY GOURMET CELLS' POISON...
...HE SEEMED TO LOSE HIS MIND AND STARTED BLOWING HIS BAZOOKA BREATH.
I DON'T KNOW HOW MANY TENS OF THOUSANDS OF METERS HE BORED OUT, BUT...
...IT MAY HAVE GONE EVEN DEEPER THAN HEAVY HOLE...
...THE HUMAN WORLD'S DEEPEST CAVE.

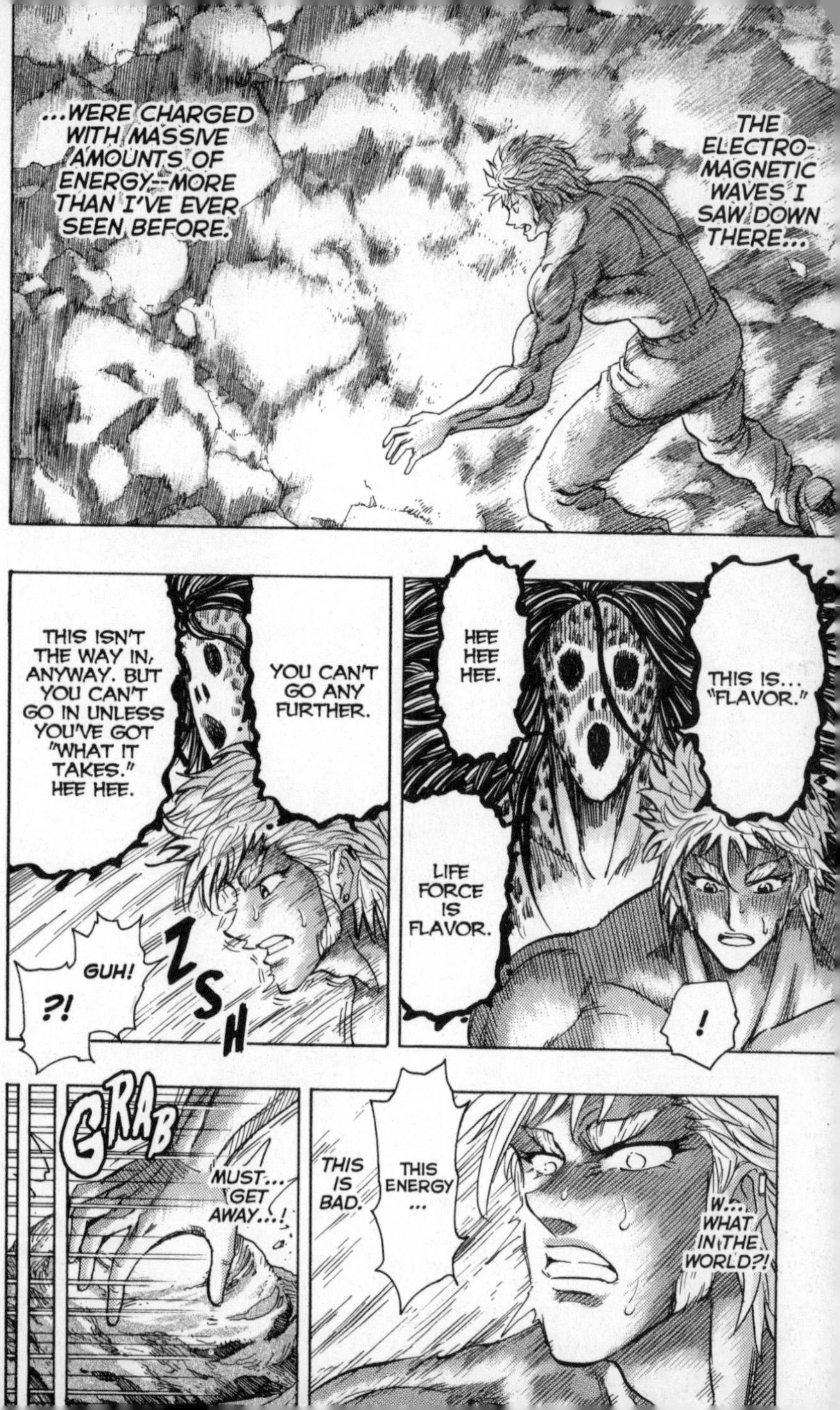
THE ELECTRO-MAGNETIC WAVES I SAW DOWN THERE...
...WERE CHARGED WITH MASSIVE AMOUNTS OF ENERGY--MORE THAN I'VE EVER SEEN BEFORE.
THIS IS... "FLAVOR."
HEE HEE HEE.
LIFE FORCE IS FLAVOR.
!
YOU CAN'T GO ANY FURTHER.
THIS ISN'T THE WAY IN, ANYWAY. BUT YOU CAN'T GO IN UNLESS YOU'VE GOT "WHAT IT TAKES." HEE HEE.
ZSH
GUH!
?!
W... WHAT IN THE WORLD?!
THIS ENERGY...
THIS IS BAD.
GRAB
MUST... GET AWAY...!

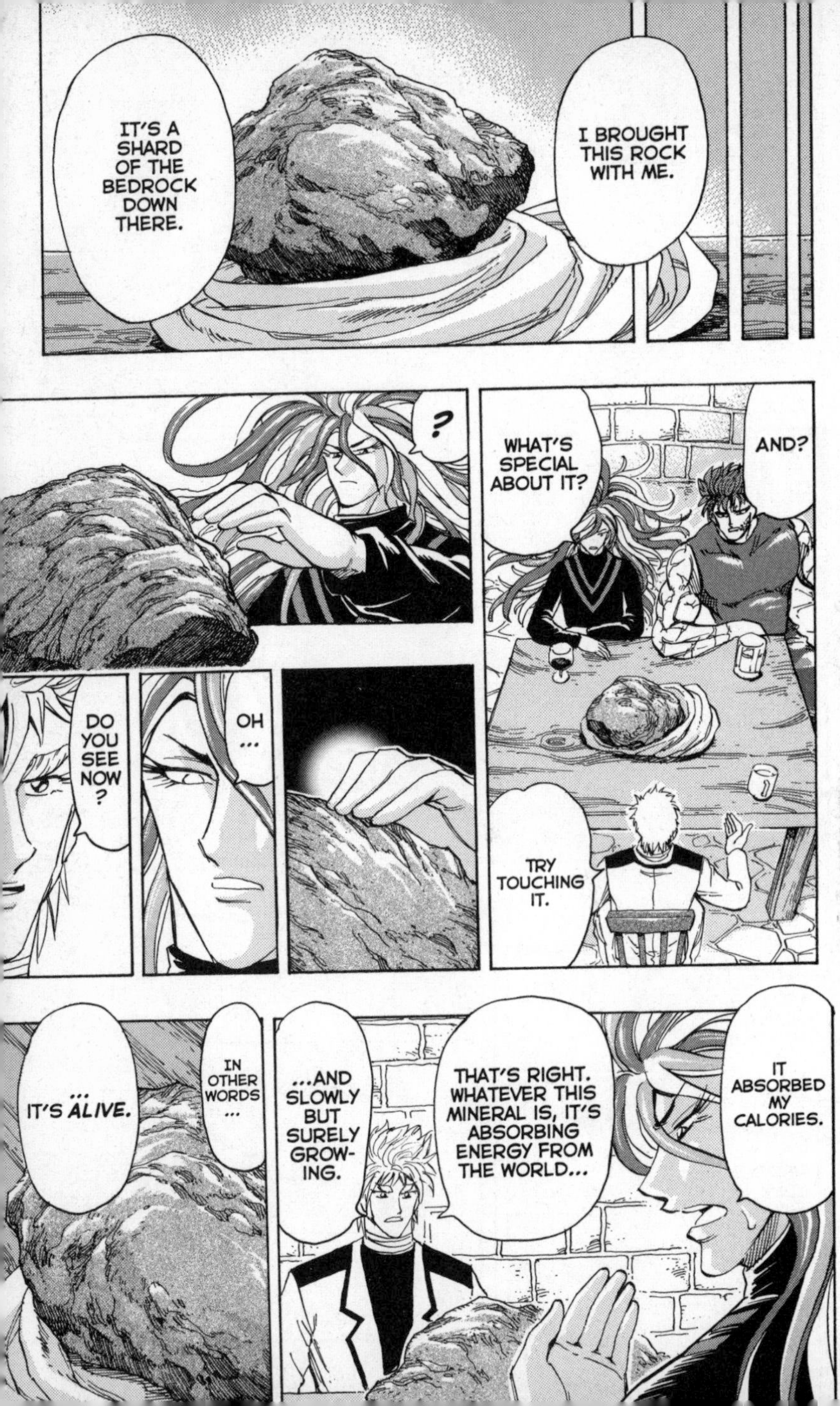
I BROUGHT THIS ROCK WITH ME.
IT'S A SHARD OF THE BEDROCK DOWN THERE.
AND?
WHAT'S SPECIAL ABOUT IT?
TRY TOUCHING IT.
?
OH ...
DO YOU SEE NOW ?
IT ABSORBED MY CALORIES.
THAT'S RIGHT. WHATEVER THIS MINERAL IS, IT'S ABSORBING ENERGY FROM THE WORLD...
...AND SLOWLY BUT SURELY GROW-ING.
IN OTHER WORDS ...
... IT'S *ALIVE.*

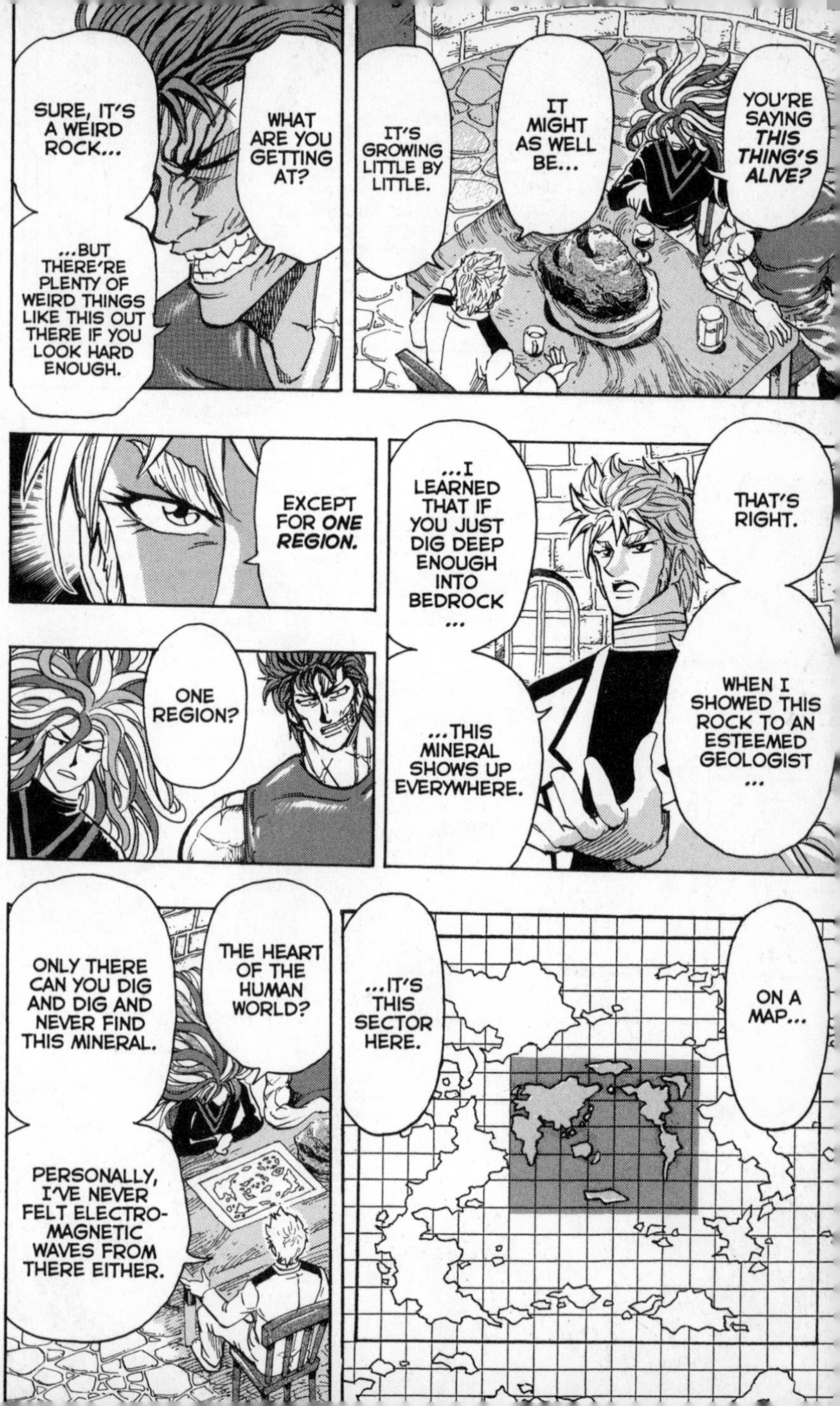
YOU'RE SAYING *THIS THING'S ALIVE?*
IT MIGHT AS WELL BE...
IT'S GROWING LITTLE BY LITTLE.
WHAT ARE YOU GETTING AT?
SURE, IT'S A WEIRD ROCK...
...BUT THERE'RE PLENTY OF WEIRD THINGS LIKE THIS OUT THERE IF YOU LOOK HARD ENOUGH.
THAT'S RIGHT.
WHEN I SHOWED THIS ROCK TO AN ESTEEMED GEOLOGIST...
...I LEARNED THAT IF YOU JUST DIG DEEP ENOUGH INTO BEDROCK...
...THIS MINERAL SHOWS UP EVERYWHERE.
EXCEPT FOR *ONE REGION.*
ONE REGION?
ON A MAP...
...IT'S THIS SECTOR HERE.
THE HEART OF THE HUMAN WORLD?
ONLY THERE CAN YOU DIG AND DIG AND NEVER FIND THIS MINERAL.
PERSONALLY, I'VE NEVER FELT ELECTRO-MAGNETIC WAVES FROM THERE EITHER.

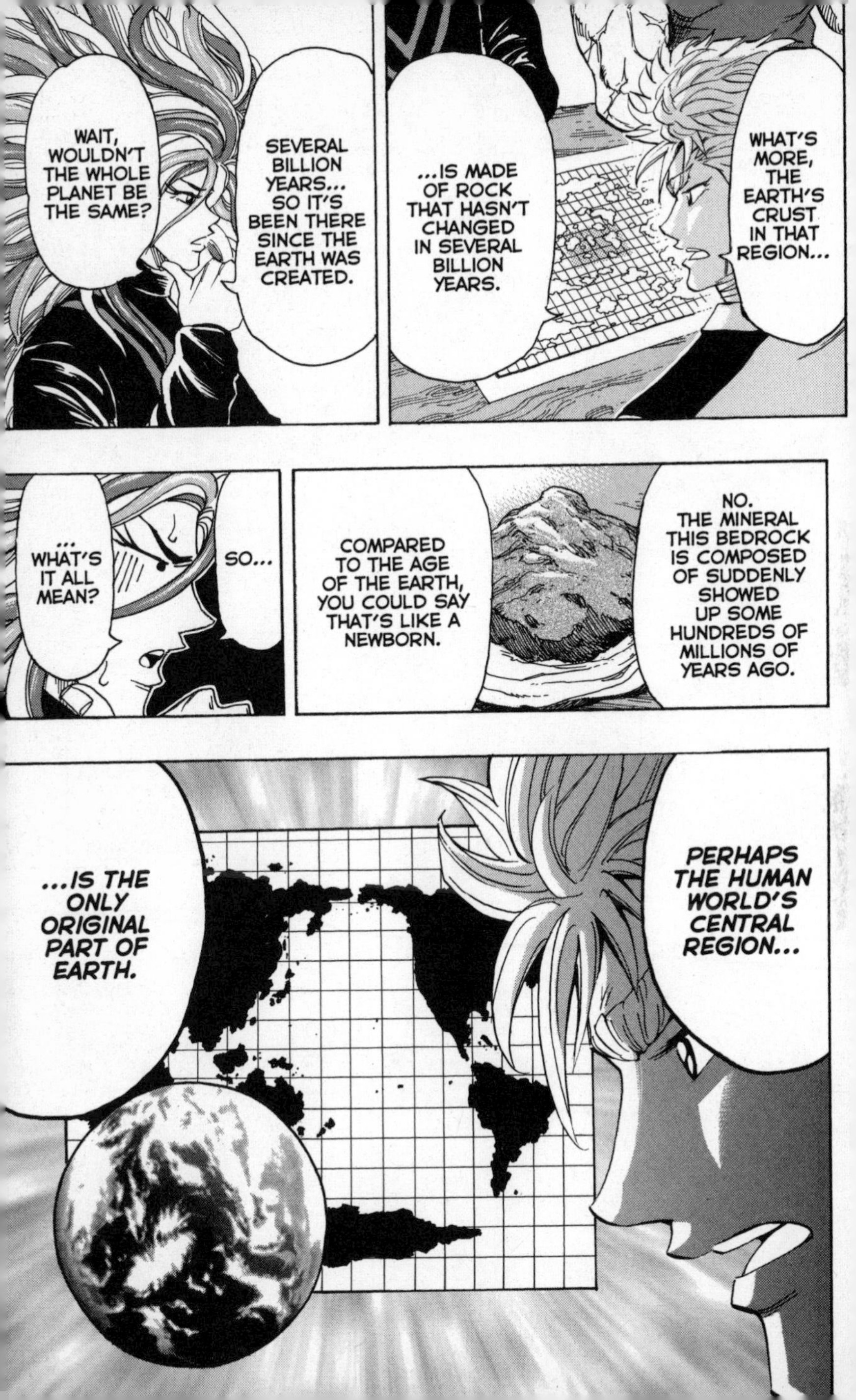
WHAT'S MORE, THE EARTH'S CRUST IN THAT REGION...
...IS MADE OF ROCK THAT HASN'T CHANGED IN SEVERAL BILLION YEARS.
SEVERAL BILLION YEARS... SO IT'S BEEN THERE SINCE THE EARTH WAS CREATED.
WAIT, WOULDN'T THE WHOLE PLANET BE THE SAME?
NO. THE MINERAL THIS BEDROCK IS COMPOSED OF SUDDENLY SHOWED UP SOME HUNDREDS OF MILLIONS OF YEARS AGO.
COMPARED TO THE AGE OF THE EARTH, YOU COULD SAY THAT'S LIKE A NEWBORN.
SO...
...WHAT'S IT ALL MEAN?
PERHAPS THE HUMAN WORLD'S CENTRAL REGION...
...IS THE ONLY ORIGINAL PART OF EARTH.

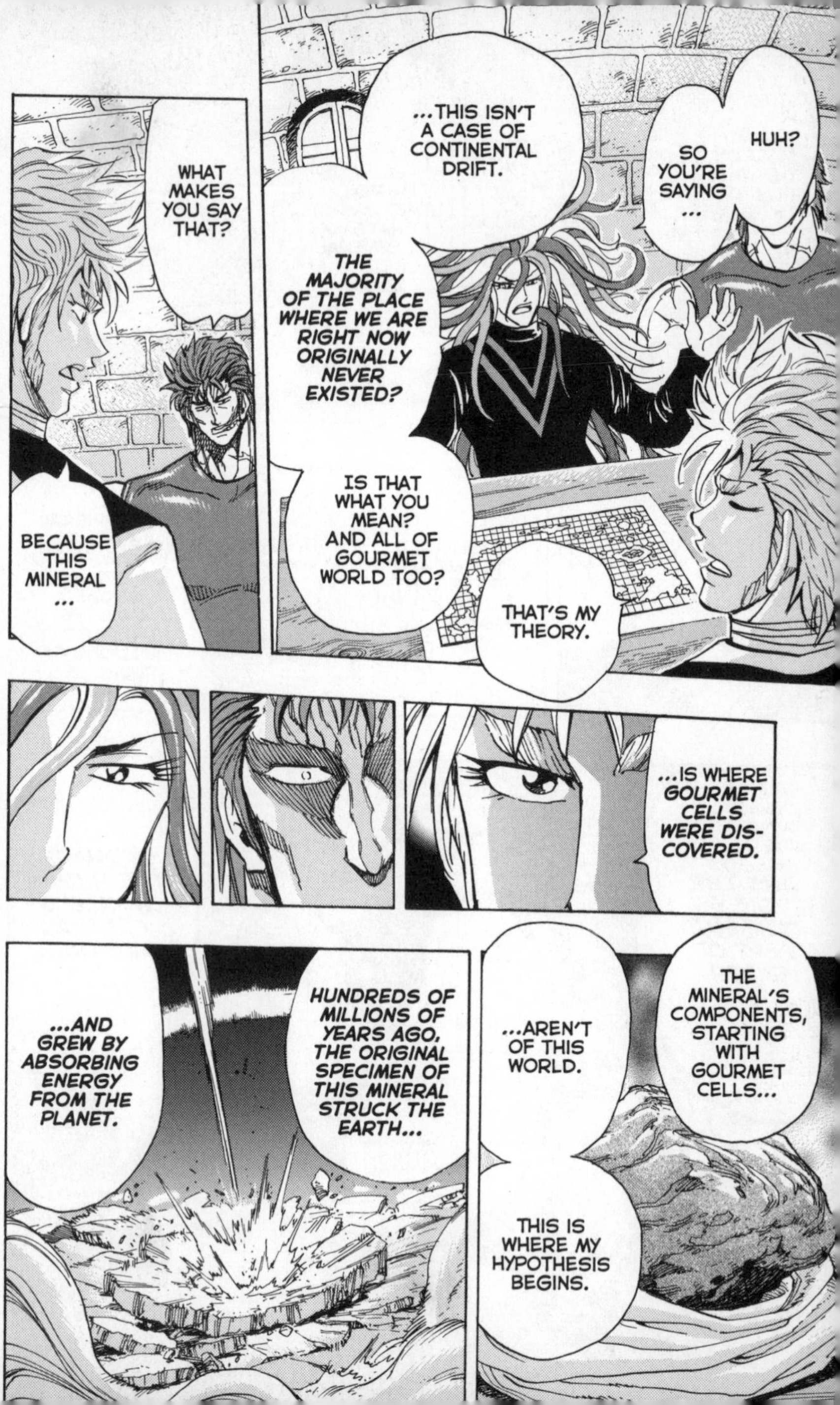
HUH?
SO YOU'RE SAYING ...
...THIS ISN'T A CASE OF CONTINENTAL DRIFT.
THE MAJORITY OF THE PLACE WHERE WE ARE RIGHT NOW ORIGINALLY NEVER EXISTED?
IS THAT WHAT YOU MEAN? AND ALL OF GOURMET WORLD TOO?
THAT'S MY THEORY.
WHAT MAKES YOU SAY THAT?
BECAUSE THIS MINERAL ...
...IS WHERE GOURMET CELLS WERE DIS-COVERED.
THE MINERAL'S COMPONENTS, STARTING WITH GOURMET CELLS...
...AREN'T OF THIS WORLD.
THIS IS WHERE MY HYPOTHESIS BEGINS.
HUNDREDS OF MILLIONS OF YEARS AGO, THE ORIGINAL SPECIMEN OF THIS MINERAL STRUCK THE EARTH...
...AND GREW BY ABSORBING ENERGY FROM THE PLANET.

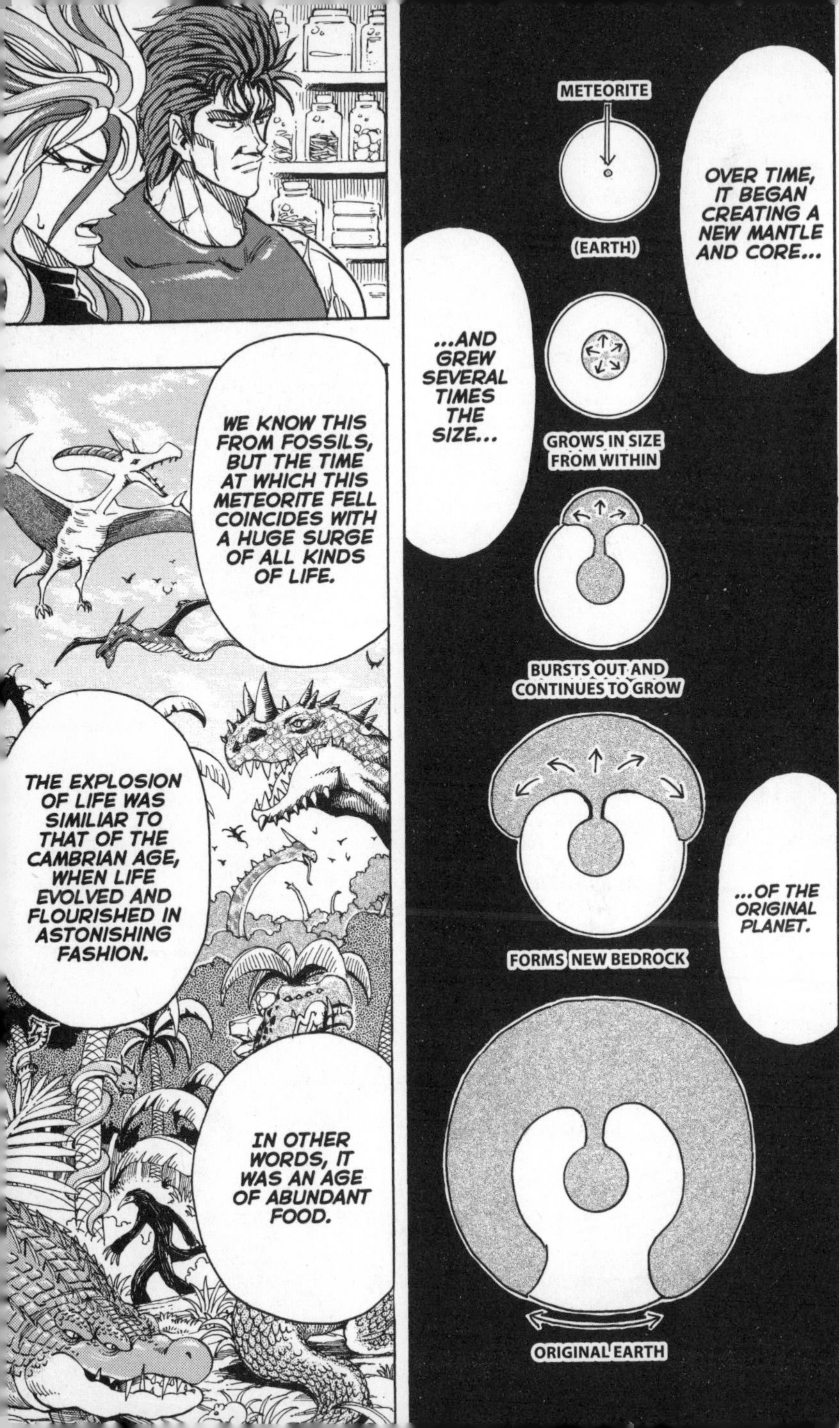
OVER TIME, IT BEGAN CREATING A NEW MANTLE AND CORE...
METEORITE
(EARTH)
...AND GREW SEVERAL TIMES THE SIZE...
GROWS IN SIZE FROM WITHIN
BURSTS OUT AND CONTINUES TO GROW
FORMS NEW BEDROCK
...OF THE ORIGINAL PLANET.
ORIGINAL EARTH
WE KNOW THIS FROM FOSSILS, BUT THE TIME AT WHICH THIS METEORITE FELL COINCIDES WITH A HUGE SURGE OF ALL KINDS OF LIFE.
THE EXPLOSION OF LIFE WAS SIMILIAR TO THAT OF THE CAMBRIAN AGE, WHEN LIFE EVOLVED AND FLOURISHED IN ASTONISHING FASHION.
IN OTHER WORDS, IT WAS AN AGE OF ABUNDANT FOOD.

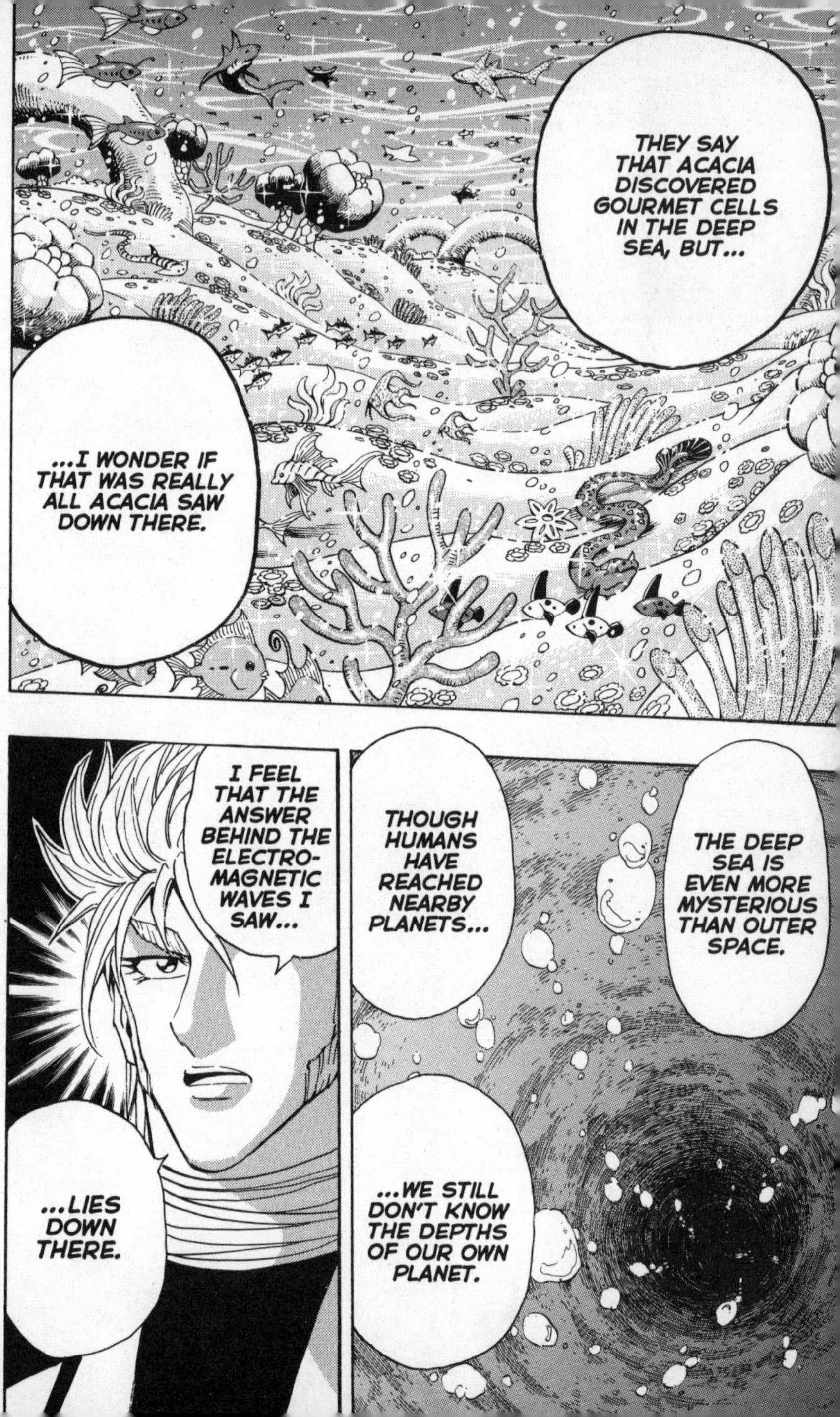
THEY SAY THAT ACACIA DISCOVERED GOURMET CELLS IN THE DEEP SEA, BUT...
...I WONDER IF THAT WAS REALLY ALL ACACIA SAW DOWN THERE.
THE DEEP SEA IS EVEN MORE MYSTERIOUS THAN OUTER SPACE.
THOUGH HUMANS HAVE REACHED NEARBY PLANETS...
...WE STILL DON'T KNOW THE DEPTHS OF OUR OWN PLANET.
I FEEL THAT THE ANSWER BEHIND THE ELECTRO-MAGNETIC WAVES I SAW...
...LIES DOWN THERE.

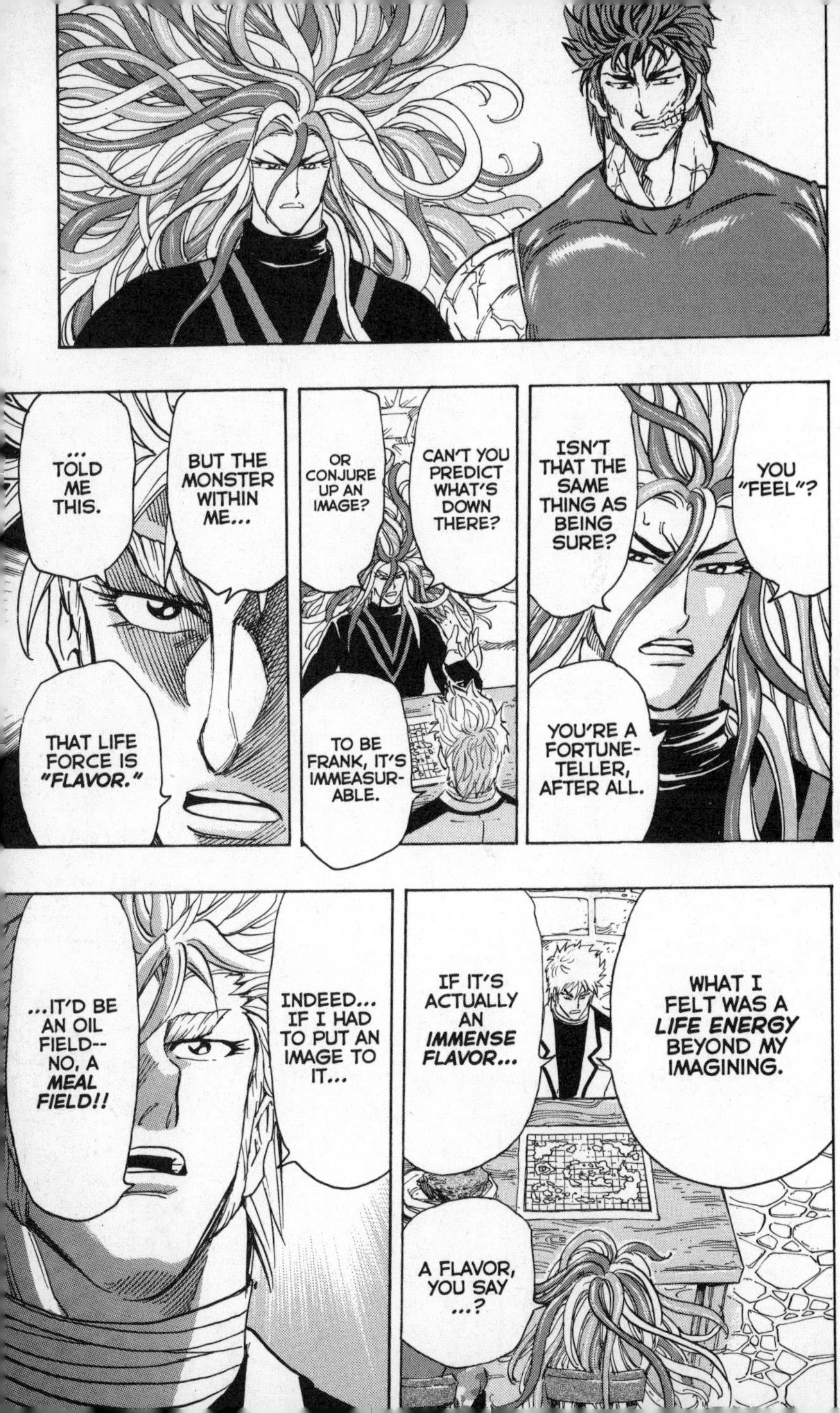
YOU "FEEL"?
ISN'T THAT THE SAME THING AS BEING SURE?
YOU'RE A FORTUNE-TELLER, AFTER ALL.
CAN'T YOU PREDICT WHAT'S DOWN THERE?
OR CONJURE UP AN IMAGE?
TO BE FRANK, IT'S IMMEASURABLE.
BUT THE MONSTER WITHIN ME...
...TOLD ME THIS.
THAT LIFE FORCE IS *"FLAVOR."*
WHAT I FELT WAS A *LIFE ENERGY* BEYOND MY IMAGINING.
IF IT'S ACTUALLY AN *IMMENSE FLAVOR...*
A FLAVOR, YOU SAY ...?
INDEED... IF I HAD TO PUT AN IMAGE TO IT...
...IT'D BE AN OIL FIELD-- NO, A *MEAL FIELD!!*

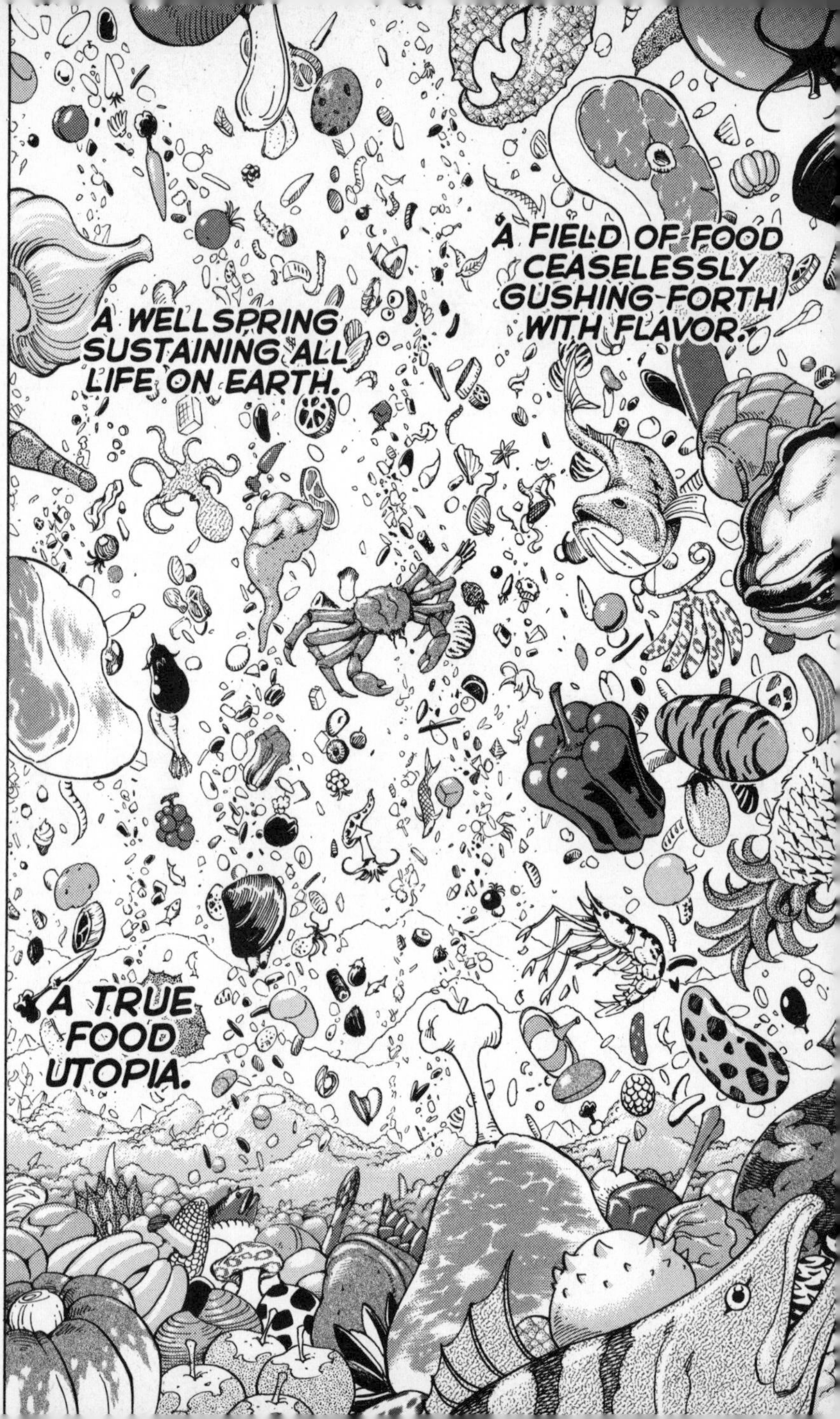
A FIELD OF FOOD CEASELESSLY GUSHING FORTH WITH FLAVOR.
A WELLSPRING SUSTAINING ALL LIFE ON EARTH.
A TRUE FOOD UTOPIA.

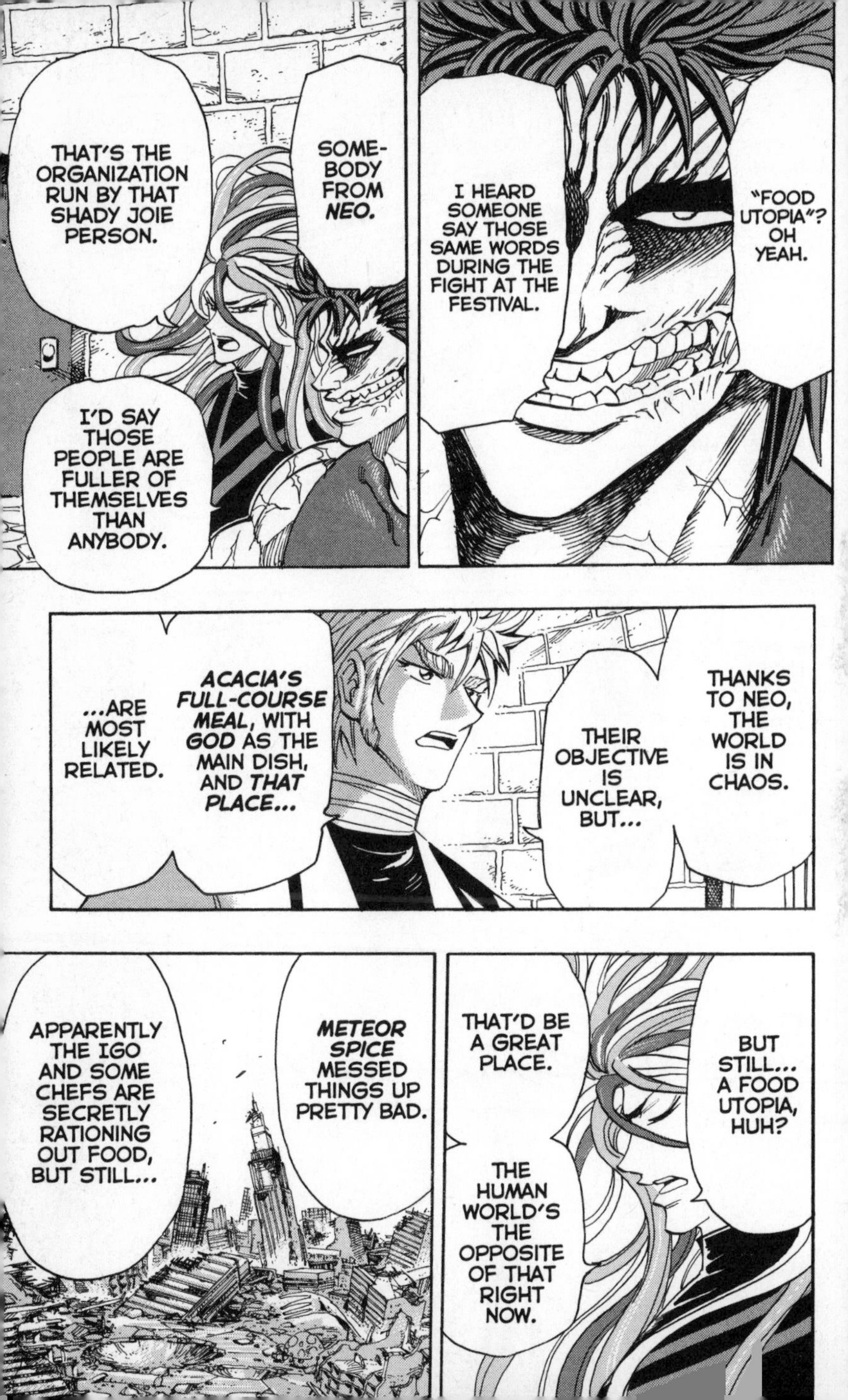
"FOOD UTOPIA"? OH YEAH.
I HEARD SOMEONE SAY THOSE SAME WORDS DURING THE FIGHT AT THE FESTIVAL.
SOME-BODY FROM *NEO.*
THAT'S THE ORGANIZATION RUN BY THAT SHADY JOIE PERSON.
I'D SAY THOSE PEOPLE ARE FULLER OF THEMSELVES THAN ANYBODY.
THANKS TO NEO, THE WORLD IS IN CHAOS.
THEIR OBJECTIVE IS UNCLEAR, BUT...
ACACIA'S FULL-COURSE MEAL, WITH *GOD* AS THE MAIN DISH, AND *THAT PLACE...*
...ARE MOST LIKELY RELATED.
BUT STILL... A FOOD UTOPIA, HUH?
THAT'D BE A GREAT PLACE.
THE HUMAN WORLD'S THE OPPOSITE OF THAT RIGHT NOW.
METEOR SPICE MESSED THINGS UP PRETTY BAD.
APPARENTLY THE IGO AND SOME CHEFS ARE SECRETLY RATIONING OUT FOOD, BUT STILL...

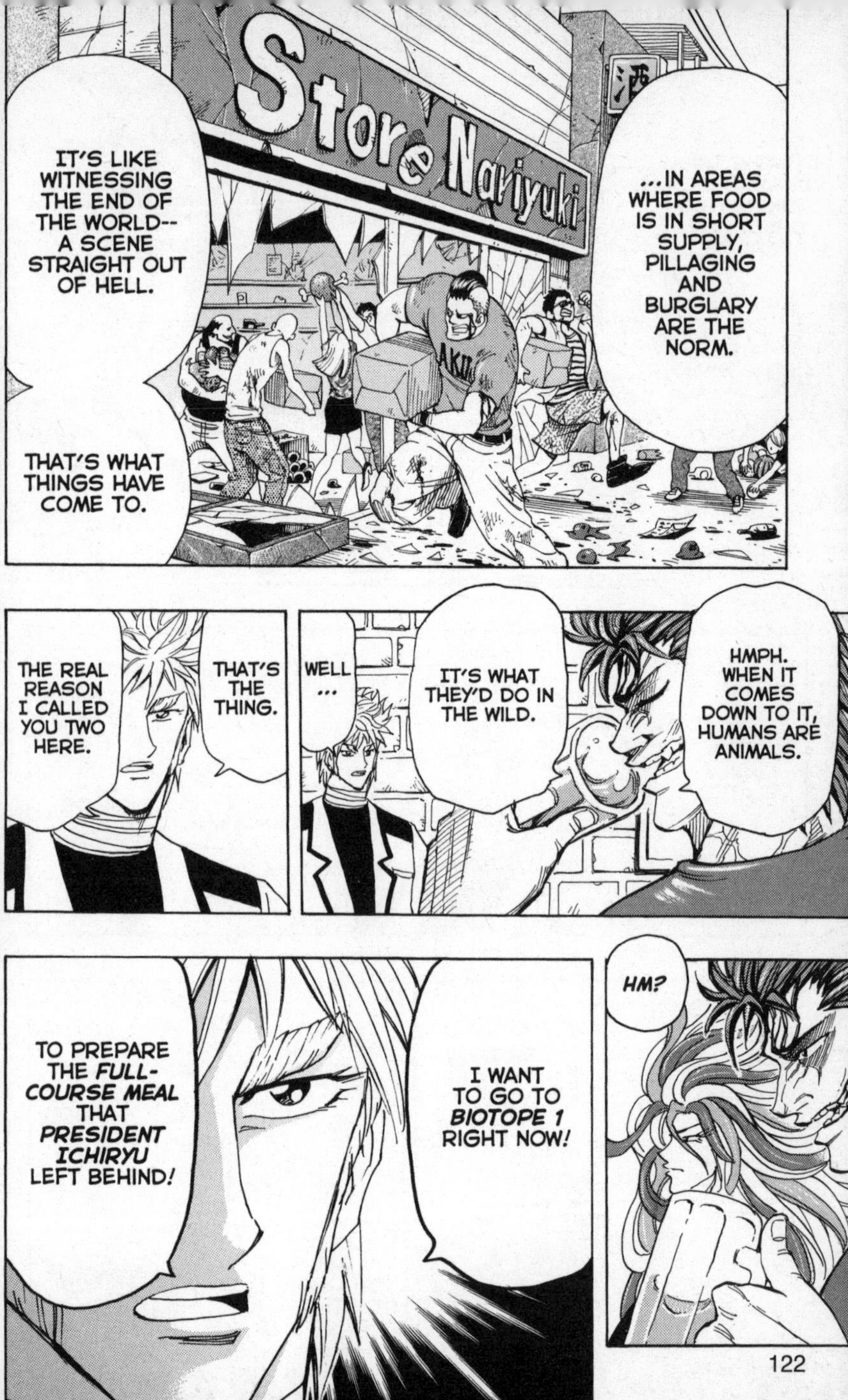
Store Nariyuki
酒
...IN AREAS WHERE FOOD IS IN SHORT SUPPLY, PILLAGING AND BURGLARY ARE THE NORM.
IT'S LIKE WITNESSING THE END OF THE WORLD-- A SCENE STRAIGHT OUT OF HELL.
THAT'S WHAT THINGS HAVE COME TO.
HMPH. WHEN IT COMES DOWN TO IT, HUMANS ARE ANIMALS.
IT'S WHAT THEY'D DO IN THE WILD.
WELL...
THAT'S THE THING.
THE REAL REASON I CALLED YOU TWO HERE.
HM?
I WANT TO GO TO *BIOTOPE 1* RIGHT NOW!
TO PREPARE THE *FULL-COURSE MEAL* THAT *PRESIDENT ICHIRYU* LEFT BEHIND!

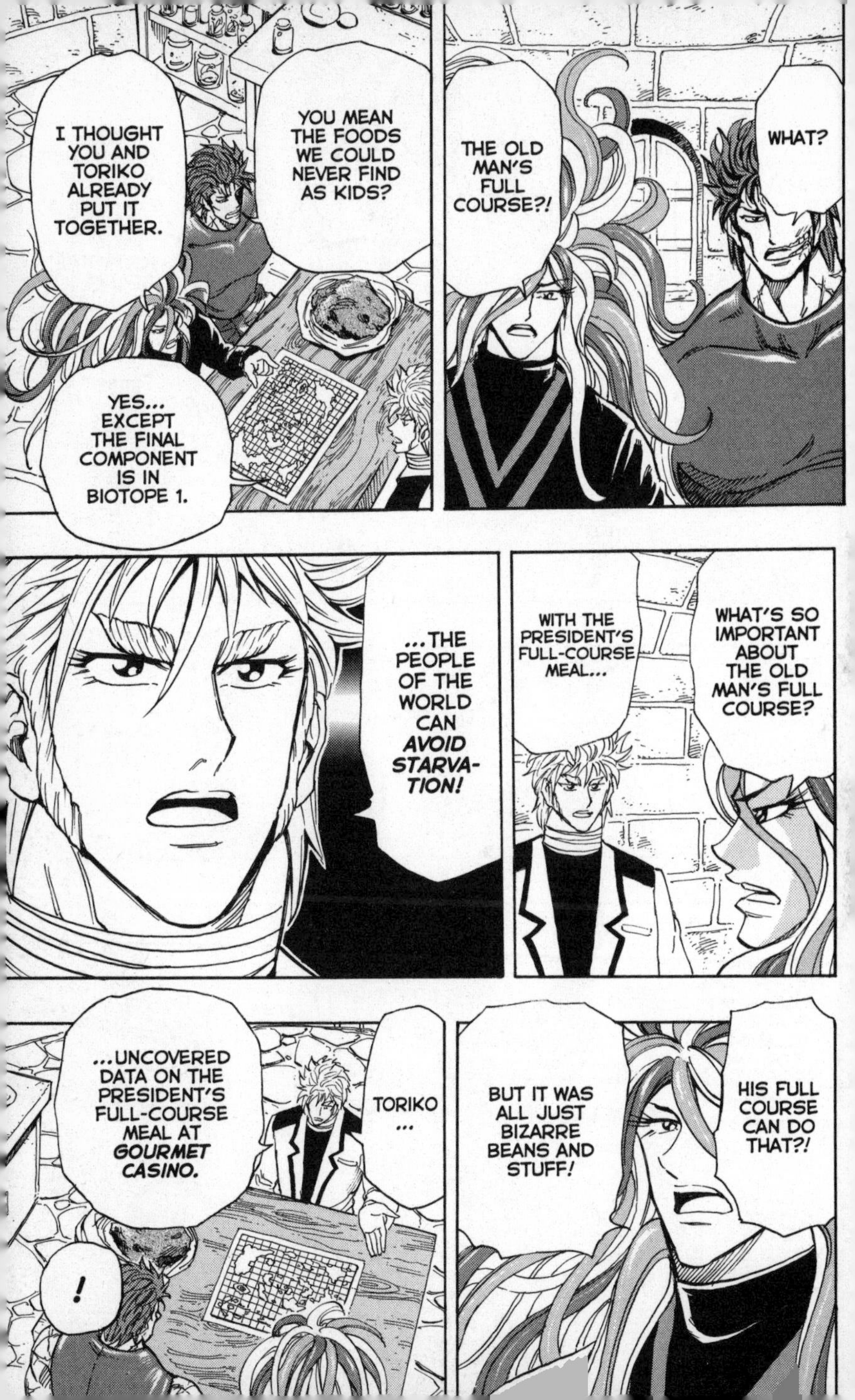
WHAT?
THE OLD MAN'S FULL COURSE?!
YOU MEAN THE FOODS WE COULD NEVER FIND AS KIDS?
I THOUGHT YOU AND TORIKO ALREADY PUT IT TOGETHER.
YES... EXCEPT THE FINAL COMPONENT IS IN BIOTOPE 1.
WHAT'S SO IMPORTANT ABOUT THE OLD MAN'S FULL COURSE?
WITH THE PRESIDENT'S FULL-COURSE MEAL...
...THE PEOPLE OF THE WORLD CAN *AVOID STARVATION!*
HIS FULL COURSE CAN DO THAT?!
BUT IT WAS ALL JUST BIZARRE BEANS AND STUFF!
TORIKO ...
...UNCOVERED DATA ON THE PRESIDENT'S FULL-COURSE MEAL AT *GOURMET CASINO.*
!

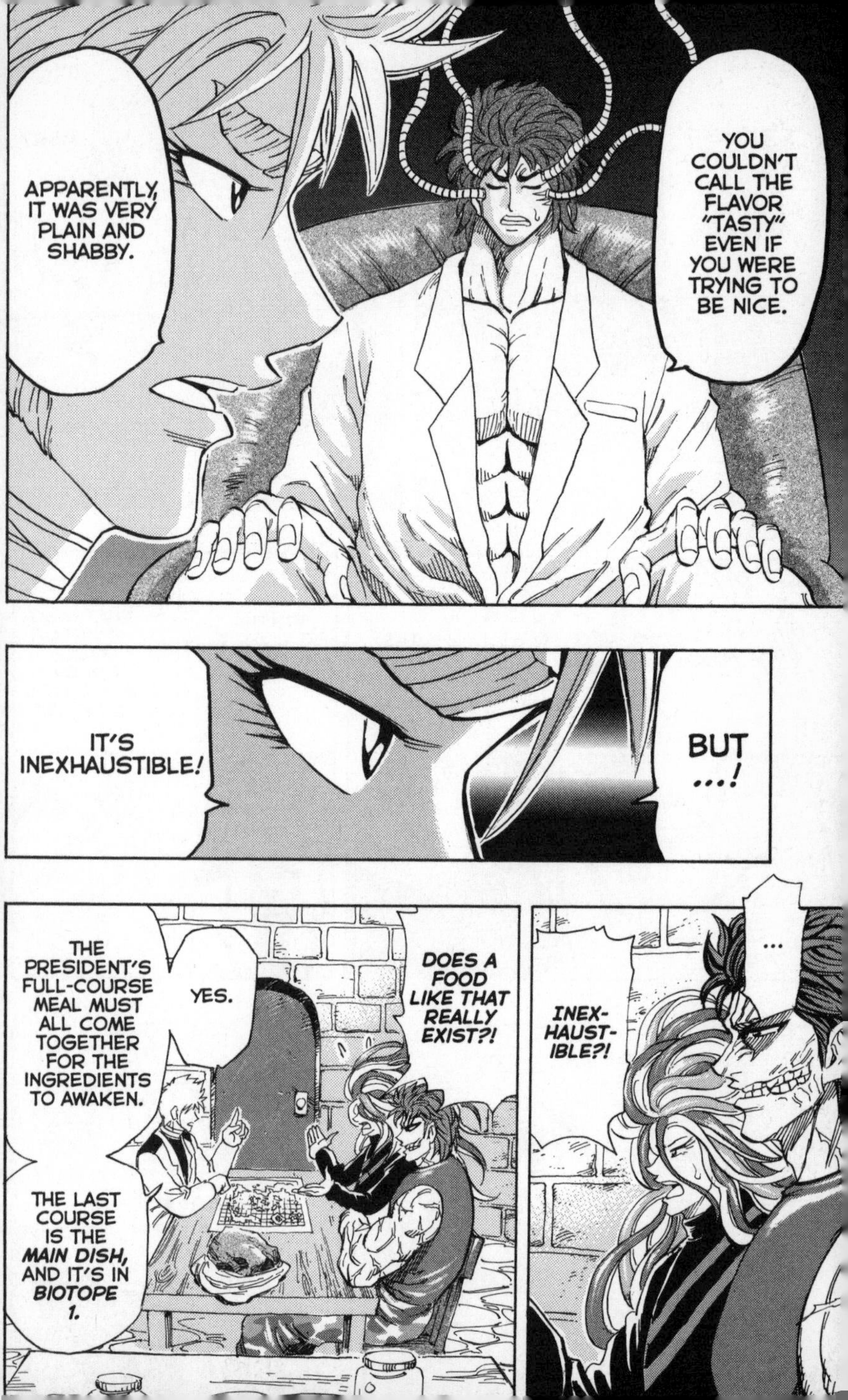
YOU COULDN'T CALL THE FLAVOR "TASTY" EVEN IF YOU WERE TRYING TO BE NICE.
APPARENTLY, IT WAS VERY PLAIN AND SHABBY.
BUT ...!
IT'S INEXHAUSTIBLE!
...
INEX-HAUST-IBLE?!
DOES A FOOD LIKE THAT REALLY EXIST?!
YES.
THE PRESIDENT'S FULL-COURSE MEAL MUST ALL COME TOGETHER FOR THE INGREDIENTS TO AWAKEN.
THE LAST COURSE IS THE *MAIN DISH,* AND IT'S IN *BIOTOPE 1.*

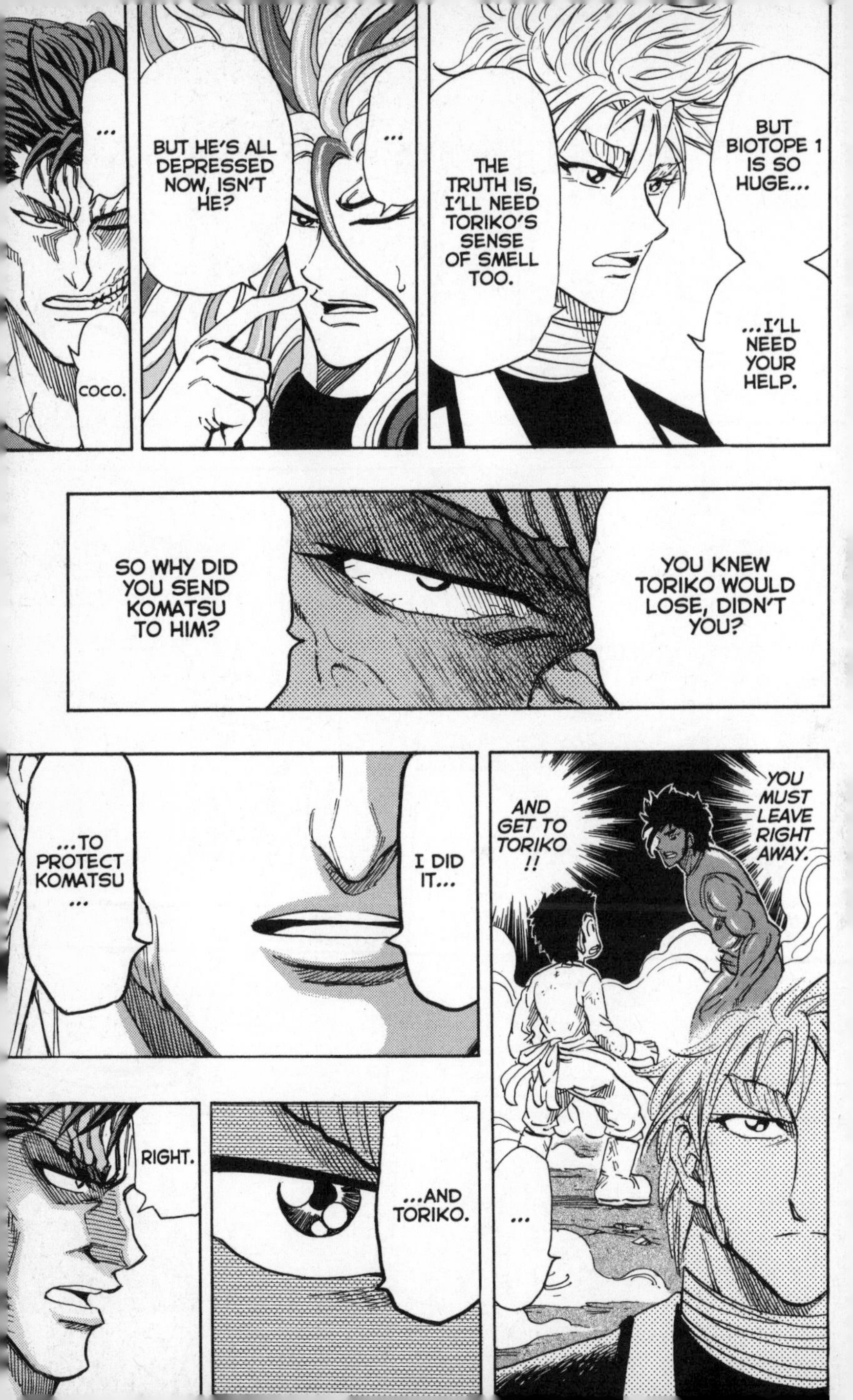
BUT BIOTOPE 1 IS SO HUGE...
...I'LL NEED YOUR HELP.
THE TRUTH IS, I'LL NEED TORIKO'S SENSE OF SMELL TOO.
...
BUT HE'S ALL DEPRESSED NOW, ISN'T HE?
...
COCO.
YOU KNEW TORIKO WOULD LOSE, DIDN'T YOU?
SO WHY DID YOU SEND KOMATSU TO HIM?
YOU MUST LEAVE RIGHT AWAY.
AND GET TO TORIKO!!
...
I DID IT...
...TO PROTECT KOMATSU...
...AND TORIKO.
RIGHT.

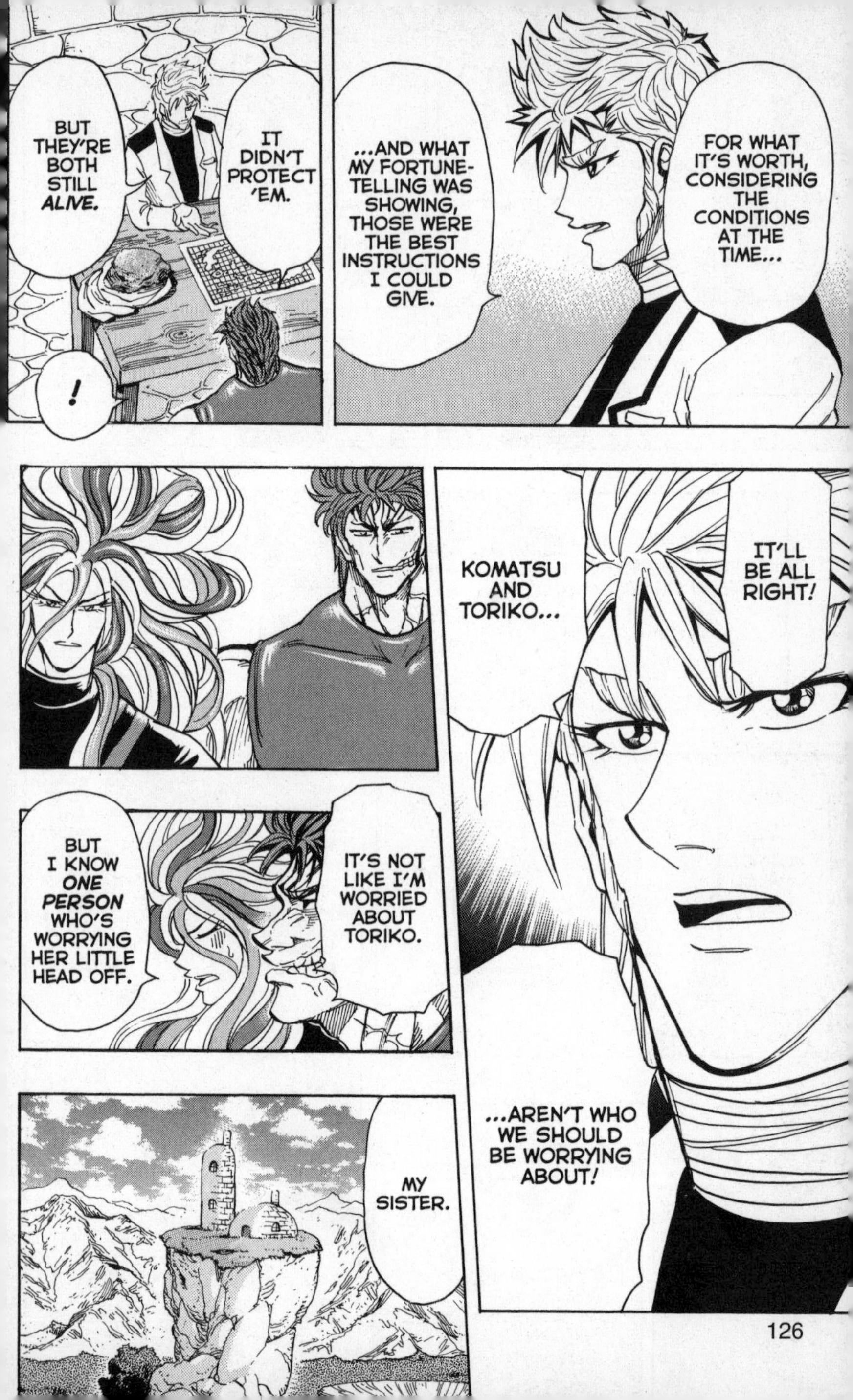
FOR WHAT IT'S WORTH, CONSIDERING THE CONDITIONS AT THE TIME...
...AND WHAT MY FORTUNE-TELLING WAS SHOWING, THOSE WERE THE BEST INSTRUCTIONS I COULD GIVE.
IT DIDN'T PROTECT 'EM.
BUT THEY'RE BOTH STILL *ALIVE.*
!
IT'LL BE ALL RIGHT!
KOMATSU AND TORIKO...
...AREN'T WHO WE SHOULD BE WORRYING ABOUT!
IT'S NOT LIKE I'M WORRIED ABOUT TORIKO.
BUT I KNOW *ONE PERSON* WHO'S WORRYING HER LITTLE HEAD OFF.
MY SISTER.

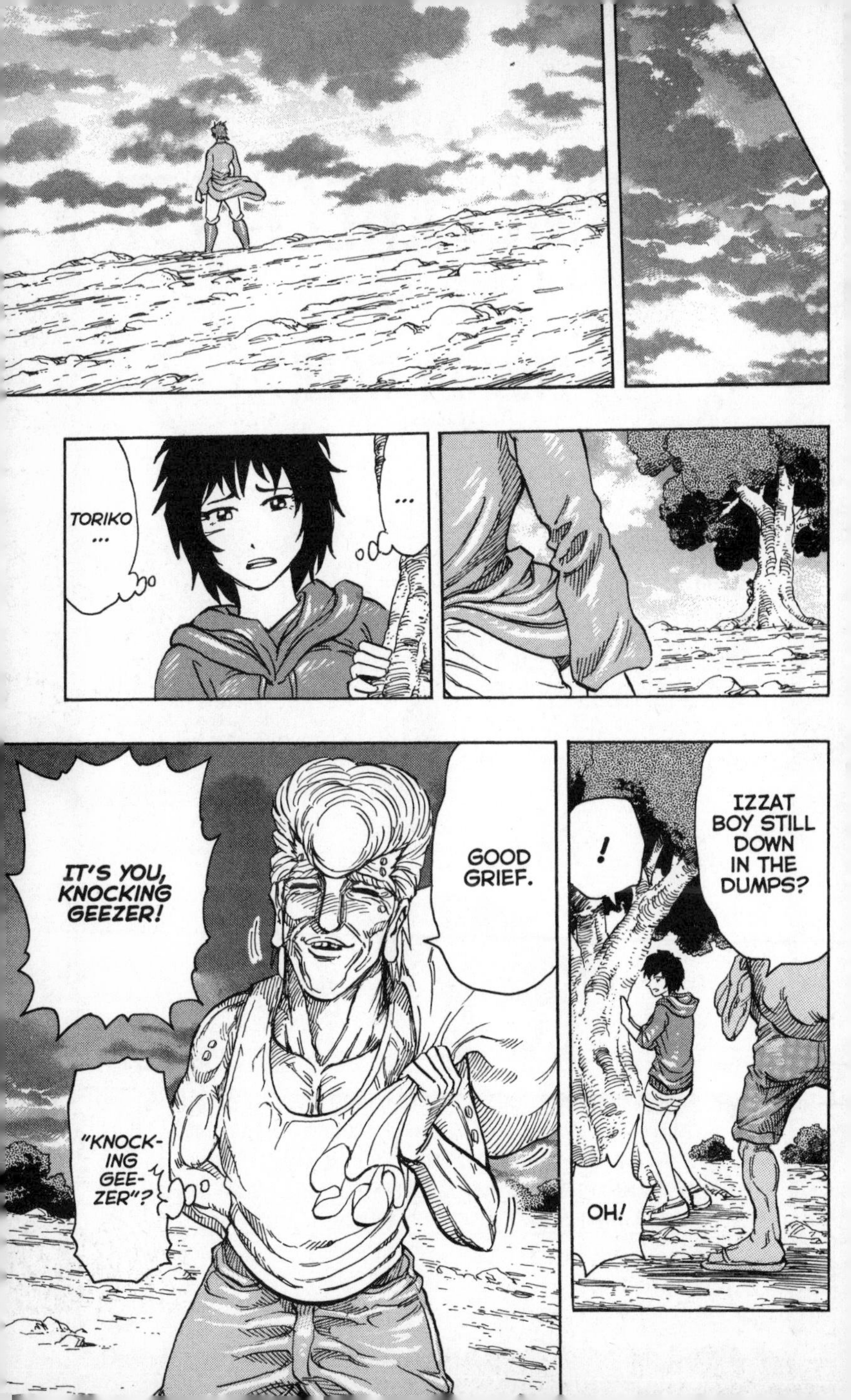
...
TORIKO ...
IZZAT BOY STILL DOWN IN THE DUMPS?
!
OH!
GOOD GRIEF.
IT'S YOU, KNOCKING GEEZER!
"KNOCKING-ING GEE-ZER"?

TORIKO

GOURMET CHECKLIST

Vol. 285

BRANDY TIGER
(MAMMAL)

CAPTURE LEVEL: 53

HABITAT: SPIRITS ARCHIPELAGO

SIZE: 5 METERS

HEIGHT: 2.5 METERS

WEIGHT: 2 TONS

PRICE: 100 G OF MEAT / 200 YEN;
1 BOTTLE OF BLOOD / 500,000 YEN

THEIR BLOOD IS SUPPOSED TO BE A HIGH-QUALITY BRANDY!

A BRANDY TIGER!!

GRR

BRANDY TIGER
(MAMMAL)
CAPTURE LEVEL 53

SCALE

A RARE TIGER WITH BLOOD THAT'S ACTUALLY HIGH-QUALITY BRANDY. ITS BODY IS QUITE POISONOUS, BUT BY THE TIME THE ANIMAL HAS REACHED A HUNDRED YEARS OF AGE, THAT POISON MATURES INTO BRANDY. IT'S SO HIGHLY DESIRED BY ALCOHOL AFICIONADOS THAT THERE ARE MANY CASES OF PEOPLE CAPTURING A BRANDY TIGER BEFORE ITS BODY HAS COMPLETELY DETOXIFIED AND DYING FROM FOOD POISONING.

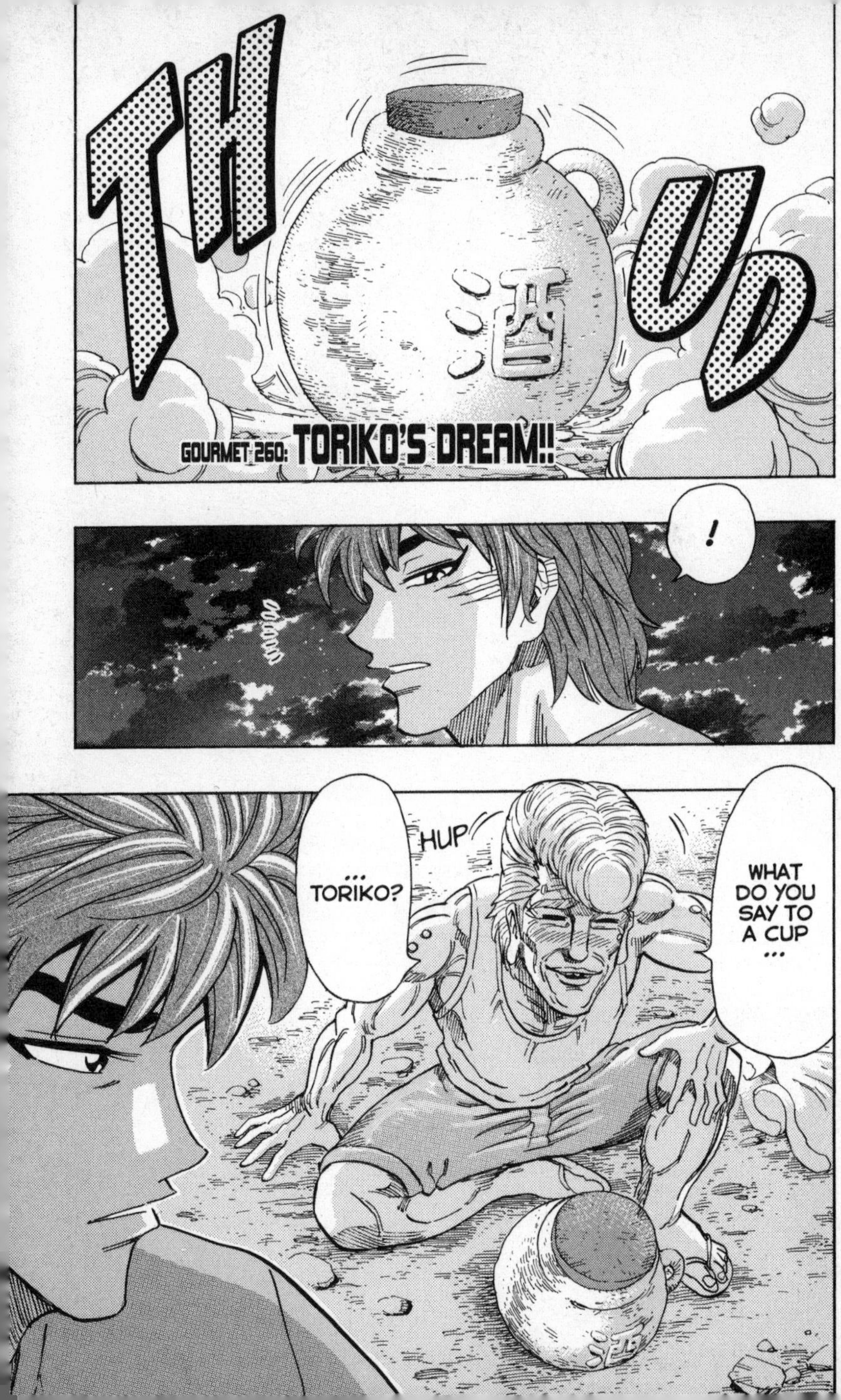
THUD
GOURMET 260: TORIKO'S DREAM!!
!
WHAT DO YOU SAY TO A CUP...
HUP
...TORIKO?

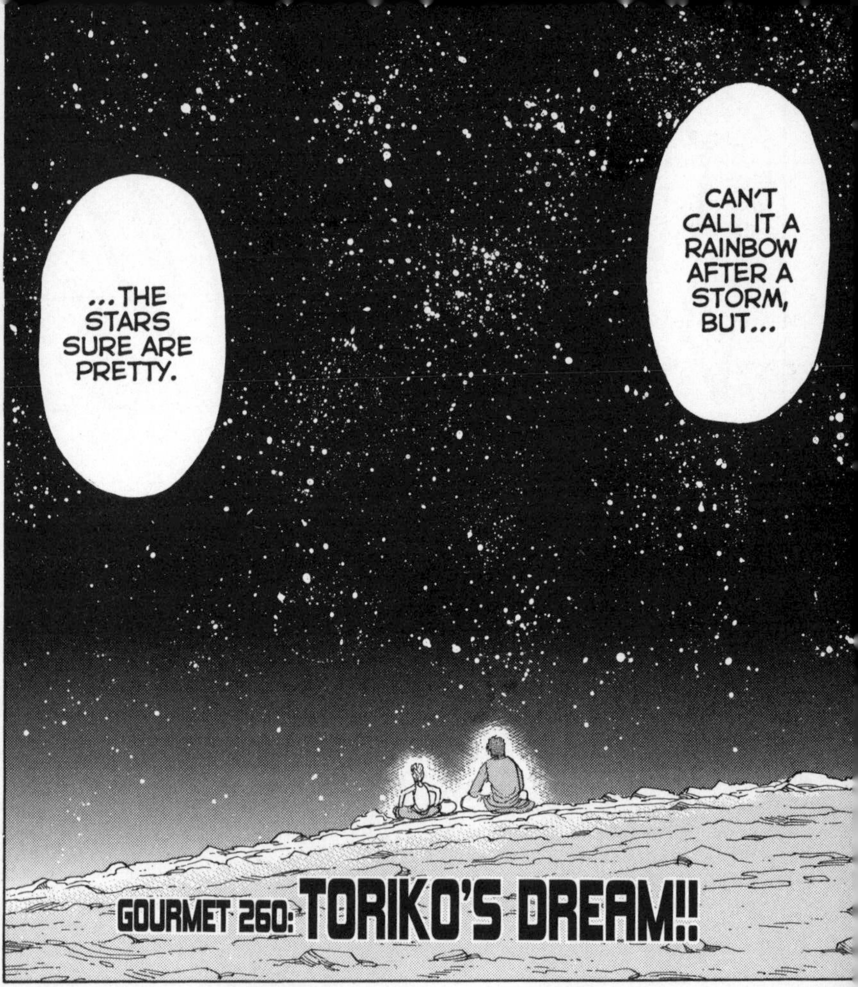
CAN'T CALL IT A RAINBOW AFTER A STORM, BUT...
...THE STARS SURE ARE PRETTY.
GOURMET 260: TORIKO'S DREAM!!

*SUBMITTED BY IZURU INUBUSHI FROM OSAKA!

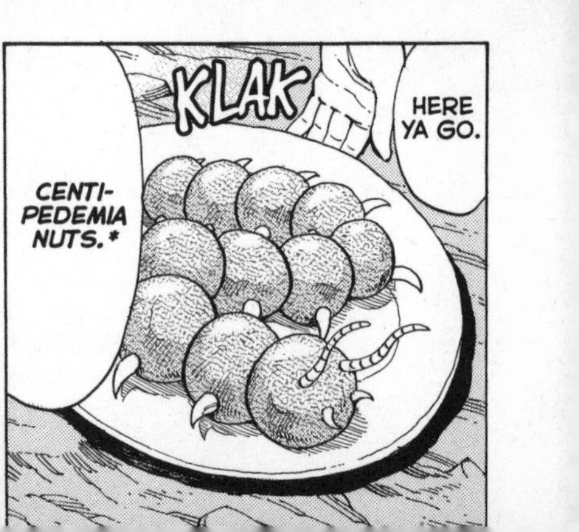
HERE YA GO.
KLAK
CENTI-PEDEMIA NUTS.*

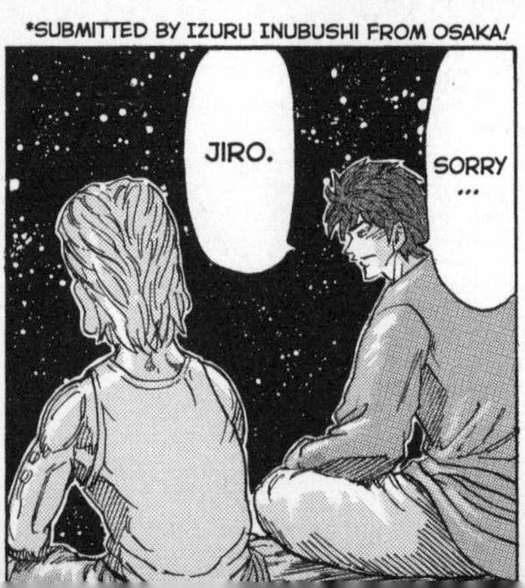
SORRY...
JIRO.

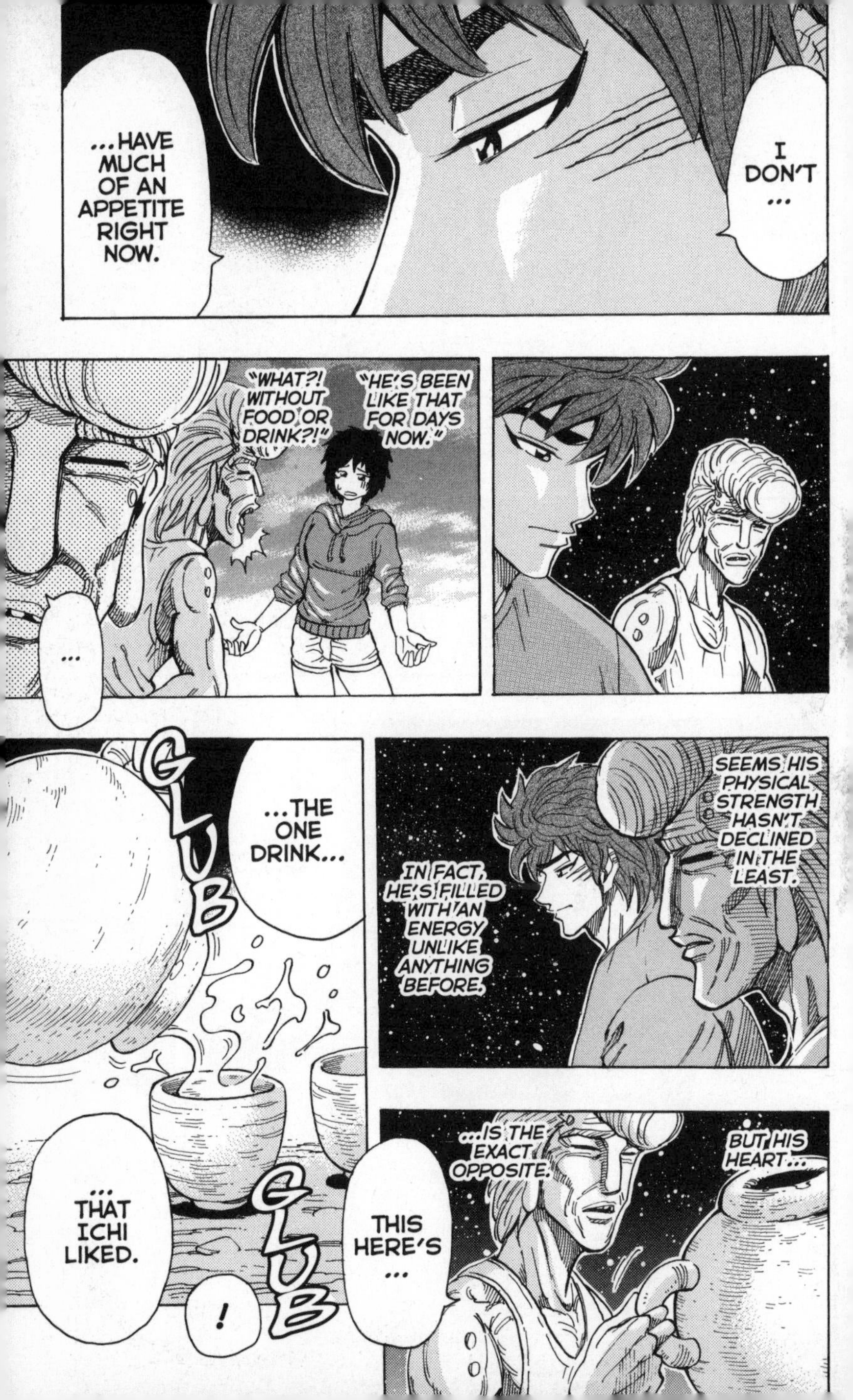
I DON'T ...
...HAVE MUCH OF AN APPETITE RIGHT NOW.
"HE'S BEEN LIKE THAT FOR DAYS NOW."
"WHAT?! WITHOUT FOOD OR DRINK?!"
...
SEEMS HIS PHYSICAL STRENGTH HASN'T DECLINED IN THE LEAST.
IN FACT, HE'S FILLED WITH AN ENERGY UNLIKE ANYTHING BEFORE.
BUT HIS HEART...
...IS THE EXACT OPPOSITE.
THIS HERE'S ...
GLUB
...THE ONE DRINK...
... THAT ICHI LIKED.
GLUB
!

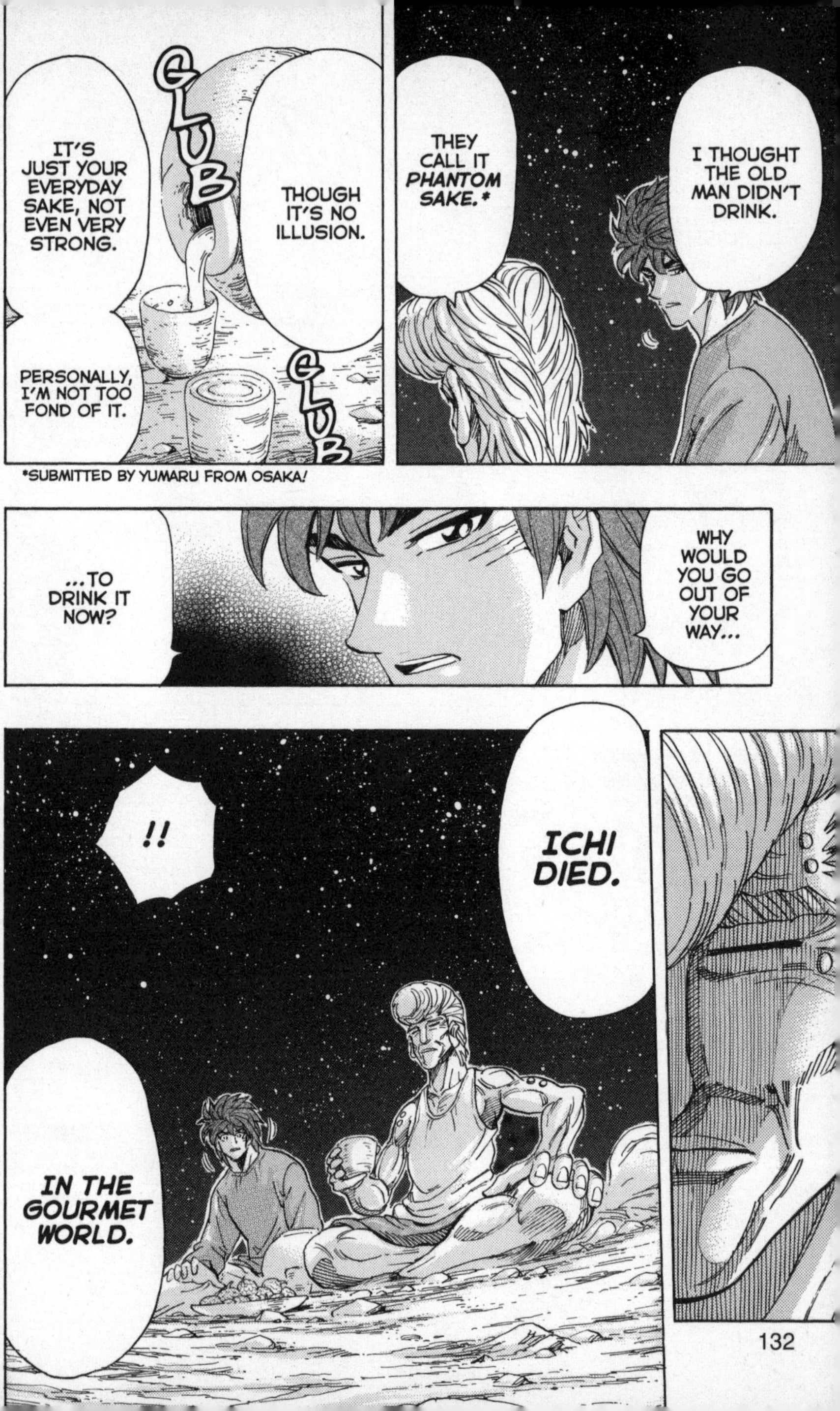
I THOUGHT THE OLD MAN DIDN'T DRINK.
THEY CALL IT *PHANTOM SAKE.**
THOUGH IT'S NO ILLUSION.
GLUB
GLUB
IT'S JUST YOUR EVERYDAY SAKE, NOT EVEN VERY STRONG.
PERSONALLY, I'M NOT TOO FOND OF IT.
WHY WOULD YOU GO OUT OF YOUR WAY...
...TO DRINK IT NOW?
ICHI DIED.
!!
IN THE GOURMET WORLD.

*SUBMITTED BY YUMARU FROM OSAKA!

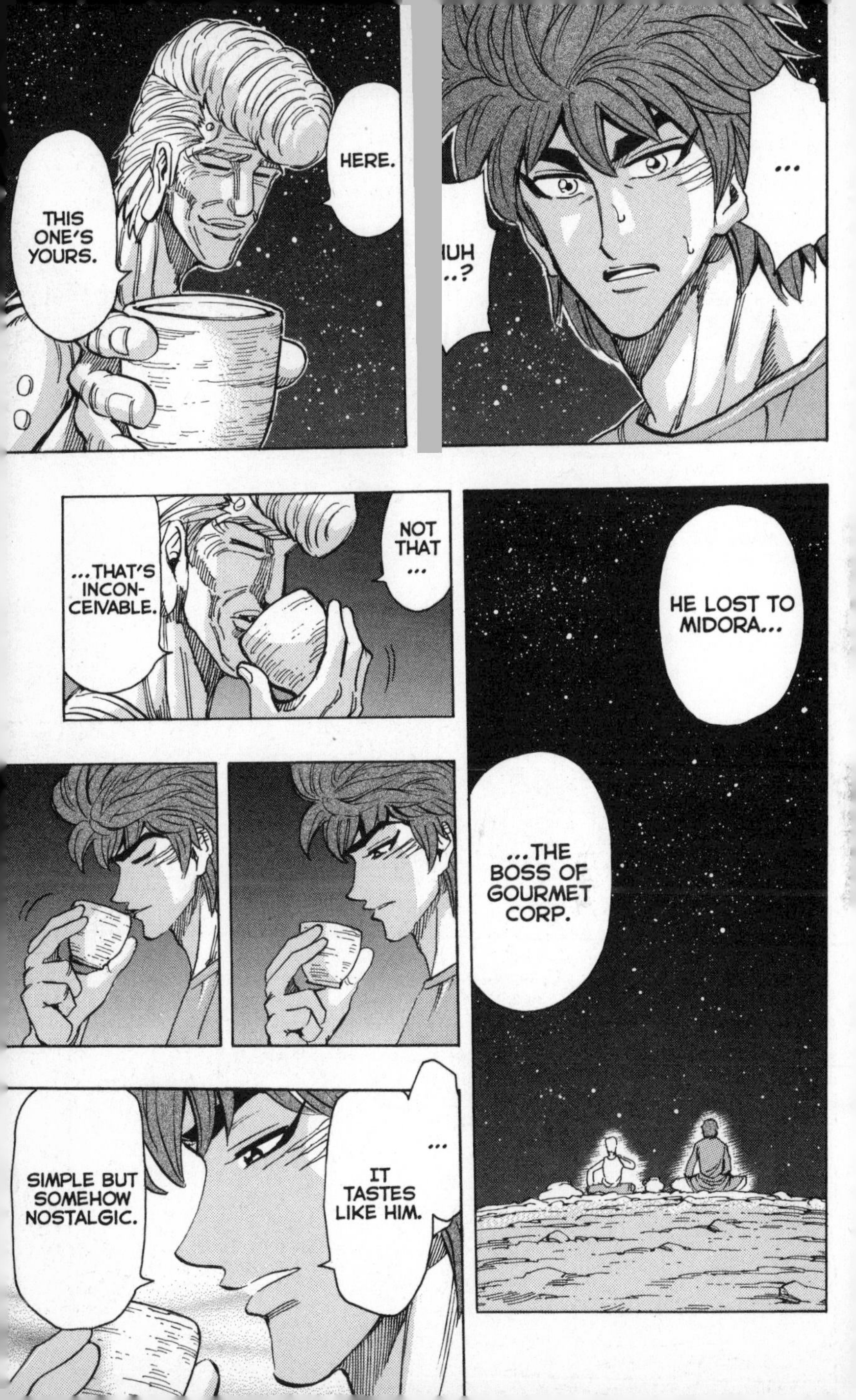
...
HUH ..?
HERE.
THIS ONE'S YOURS.
HE LOST TO MIDORA...
...THE BOSS OF GOURMET CORP.
NOT THAT ...
...THAT'S INCONCEIVABLE.
...
IT TASTES LIKE HIM.
SIMPLE BUT SOMEHOW NOSTALGIC.

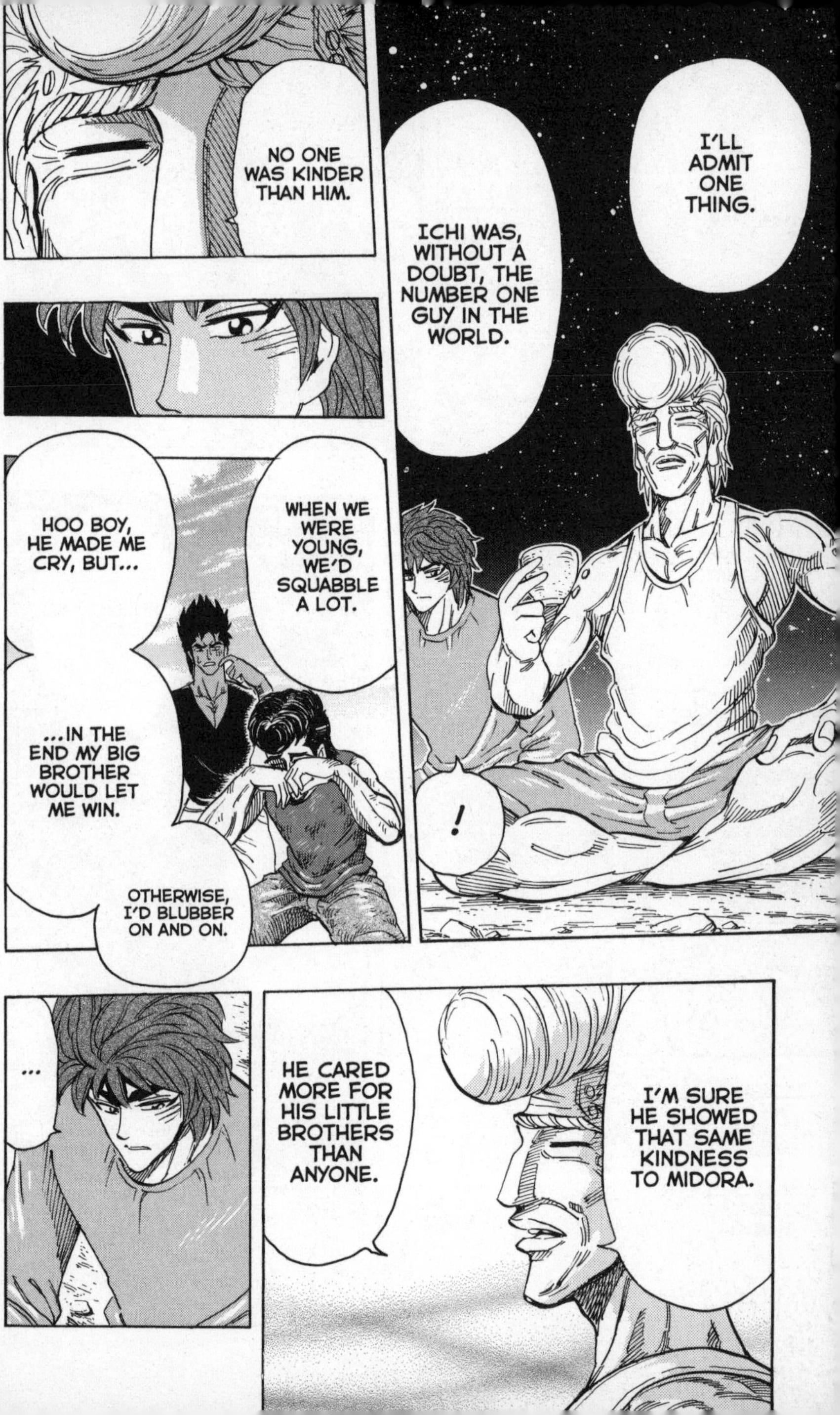
I'LL ADMIT ONE THING.
ICHI WAS, WITHOUT A DOUBT, THE NUMBER ONE GUY IN THE WORLD.
!
NO ONE WAS KINDER THAN HIM.
WHEN WE WERE YOUNG, WE'D SQUABBLE A LOT.
HOO BOY, HE MADE ME CRY, BUT...
...IN THE END MY BIG BROTHER WOULD LET ME WIN.
OTHERWISE, I'D BLUBBER ON AND ON.
I'M SURE HE SHOWED THAT SAME KINDNESS TO MIDORA.
HE CARED MORE FOR HIS LITTLE BROTHERS THAN ANYONE.
...

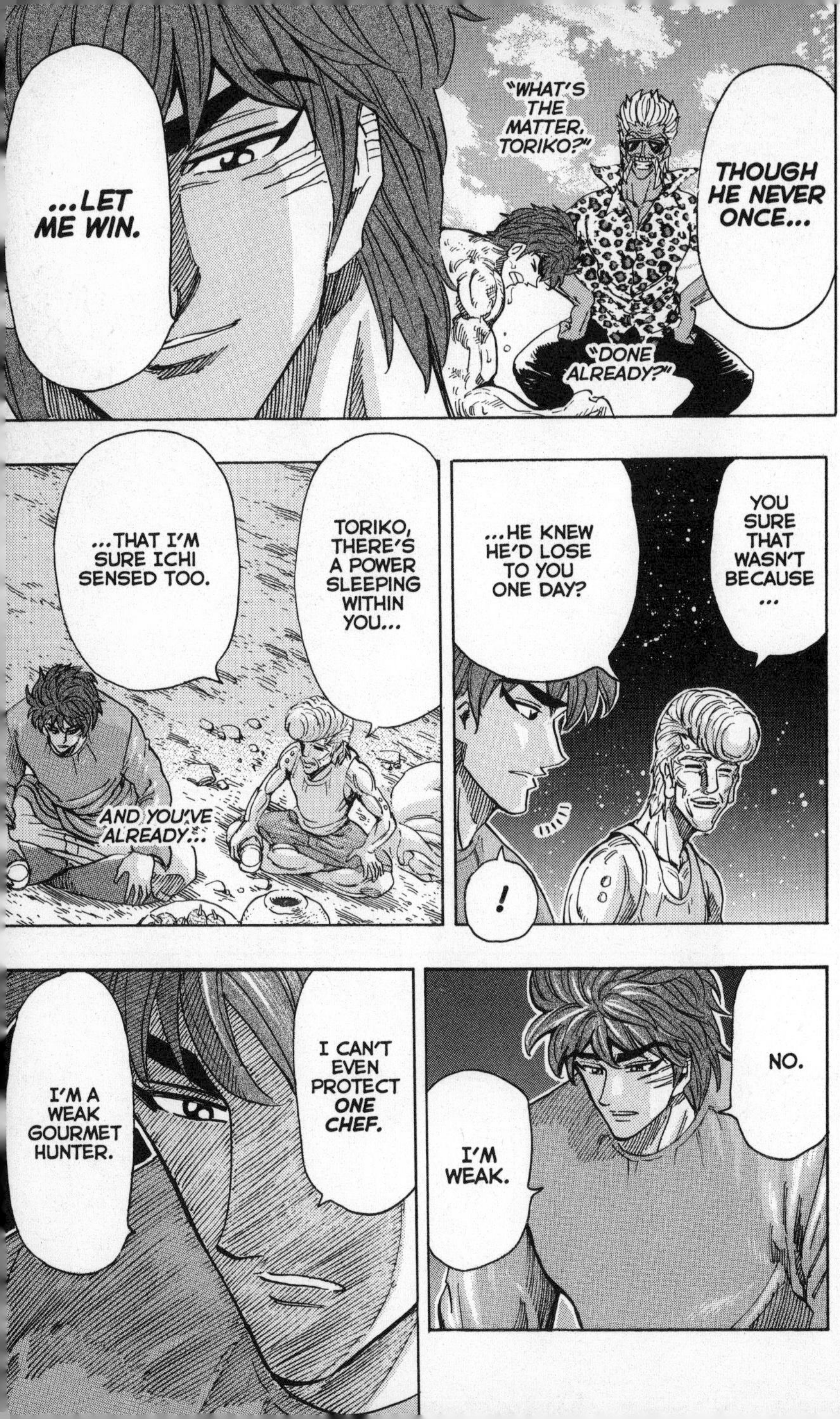
THOUGH HE NEVER ONCE...
"WHAT'S THE MATTER, TORIKO?"
"DONE ALREADY?"
...LET ME WIN.
YOU SURE THAT WASN'T BECAUSE ...
...HE KNEW HE'D LOSE TO YOU ONE DAY?
!
TORIKO, THERE'S A POWER SLEEPING WITHIN YOU...
...THAT I'M SURE ICHI SENSED TOO.
AND YOU'VE ALREADY...
NO.
I'M WEAK.
I CAN'T EVEN PROTECT ONE CHEF.
I'M A WEAK GOURMET HUNTER.

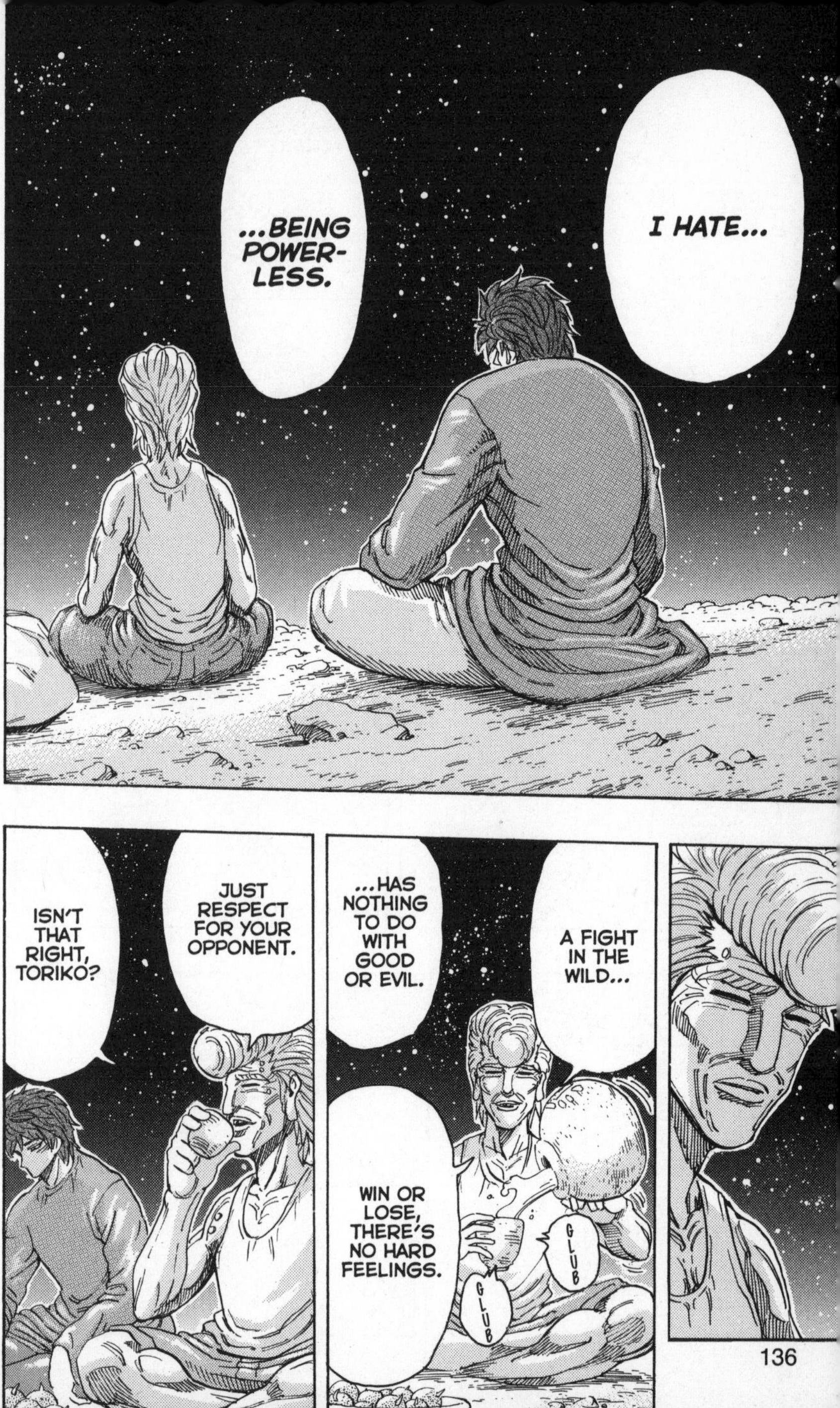
I HATE...
...BEING POWER-LESS.
A FIGHT IN THE WILD...
...HAS NOTHING TO DO WITH GOOD OR EVIL.
WIN OR LOSE, THERE'S NO HARD FEELINGS.
GLUB
GLUB
JUST RESPECT FOR YOUR OPPONENT.
ISN'T THAT RIGHT, TORIKO?

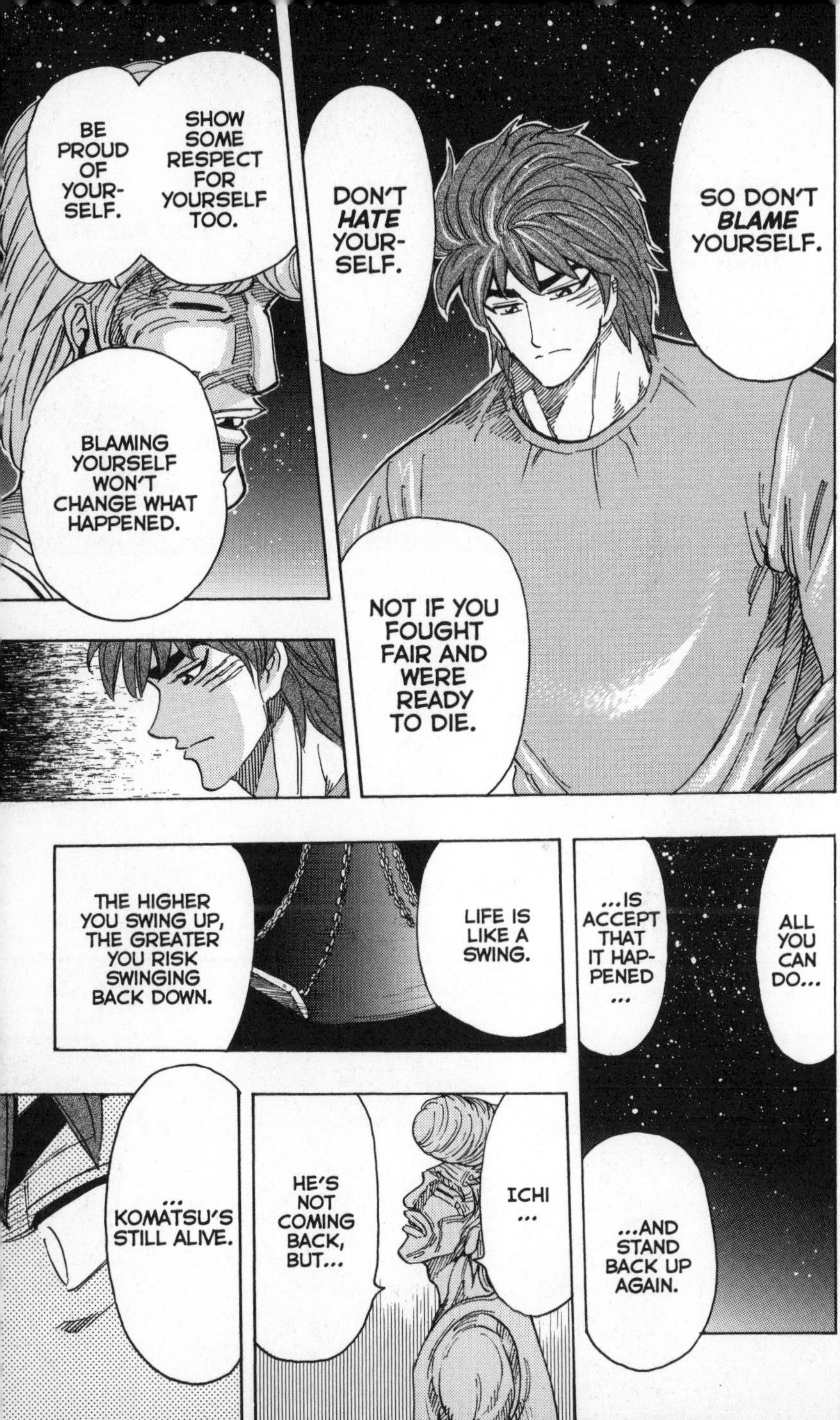
SO DON'T *BLAME* YOURSELF.
DON'T *HATE* YOURSELF.
NOT IF YOU FOUGHT FAIR AND WERE READY TO DIE.
SHOW SOME RESPECT FOR YOURSELF TOO.
BE PROUD OF YOURSELF.
BLAMING YOURSELF WON'T CHANGE WHAT HAPPENED.
ALL YOU CAN DO...
...IS ACCEPT THAT IT HAPPENED...
...AND STAND BACK UP AGAIN.
LIFE IS LIKE A SWING.
THE HIGHER YOU SWING UP, THE GREATER YOU RISK SWINGING BACK DOWN.
ICHI...
HE'S NOT COMING BACK, BUT...
...KOMATSU'S STILL ALIVE.

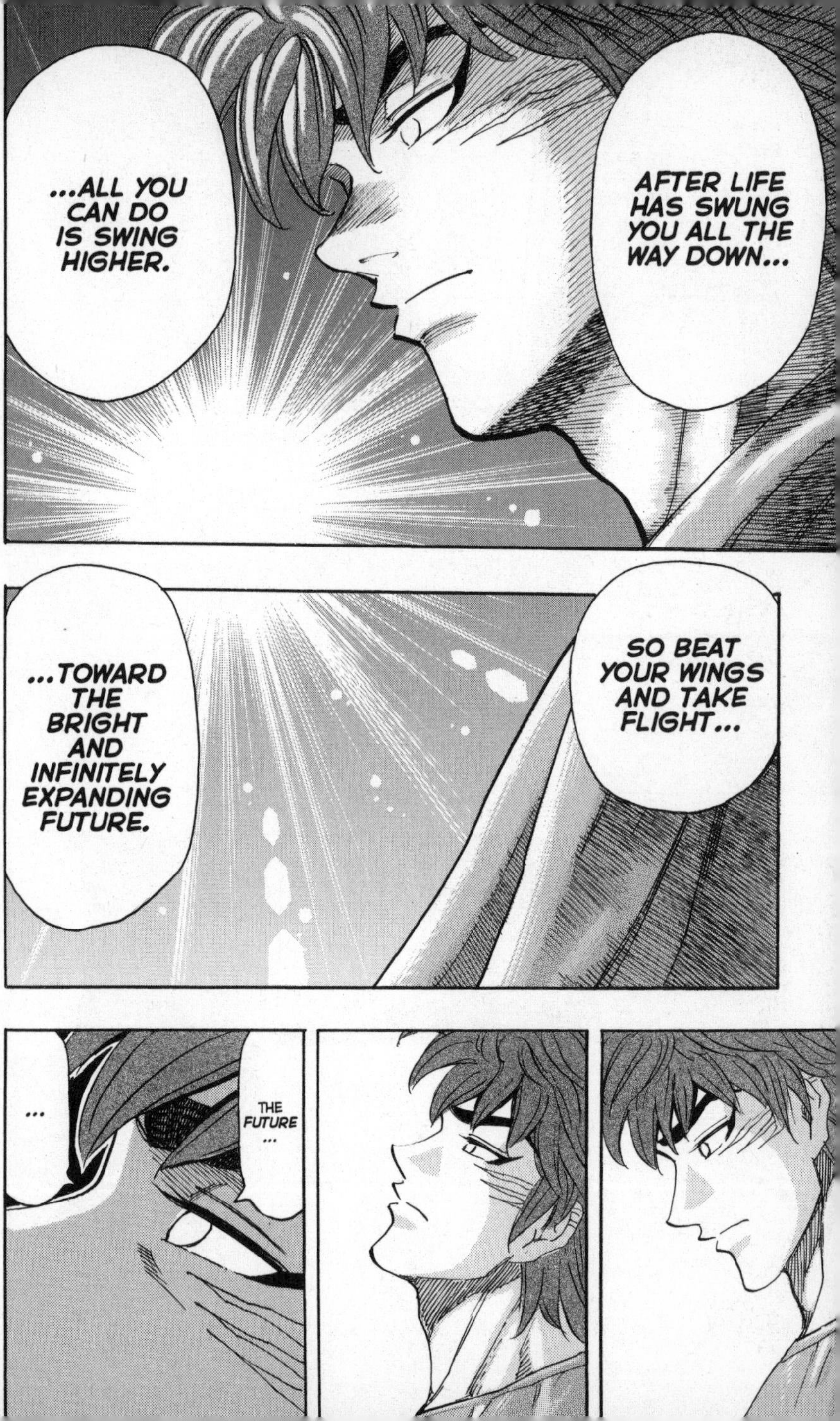
AFTER LIFE HAS SWUNG YOU ALL THE WAY DOWN...
...ALL YOU CAN DO IS SWING HIGHER.
SO BEAT YOUR WINGS AND TAKE FLIGHT...
...TOWARD THE BRIGHT AND INFINITELY EXPANDING FUTURE.
THE FUTURE ...
...

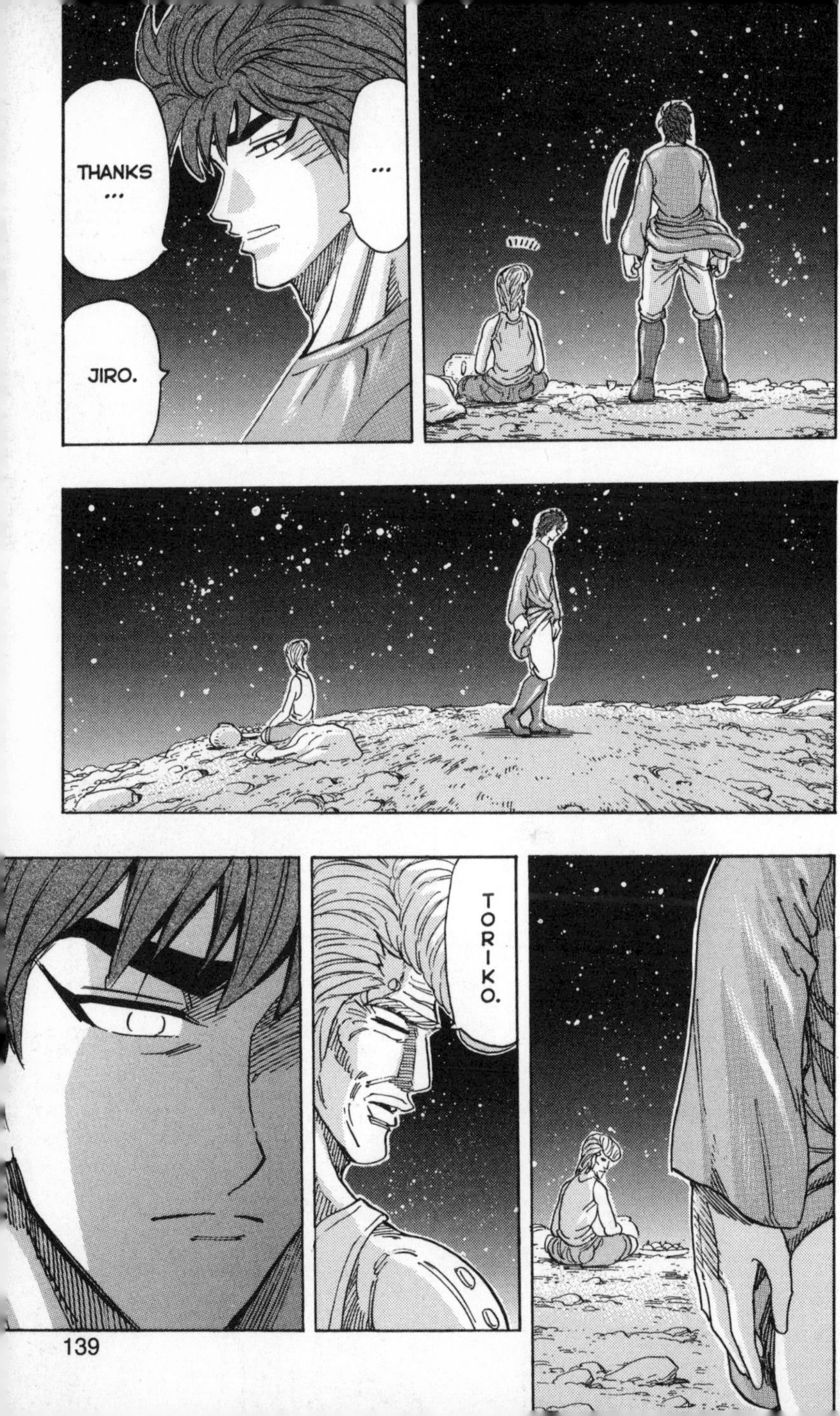
...
THANKS ...
JIRO.
TORIKO.

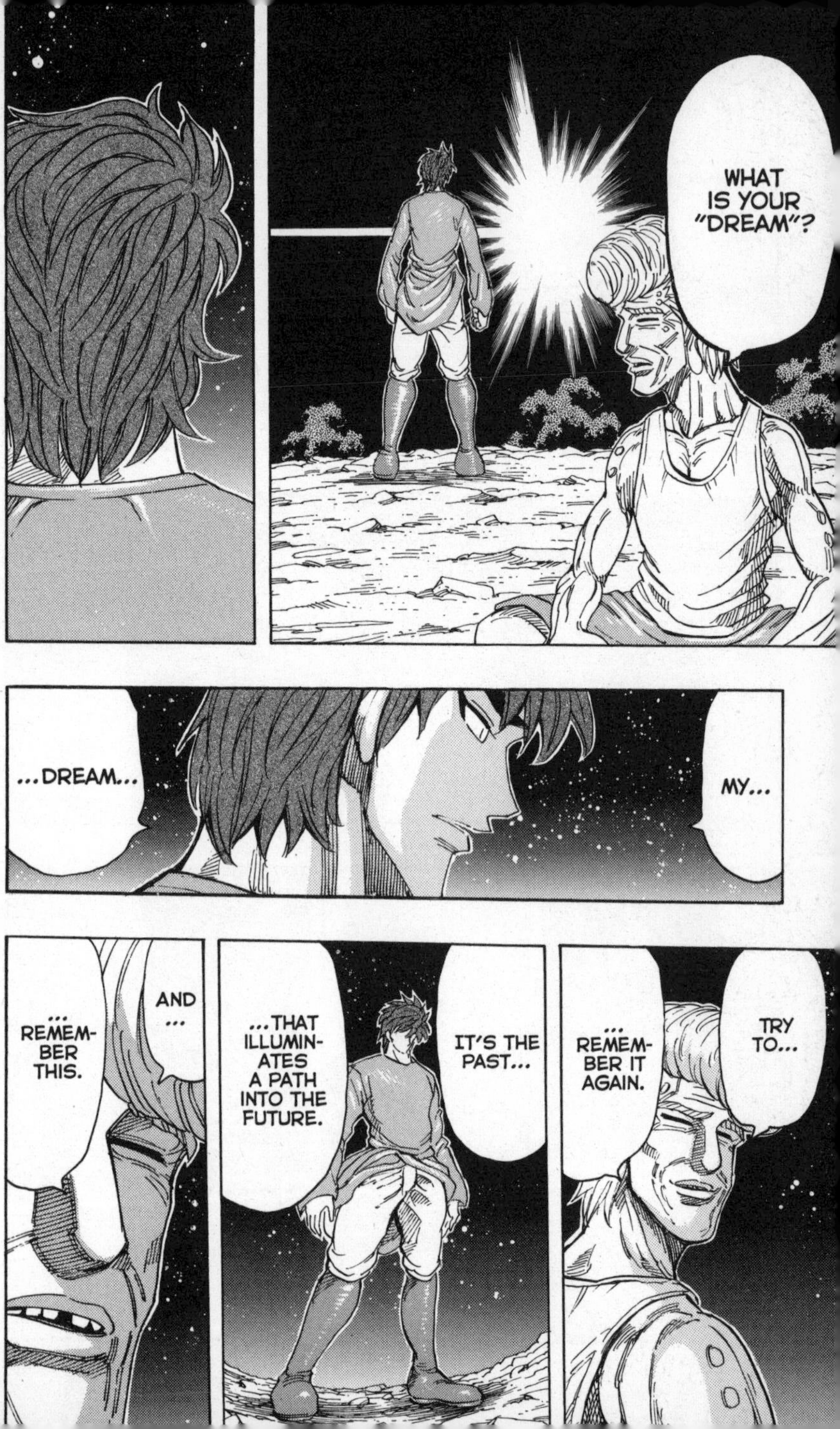
WHAT IS YOUR "DREAM"?
MY...
...DREAM...
TRY TO...
...REMEMBER IT AGAIN.
IT'S THE PAST...
...THAT ILLUMINATES A PATH INTO THE FUTURE.
AND...
...REMEMBER THIS.

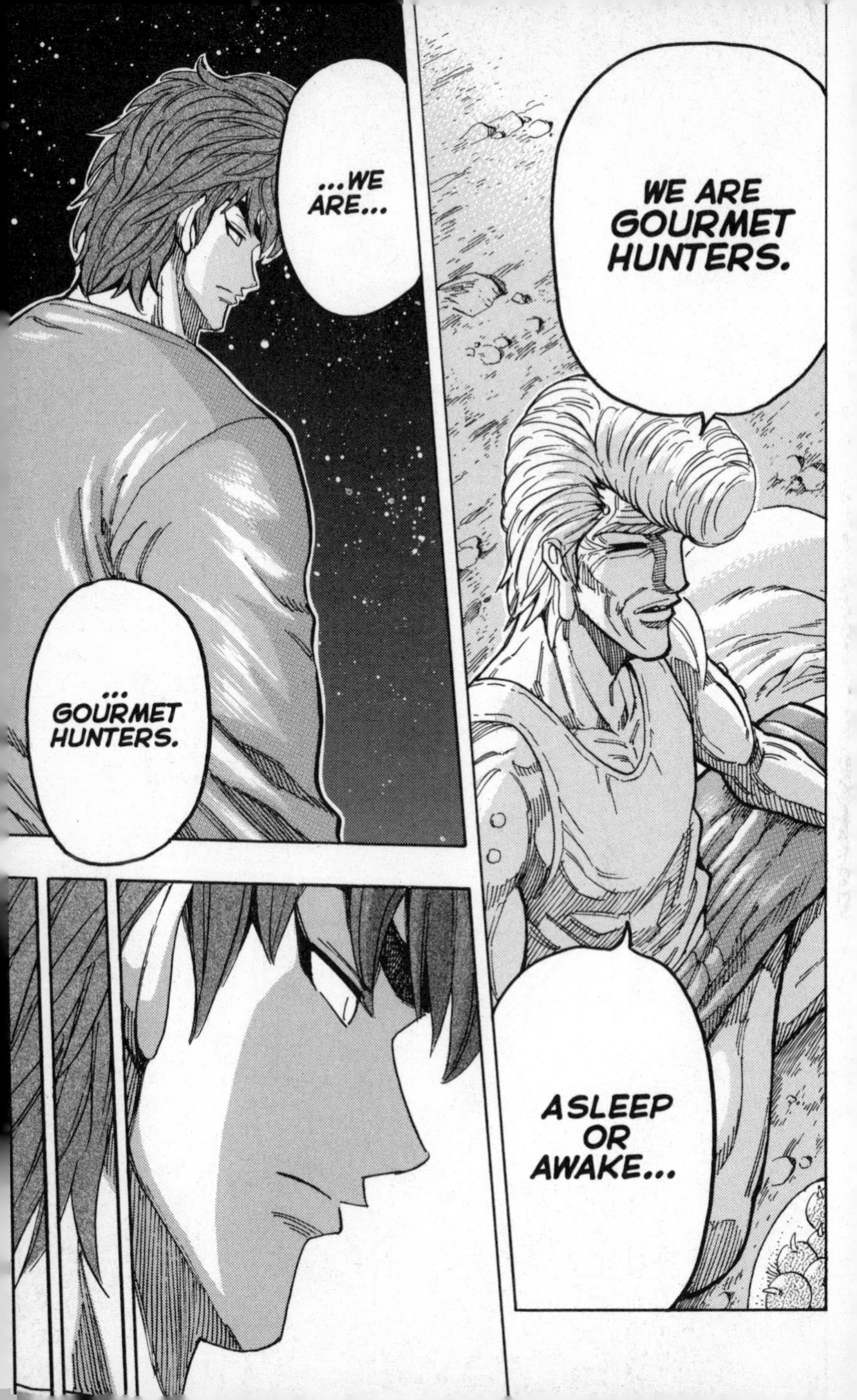
WE ARE GOURMET HUNTERS.
ASLEEP OR AWAKE...
...WE ARE...
...GOURMET HUNTERS.

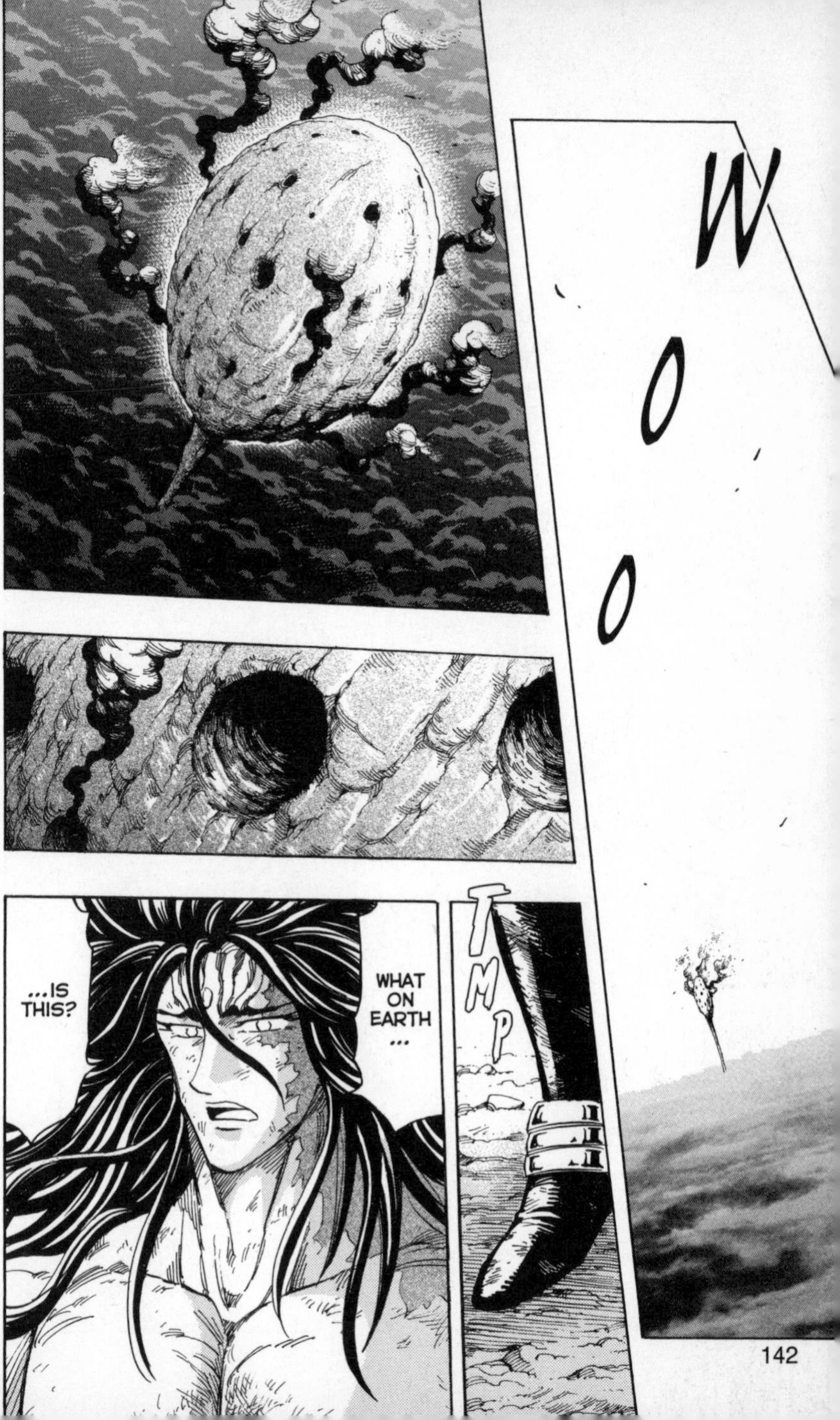
WOOO
TMP
WHAT ON EARTH ...
...IS THIS?

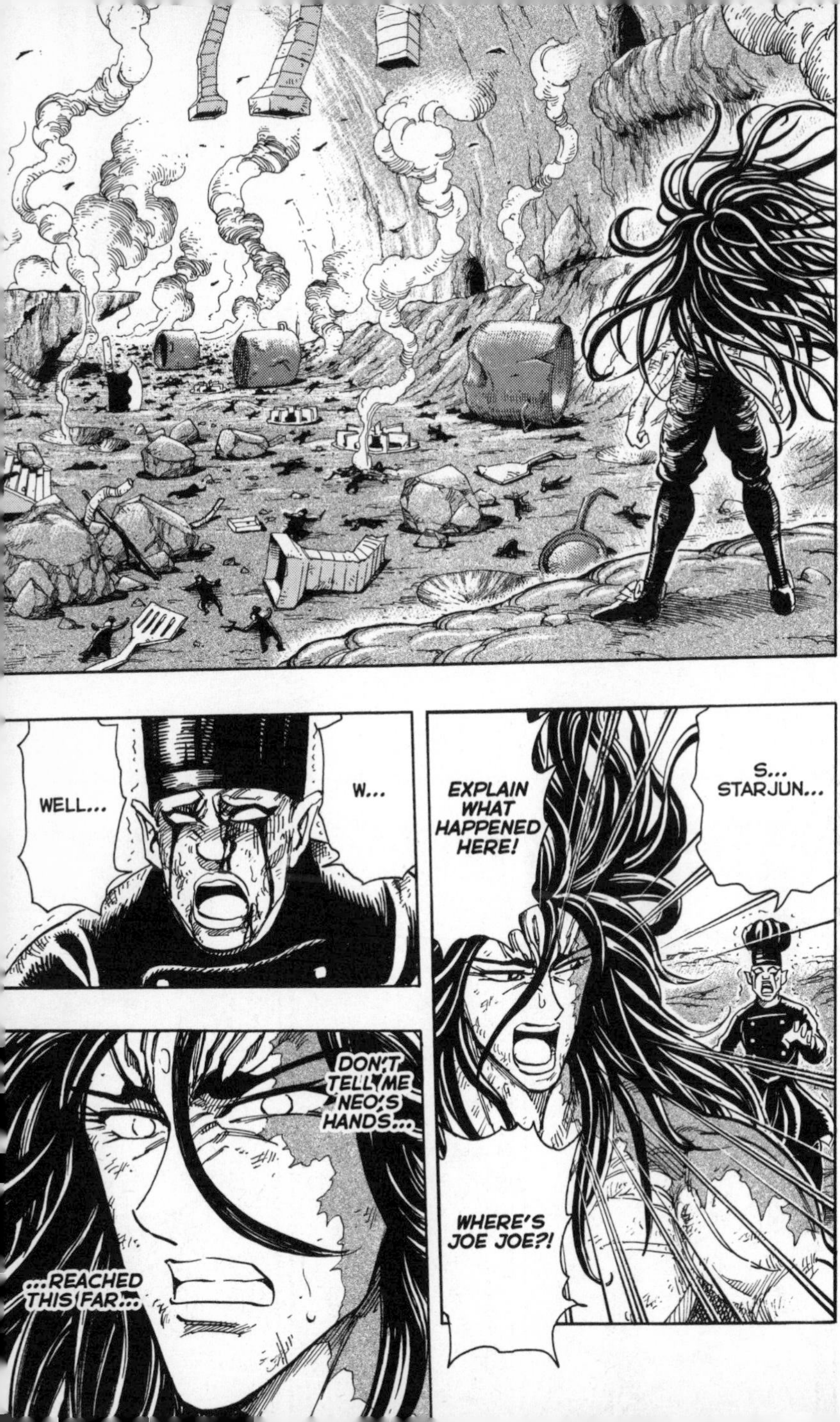
S... STARJUN...
EXPLAIN WHAT HAPPENED HERE!
WHERE'S JOE JOE?!
W...
WELL...
DON'T TELL ME NEO'S HANDS...
...REACHED THIS FAR...

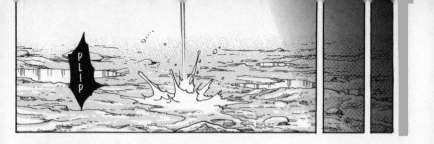

IT LOOKS LIKE YOU'VE COME AROUND.

UNH
...

...

144

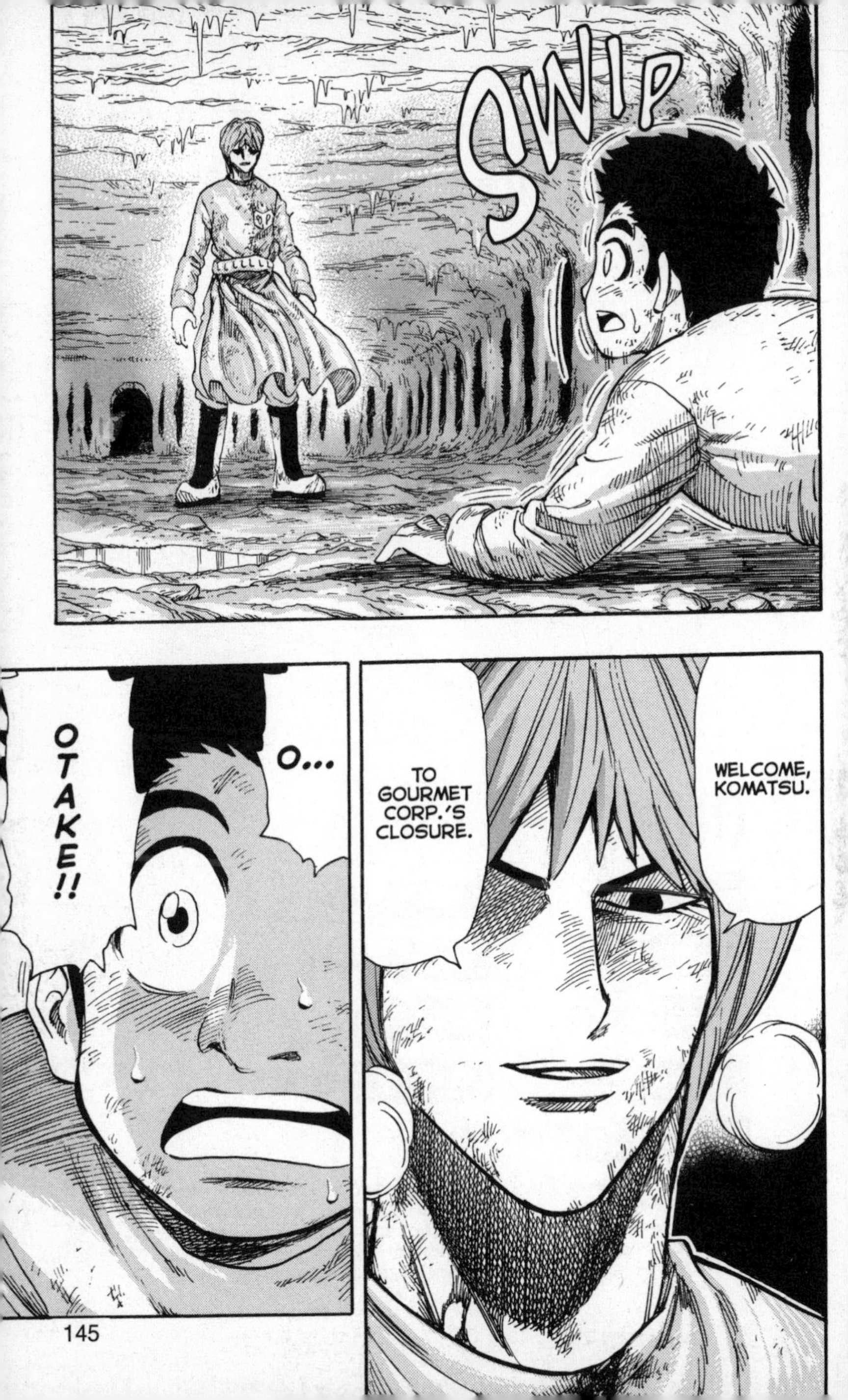
SWIP
WELCOME, KOMATSU.
TO GOURMET CORP.'S CLOSURE.
O...
OTAKE!!

CHARACTER PROFILE

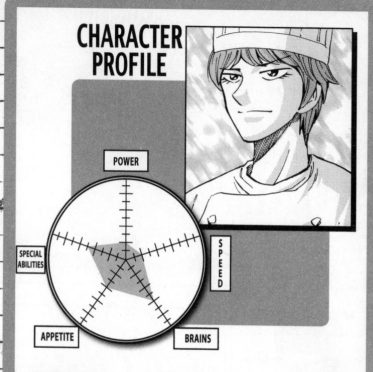

POWER

SPECIAL
ABILITIES

SPEED

APPETITE

BRAINS

OTAKE

AGE:	25	**BIRTHDAY:**	MAY 5
BLOOD TYPE:	AB	**SIGN:**	TAURUS
HEIGHT:	165 CM	**WEIGHT:**	58 KG
EYESIGHT:	20/20	**SHOE SIZE:**	26 CM

SPECIAL MOVES/ABILITIES: • Unknown

The owner-chef of the seven-star restaurant Faiytale Castle and #99 on the World Chef Ranking. He and Komatsu trained together when they were just starting out. They shared the aspiration of becoming a chef who could grant great joy to thousands with his delicious cooking, but after starting his own restaurant, his ambitions changed to those of commercialism and reaching the top of the World Chef Ranking. He is currently with Gourmet Corp., had Gourmet Cells injected into him and is an adversary of Komatsu and the others.

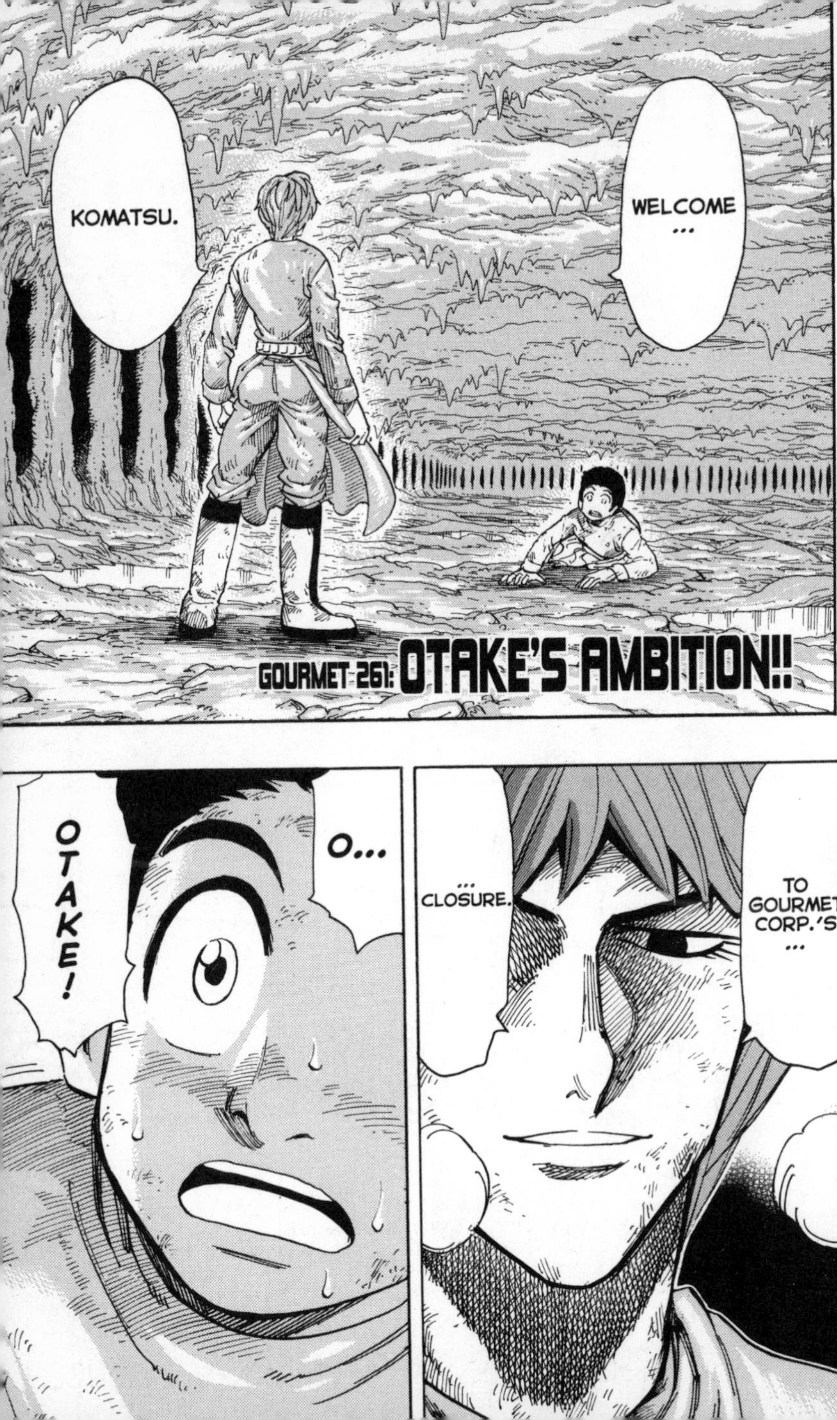
WELCOME ...
KOMATSU.
GOURMET 261: OTAKE'S AMBITION!!
TO GOURMET CORP.'S ...
... CLOSURE.
O...
OTAKE!

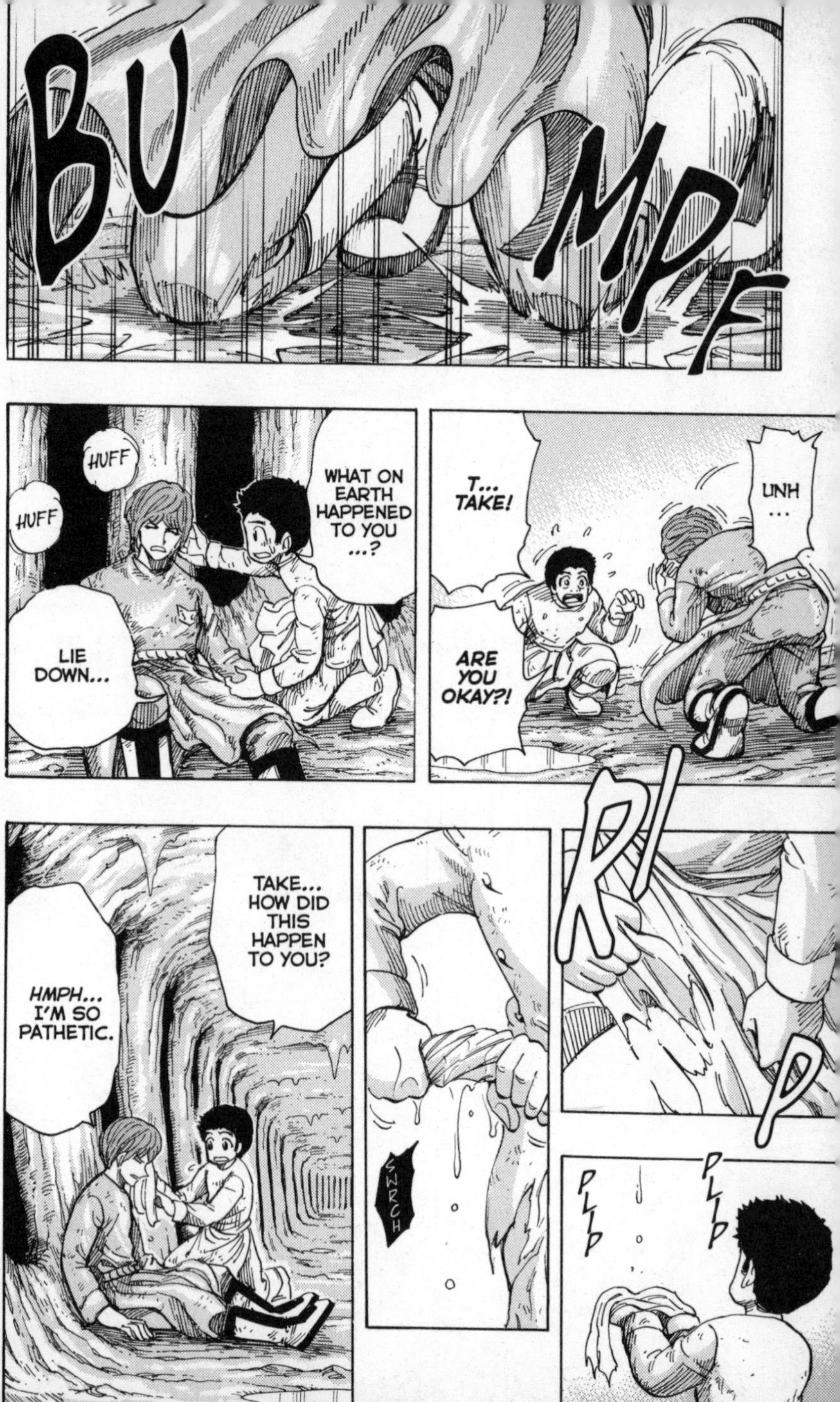
BUMPF
UNH ...
T... TAKE!
ARE YOU OKAY?!
WHAT ON EARTH HAPPENED TO YOU ...?
HUFF
HUFF
LIE DOWN...
RIP
PLIP
PLIP
SWRCH
TAKE... HOW DID THIS HAPPEN TO YOU?
HMPH... I'M SO PATHETIC.

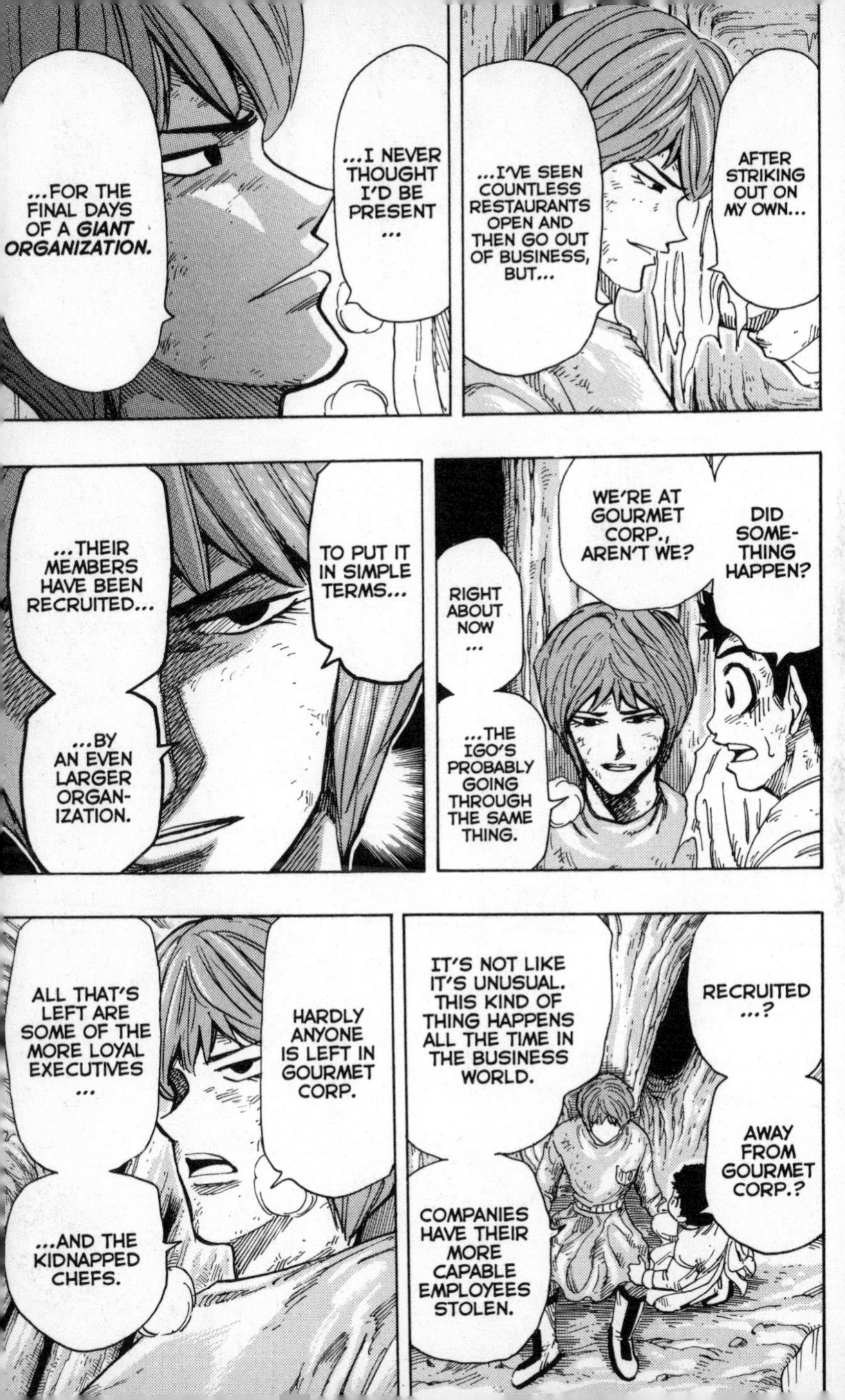
AFTER STRIKING OUT ON MY OWN...
...I'VE SEEN COUNTLESS RESTAURANTS OPEN AND THEN GO OUT OF BUSINESS, BUT...
...I NEVER THOUGHT I'D BE PRESENT ...
...FOR THE FINAL DAYS OF A *GIANT ORGANIZATION.*
DID SOME-THING HAPPEN?
WE'RE AT GOURMET CORP., AREN'T WE?
RIGHT ABOUT NOW ...
...THE IGO'S PROBABLY GOING THROUGH THE SAME THING.
TO PUT IT IN SIMPLE TERMS...
...THEIR MEMBERS HAVE BEEN RECRUITED...
...BY AN EVEN LARGER ORGAN-IZATION.
RECRUITED ...?
AWAY FROM GOURMET CORP.?
IT'S NOT LIKE IT'S UNUSUAL. THIS KIND OF THING HAPPENS ALL THE TIME IN THE BUSINESS WORLD.
COMPANIES HAVE THEIR MORE CAPABLE EMPLOYEES STOLEN.
HARDLY ANYONE IS LEFT IN GOURMET CORP.
ALL THAT'S LEFT ARE SOME OF THE MORE LOYAL EXECUTIVES ...
...AND THE KIDNAPPED CHEFS.

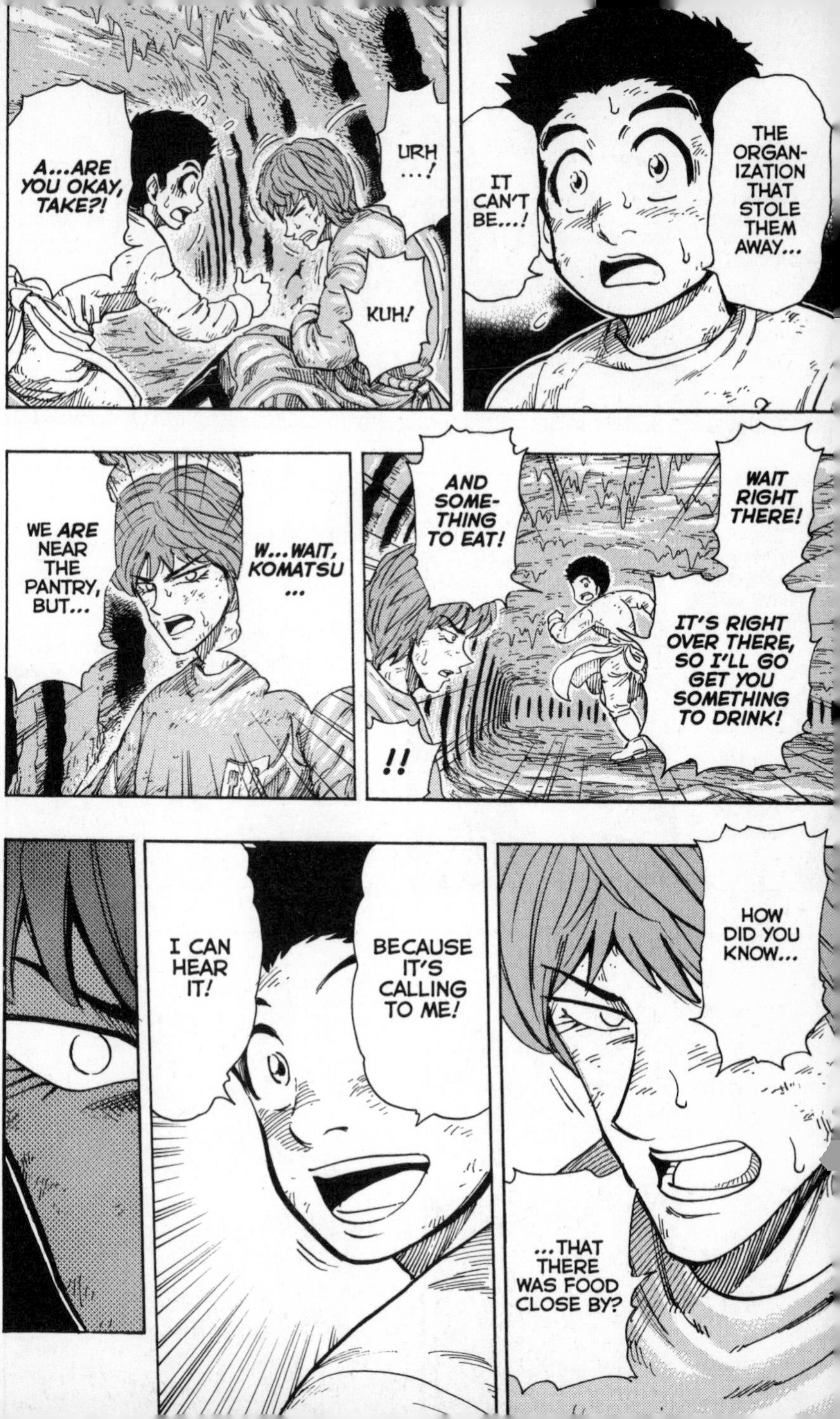
THE ORGANIZATION THAT STOLE THEM AWAY...
IT CAN'T BE...!
URH ...!
A...ARE YOU OKAY, TAKE?!
KUH!
WAIT RIGHT THERE!
IT'S RIGHT OVER THERE, SO I'LL GO GET YOU SOMETHING TO DRINK!
AND SOMETHING TO EAT!
!!
W...WAIT, KOMATSU...
WE ARE NEAR THE PANTRY, BUT...
HOW DID YOU KNOW...
...THAT THERE WAS FOOD CLOSE BY?
BECAUSE IT'S CALLING TO ME!
I CAN HEAR IT!

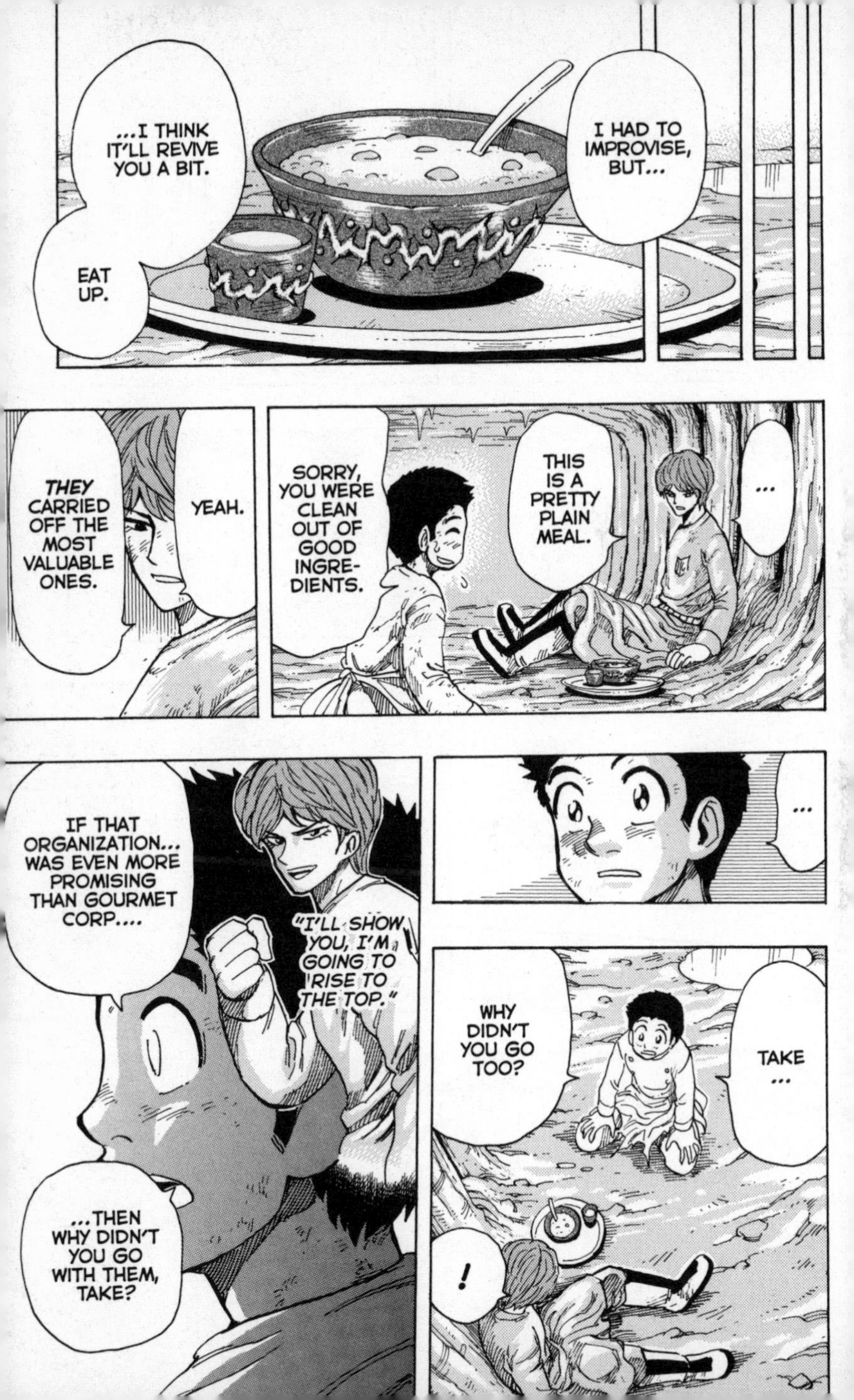
I HAD TO IMPROVISE, BUT...
...I THINK IT'LL REVIVE YOU A BIT.
EAT UP.
...
THIS IS A PRETTY PLAIN MEAL.
SORRY, YOU WERE CLEAN OUT OF GOOD INGREDIENTS.
YEAH.
THEY CARRIED OFF THE MOST VALUABLE ONES.
...
TAKE ...
WHY DIDN'T YOU GO TOO?
!
IF THAT ORGANIZATION... WAS EVEN MORE PROMISING THAN GOURMET CORP....
"I'LL SHOW YOU, I'M GOING TO RISE TO THE TOP."
...THEN WHY DIDN'T YOU GO WITH THEM, TAKE?

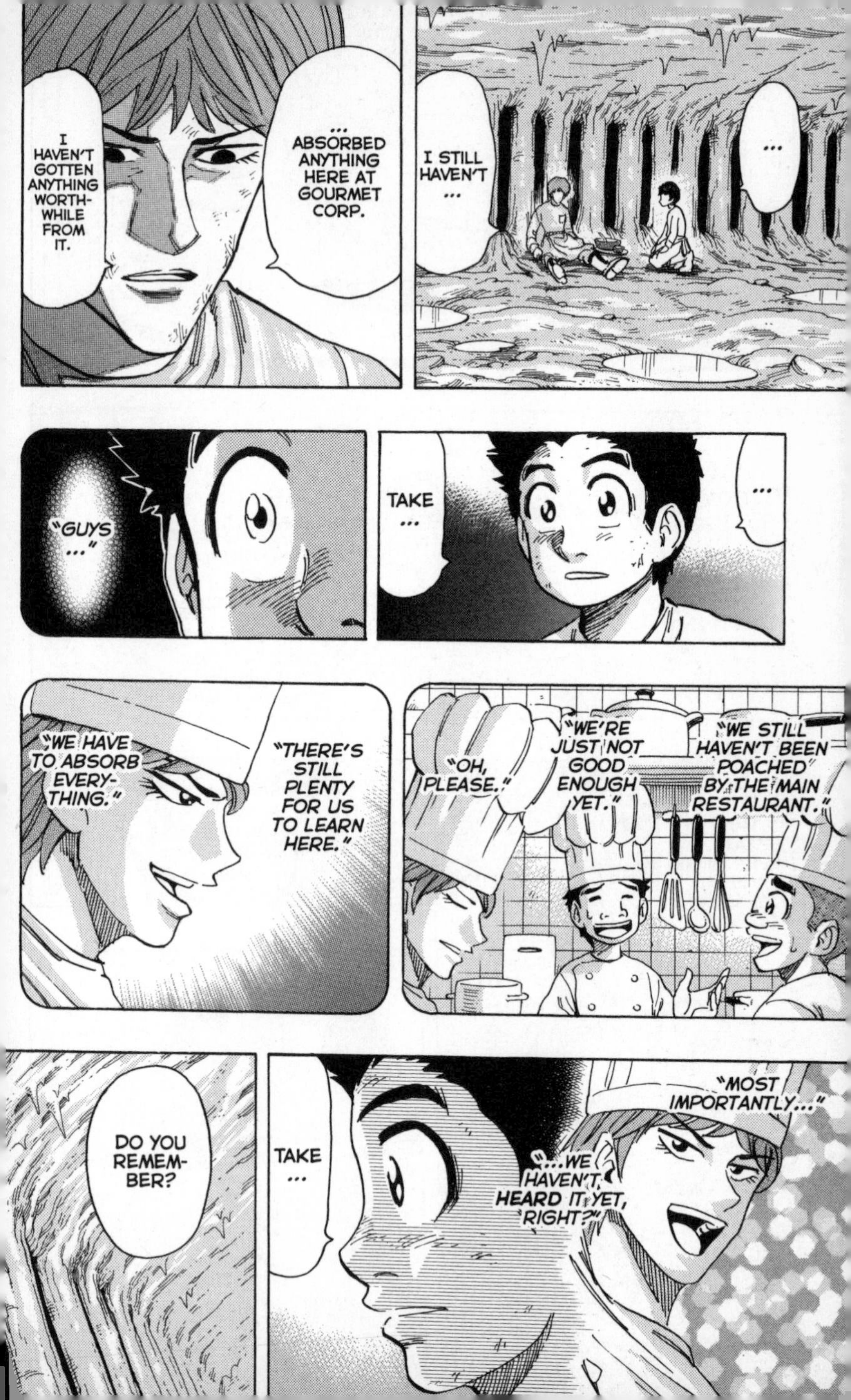
...
I STILL HAVEN'T ...
... ABSORBED ANYTHING HERE AT GOURMET CORP.
I HAVEN'T GOTTEN ANYTHING WORTHWHILE FROM IT.
...
TAKE ...
“GUYS ...”
“WE STILL HAVEN'T BEEN POACHED BY THE MAIN RESTAURANT.”
“WE'RE JUST NOT GOOD ENOUGH YET.”
“OH, PLEASE.”
“THERE'S STILL PLENTY FOR US TO LEARN HERE.”
“WE HAVE TO ABSORB EVERYTHING.”
“MOST IMPORTANTLY...”
“...WE HAVEN'T HEARD IT YET, RIGHT?”
TAKE ...
DO YOU REMEMBER?

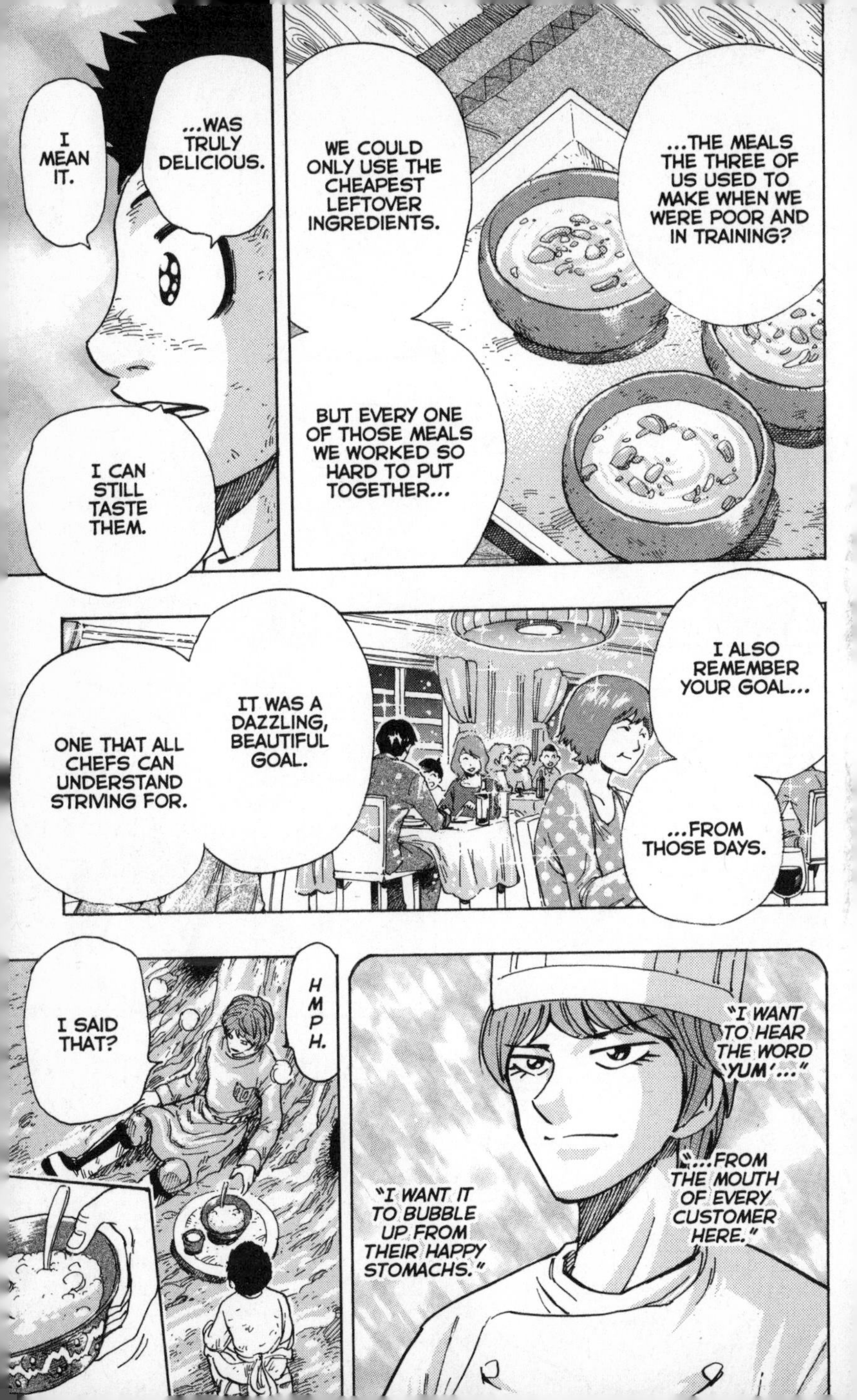

...THE MEALS THE THREE OF US USED TO MAKE WHEN WE WERE POOR AND IN TRAINING?
WE COULD ONLY USE THE CHEAPEST LEFTOVER INGREDIENTS.
BUT EVERY ONE OF THOSE MEALS WE WORKED SO HARD TO PUT TOGETHER...
...WAS TRULY DELICIOUS.
I MEAN IT.
I CAN STILL TASTE THEM.
I ALSO REMEMBER YOUR GOAL...
...FROM THOSE DAYS.
IT WAS A DAZZLING, BEAUTIFUL GOAL.
ONE THAT ALL CHEFS CAN UNDERSTAND STRIVING FOR.
"I WANT TO HEAR THE WORD 'YUM'..."
"...FROM THE MOUTH OF EVERY CUSTOMER HERE."
"I WANT IT TO BUBBLE UP FROM THEIR HAPPY STOMACHS."
HMPH.
I SAID THAT?

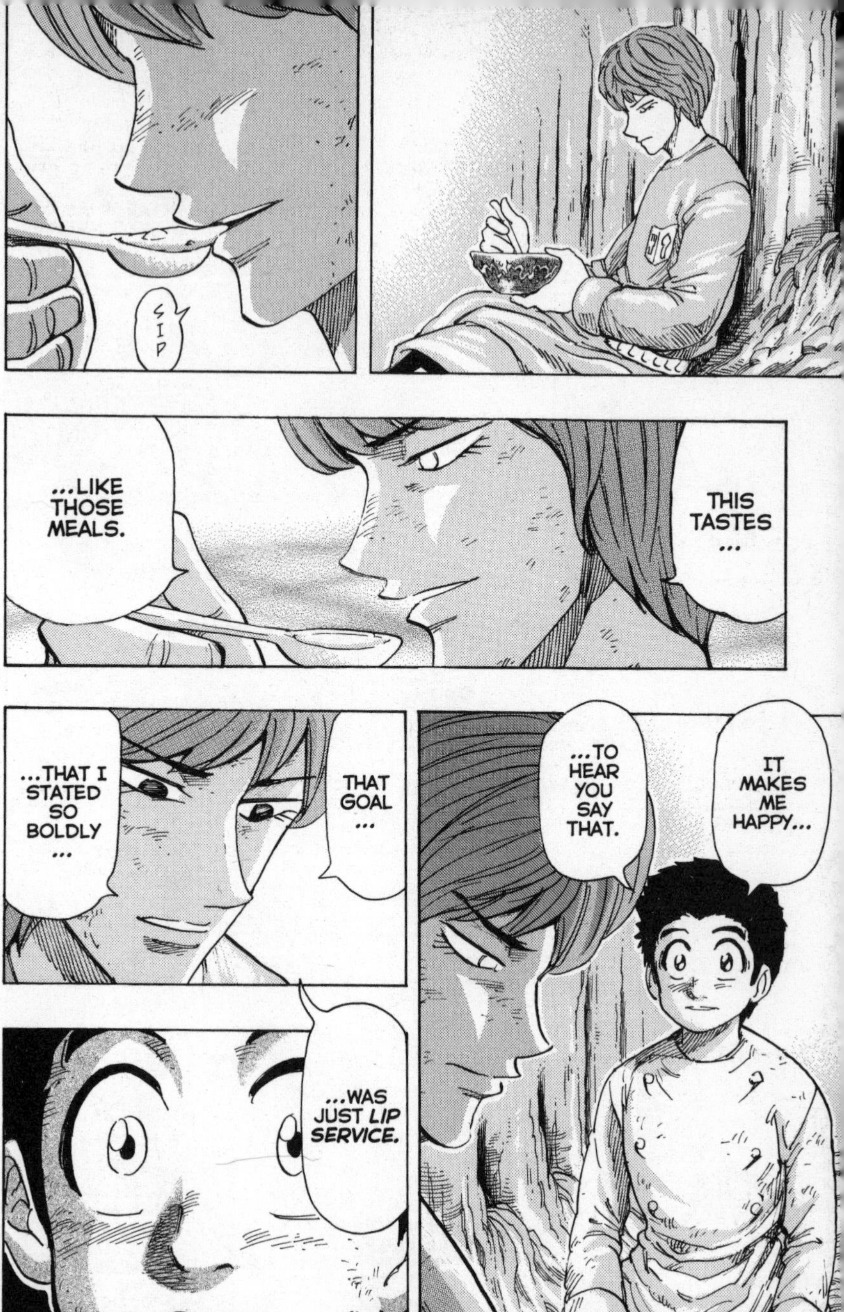
SIP
THIS TASTES...
...LIKE THOSE MEALS.
IT MAKES ME HAPPY...
...TO HEAR YOU SAY THAT.
THAT GOAL...
...THAT I STATED SO BOLDLY...
...WAS JUST *LIP SERVICE.*

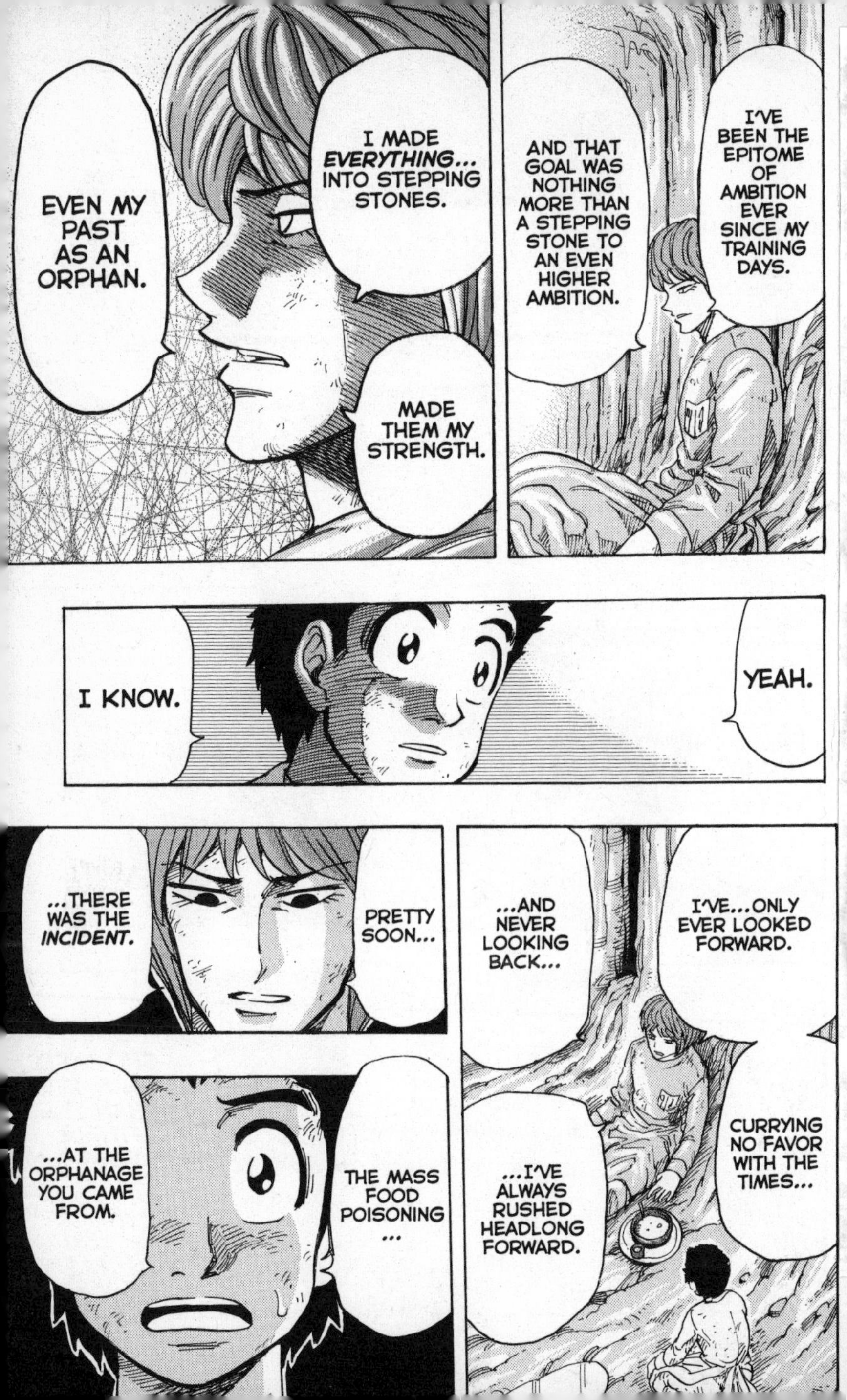
I'VE BEEN THE EPITOME OF AMBITION EVER SINCE MY TRAINING DAYS.
AND THAT GOAL WAS NOTHING MORE THAN A STEPPING STONE TO AN EVEN HIGHER AMBITION.
I MADE *EVERYTHING*... INTO STEPPING STONES.
MADE THEM MY STRENGTH.
EVEN MY PAST AS AN ORPHAN.
YEAH.
I KNOW.
I'VE...ONLY EVER LOOKED FORWARD.
...AND NEVER LOOKING BACK...
CURRYING NO FAVOR WITH THE TIMES...
...I'VE ALWAYS RUSHED HEADLONG FORWARD.
PRETTY SOON...
...THERE WAS THE *INCIDENT*.
THE MASS FOOD POISONING...
...AT THE ORPHANAGE YOU CAME FROM.

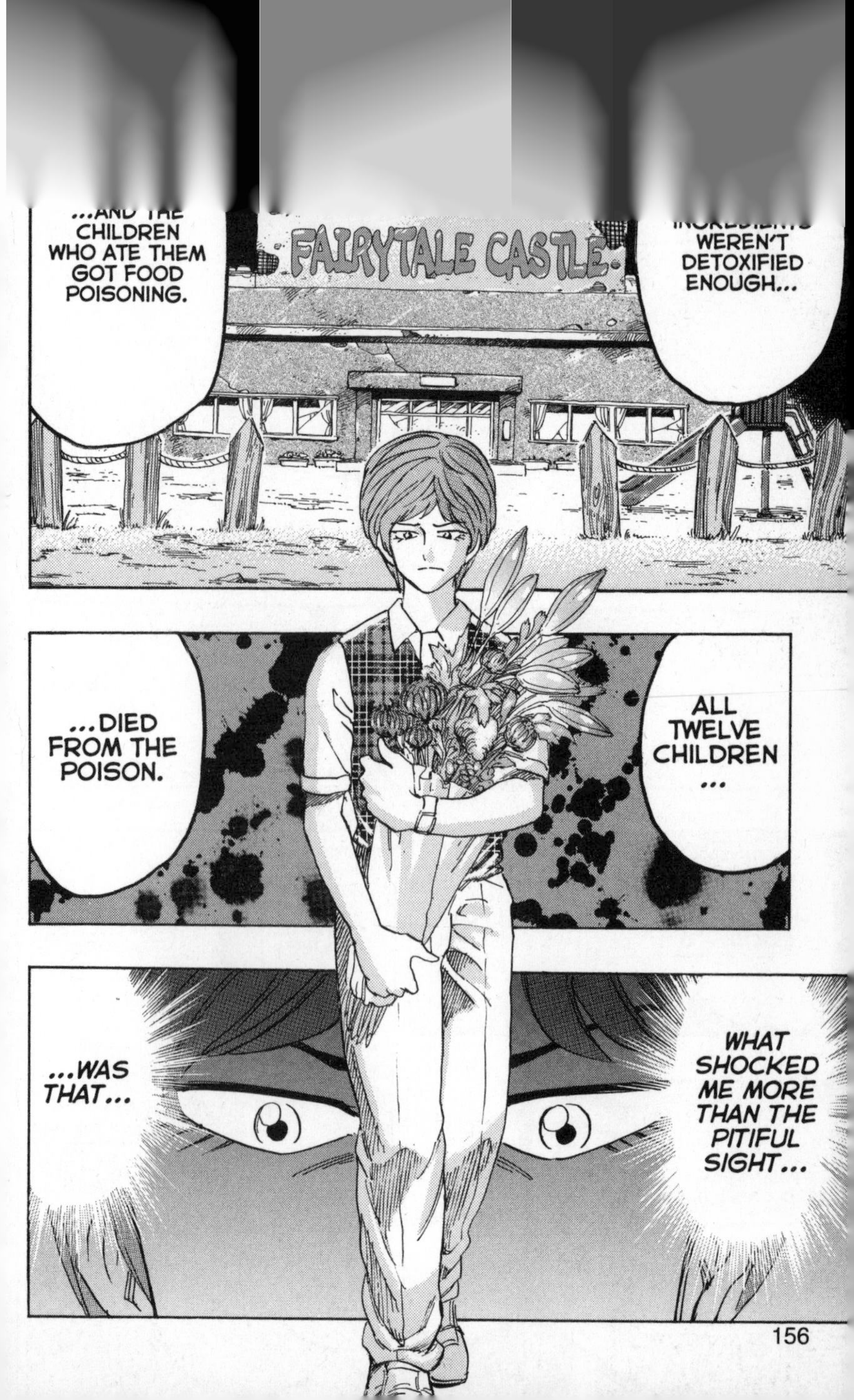
WEREN'T DETOXIFIED ENOUGH...
FAIRYTALE CASTLE
CHILDREN WHO ATE THEM GOT FOOD POISONING.
ALL TWELVE CHILDREN...
...DIED FROM THE POISON.
WHAT SHOCKED ME MORE THAN THE PITIFUL SIGHT...
...WAS THAT...

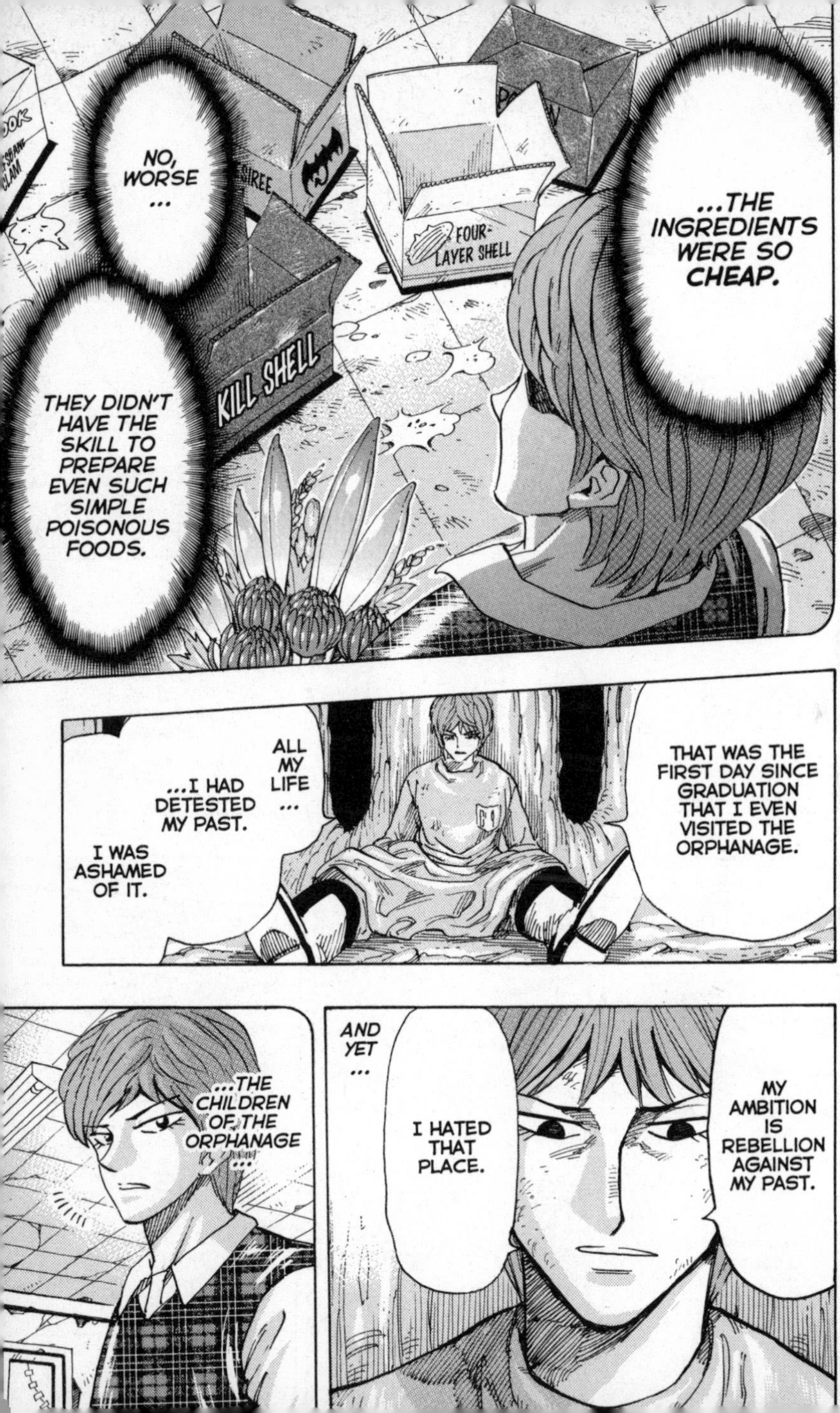
...THE INGREDIENTS WERE SO CHEAP.
FOUR-LAYER SHELL
NO, WORSE...
KILL SHELL
THEY DIDN'T HAVE THE SKILL TO PREPARE EVEN SUCH SIMPLE POISONOUS FOODS.
THAT WAS THE FIRST DAY SINCE GRADUATION THAT I EVEN VISITED THE ORPHANAGE.
ALL MY LIFE...
...I HAD DETESTED MY PAST.
I WAS ASHAMED OF IT.
MY AMBITION IS REBELLION AGAINST MY PAST.
I HATED THAT PLACE.
AND YET...
...THE CHILDREN OF THE ORPHANAGE...

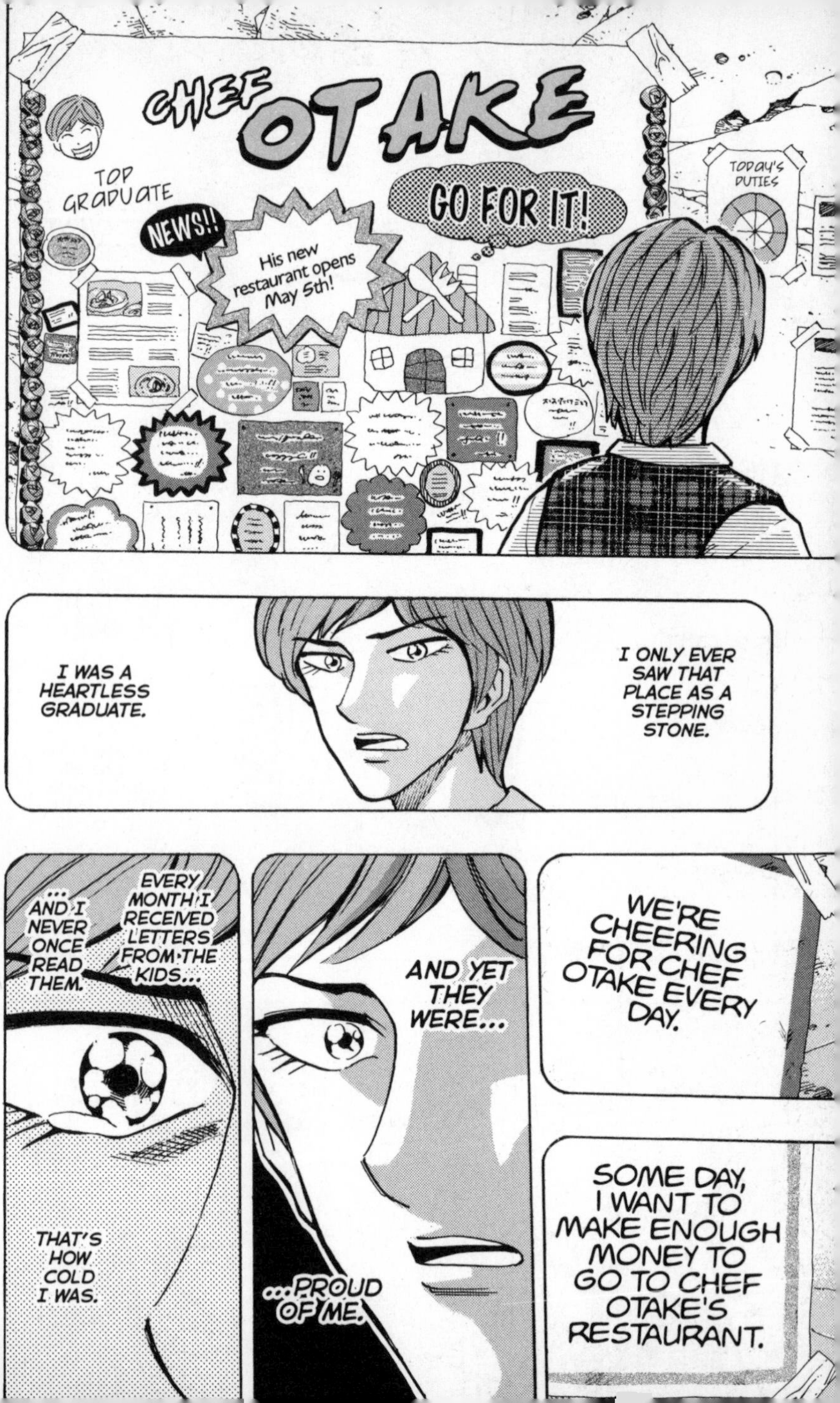
TODAY'S DUTIES
GO FOR IT!
CHEF OTAKE
TOP GRADUATE
NEWS!!
His new restaurant opens May 5th!
I ONLY EVER SAW THAT PLACE AS A STEPPING STONE.
I WAS A HEARTLESS GRADUATE.
WE'RE CHEERING FOR CHEF OTAKE EVERY DAY.
SOME DAY, I WANT TO MAKE ENOUGH MONEY TO GO TO CHEF OTAKE'S RESTAURANT.
AND YET THEY WERE...
...PROUD OF ME.
EVERY MONTH I RECEIVED LETTERS FROM THE KIDS...
...AND I NEVER ONCE READ THEM.
THAT'S HOW COLD I WAS.

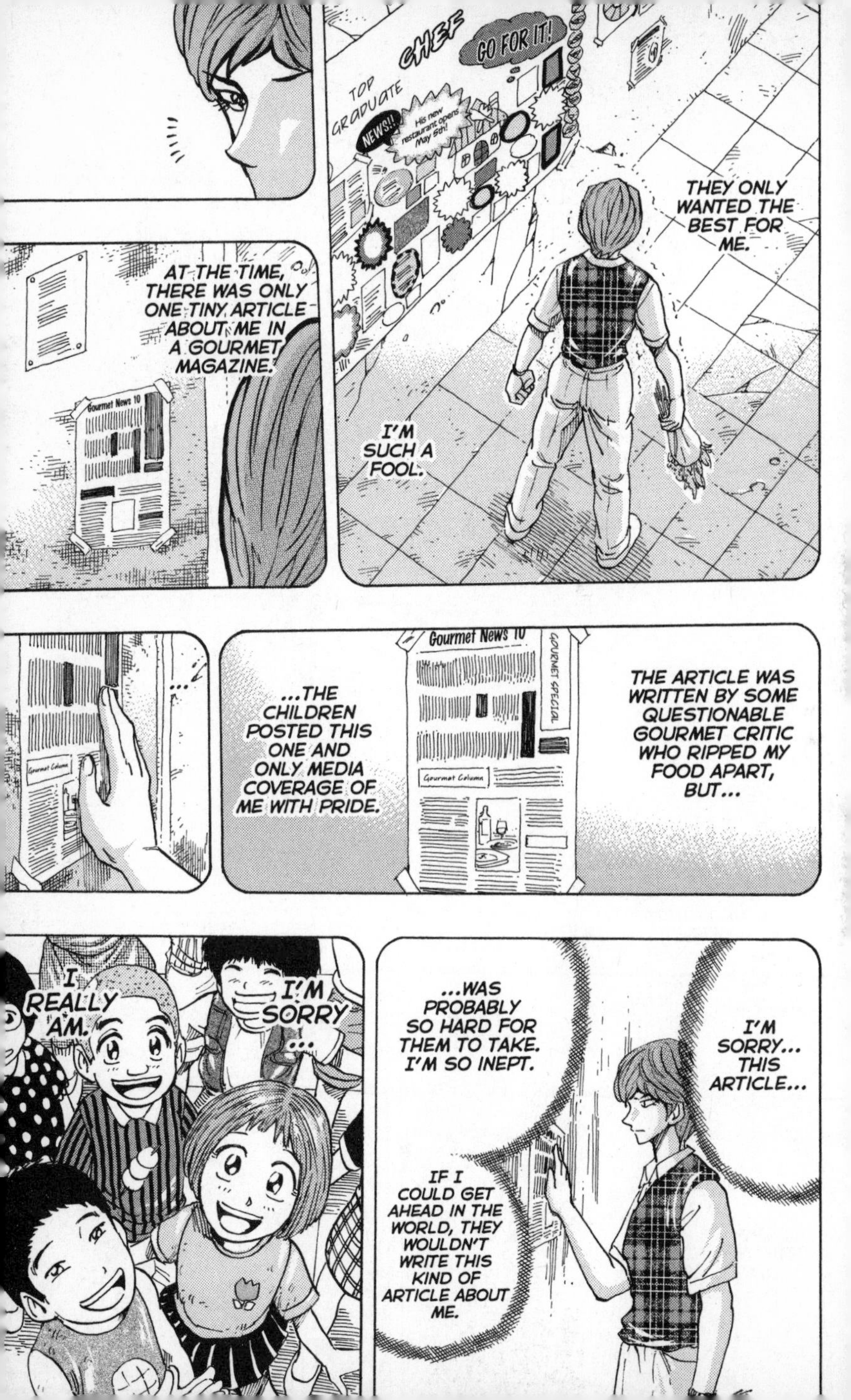
TOP GRADUATE CHEF
GO FOR IT!
NEWS!!
His new restaurant opens May 5th!
THEY ONLY WANTED THE BEST FOR ME.
I'M SUCH A FOOL.
AT THE TIME, THERE WAS ONLY ONE TINY ARTICLE ABOUT ME IN A GOURMET MAGAZINE.
Gourmet News 10
THE ARTICLE WAS WRITTEN BY SOME QUESTIONABLE GOURMET CRITIC WHO RIPPED MY FOOD APART, BUT...
Gourmet News 10
GOURMET SPECIAL
Gourmet Column
...THE CHILDREN POSTED THIS ONE AND ONLY MEDIA COVERAGE OF ME WITH PRIDE.
...
Gourmet Column
I'M SORRY... THIS ARTICLE...
...WAS PROBABLY SO HARD FOR THEM TO TAKE. I'M SO INEPT.
IF I COULD GET AHEAD IN THE WORLD, THEY WOULDN'T WRITE THIS KIND OF ARTICLE ABOUT ME.
I'M SORRY...
I REALLY AM.

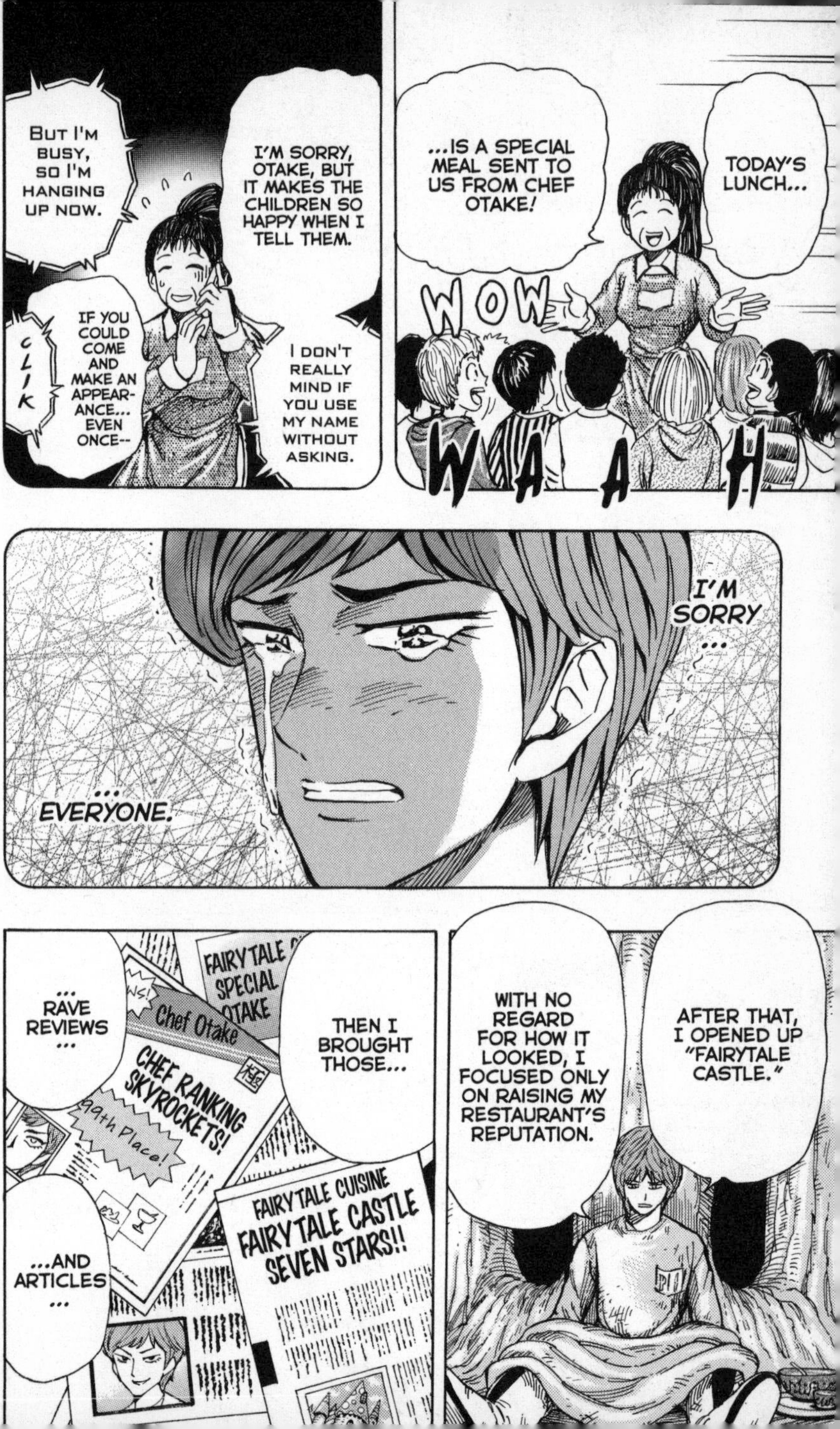
TODAY'S LUNCH...
...IS A SPECIAL MEAL SENT TO US FROM CHEF OTAKE!
WOW
WAAH
I'M SORRY, OTAKE, BUT IT MAKES THE CHILDREN SO HAPPY WHEN I TELL THEM.
BUT I'M BUSY, SO I'M HANGING UP NOW.
I DON'T REALLY MIND IF YOU USE MY NAME WITHOUT ASKING.
IF YOU COULD COME AND MAKE AN APPEARANCE... EVEN ONCE--
CLIK
I'M SORRY...
...EVERYONE.
AFTER THAT, I OPENED UP "FAIRYTALE CASTLE."
WITH NO REGARD FOR HOW IT LOOKED, I FOCUSED ONLY ON RAISING MY RESTAURANT'S REPUTATION.
THEN I BROUGHT THOSE...
FAIRYTALE SPECIAL OTAKE
Chef Otake
CHEF RANKING SKYROCKETS!
99th Place!
...RAVE REVIEWS...
FAIRYTALE CUISINE
FAIRYTALE CASTLE SEVEN STARS!!
...AND ARTICLES...

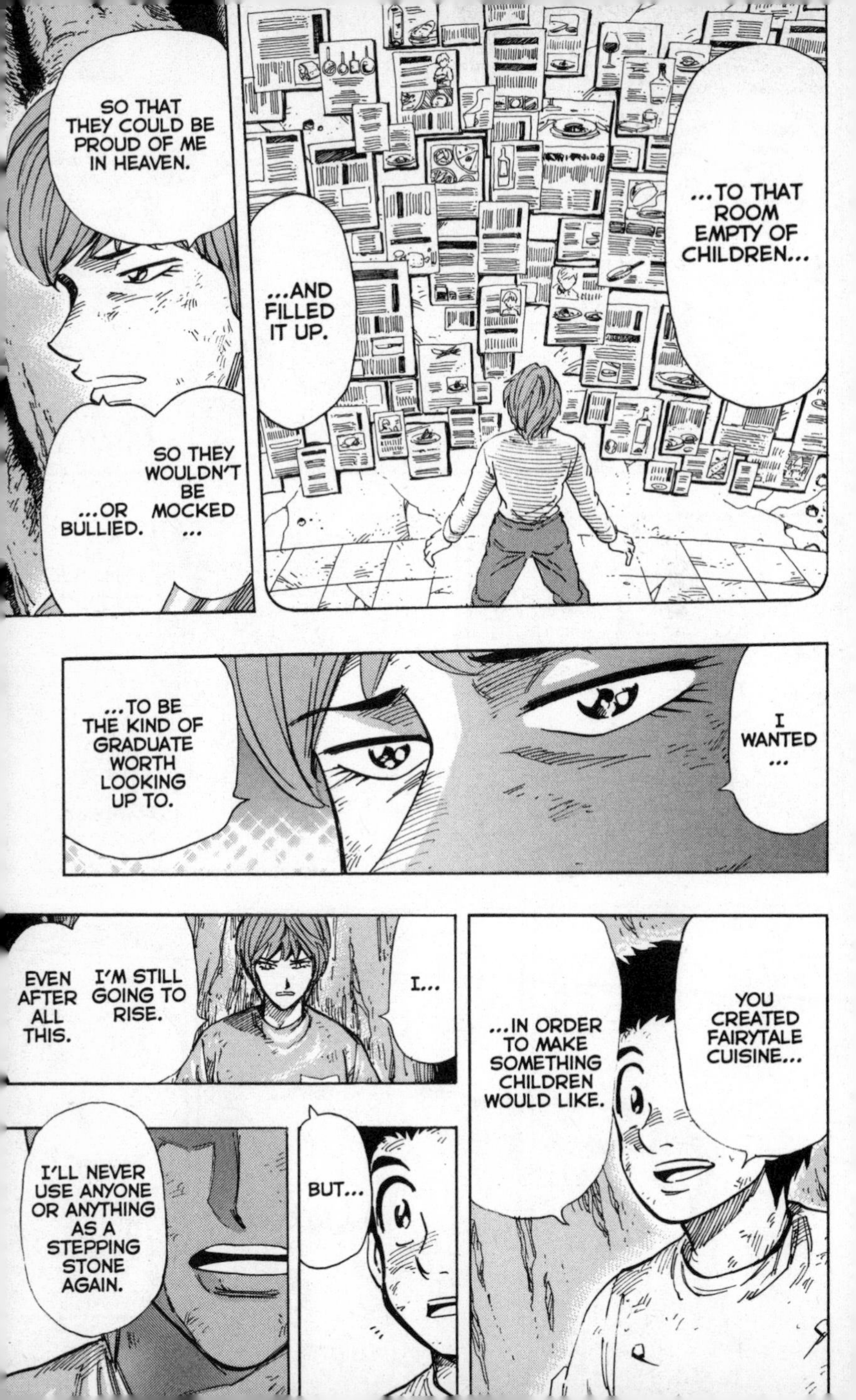
...TO THAT ROOM EMPTY OF CHILDREN...
...AND FILLED IT UP.
SO THAT THEY COULD BE PROUD OF ME IN HEAVEN.
SO THEY WOULDN'T BE MOCKED...
...OR BULLIED.
I WANTED...
...TO BE THE KIND OF GRADUATE WORTH LOOKING UP TO.
YOU CREATED FAIRYTALE CUISINE...
...IN ORDER TO MAKE SOMETHING CHILDREN WOULD LIKE.
I...
I'M STILL GOING TO RISE.
EVEN AFTER ALL THIS.
BUT...
I'LL NEVER USE ANYONE OR ANYTHING AS A STEPPING STONE AGAIN.

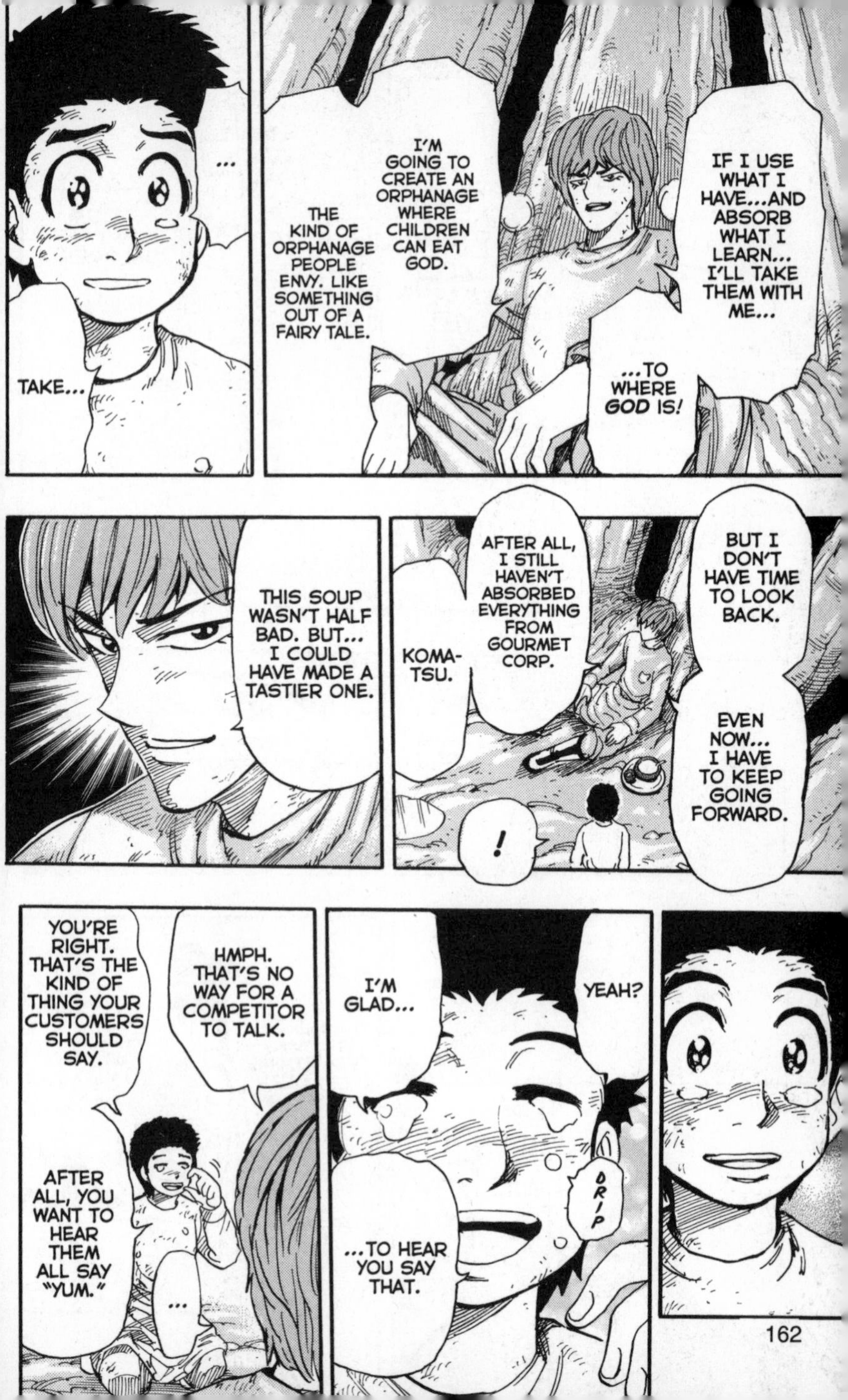
IF I USE WHAT I HAVE...AND ABSORB WHAT I LEARN... I'LL TAKE THEM WITH ME...
...TO WHERE GOD IS!
I'M GOING TO CREATE AN ORPHANAGE WHERE CHILDREN CAN EAT GOD.
THE KIND OF ORPHANAGE PEOPLE ENVY. LIKE SOMETHING OUT OF A FAIRY TALE.
...
TAKE...
BUT I DON'T HAVE TIME TO LOOK BACK.
EVEN NOW... I HAVE TO KEEP GOING FORWARD.
AFTER ALL, I STILL HAVEN'T ABSORBED EVERYTHING FROM GOURMET CORP.
KOMATSU.
!
THIS SOUP WASN'T HALF BAD. BUT... I COULD HAVE MADE A TASTIER ONE.
YEAH?
I'M GLAD...
DRIP
...TO HEAR YOU SAY THAT.
HMPH. THAT'S NO WAY FOR A COMPETITOR TO TALK.
YOU'RE RIGHT. THAT'S THE KIND OF THING YOUR CUSTOMERS SHOULD SAY.
AFTER ALL, YOU WANT TO HEAR THEM ALL SAY "YUM."
...

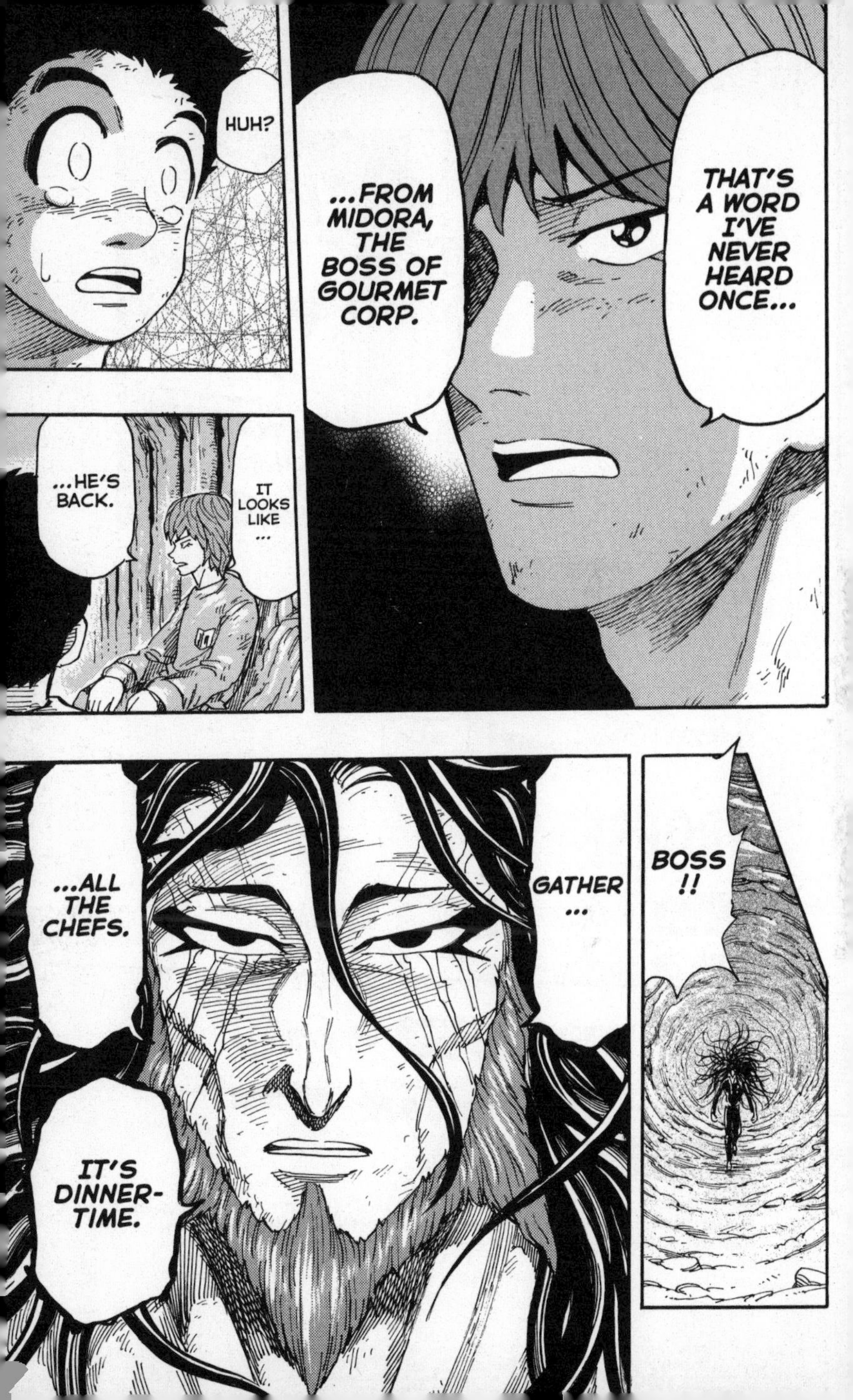
THAT'S A WORD I'VE NEVER HEARD ONCE...
...FROM MIDORA, THE BOSS OF GOURMET CORP.
HUH?
IT LOOKS LIKE...
...HE'S BACK.
BOSS!!
GATHER...
...ALL THE CHEFS.
IT'S DINNER-TIME.

CHARACTER PROFILE

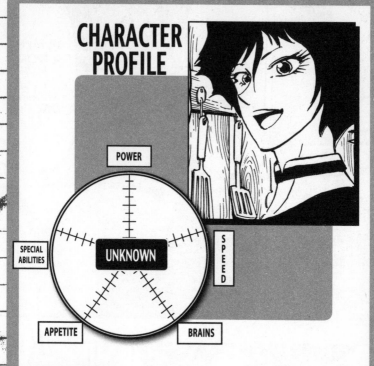

POWER

SPECIAL ABILITIES

UNKNOWN

SPEED

APPETITE

BRAINS

FROESE

AGE:	UNKNOWN	BIRTHDAY:	UNKNOWN
BLOOD TYPE:	UNKNOWN	SIGN:	UNKNOWN
HEIGHT:	UNKNOWN	WEIGHT:	UNKNOWN
EYESIGHT:	UNKNOWN	SHOE SIZE:	UNKNOWN

SPECIAL MOVES/ABILITIES: • God Cooking

Gourmet God Acacia's legendary chef partner. Long after her death, she is still revered by chefs and those who knew her as the "God Chef." She acted as a mother to Ichiryu, Jiro and Midora during their training. Along with Acacia, she is credited with laying the foundation of the Age of Gourmet.

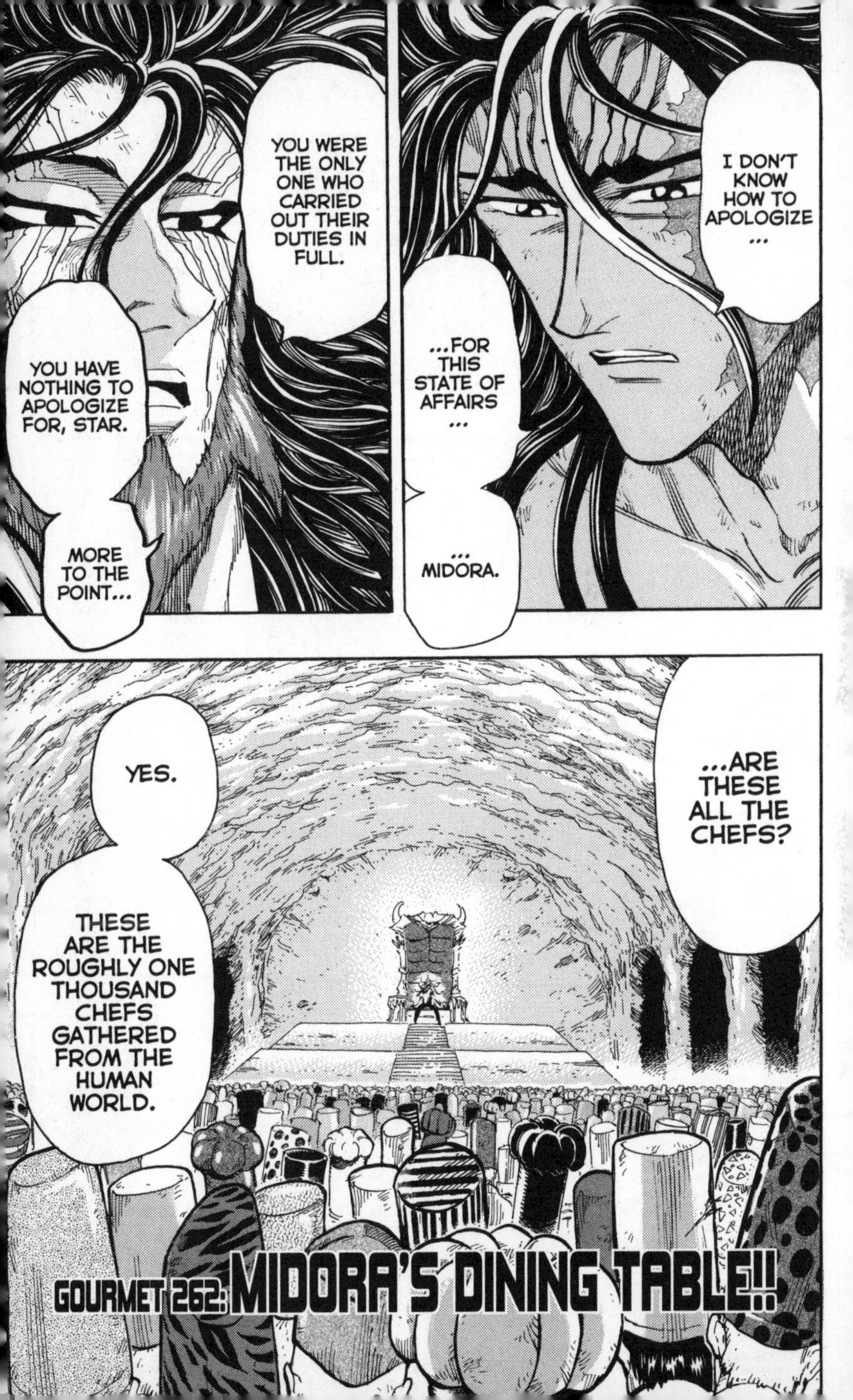
I DON'T KNOW HOW TO APOLOGIZE ...
...FOR THIS STATE OF AFFAIRS ...
... MIDORA.
YOU WERE THE ONLY ONE WHO CARRIED OUT THEIR DUTIES IN FULL.
YOU HAVE NOTHING TO APOLOGIZE FOR, STAR.
MORE TO THE POINT...
...ARE THESE ALL THE CHEFS?
YES.
THESE ARE THE ROUGHLY ONE THOUSAND CHEFS GATHERED FROM THE HUMAN WORLD.
GOURMET 262: MIDORA'S DINING TABLE!!

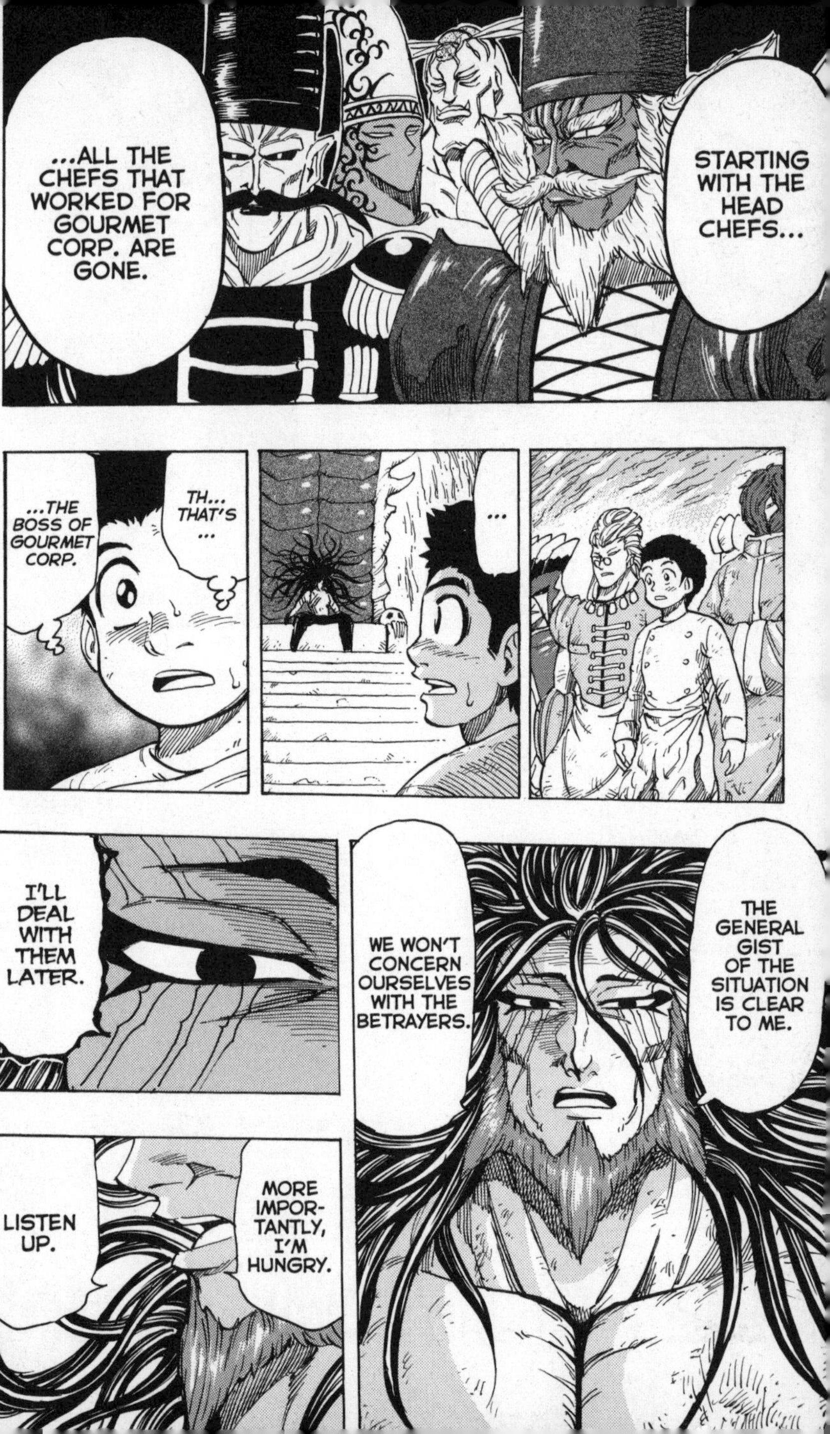
STARTING WITH THE HEAD CHEFS...
...ALL THE CHEFS THAT WORKED FOR GOURMET CORP. ARE GONE.
...
TH... THAT'S ...
...THE BOSS OF GOURMET CORP.
THE GENERAL GIST OF THE SITUATION IS CLEAR TO ME.
WE WON'T CONCERN OURSELVES WITH THE BETRAYERS.
I'LL DEAL WITH THEM LATER.
MORE IMPOR-TANTLY, I'M HUNGRY.
LISTEN UP.

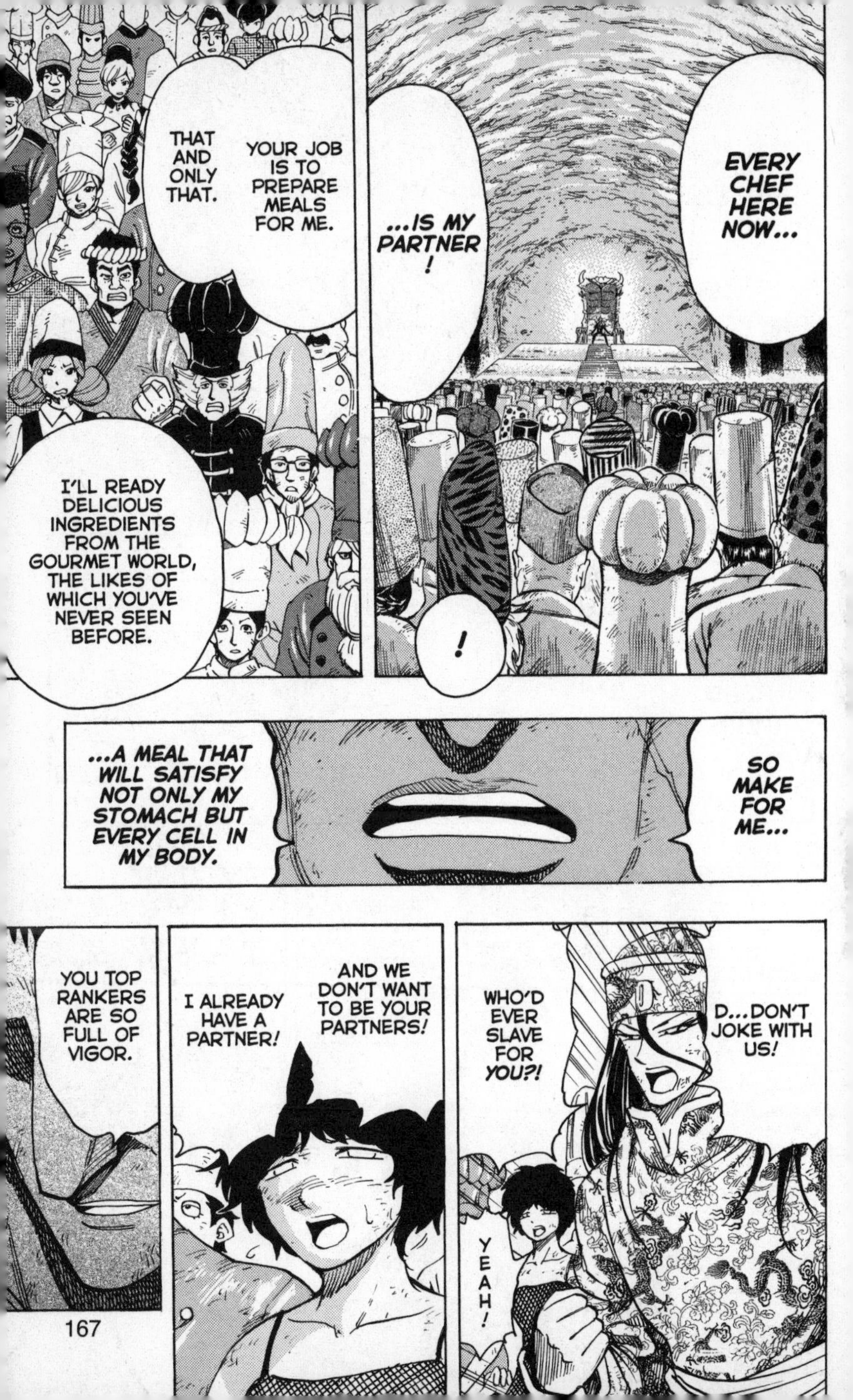
EVERY CHEF HERE NOW...
...IS MY PARTNER!
!
YOUR JOB IS TO PREPARE MEALS FOR ME.
THAT AND ONLY THAT.
I'LL READY DELICIOUS INGREDIENTS FROM THE GOURMET WORLD, THE LIKES OF WHICH YOU'VE NEVER SEEN BEFORE.
SO MAKE FOR ME...
...A MEAL THAT WILL SATISFY NOT ONLY MY STOMACH BUT EVERY CELL IN MY BODY.
D...DON'T JOKE WITH US!
WHO'D EVER SLAVE FOR YOU?!
YEAH!
AND WE DON'T WANT TO BE YOUR PARTNERS!
I ALREADY HAVE A PARTNER!
YOU TOP RANKERS ARE SO FULL OF VIGOR.

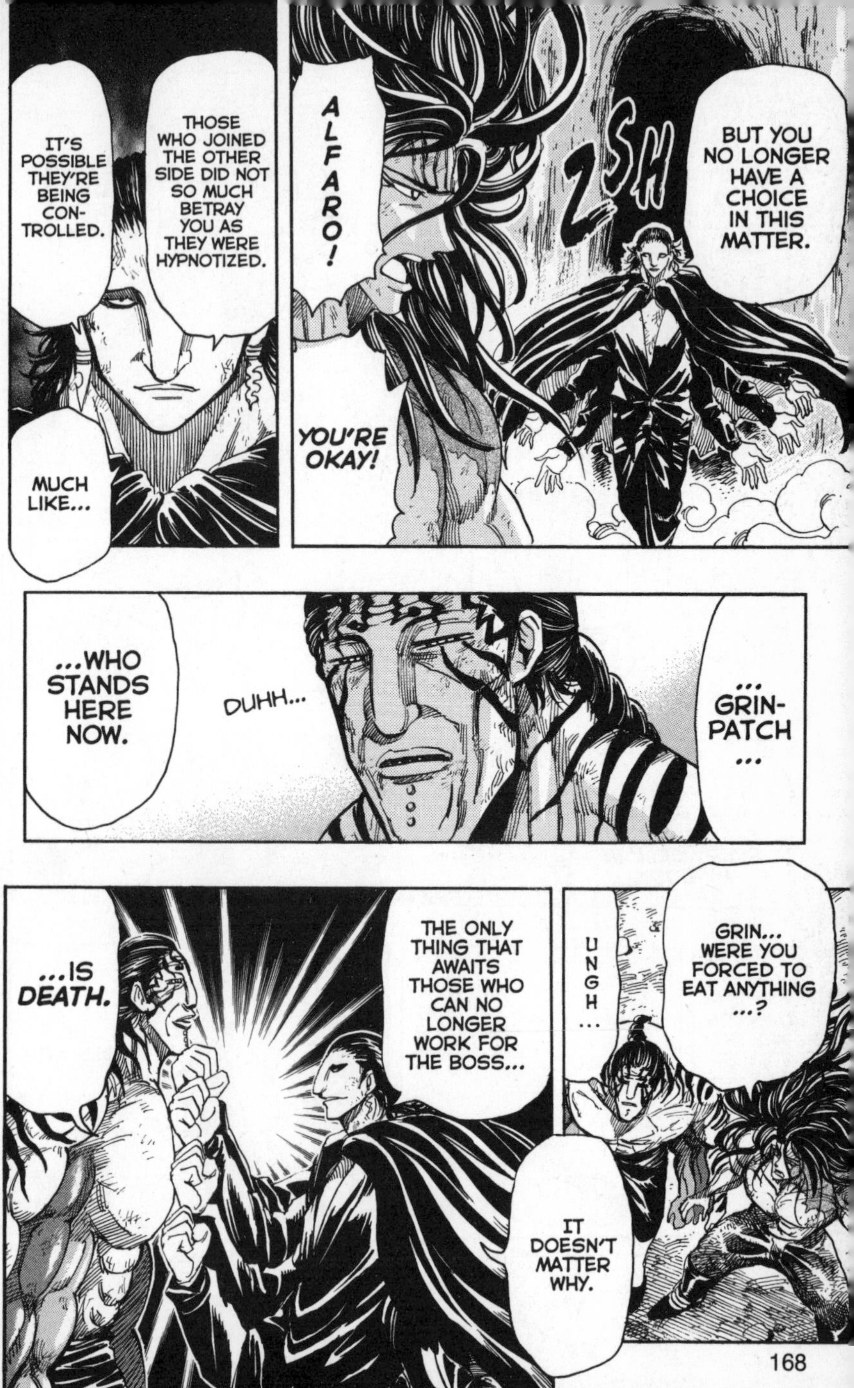
BUT YOU NO LONGER HAVE A CHOICE IN THIS MATTER.
ZSH
ALFARO!
YOU'RE OKAY!
THOSE WHO JOINED THE OTHER SIDE DID NOT SO MUCH BETRAY YOU AS THEY WERE HYPNOTIZED.
IT'S POSSIBLE THEY'RE BEING CON-TROLLED.
MUCH LIKE...
...GRIN-PATCH...
DUHH...
...WHO STANDS HERE NOW.
GRIN... WERE YOU FORCED TO EAT ANYTHING...?
UNGH...
IT DOESN'T MATTER WHY.
THE ONLY THING THAT AWAITS THOSE WHO CAN NO LONGER WORK FOR THE BOSS...
...IS DEATH.

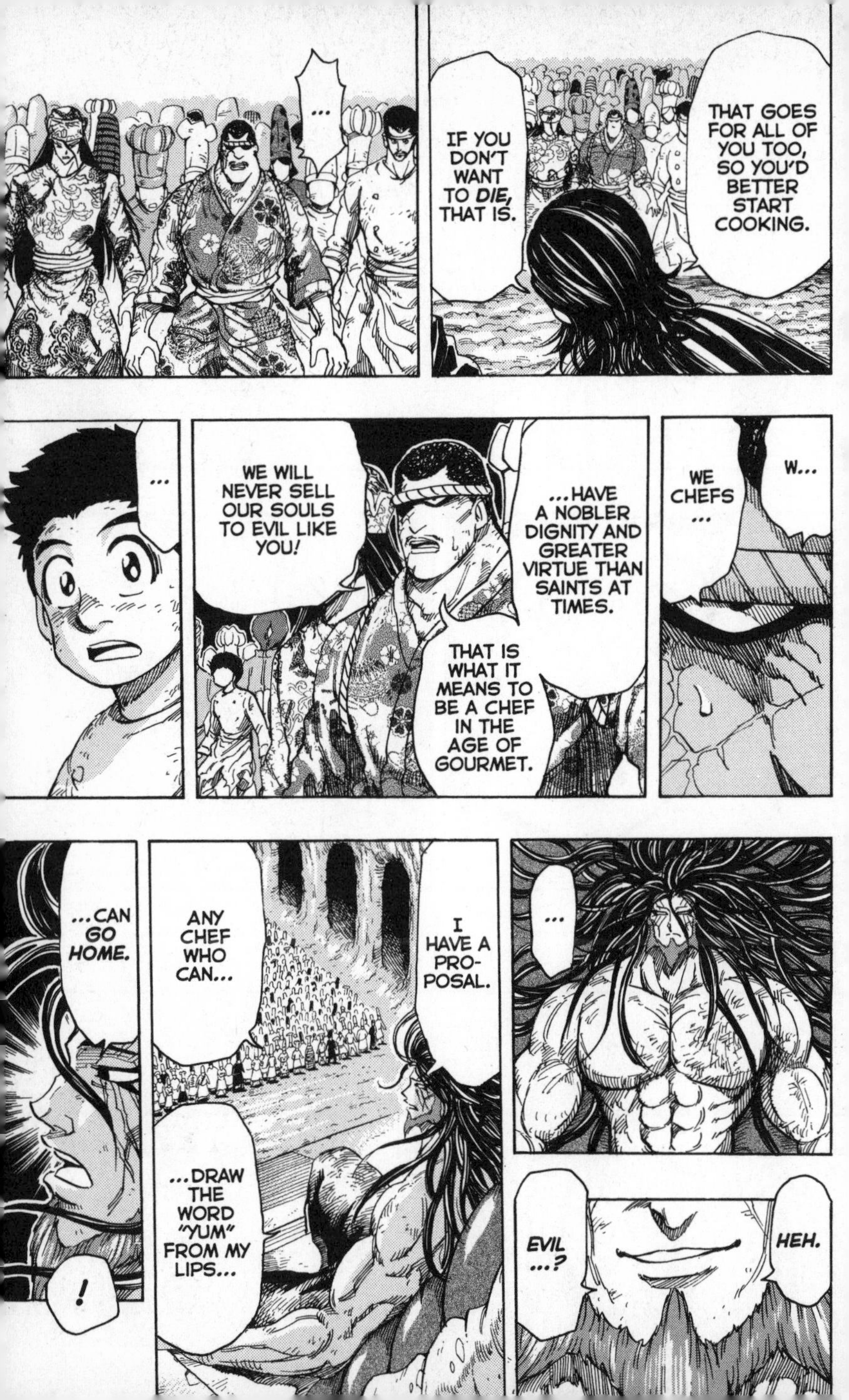
THAT GOES FOR ALL OF YOU TOO, SO YOU'D BETTER START COOKING.
IF YOU DON'T WANT TO *DIE*, THAT IS.
...
W...
WE CHEFS...
...HAVE A NOBLER DIGNITY AND GREATER VIRTUE THAN SAINTS AT TIMES.
THAT IS WHAT IT MEANS TO BE A CHEF IN THE AGE OF GOURMET.
WE WILL NEVER SELL OUR SOULS TO EVIL LIKE YOU!
...
...
HEH.
EVIL...?
I HAVE A PROPOSAL.
ANY CHEF WHO CAN...
...DRAW THE WORD "YUM" FROM MY LIPS...
...CAN GO *HOME.*
!

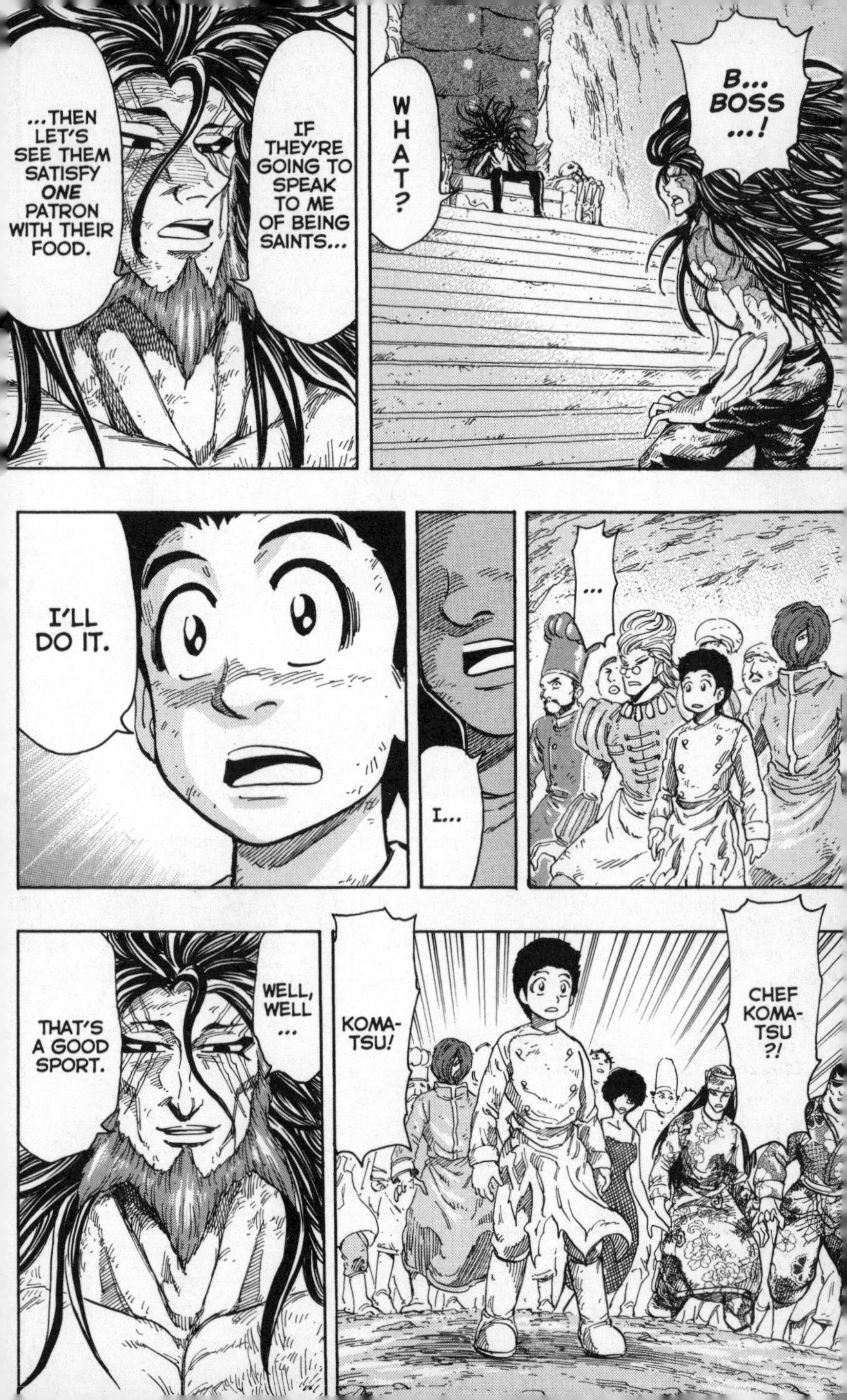
B... BOSS ...!
WHAT?
IF THEY'RE GOING TO SPEAK TO ME OF BEING SAINTS...
...THEN LET'S SEE THEM SATISFY *ONE* PATRON WITH THEIR FOOD.
...
I...
I'LL DO IT.
CHEF KOMA-TSU ?!
KOMA-TSU!
WELL, WELL ...
THAT'S A GOOD SPORT.

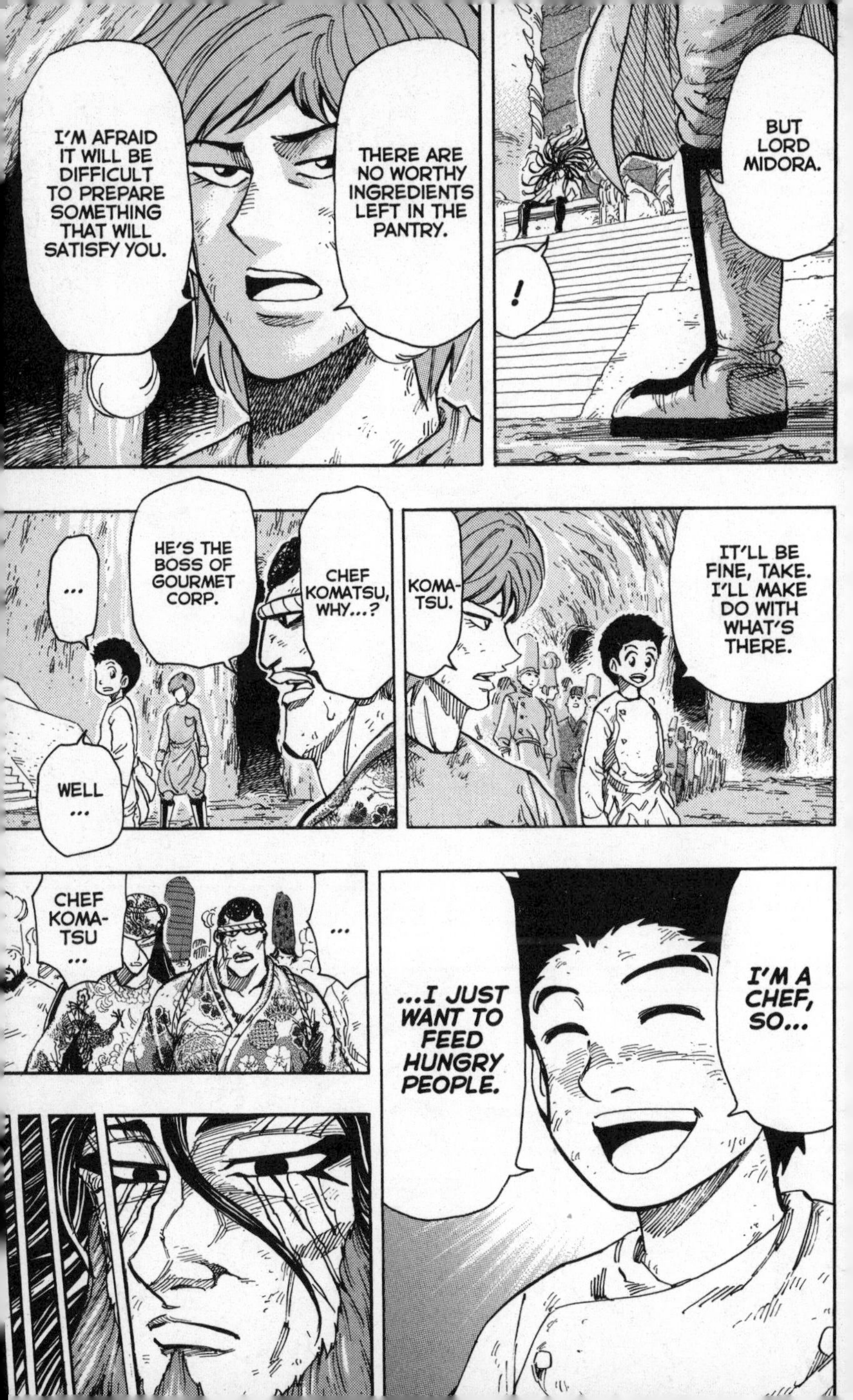
BUT LORD MIDORA.
!
THERE ARE NO WORTHY INGREDIENTS LEFT IN THE PANTRY.
I'M AFRAID IT WILL BE DIFFICULT TO PREPARE SOMETHING THAT WILL SATISFY YOU.
IT'LL BE FINE, TAKE. I'LL MAKE DO WITH WHAT'S THERE.
KOMA-TSU.
CHEF KOMATSU, WHY...?
HE'S THE BOSS OF GOURMET CORP.
...
WELL...
I'M A CHEF, SO...
...I JUST WANT TO FEED HUNGRY PEOPLE.
...
CHEF KOMA-TSU...

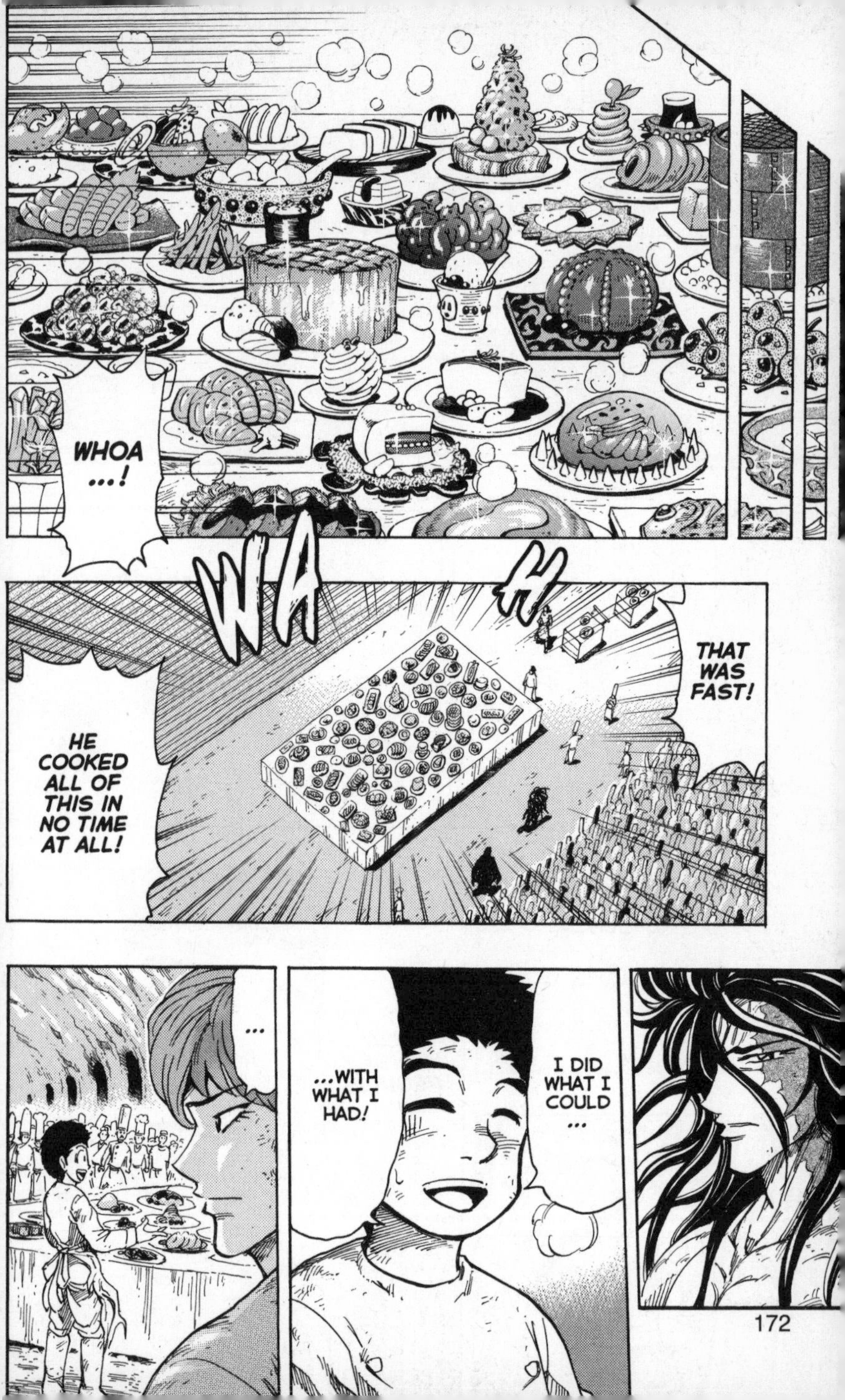
WHOA ...!
WA H
THAT WAS FAST!
HE COOKED ALL OF THIS IN NO TIME AT ALL!
I DID WHAT I COULD ...
...WITH WHAT I HAD!
...

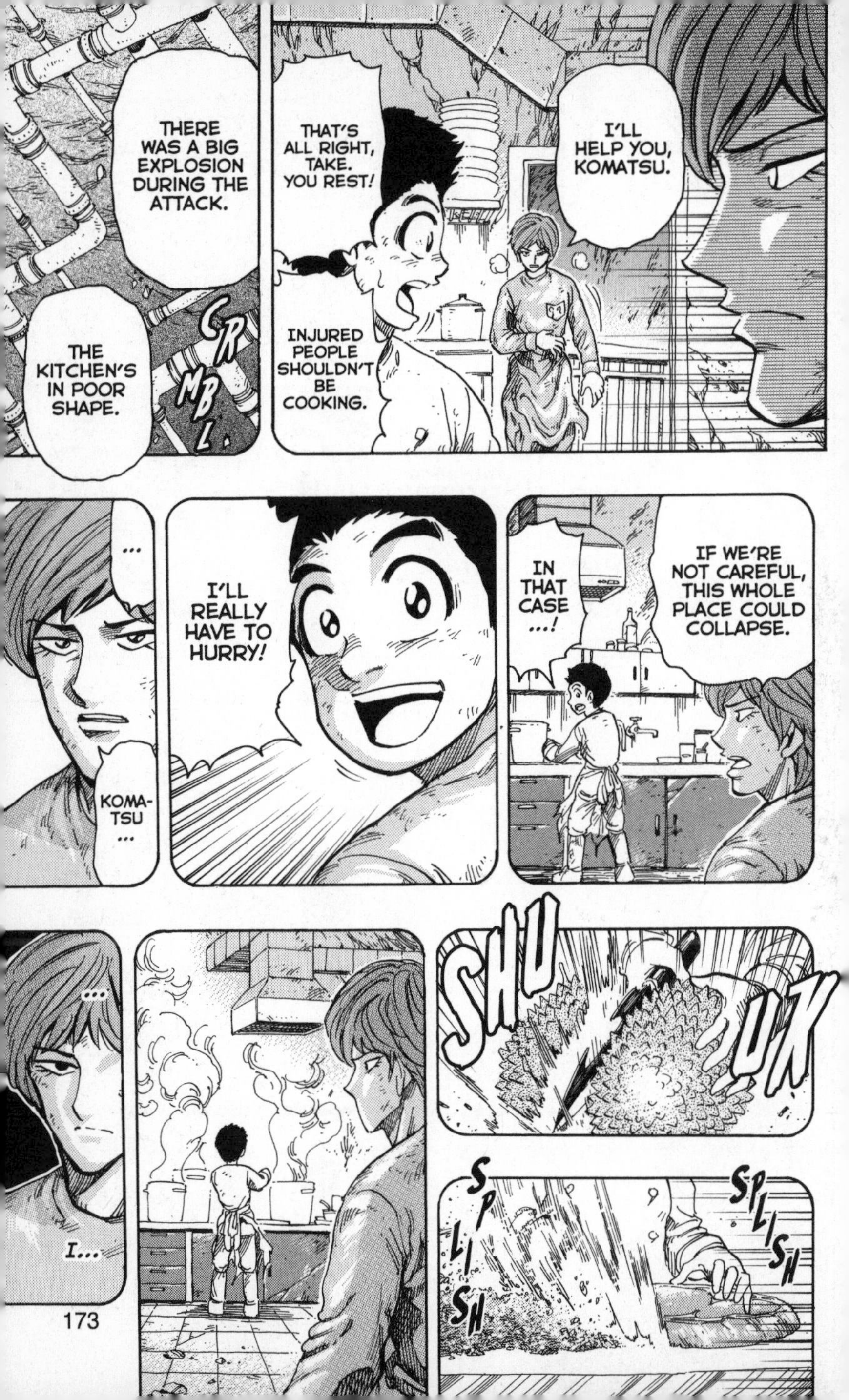
I'LL HELP YOU, KOMATSU.
THAT'S ALL RIGHT, TAKE. YOU REST!
INJURED PEOPLE SHOULDN'T BE COOKING.
THERE WAS A BIG EXPLOSION DURING THE ATTACK.
THE KITCHEN'S IN POOR SHAPE.
CRMBL
IF WE'RE NOT CAREFUL, THIS WHOLE PLACE COULD COLLAPSE.
IN THAT CASE ...!
I'LL REALLY HAVE TO HURRY!
...
KOMATSU ...
SHUNK
SPLISH
SPLISH
...
I...

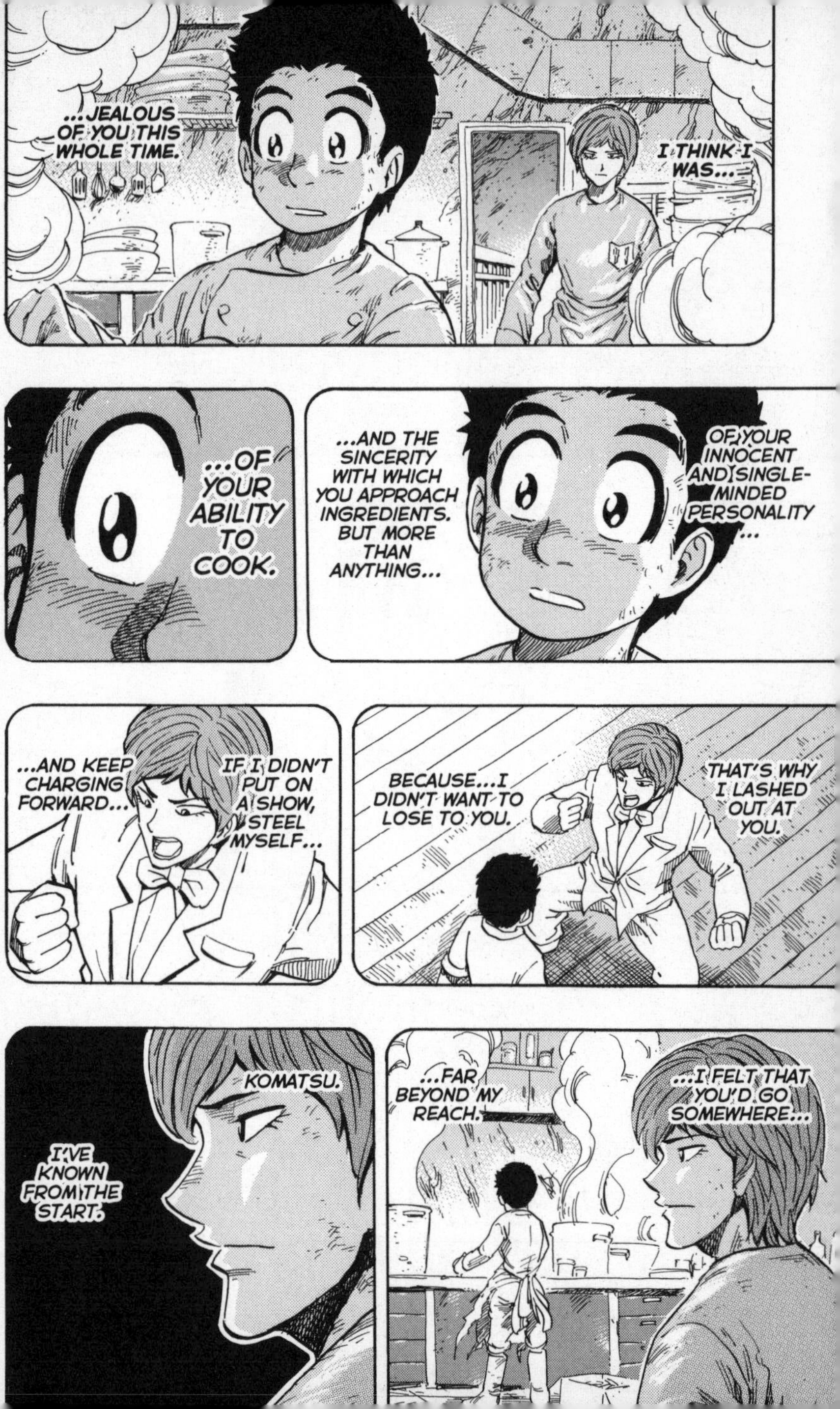
I THINK I WAS...
...JEALOUS OF YOU THIS WHOLE TIME.
OF YOUR INNOCENT AND SINGLE-MINDED PERSONALITY...
...AND THE SINCERITY WITH WHICH YOU APPROACH INGREDIENTS. BUT MORE THAN ANYTHING...
...OF YOUR ABILITY TO COOK.
THAT'S WHY I LASHED OUT AT YOU.
BECAUSE...I DIDN'T WANT TO LOSE TO YOU.
IF I DIDN'T PUT ON A SHOW, STEEL MYSELF...
...AND KEEP CHARGING FORWARD...
...I FELT THAT YOU'D GO SOMEWHERE...
...FAR BEYOND MY REACH.
KOMATSU.
I'VE KNOWN FROM THE START.

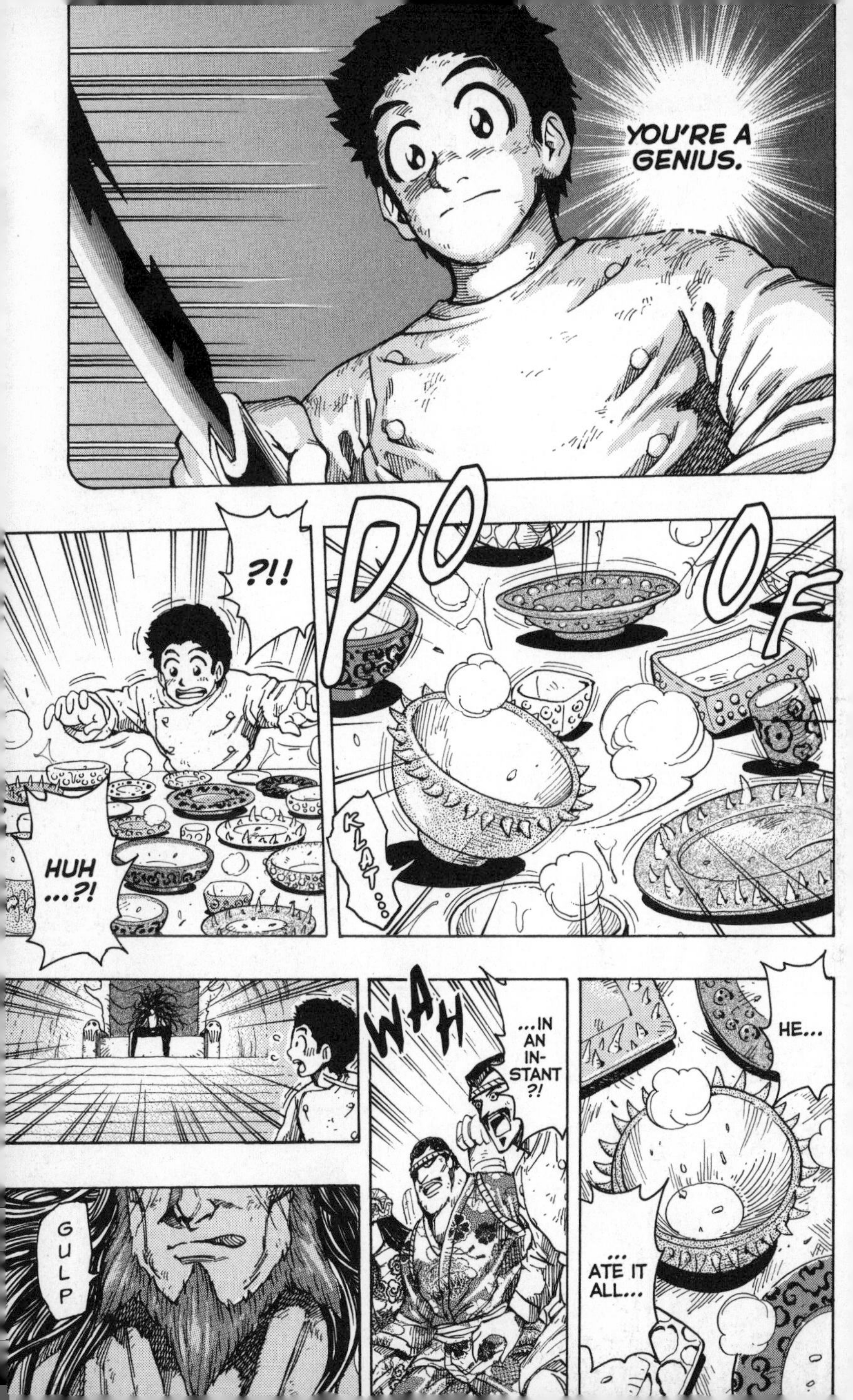
YOU'RE A GENIUS.
POOF
KLAT...
?!!
HUH ...?!
HE...
... ATE IT ALL...
WAH
...IN AN IN-STANT ?!
GULP

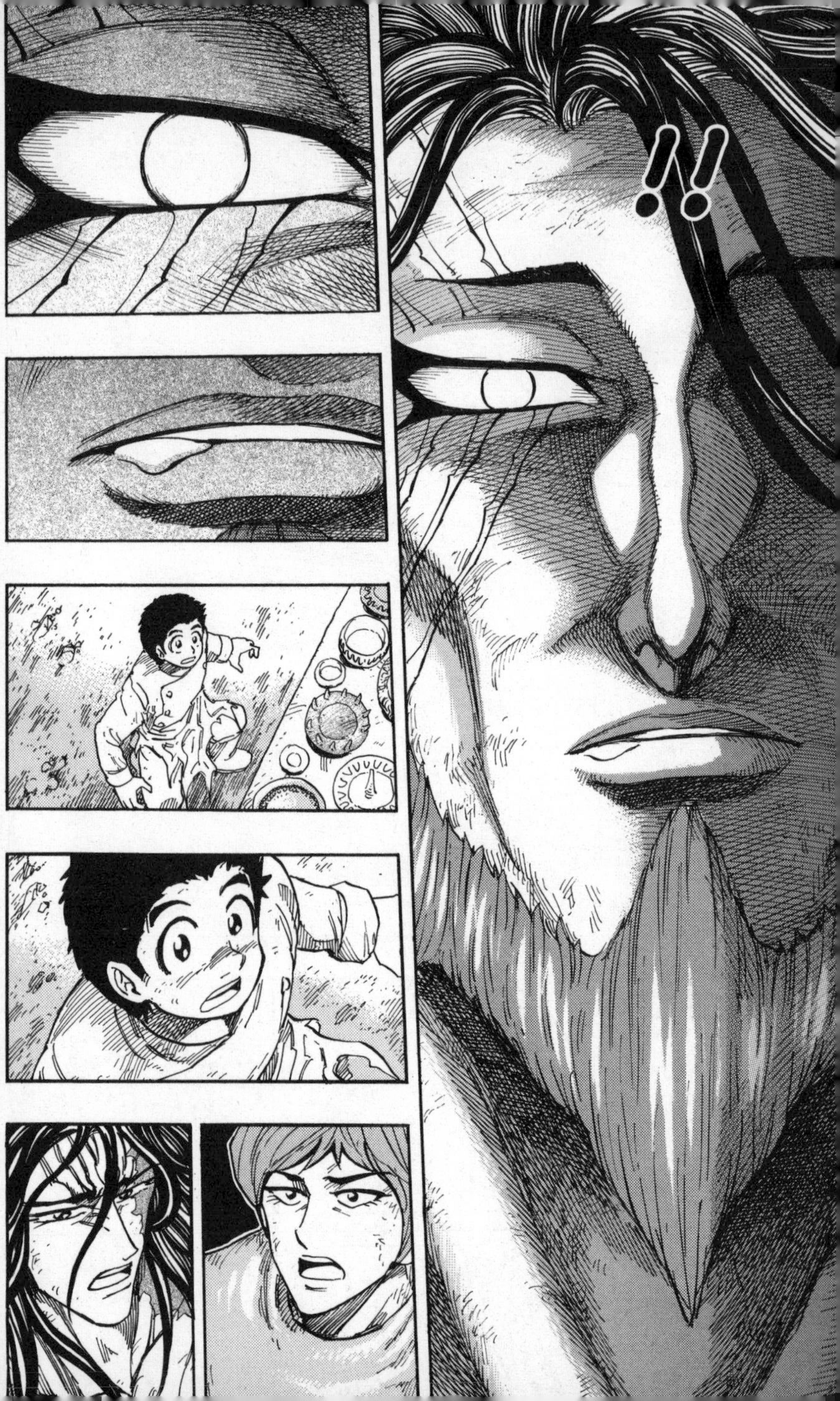
!!

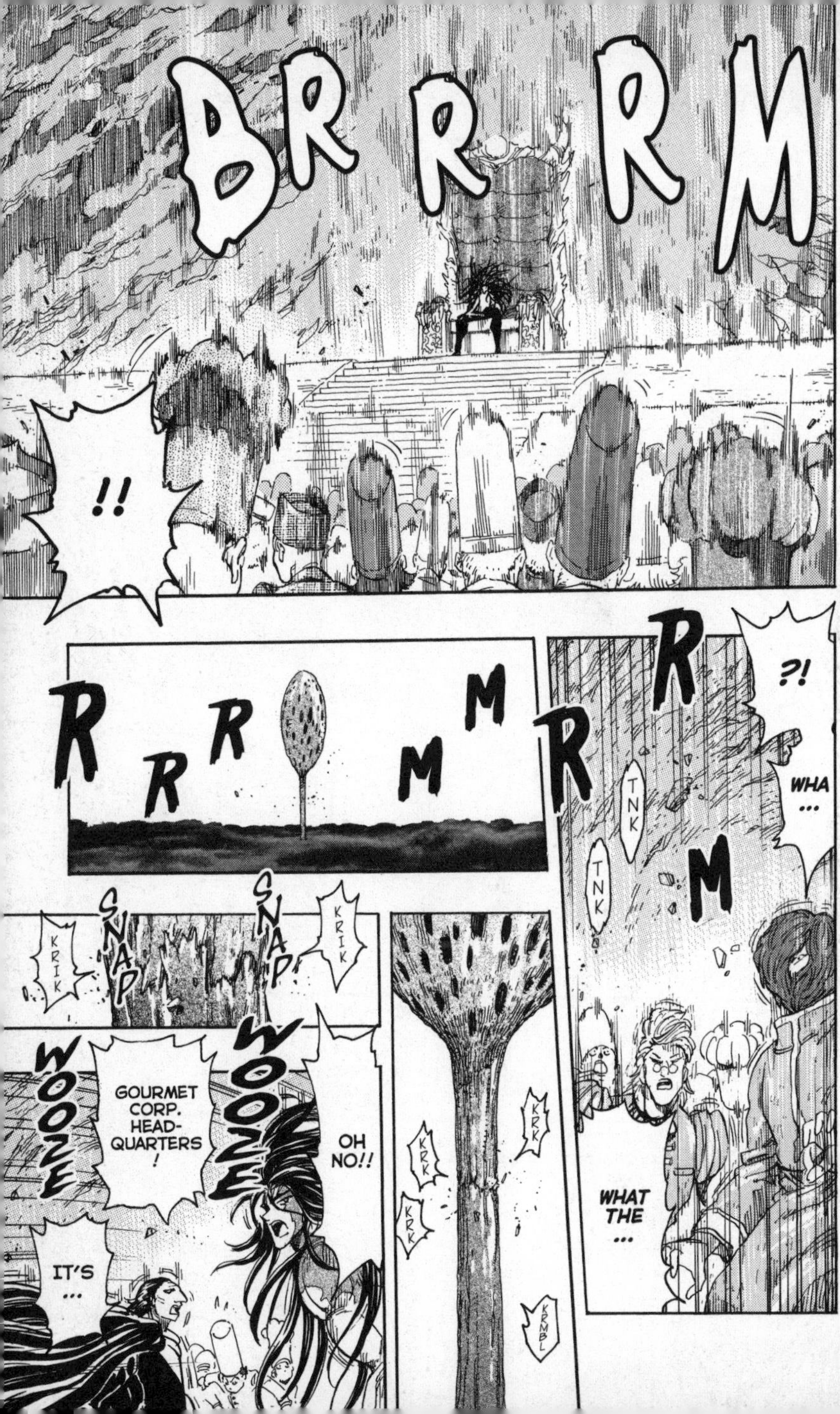
BRRRRM
!!
RRM
?!
WHA...
TNK
TNK
WHAT THE...
RRRMM
KRK
KRK
KRK
KRMBL
KRIK
SNAP
SNAP
KRIK
WOOOZE
OH NO!!
GOURMET CORP. HEAD-QUARTERS!
WOOOZE
IT'S...

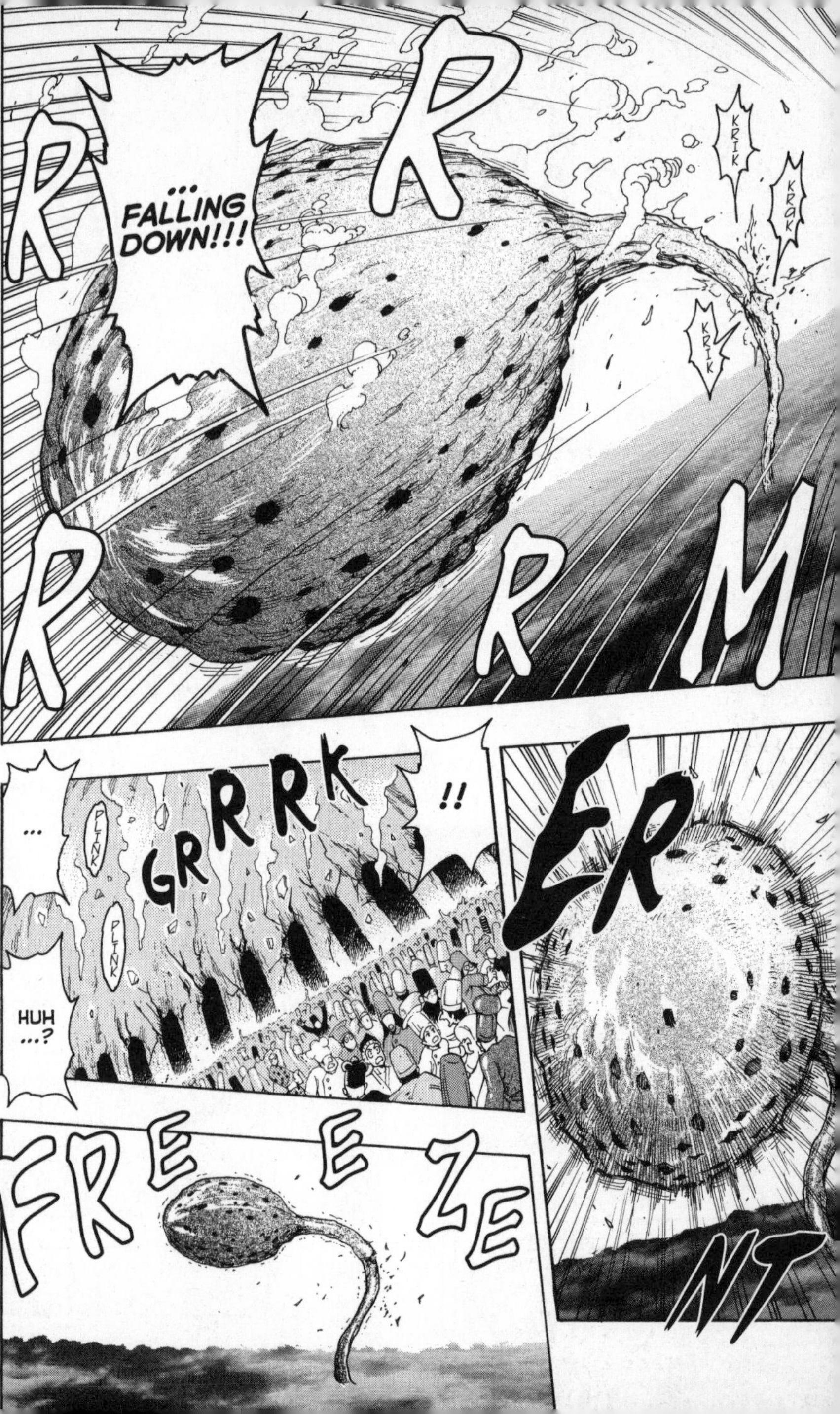

KRAK
KRIK
KRIK
... FALLING DOWN!!!
RRRRM
ERNT
!!
GRRRK
PLINK
PLINK
...
HUH ...?
FREEZE

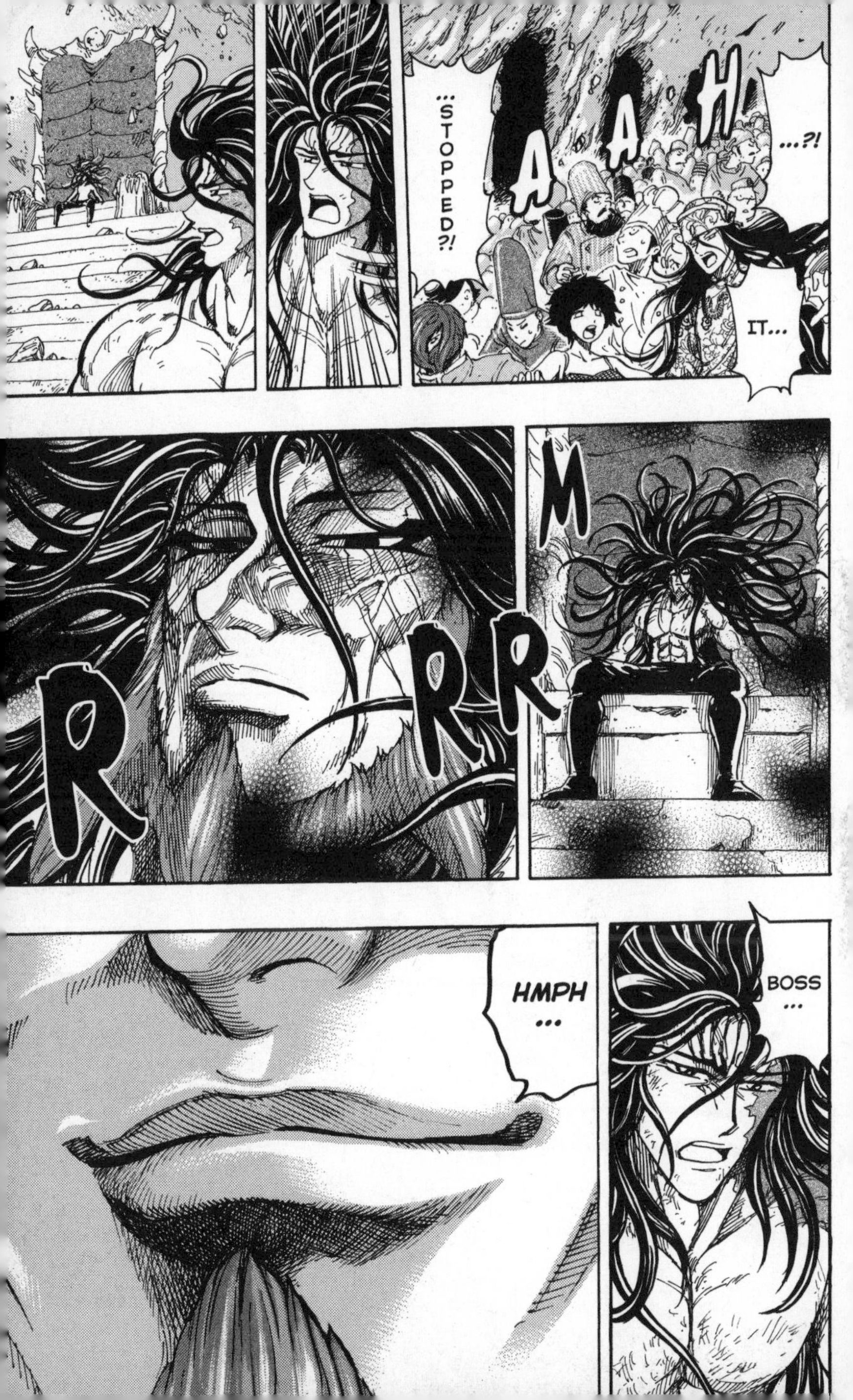

AAH
...?!
IT...
...STOPPED?!
RRRM
BOSS...
HMPH...

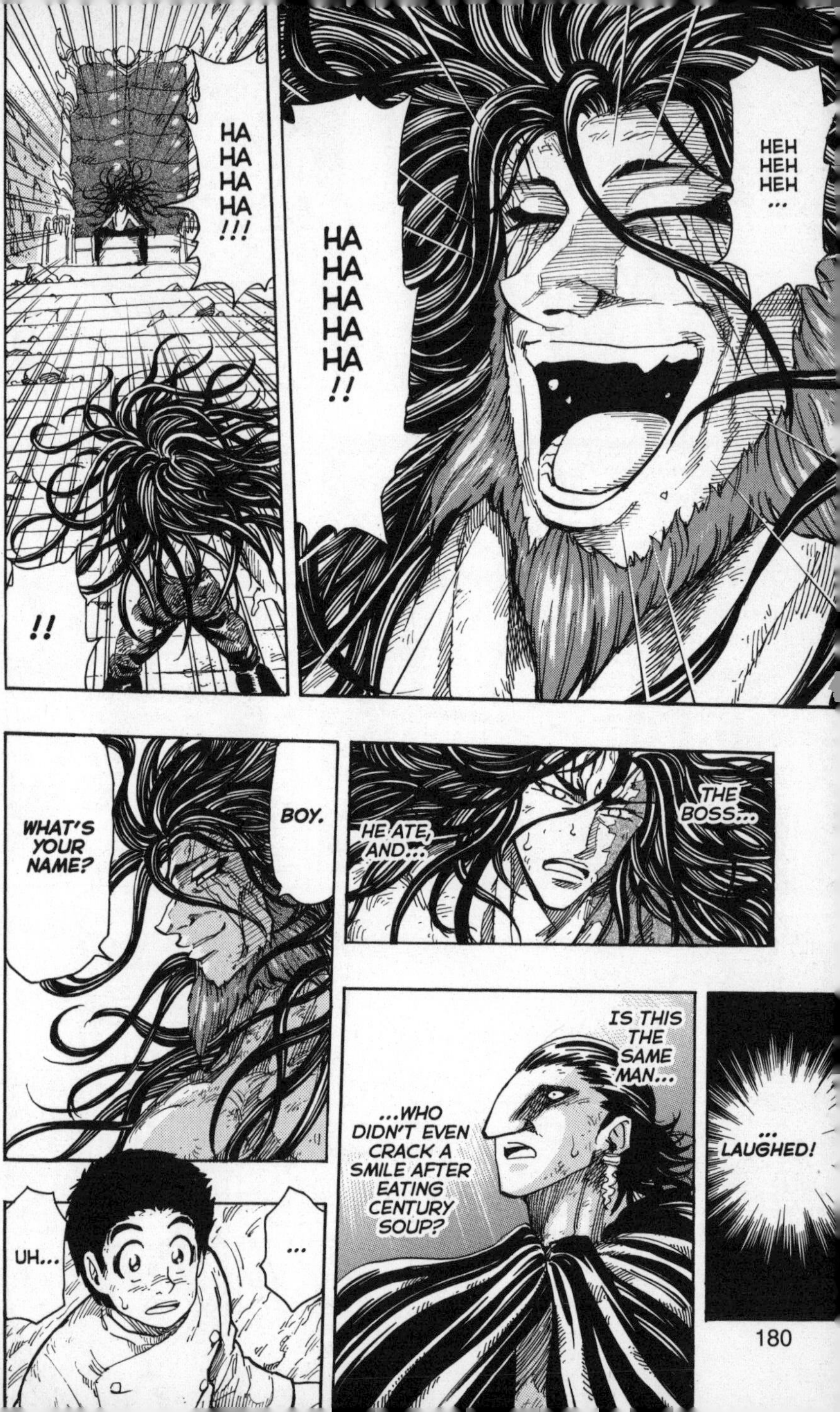
HEH HEH HEH...
HA HA HA HA HA!!
HA HA HA HA!!!
!!
THE BOSS...
HE ATE, AND...
...LAUGHED!
IS THIS THE SAME MAN...
...WHO DIDN'T EVEN CRACK A SMILE AFTER EATING CENTURY SOUP?
BOY.
WHAT'S YOUR NAME?
...
UH...

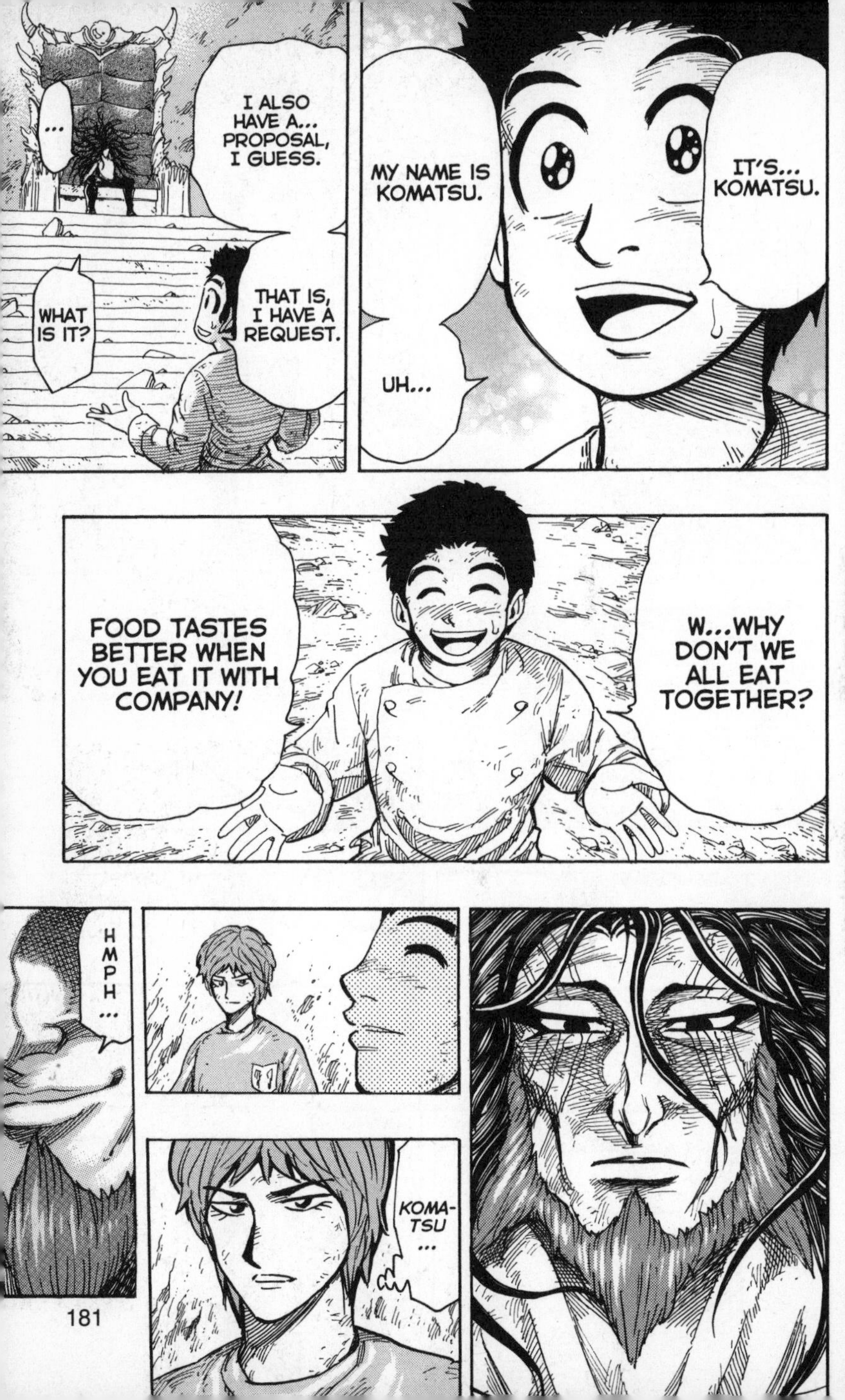
IT'S... KOMATSU.
MY NAME IS KOMATSU.
UH...
I ALSO HAVE A... PROPOSAL, I GUESS.
...
THAT IS, I HAVE A REQUEST.
WHAT IS IT?
W...WHY DON'T WE ALL EAT TOGETHER?
FOOD TASTES BETTER WHEN YOU EAT IT WITH COMPANY!
KOMA-TSU...
HMPH...

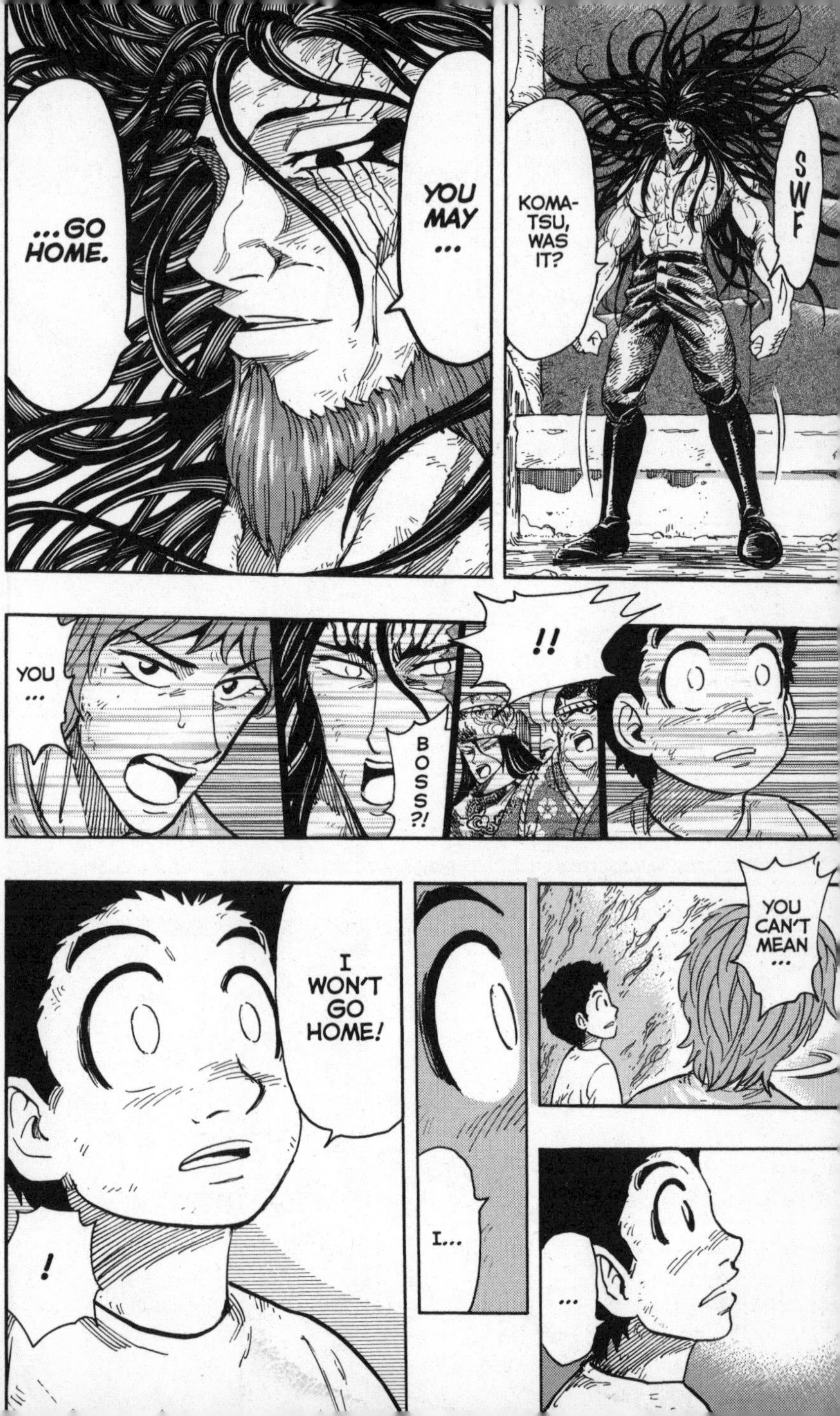
SWF
KOMATSU, WAS IT?
YOU MAY...
...GO HOME.
!!
BOSS?!
YOU...
YOU CAN'T MEAN...
...
I...
I WON'T GO HOME!
!

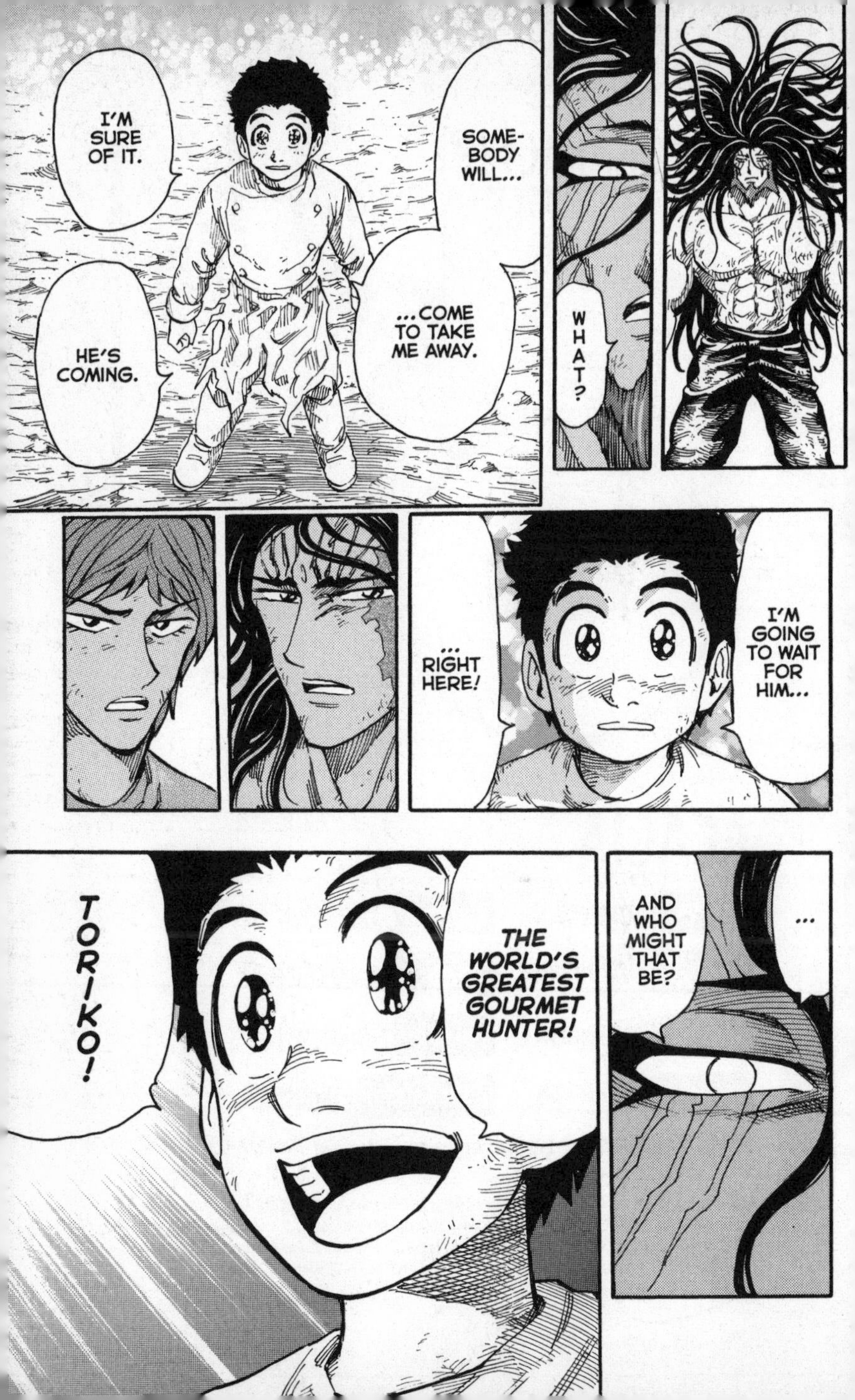
WHAT?
SOME-BODY WILL...
...COME TO TAKE ME AWAY.
I'M SURE OF IT.
HE'S COMING.
I'M GOING TO WAIT FOR HIM...
...RIGHT HERE!
...
AND WHO MIGHT THAT BE?
THE WORLD'S GREATEST GOURMET HUNTER!
TORIKO!

CHARACTER PROFILE

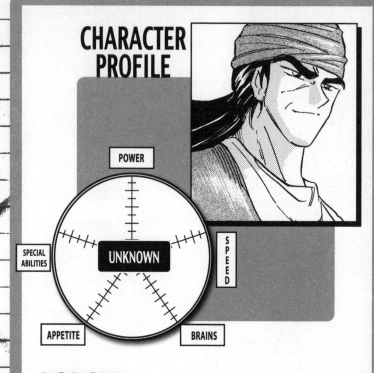

POWER

SPECIAL ABILITIES

SPEED

UNKNOWN

APPETITE

BRAINS

ACACIA

AGE:	UNKNOWN	**BIRTHDAY:**	UNKNOWN
BLOOD TYPE:	UNKNOWN	**SIGN:**	UNKNOWN
HEIGHT:	UNKNOWN	**WEIGHT:**	UNKNOWN
EYESIGHT:	UNKNOWN	**SHOE SIZE:**	UNKNOWN

SPECIAL MOVES/ABILITIES:
- Unknown

The founder of the Age of Gourmet. He discovered Gourmet Cells and is worshiped as the Gourmet God. He greatly advanced society through his many discoveries of gourmet foods as well as food preparation methods, and left a legacy through his disciples Ichiryu, Jiro and Midora. A desperate contest has broken out over the acquisition of his Main Dish, God. The influence he has had over the Age of Gourmet is immeasurable.

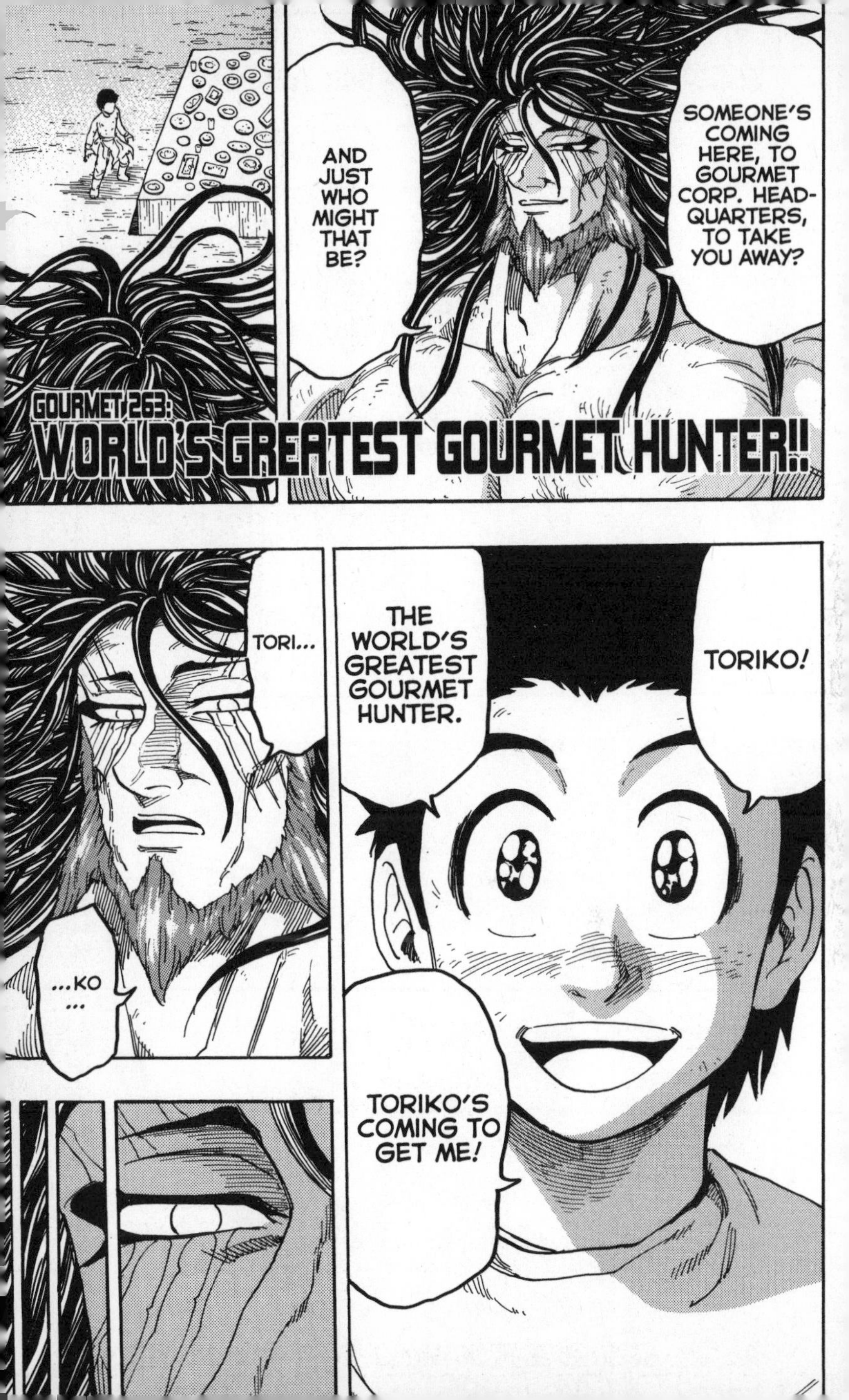

SOMEONE'S COMING HERE, TO GOURMET CORP. HEAD-QUARTERS, TO TAKE YOU AWAY?
AND JUST WHO MIGHT THAT BE?
GOURMET 263:
WORLD'S GREATEST GOURMET HUNTER!!
TORIKO!
THE WORLD'S GREATEST GOURMET HUNTER.
TORIKO'S COMING TO GET ME!
TORI...
...KO ...

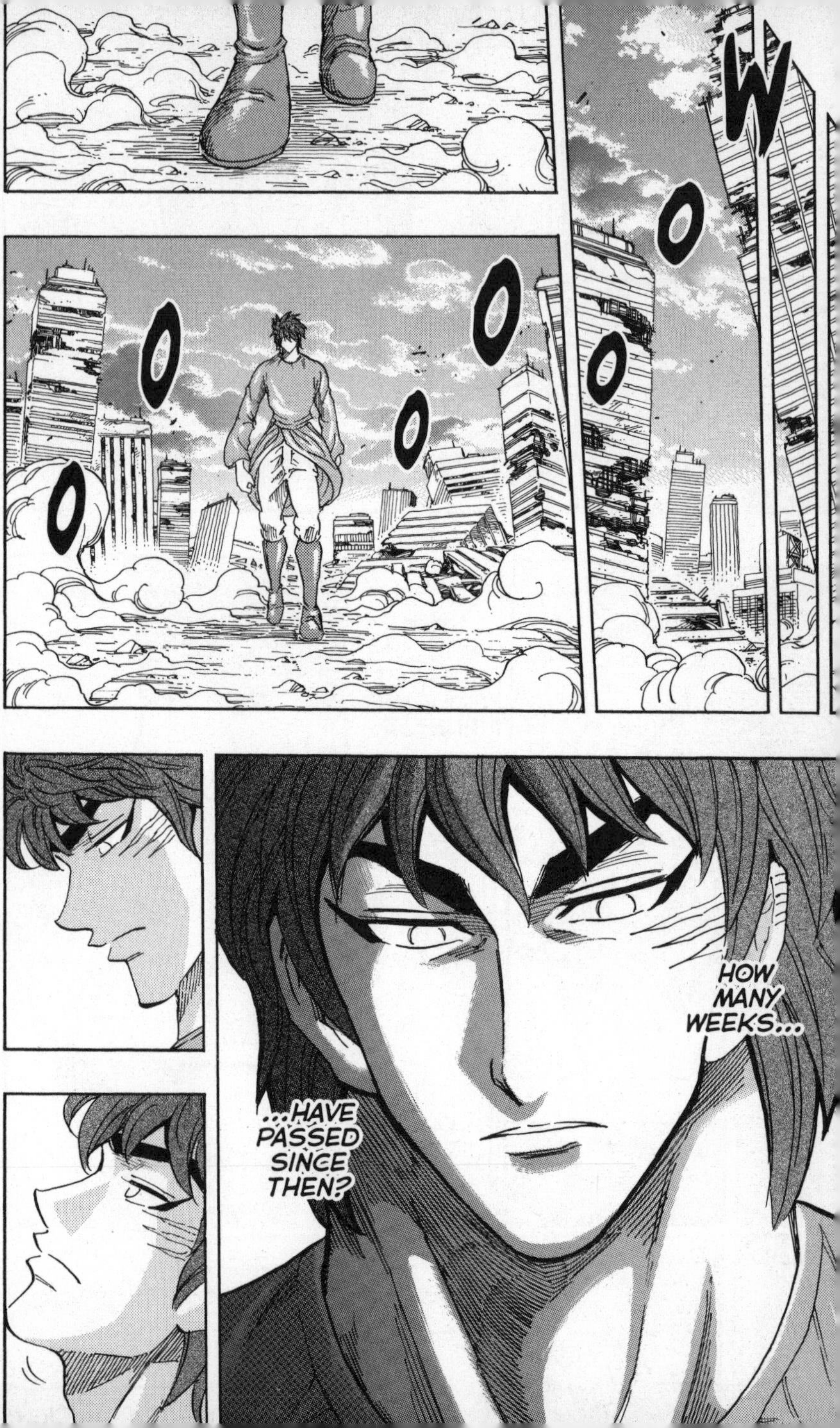
WOOOOOO
HOW MANY WEEKS...
...HAVE PASSED SINCE THEN?

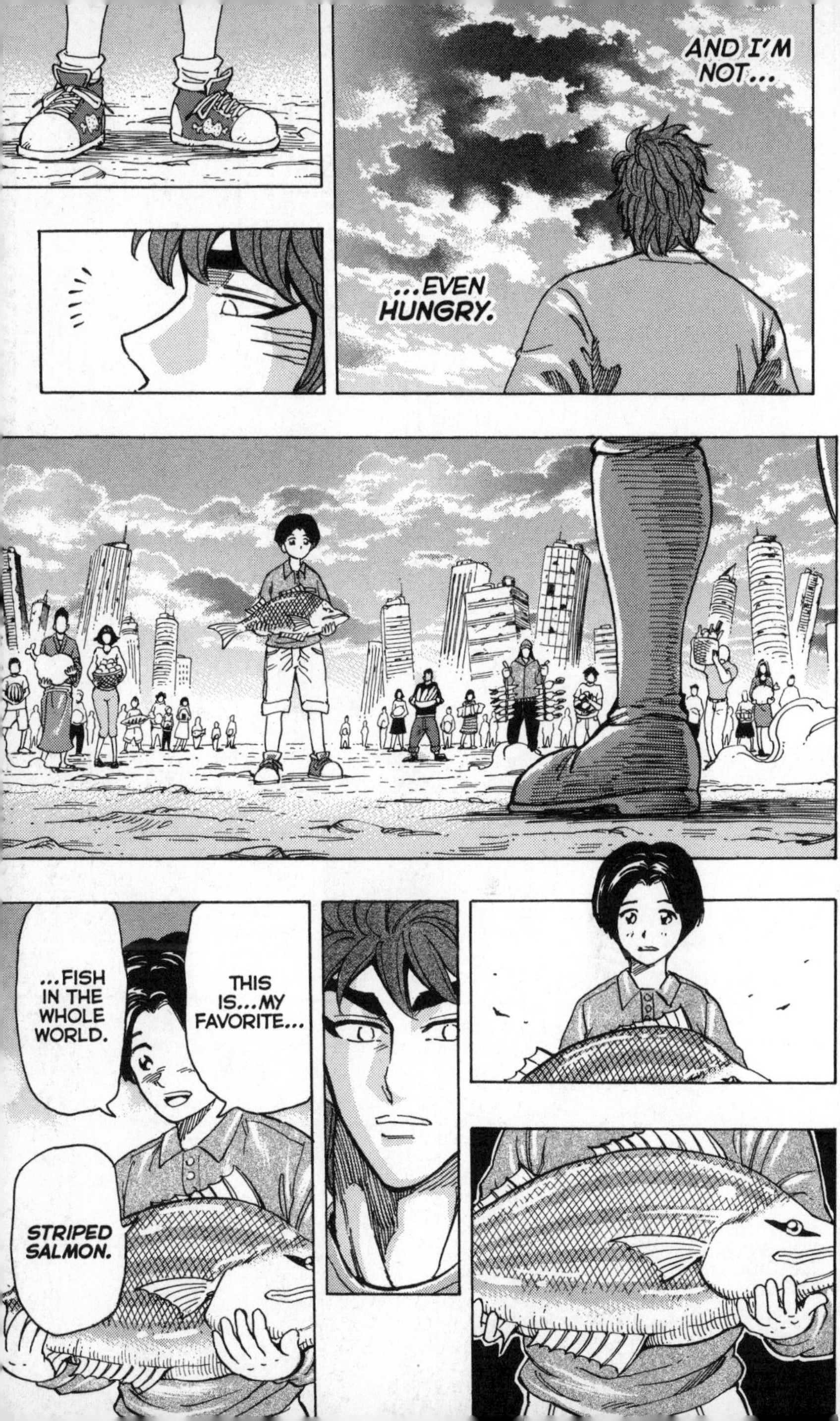
AND I'M NOT...
...EVEN HUNGRY.
THIS IS...MY FAVORITE...
...FISH IN THE WHOLE WORLD.
STRIPED SALMON.

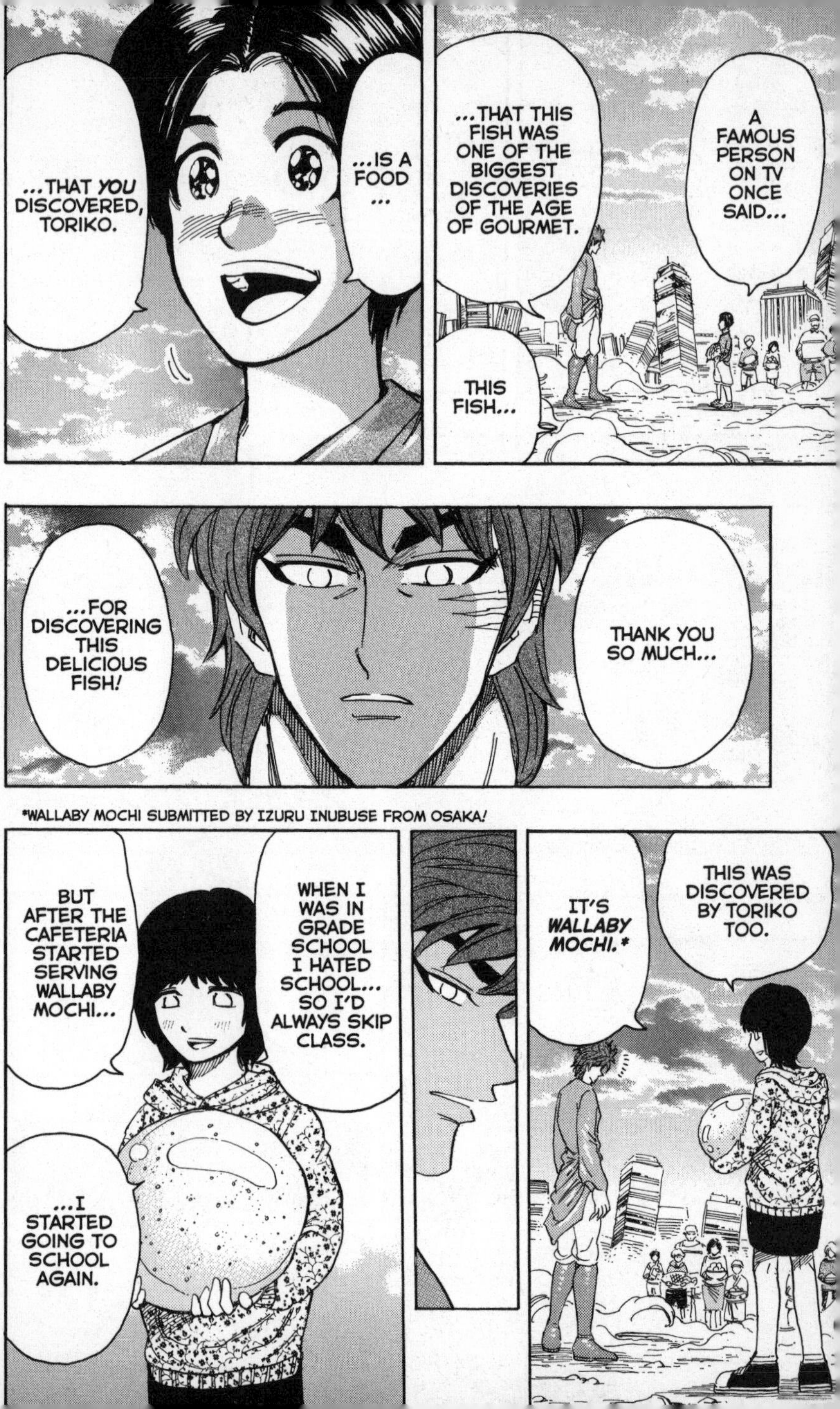
A FAMOUS PERSON ON TV ONCE SAID...
...THAT THIS FISH WAS ONE OF THE BIGGEST DISCOVERIES OF THE AGE OF GOURMET.
THIS FISH...
...IS A FOOD ...
...THAT *YOU* DISCOVERED, TORIKO.
THANK YOU SO MUCH...
...FOR DISCOVERING THIS DELICIOUS FISH!
THIS WAS DISCOVERED BY TORIKO TOO.
IT'S *WALLABY MOCHI.**
WHEN I WAS IN GRADE SCHOOL I HATED SCHOOL... SO I'D ALWAYS SKIP CLASS.
BUT AFTER THE CAFETERIA STARTED SERVING WALLABY MOCHI...
...I STARTED GOING TO SCHOOL AGAIN.

*WALLABY MOCHI SUBMITTED BY IZURU INUBUSE FROM OSAKA!

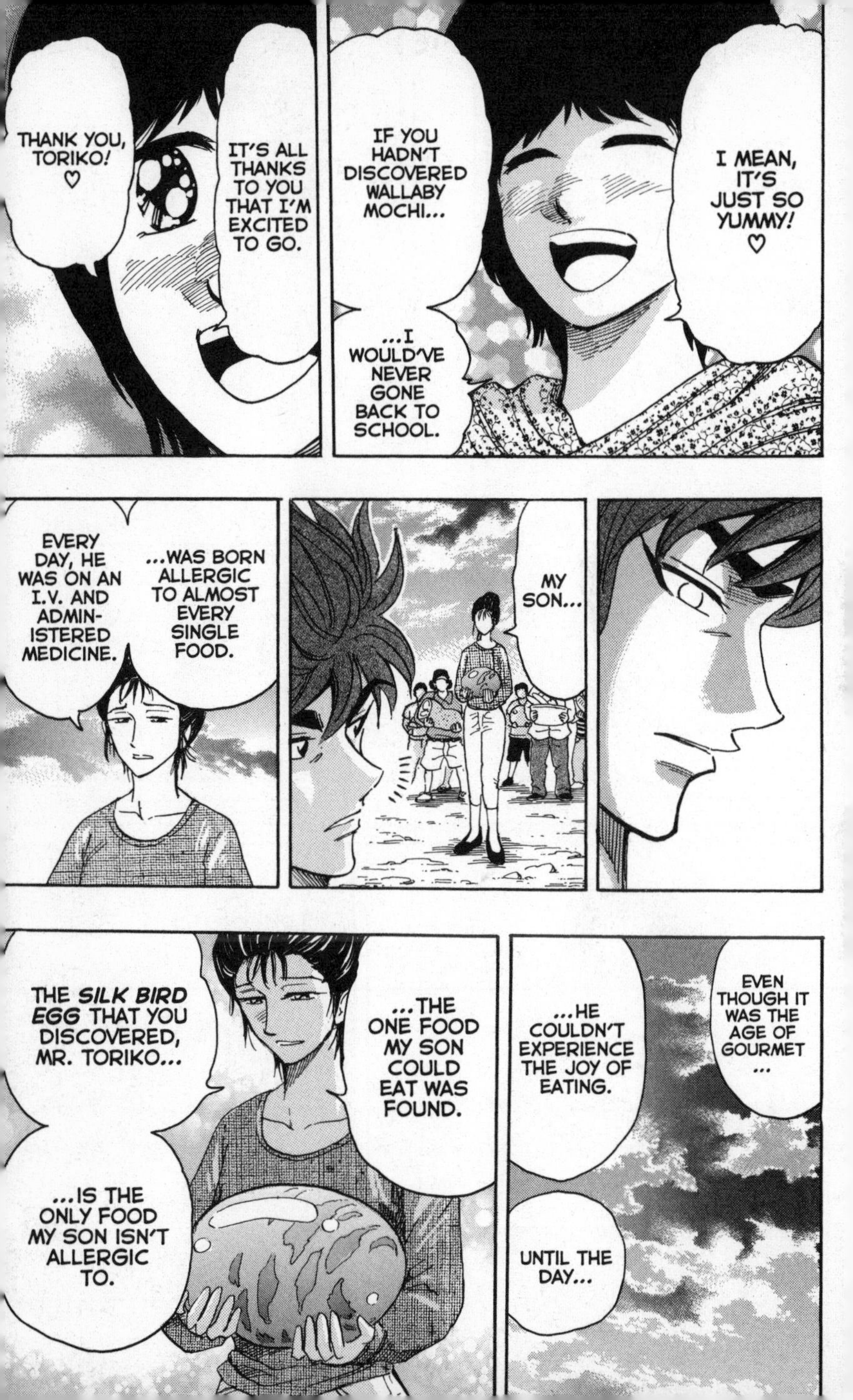
I MEAN, IT'S JUST SO YUMMY! ♡
IF YOU HADN'T DISCOVERED WALLABY MOCHI...
...I WOULD'VE NEVER GONE BACK TO SCHOOL.
IT'S ALL THANKS TO YOU THAT I'M EXCITED TO GO.
THANK YOU, TORIKO! ♡
MY SON...
...WAS BORN ALLERGIC TO ALMOST EVERY SINGLE FOOD.
EVERY DAY, HE WAS ON AN I.V. AND ADMIN-ISTERED MEDICINE.
EVEN THOUGH IT WAS THE AGE OF GOURMET...
...HE COULDN'T EXPERIENCE THE JOY OF EATING.
UNTIL THE DAY...
...THE ONE FOOD MY SON COULD EAT WAS FOUND.
THE *SILK BIRD EGG* THAT YOU DISCOVERED, MR. TORIKO...
...IS THE ONLY FOOD MY SON ISN'T ALLERGIC TO.

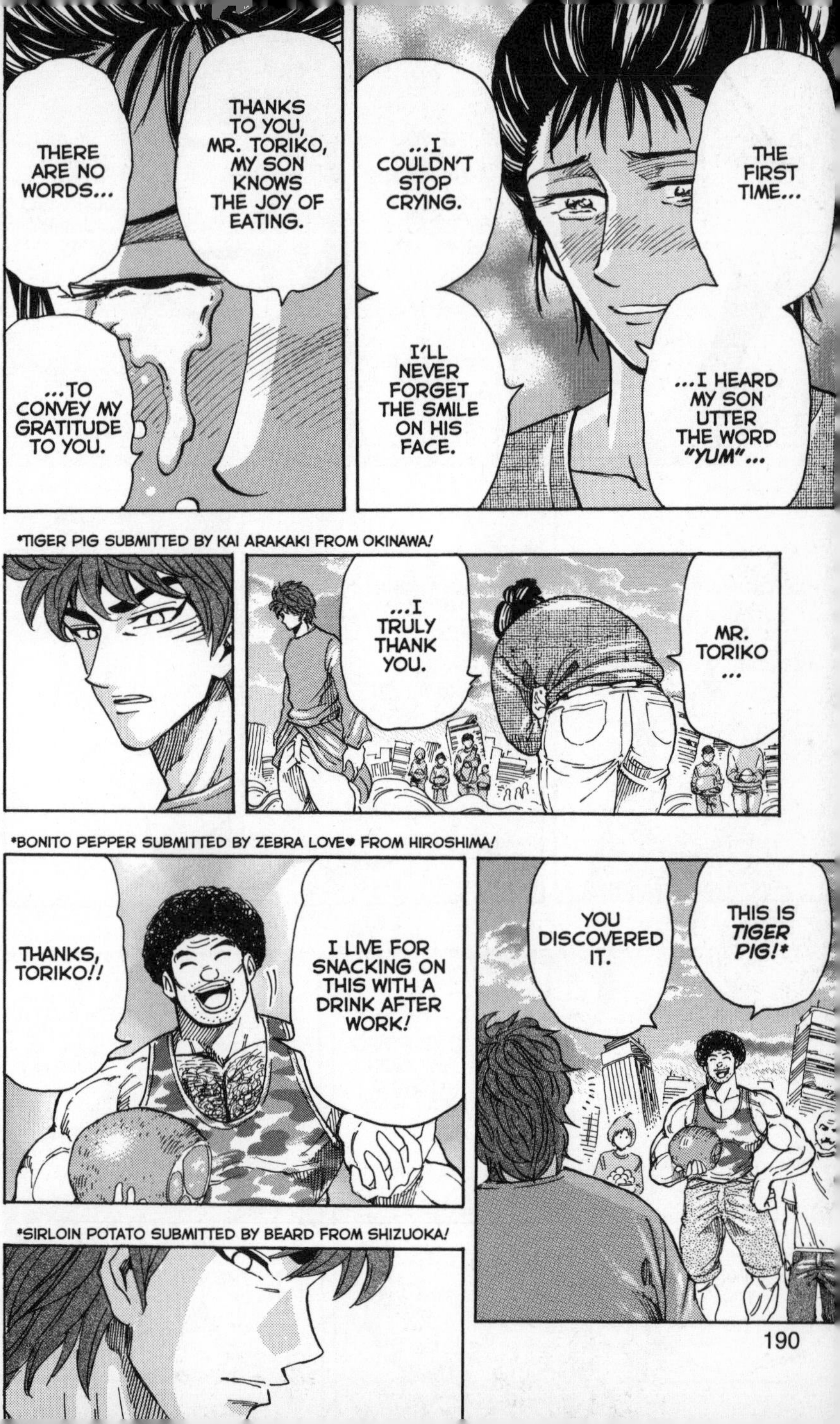
THE FIRST TIME...
...I HEARD MY SON UTTER THE WORD *"YUM"*...
...I COULDN'T STOP CRYING.
I'LL NEVER FORGET THE SMILE ON HIS FACE.
THANKS TO YOU, MR. TORIKO, MY SON KNOWS THE JOY OF EATING.
THERE ARE NO WORDS...
...TO CONVEY MY GRATITUDE TO YOU.
*TIGER PIG SUBMITTED BY KAI ARAKAKI FROM OKINAWA!
MR. TORIKO...
...I TRULY THANK YOU.
*BONITO PEPPER SUBMITTED BY ZEBRA LOVE♥ FROM HIROSHIMA!
THIS IS *TIGER PIG!**
YOU DISCOVERED IT.
I LIVE FOR SNACKING ON THIS WITH A DRINK AFTER WORK!
THANKS, TORIKO!!
*SIRLOIN POTATO SUBMITTED BY BEARD FROM SHIZUOKA!

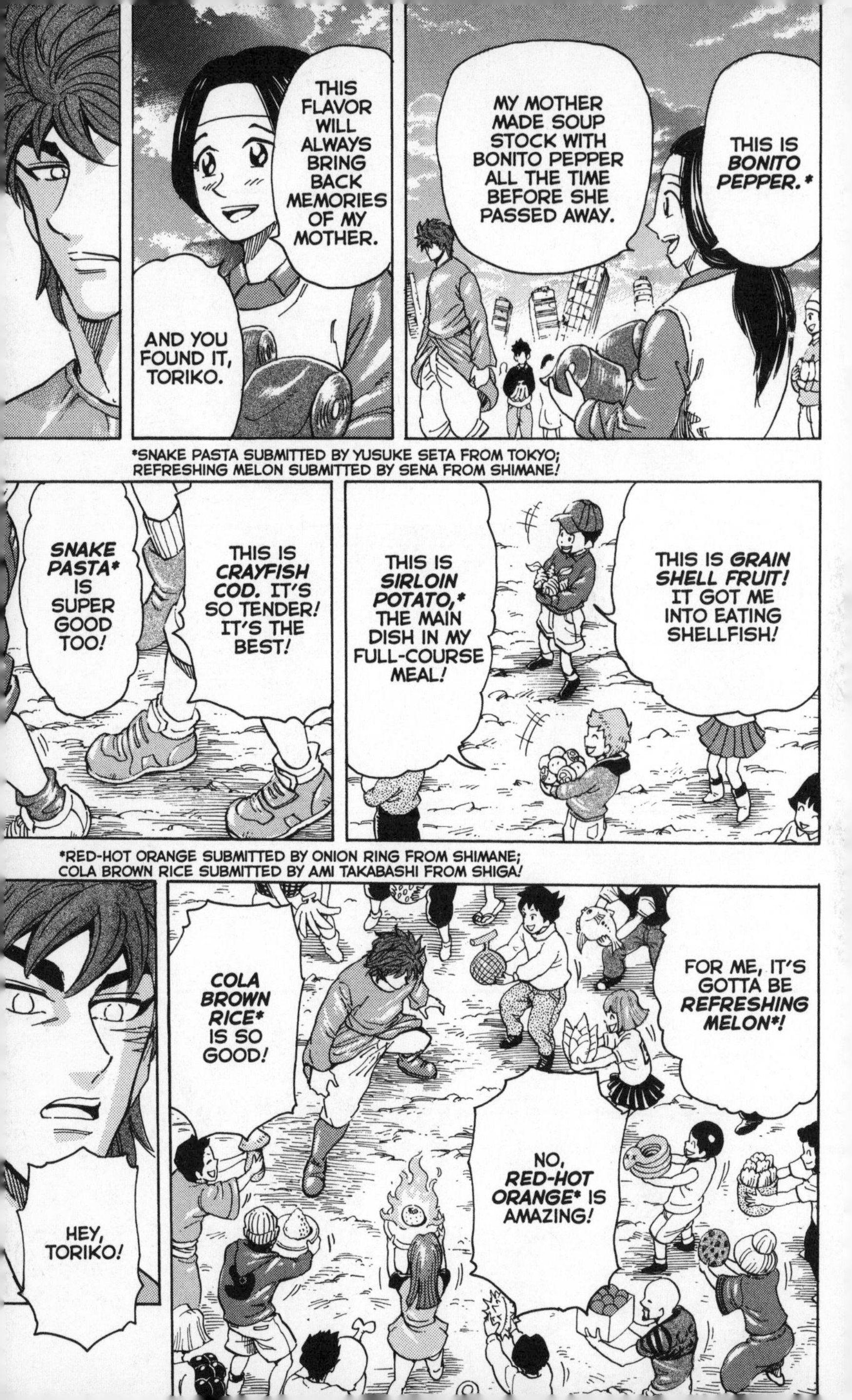
THIS IS BONITO PEPPER.*
MY MOTHER MADE SOUP STOCK WITH BONITO PEPPER ALL THE TIME BEFORE SHE PASSED AWAY.
THIS FLAVOR WILL ALWAYS BRING BACK MEMORIES OF MY MOTHER.
AND YOU FOUND IT, TORIKO.
*SNAKE PASTA SUBMITTED BY YUSUKE SETA FROM TOKYO; REFRESHING MELON SUBMITTED BY SENA FROM SHIMANE!
THIS IS GRAIN SHELL FRUIT! IT GOT ME INTO EATING SHELLFISH!
THIS IS SIRLOIN POTATO,* THE MAIN DISH IN MY FULL-COURSE MEAL!
THIS IS CRAYFISH COD. IT'S SO TENDER! IT'S THE BEST!
SNAKE PASTA* IS SUPER GOOD TOO!
*RED-HOT ORANGE SUBMITTED BY ONION RING FROM SHIMANE; COLA BROWN RICE SUBMITTED BY AMI TAKABASHI FROM SHIGA!
FOR ME, IT'S GOTTA BE REFRESHING MELON*!
NO, RED-HOT ORANGE* IS AMAZING!
COLA BROWN RICE* IS SO GOOD!
HEY, TORIKO!

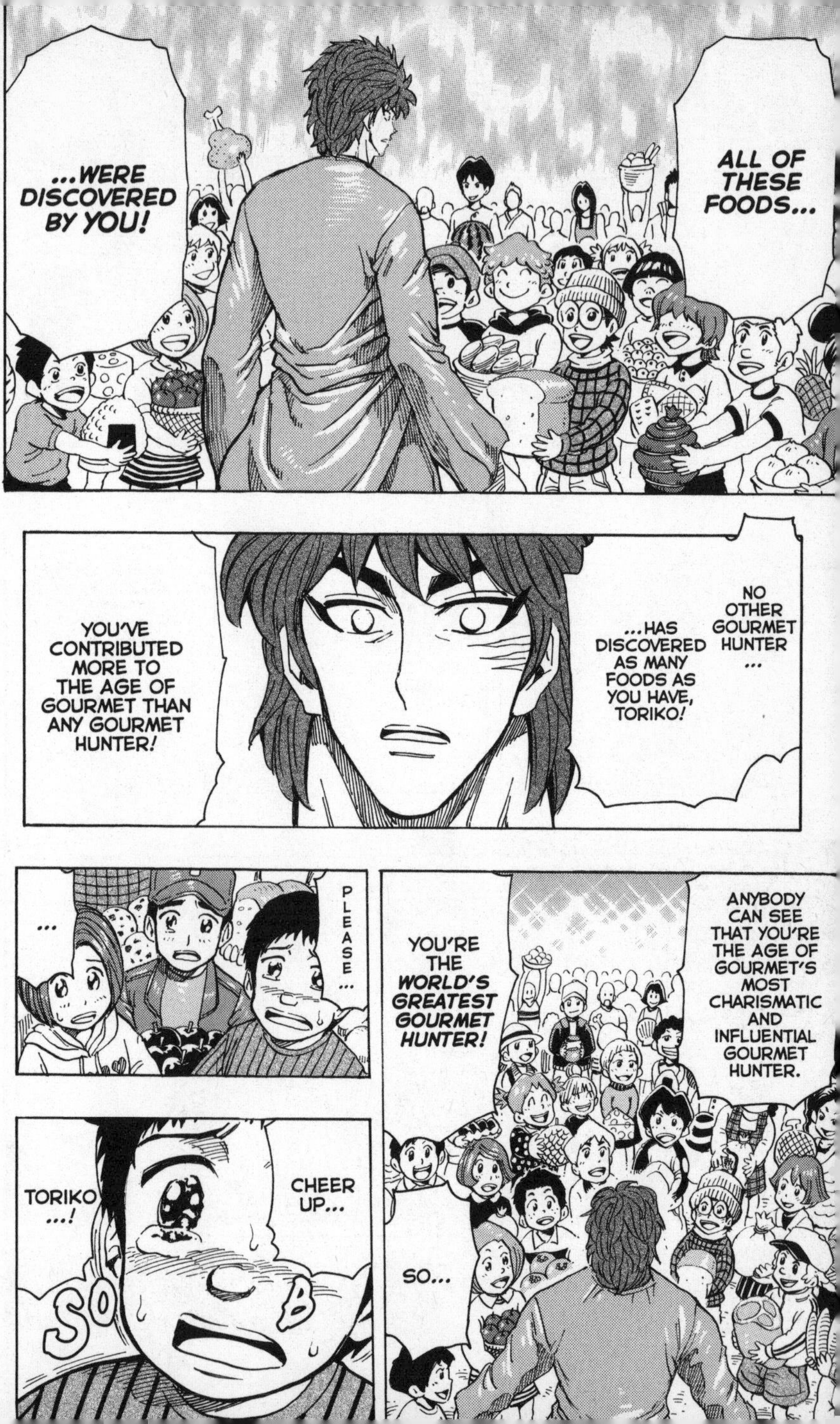
ALL OF THESE FOODS...
...WERE DISCOVERED BY YOU!
NO OTHER GOURMET HUNTER ...
...HAS DISCOVERED AS MANY FOODS AS YOU HAVE, TORIKO!
YOU'VE CONTRIBUTED MORE TO THE AGE OF GOURMET THAN ANY GOURMET HUNTER!
ANYBODY CAN SEE THAT YOU'RE THE AGE OF GOURMET'S MOST CHARISMATIC AND INFLUENTIAL GOURMET HUNTER.
YOU'RE THE *WORLD'S GREATEST GOURMET HUNTER!*
SO...
PLEASE...
...
CHEER UP...
TORIKO ...!
SOB

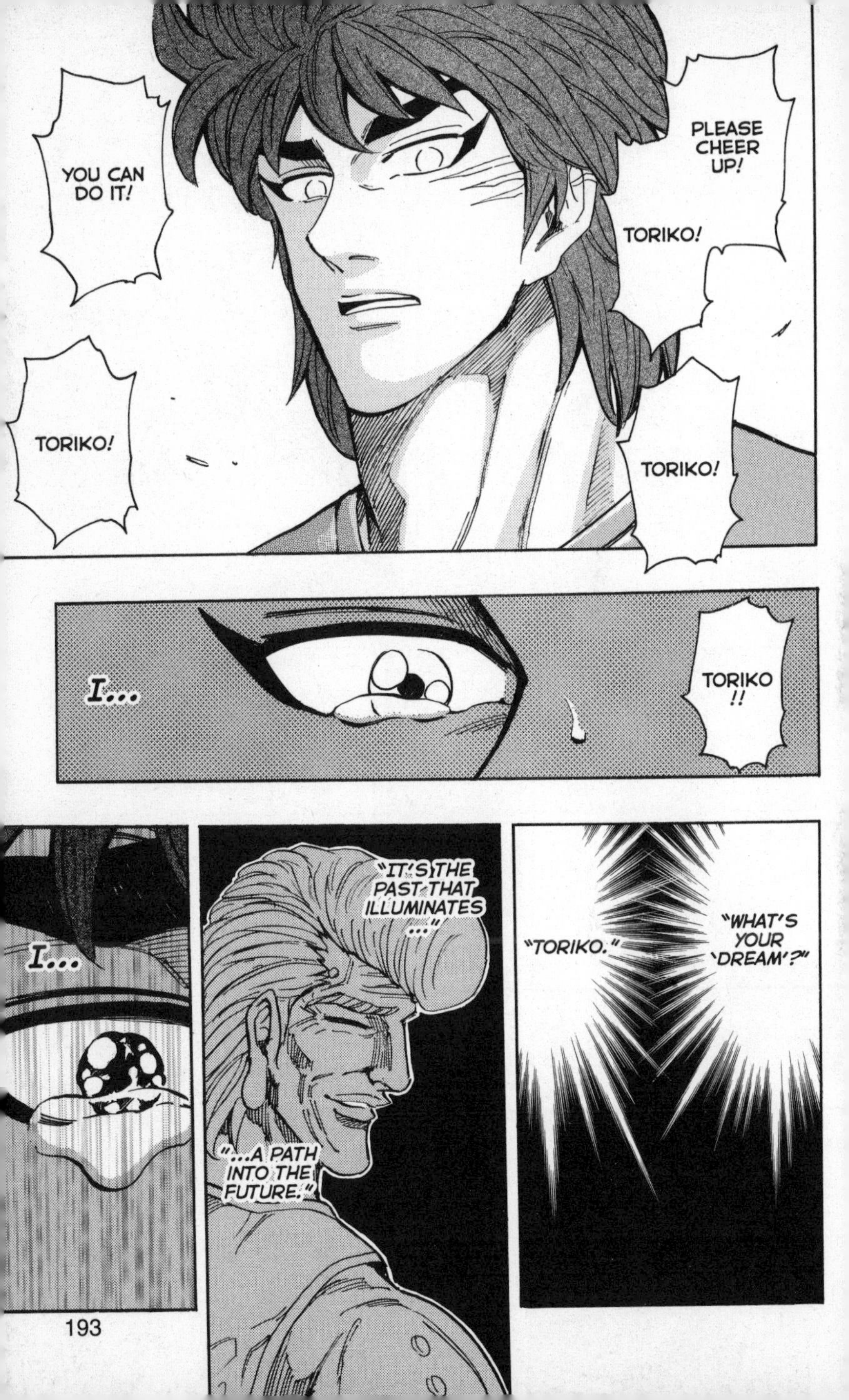
PLEASE CHEER UP!
YOU CAN DO IT!
TORIKO!
TORIKO!
TORIKO!
TORIKO!!
I...
"WHAT'S YOUR 'DREAM'?"
"TORIKO."
"IT'S THE PAST THAT ILLUMINATES..."
"...A PATH INTO THE FUTURE."
I...

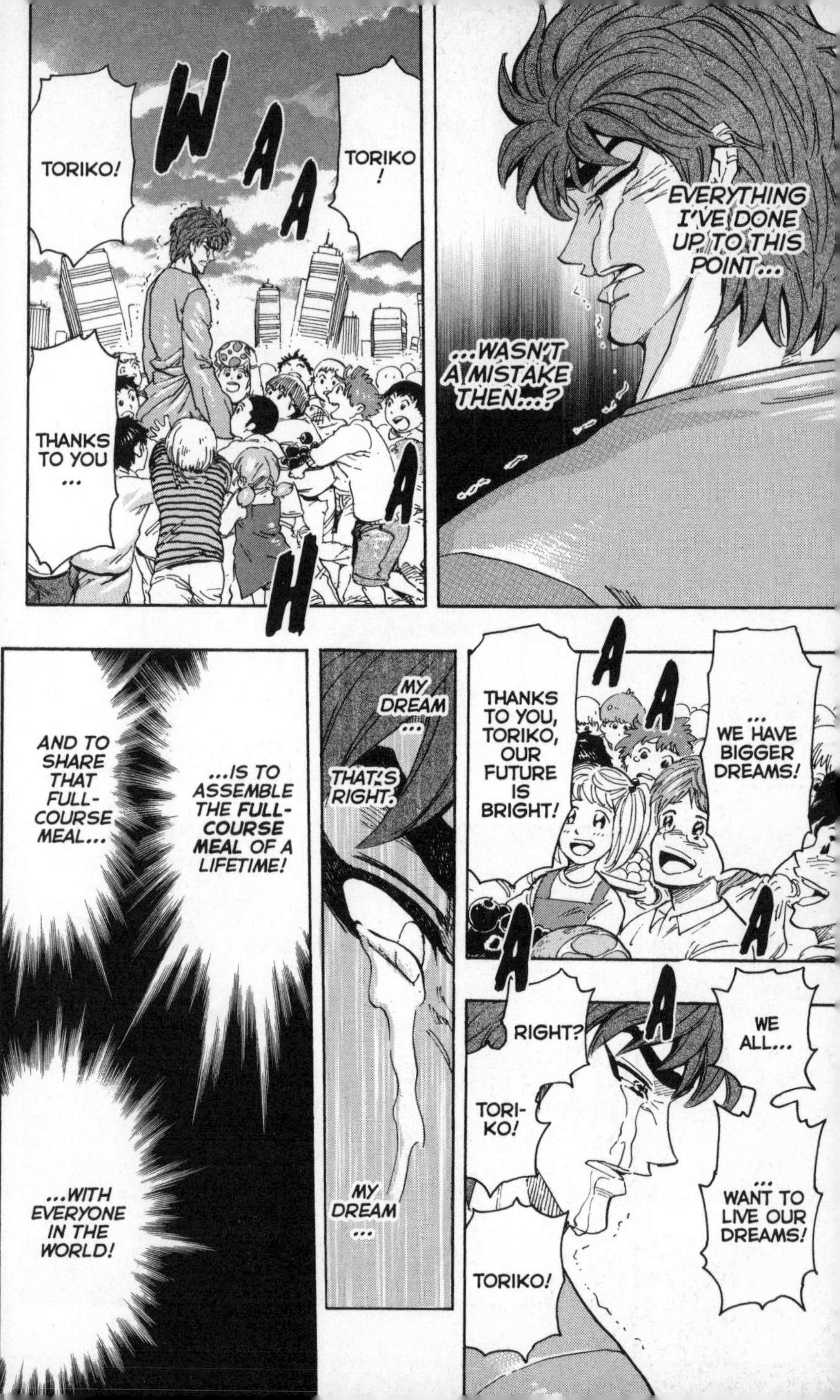
EVERYTHING I'VE DONE UP TO THIS POINT...
...WASN'T A MISTAKE THEN...?
TORIKO!
WAAAAAH
TORIKO!
THANKS TO YOU...
...WE HAVE BIGGER DREAMS!
THANKS TO YOU, TORIKO, OUR FUTURE IS BRIGHT!
AAAAAA
WE ALL...
RIGHT?
TORI-KO!
...WANT TO LIVE OUR DREAMS!
TORIKO!
MY DREAM...
THAT'S RIGHT.
MY DREAM...
...IS TO ASSEMBLE THE FULL-COURSE MEAL OF A LIFETIME!
AND TO SHARE THAT FULL-COURSE MEAL...
...WITH EVERYONE IN THE WORLD!

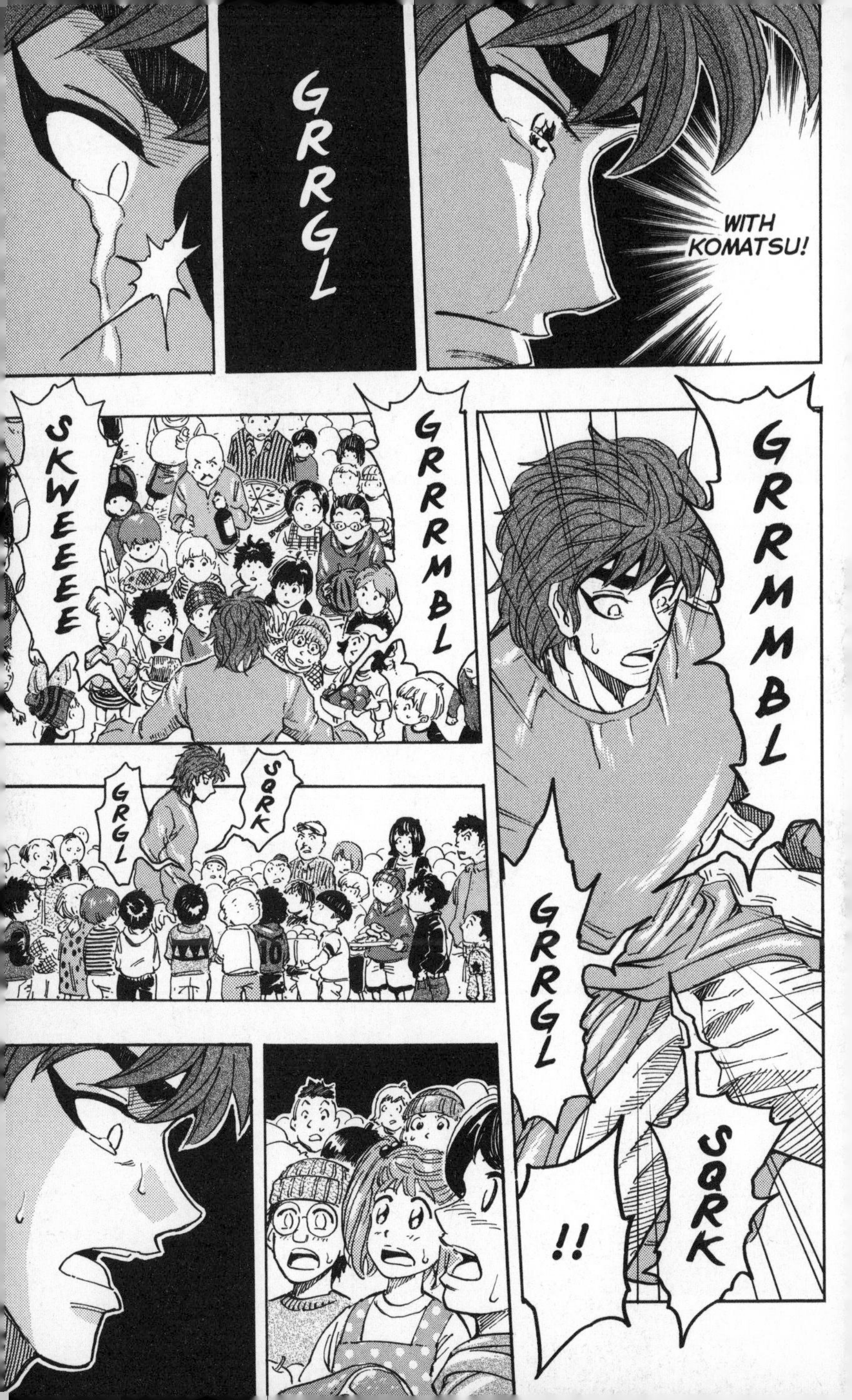
WITH KOMATSU!
GRRRGL
GRRRMMBL
GRRRGL
SQRK
!!
GRRRMMBL
SKWEEEEE
SQRK
GRGL

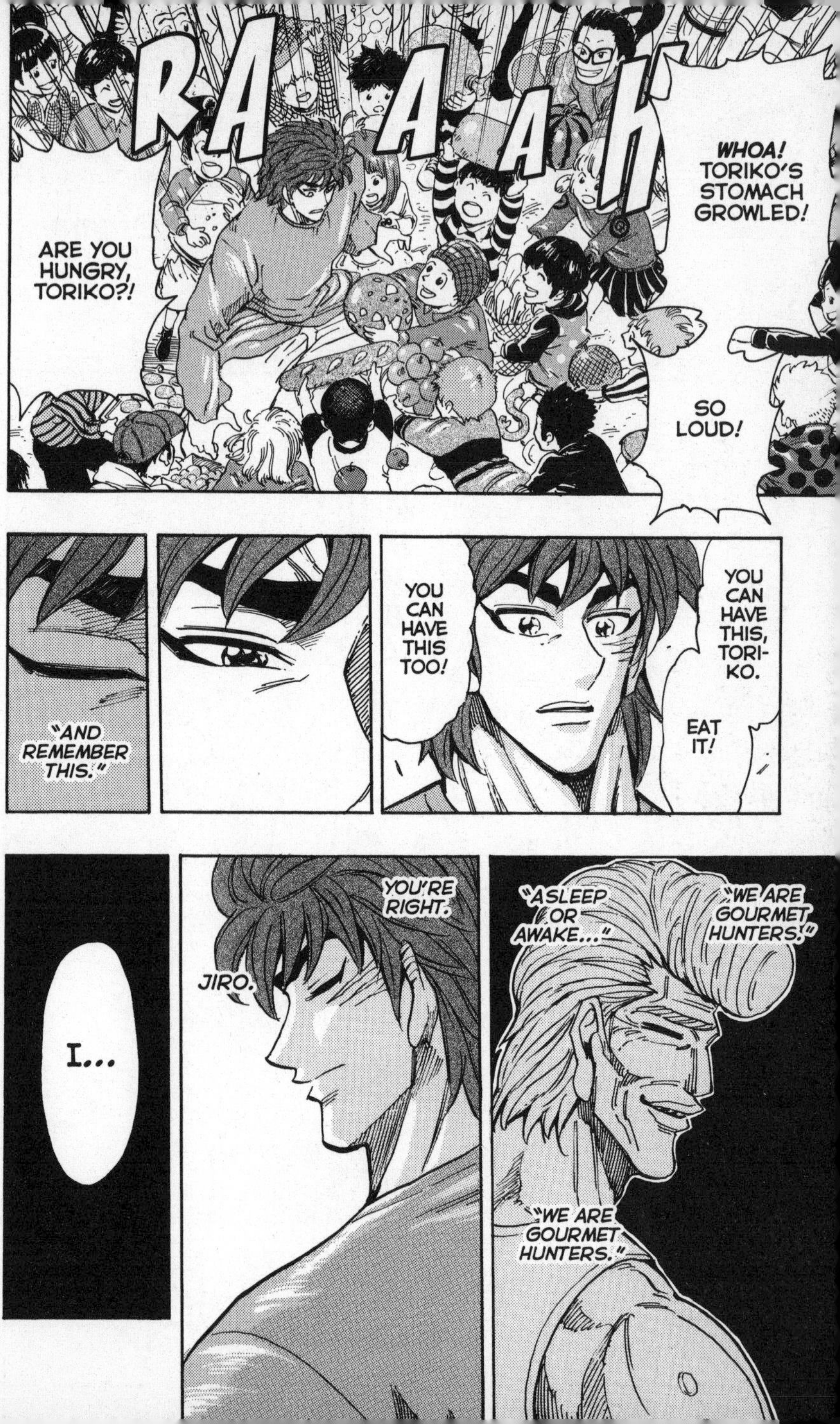
RAAAH
WHOA! TORIKO'S STOMACH GROWLED!
ARE YOU HUNGRY, TORIKO?!
SO LOUD!
YOU CAN HAVE THIS, TORI-KO.
YOU CAN HAVE THIS TOO!
EAT IT!
"AND REMEMBER THIS."
"WE ARE GOURMET HUNTERS!"
"ASLEEP OR AWAKE..."
"WE ARE GOURMET HUNTERS."
YOU'RE RIGHT.
JIRO.
I...

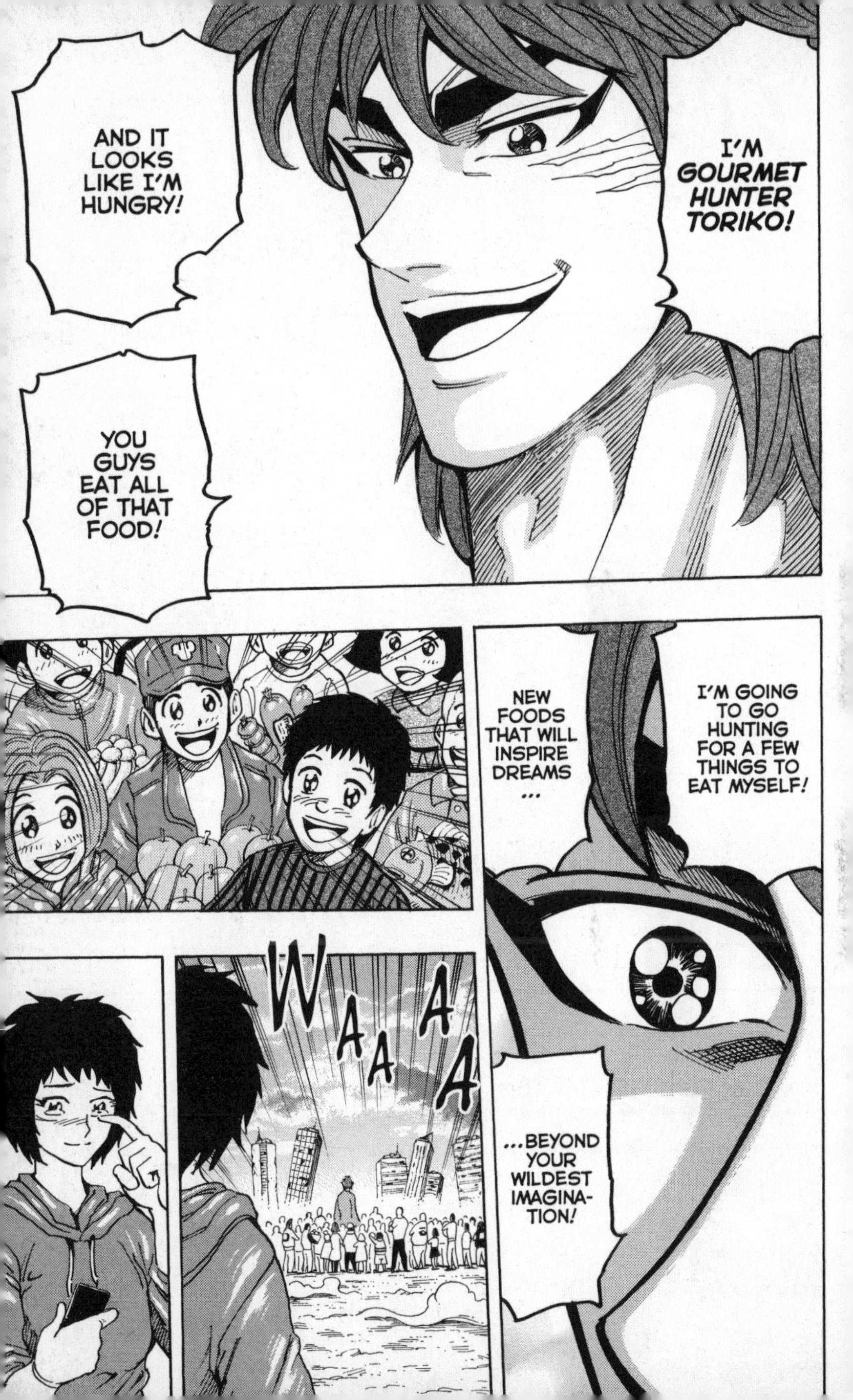
I'M GOURMET HUNTER TORIKO!
AND IT LOOKS LIKE I'M HUNGRY!
YOU GUYS EAT ALL OF THAT FOOD!
I'M GOING TO GO HUNTING FOR A FEW THINGS TO EAT MYSELF!
NEW FOODS THAT WILL INSPIRE DREAMS ...
...BEYOND YOUR WILDEST IMAGINATION!
WAAAA

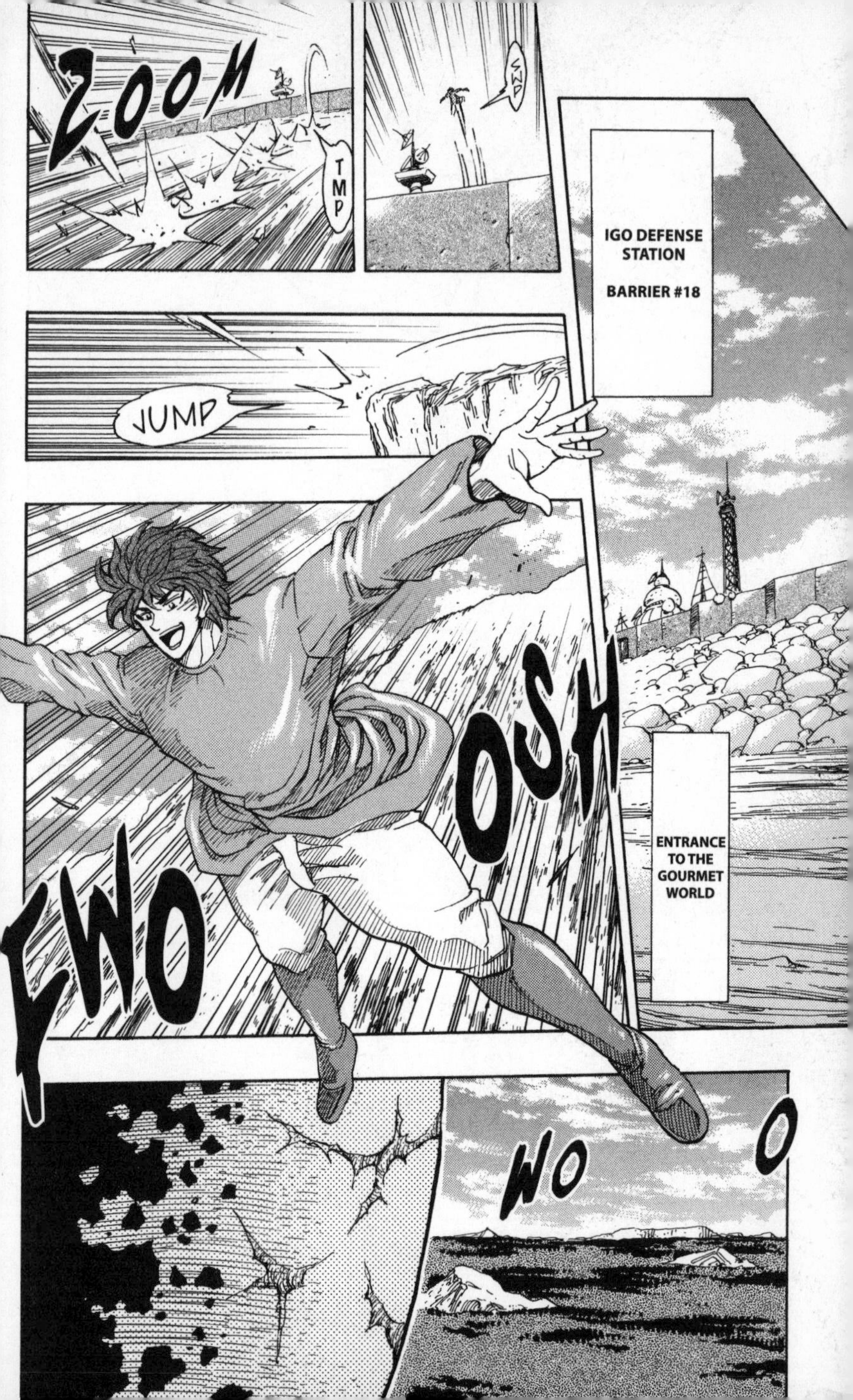
IGO DEFENSE STATION
BARRIER #18
ENTRANCE TO THE GOURMET WORLD
SWP
ZOOM
TMP
JUMP
FWOOSH
WOOO

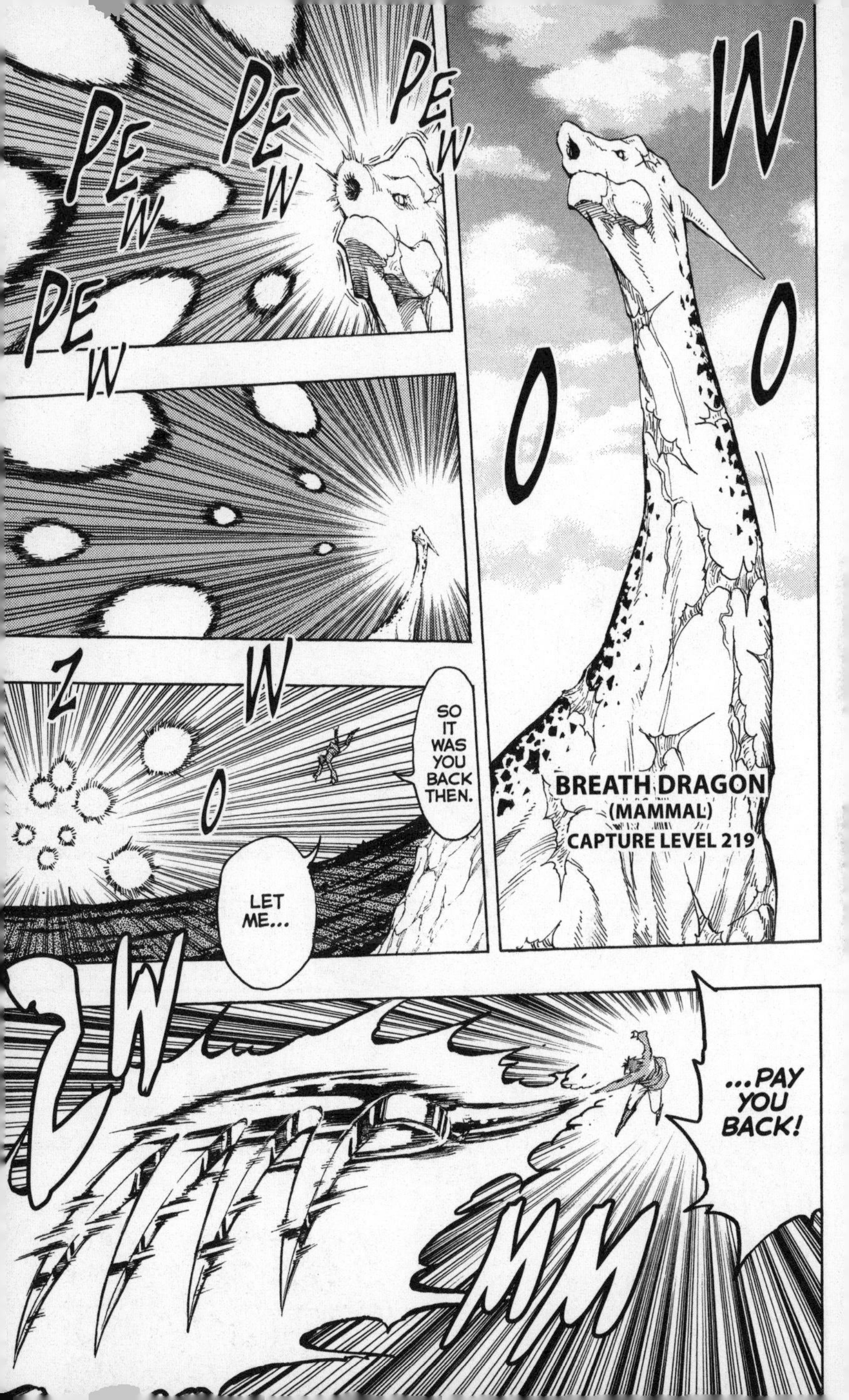
WOO
BREATH DRAGON
(MAMMAL)
CAPTURE LEVEL 219
PEW PEW PEW PEW
ZWO
SO IT WAS YOU BACK THEN.
LET ME...
ZW
...PAY YOU BACK!
MM

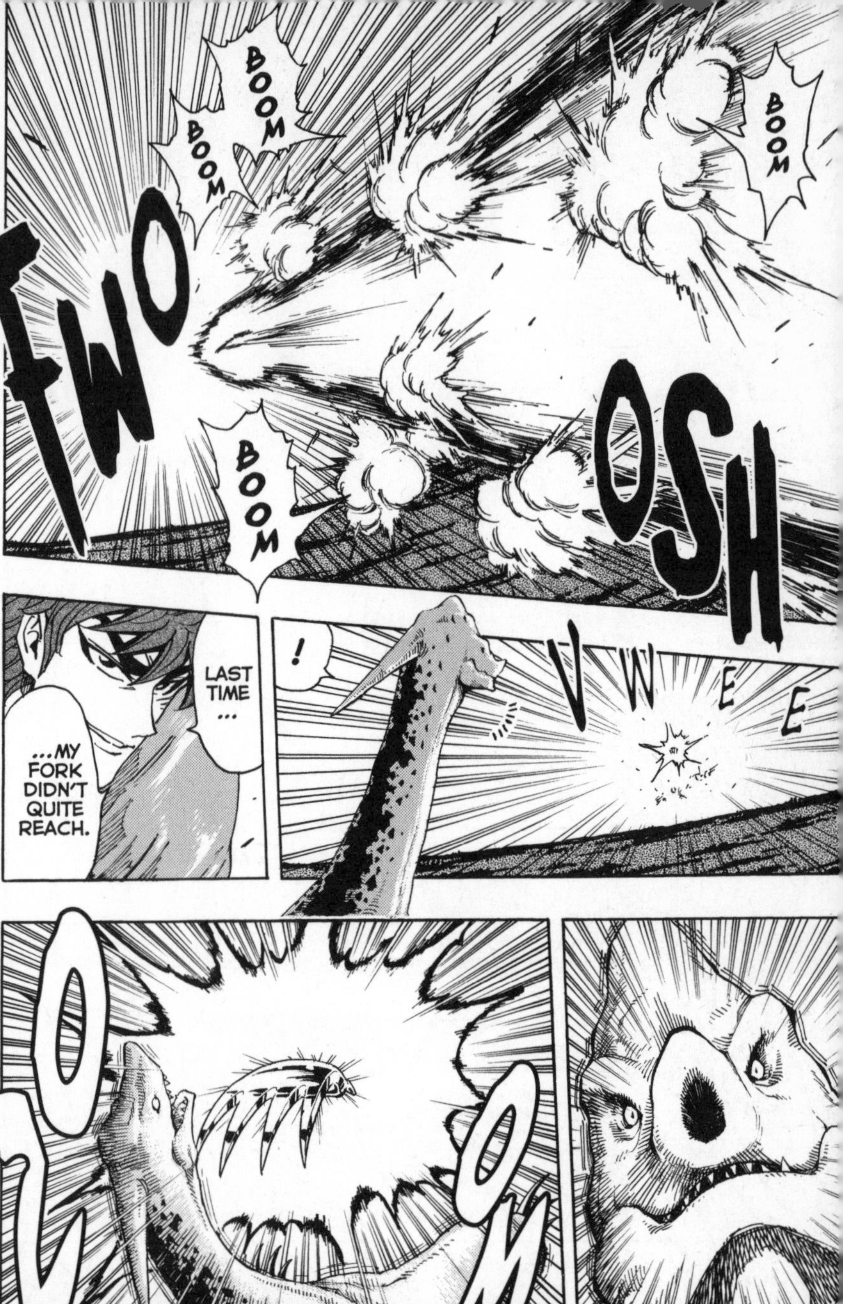
BOOM
BOOM
BOOM
FWOOSH
BOOM
!
VWEE
LAST TIME...
...MY FORK DIDN'T QUITE REACH.
ZOOM

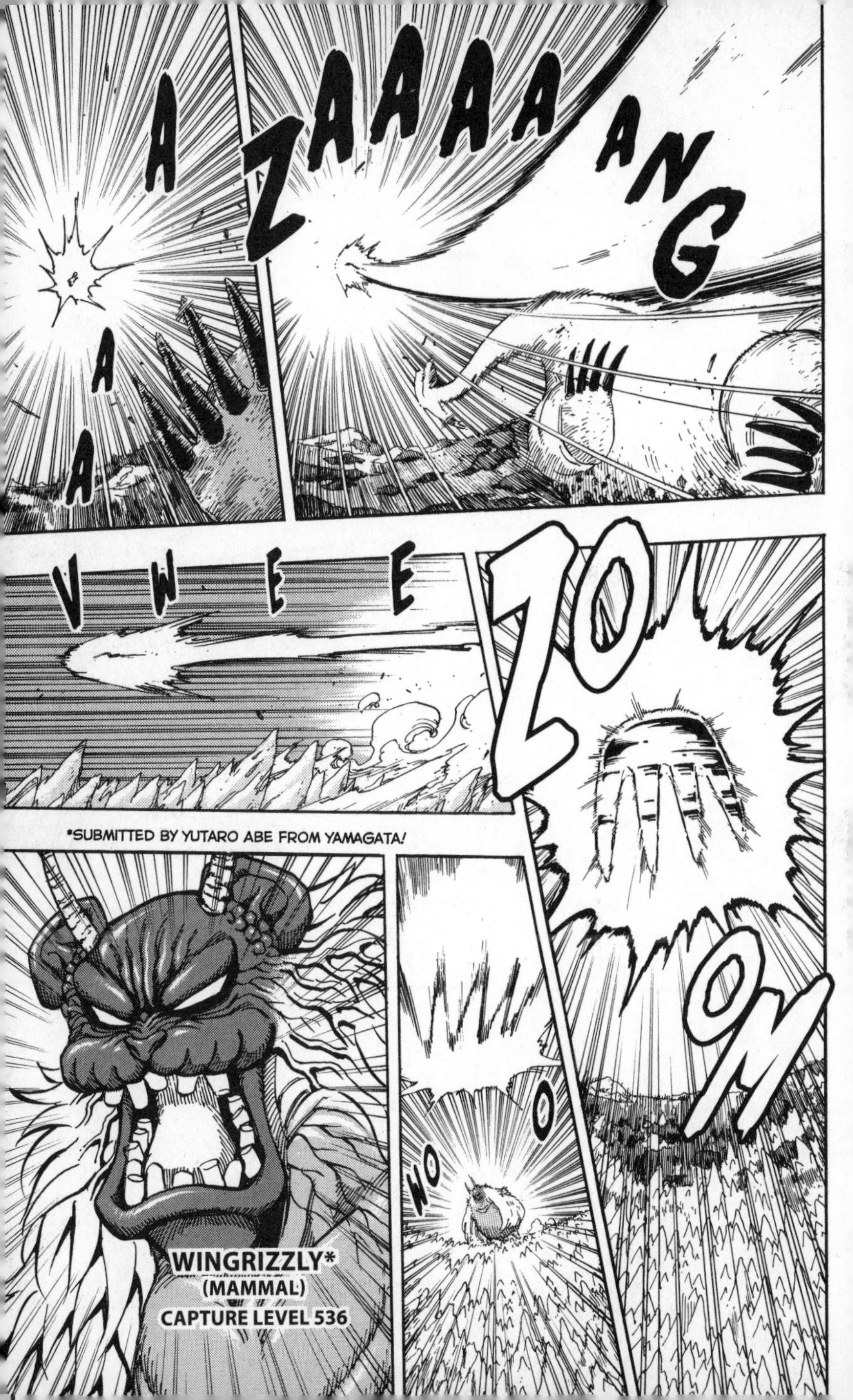
AZAAAAAANG
AA
ZOOM
VWEE
*SUBMITTED BY YUTARO ABE FROM YAMAGATA!
WINGRIZZLY*
(MAMMAL)
CAPTURE LEVEL 536

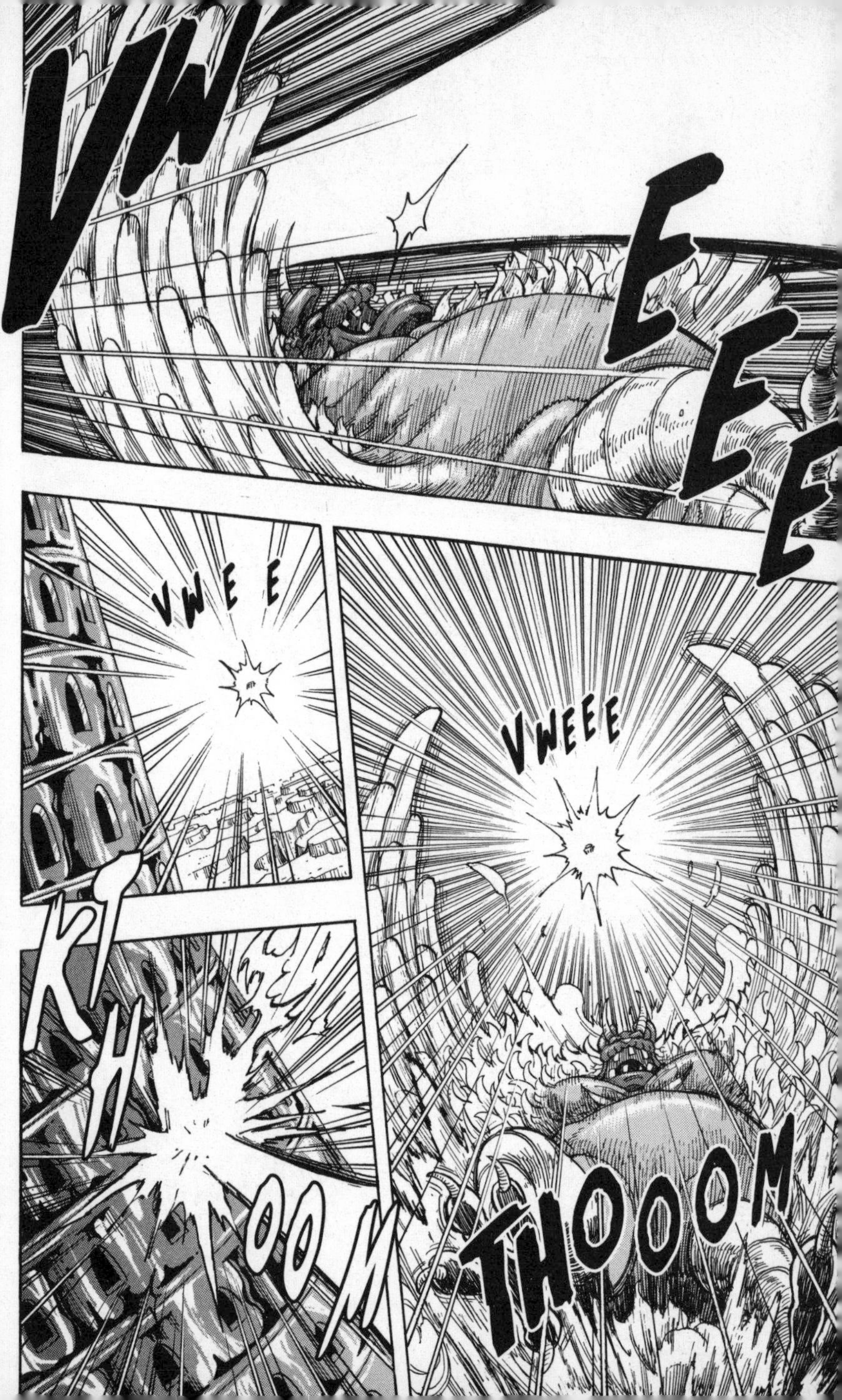
VWEEEE
VWEEE
VWEEE
THOOOM
KHOOM

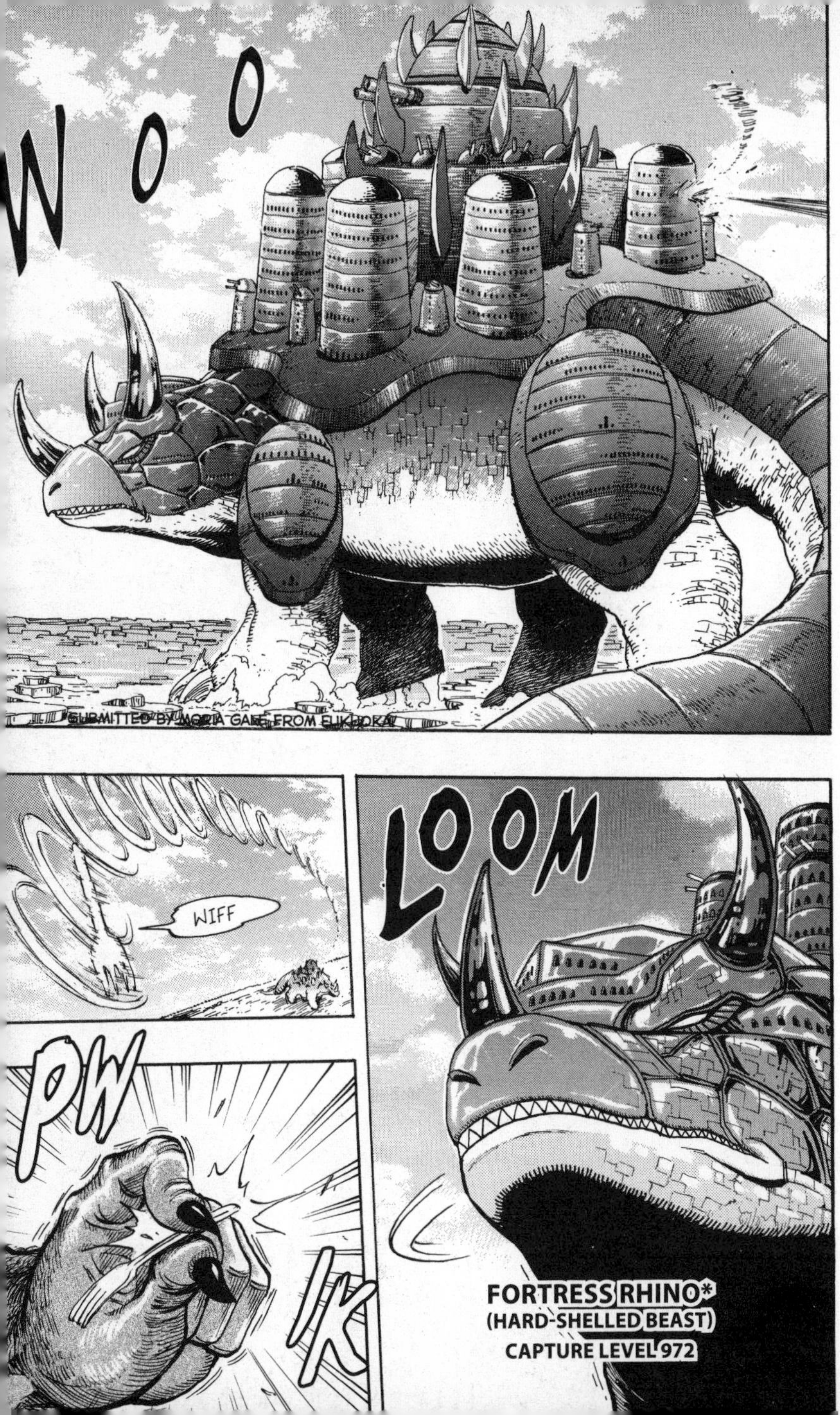
WOO
SUBMITTED BY MORIA GAKE FROM FUKUOKA
LOOM
FORTRESS RHINO*
(HARD-SHELLED BEAST)
CAPTURE LEVEL 972
WIFF
PWK

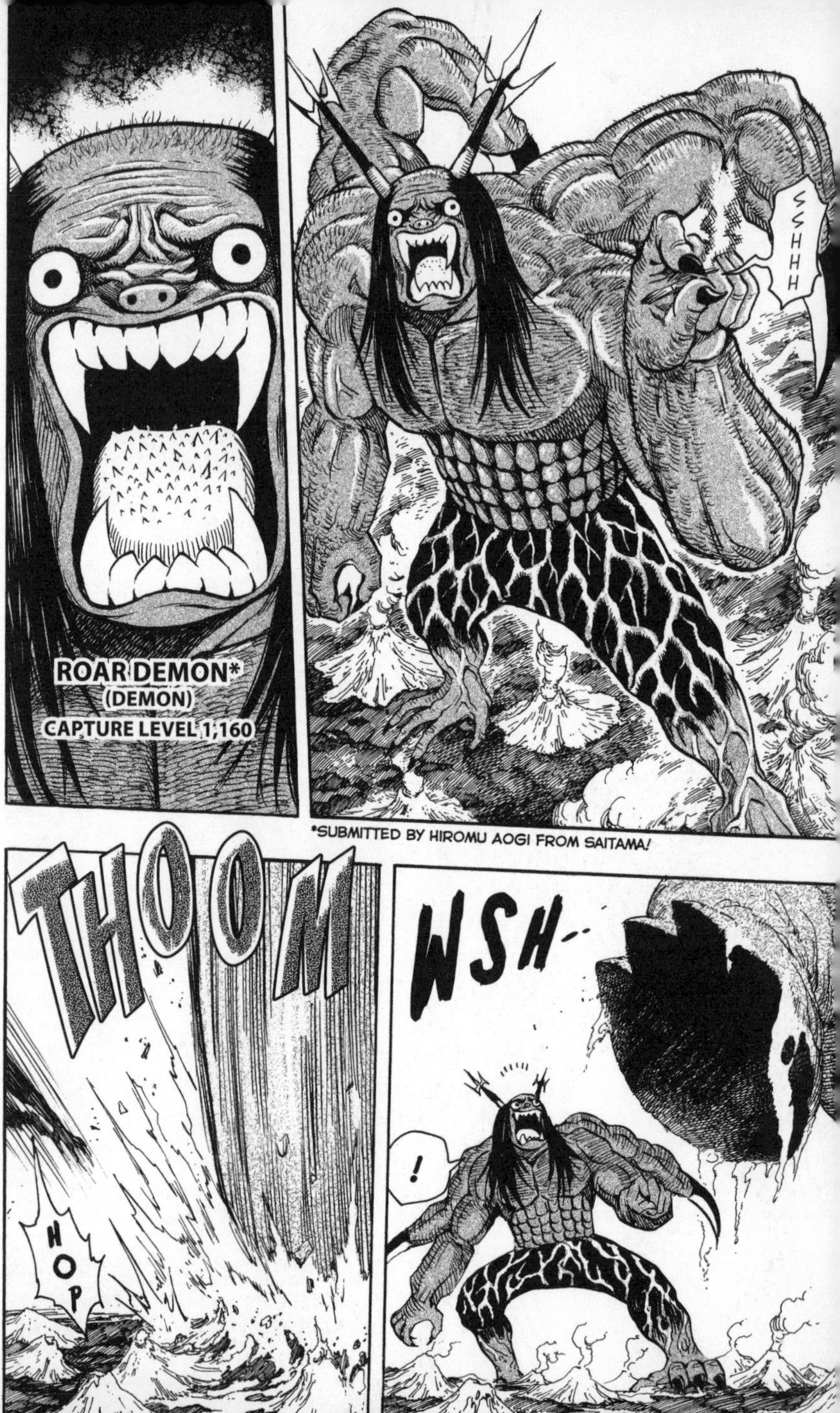
SSHHH
ROAR DEMON*
(DEMON)
CAPTURE LEVEL 1,160
*SUBMITTED BY HIROMU AOGI FROM SAITAMA!
WSH-
!
THOOM
HOP

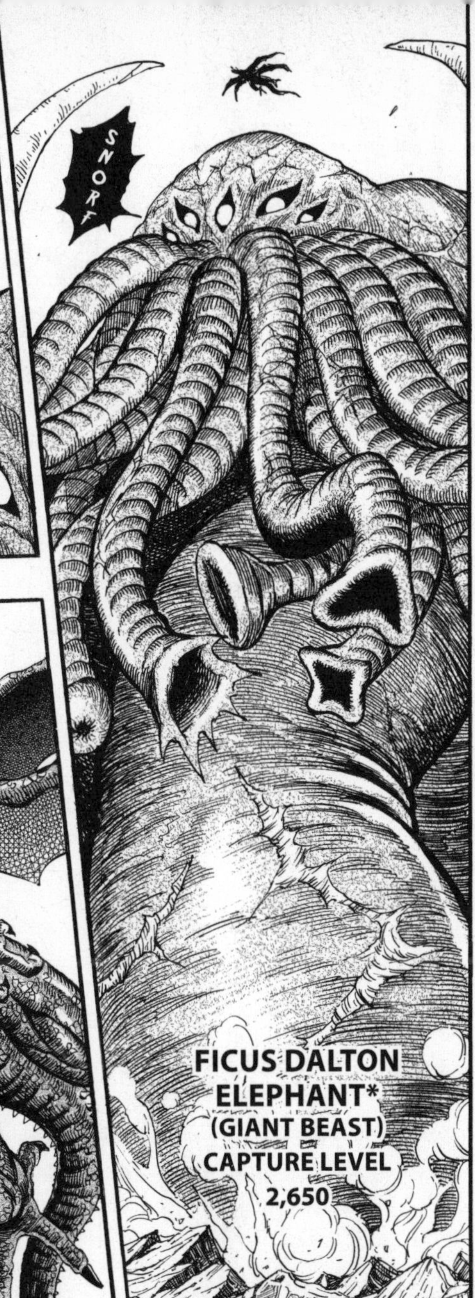
SNORF
FICUS DALTON ELEPHANT* (GIANT BEAST) CAPTURE LEVEL 2,650

*SUBMITTED BY TETSUYA YAMAOKA FROM HYOGA!

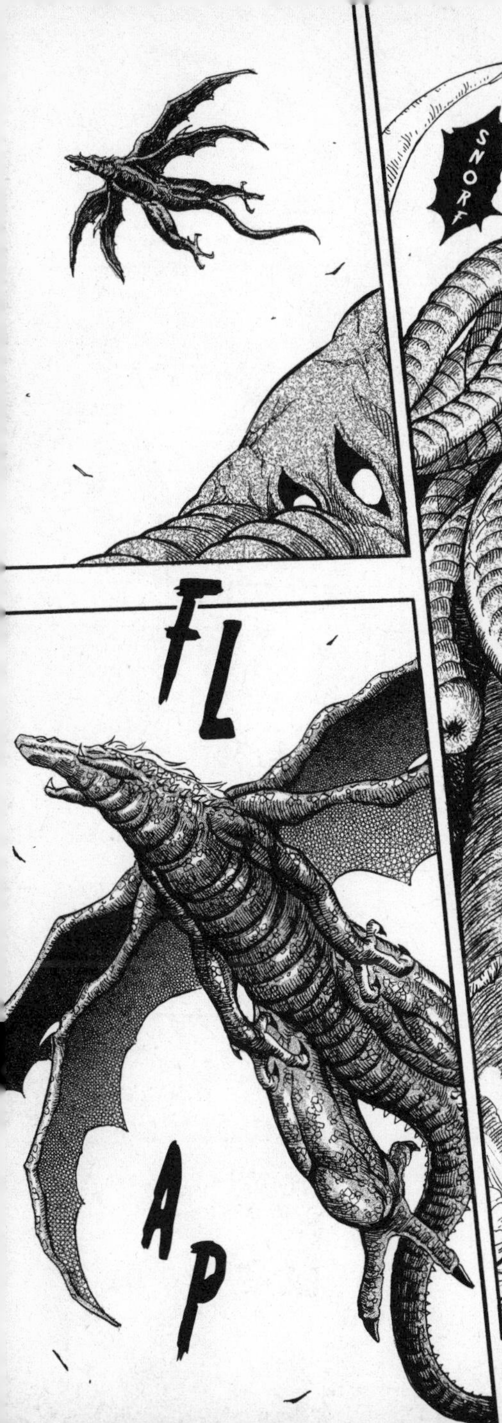
FLAP

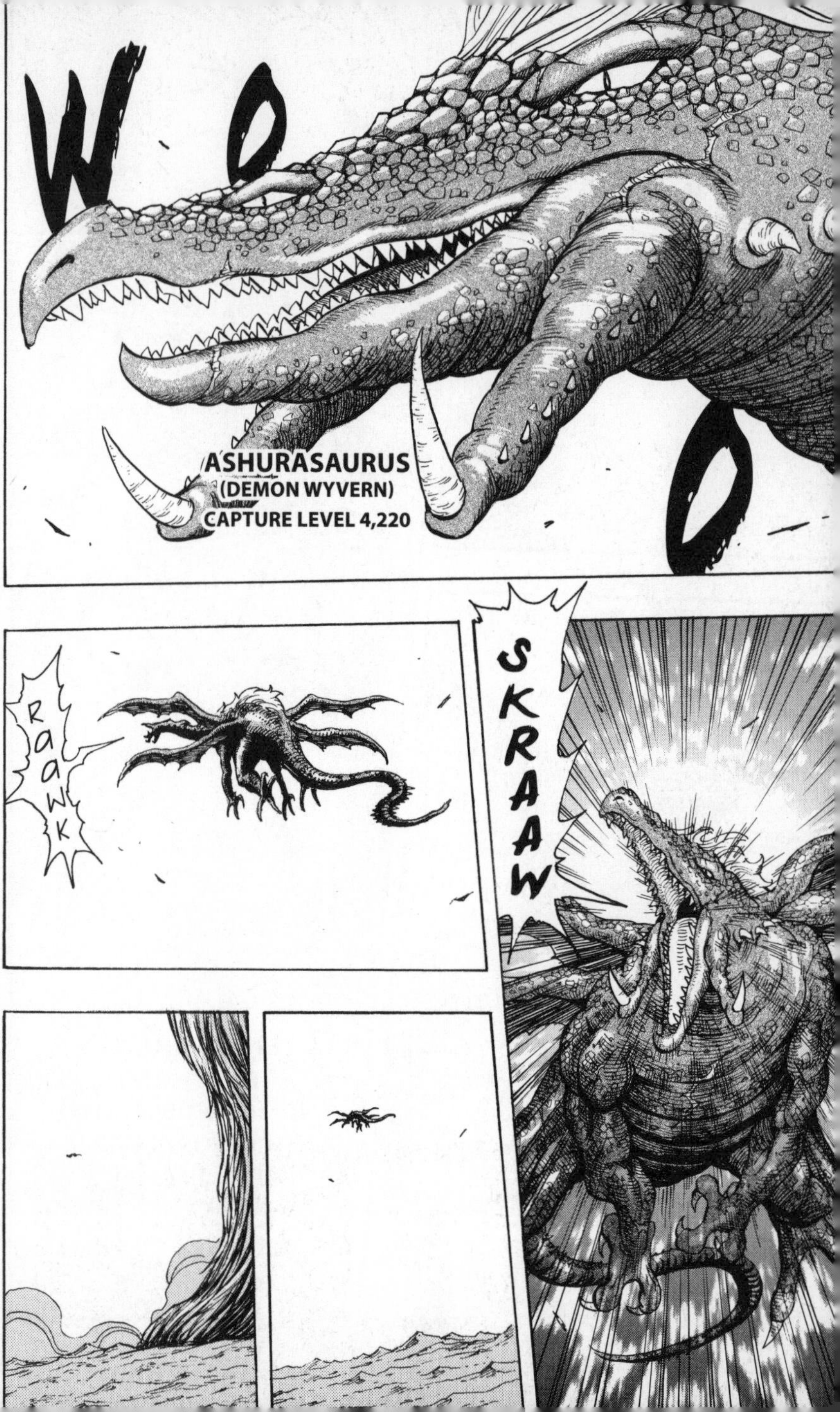
WOO
ASHURASAURUS
(DEMON WYVERN)
CAPTURE LEVEL 4,220
SKRAAW
Raaawk

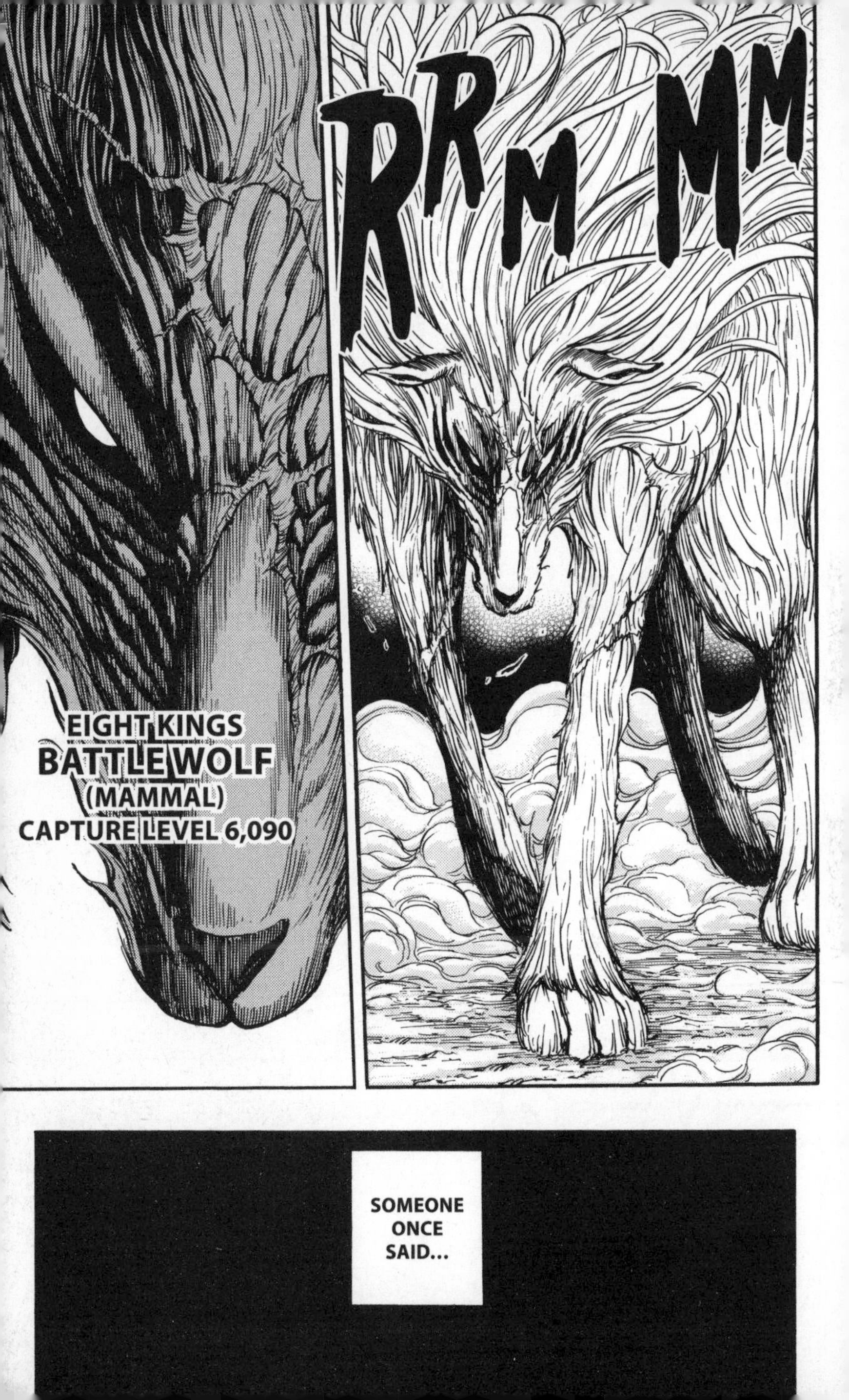
RRMMMM
EIGHT KINGS
BATTLE WOLF
(MAMMAL)
CAPTURE LEVEL 6,090
SOMEONE ONCE SAID...

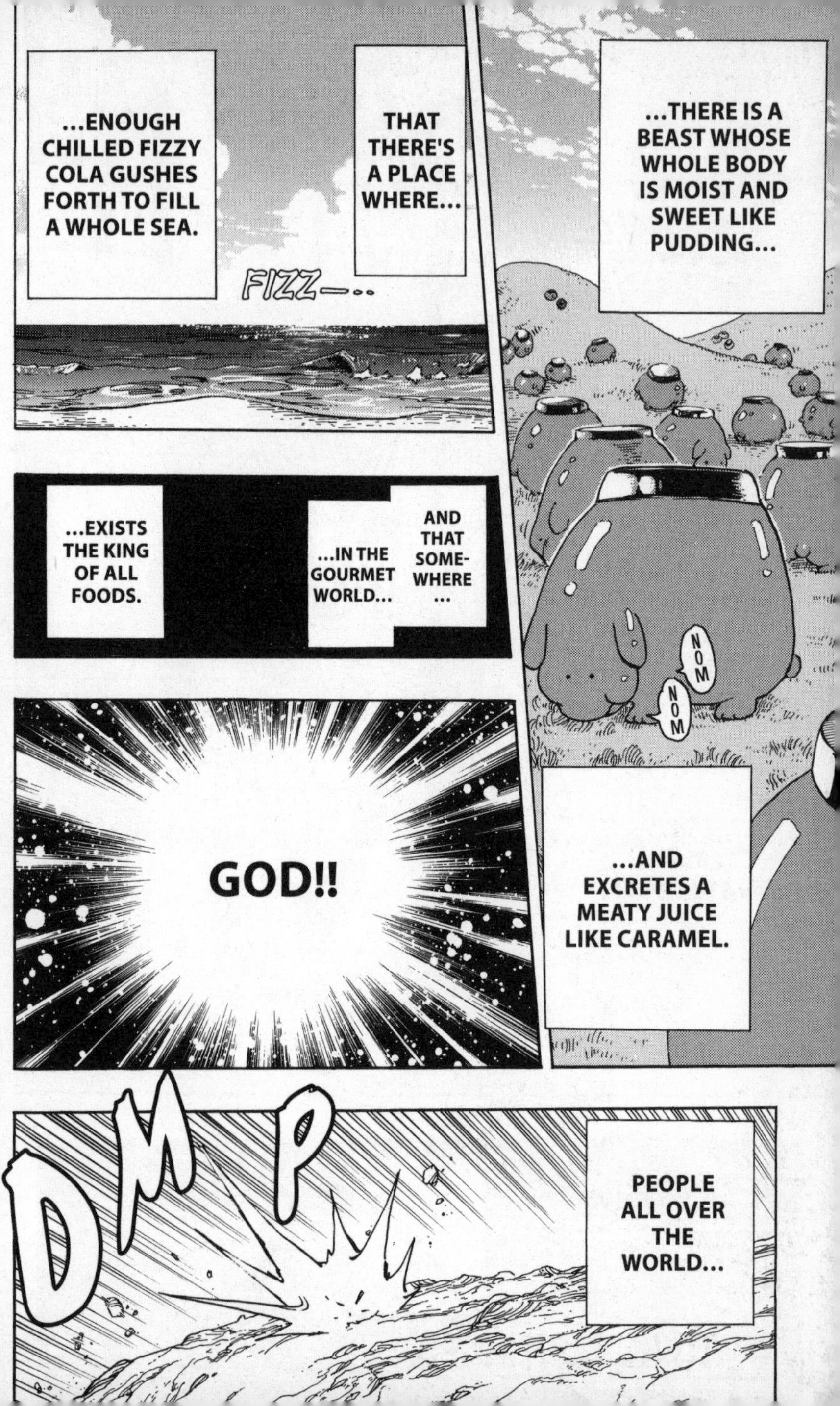

...THERE IS A BEAST WHOSE WHOLE BODY IS MOIST AND SWEET LIKE PUDDING...
NOM
NOM
...AND EXCRETES A MEATY JUICE LIKE CARAMEL.
THAT THERE'S A PLACE WHERE...
...ENOUGH CHILLED FIZZY COLA GUSHES FORTH TO FILL A WHOLE SEA.
FIZZ—..
AND THAT SOME-WHERE ...
...IN THE GOURMET WORLD...
...EXISTS THE KING OF ALL FOODS.
GOD!!
PEOPLE ALL OVER THE WORLD...
DMP

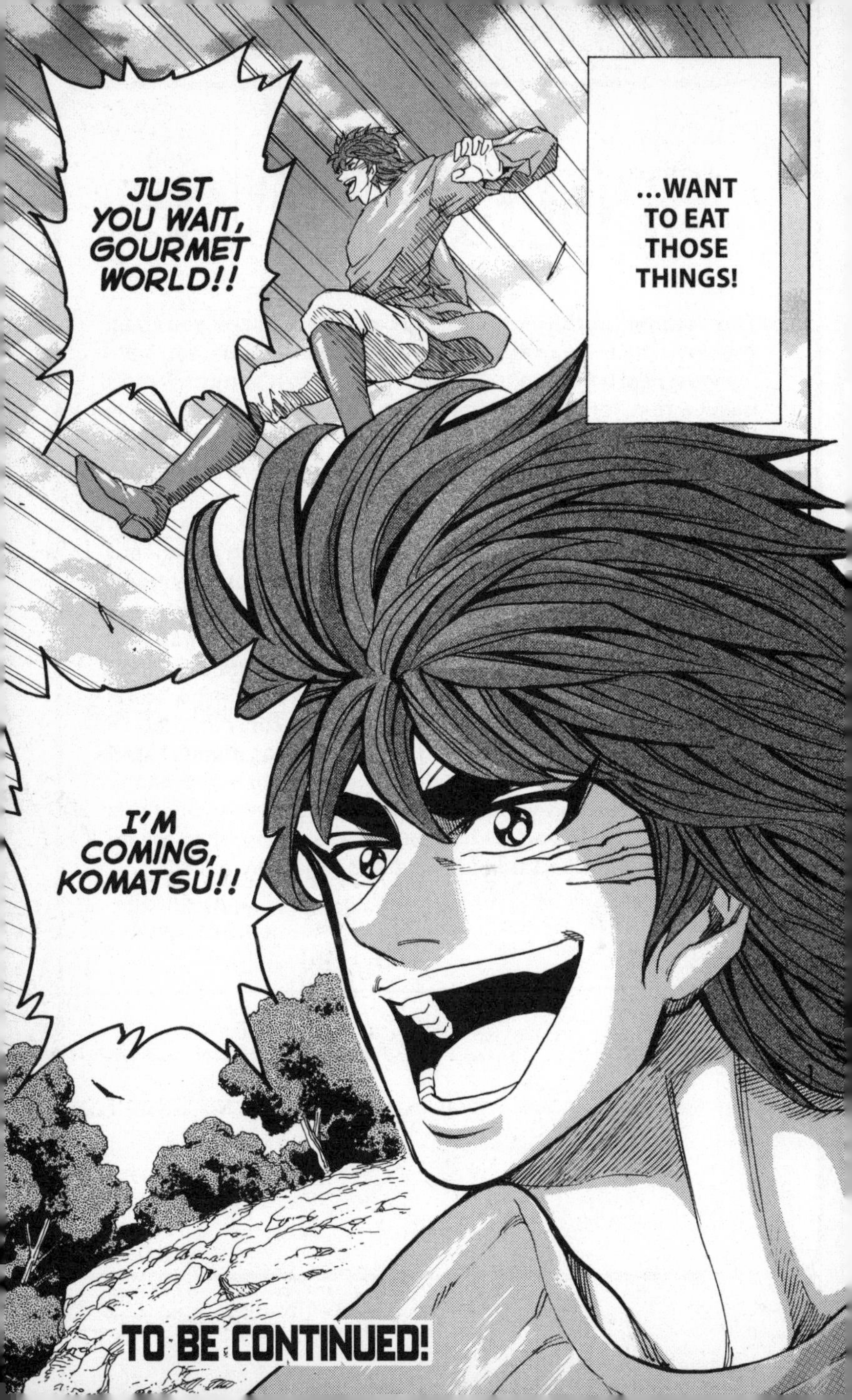
...WANT TO EAT THOSE THINGS!
JUST YOU WAIT, GOURMET WORLD!!
I'M COMING, KOMATSU!!
TO BE CONTINUED!

SHIMABU SPEAKS

This volume concludes the first arc of *Toriko*. Thank you to all the readers who read all the way to this 29th volume. You have my most heartfelt thanks. Really, I appreciate it so much. I can't believe that Toriko has gone on for close to six years. This is the longest serialization I've had in a weekly magazine and it's deeply moving for me. Yep. In more ways than I can say…

That being said, Toriko isn't done yet, and (as of the next chapter) the "Gourmet World Arc" will begin! I'm going to iron out all my feelings, change my attitude and really put my heart into it again! I'm about to turn forty, and my stamina isn't what it used to be in my twenties, but no matter what I'm going to draw *Toriko* to its conclusion (and if it stops before that, then I'm super sorry)!! I'd also like to start working on another story. I know, it's very overambitious of me to even consider that. I'd like to do some more one-shots or the kind of gag manga I used to do back in the day. All I can do is work hard to make manga that readers will enjoy! And with that, take care, everyone! This is Shimabu, signing off and always only realizing when my favorite shoes fall apart that I should've bought two pairs!!

END

COMING NEXT VOLUME

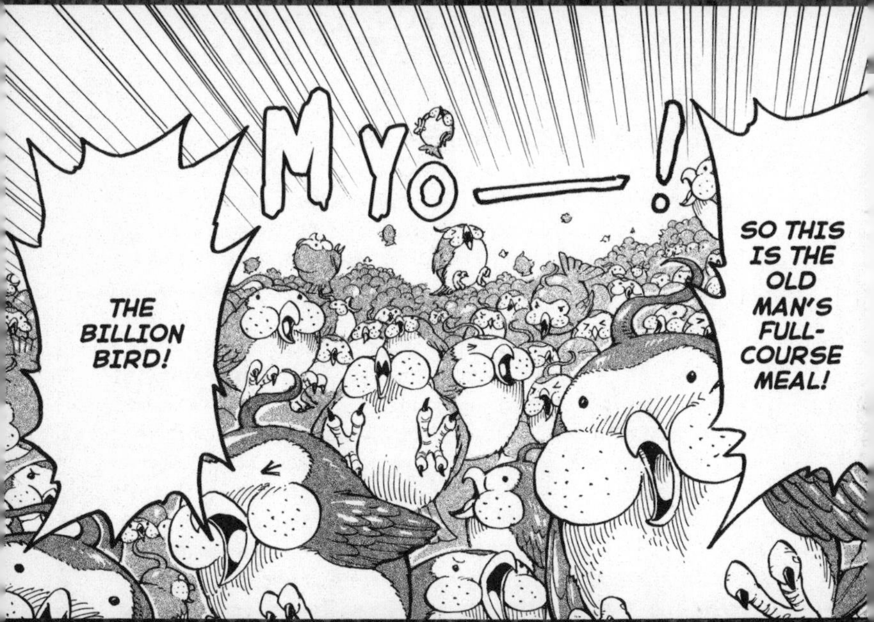
MYO—!
SO THIS IS THE OLD MAN'S FULL-COURSE MEAL!
THE BILLION BIRD!

ONWARD TO THE GOURMET WORLD

The Age of Gourmet is over. More than eighteen months after Meteor Spice destroyed much of the Human World, people struggle to find new food sources. The former President's Full-Course Meal, the Billion Bird, would provide enough food to feed the world—*if* the fowl didn't taste so foul! Can Toriko and friends turn this ugly duckling into the swan of cuisine?

AVAILABLE OCTOBER 2015!

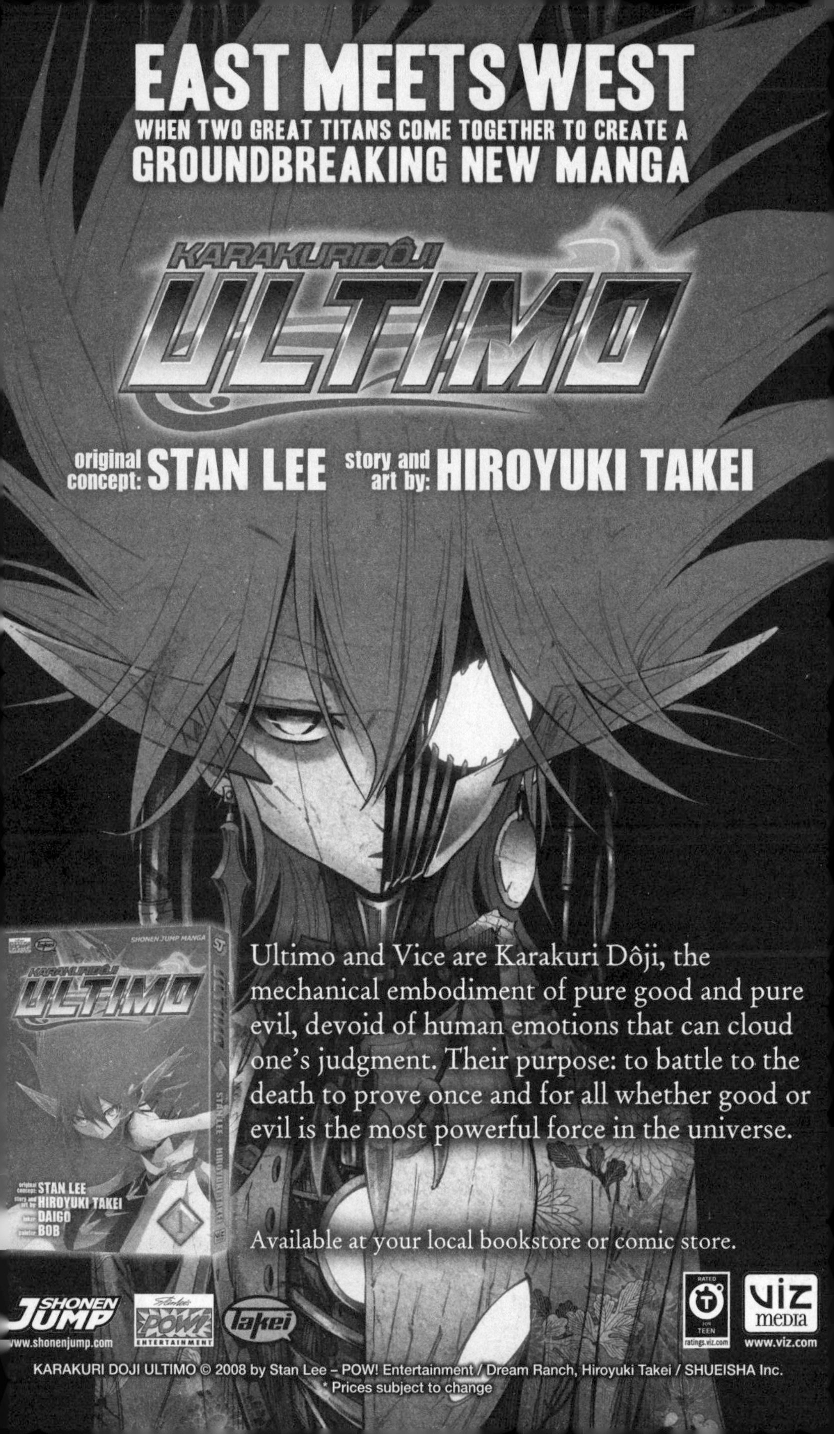

EAST MEETS WEST
WHEN TWO GREAT TITANS COME TOGETHER TO CREATE A
GROUNDBREAKING NEW MANGA
KARAKURIDÔJI
ULTIMO
original concept: STAN LEE
story and art by: HIROYUKI TAKEI
SHONEN JUMP MANGA
KARAKURIDÔJI ULTIMO
original concept STAN LEE
story and art by HIROYUKI TAKEI
inker DAIGO
painter BOB
Ultimo and Vice are Karakuri Dôji, the mechanical embodiment of pure good and pure evil, devoid of human emotions that can cloud one's judgment. Their purpose: to battle to the death to prove once and for all whether good or evil is the most powerful force in the universe.
Available at your local bookstore or comic store.
SHONEN JUMP
www.shonenjump.com
POW! ENTERTAINMENT
Takei
RATED T FOR TEEN
ratings.viz.com
VIZ media
www.viz.com
KARAKURI DOJI ULTIMO © 2008 by Stan Lee – POW! Entertainment / Dream Ranch, Hiroyuki Takei / SHUEISHA Inc.
* Prices subject to change

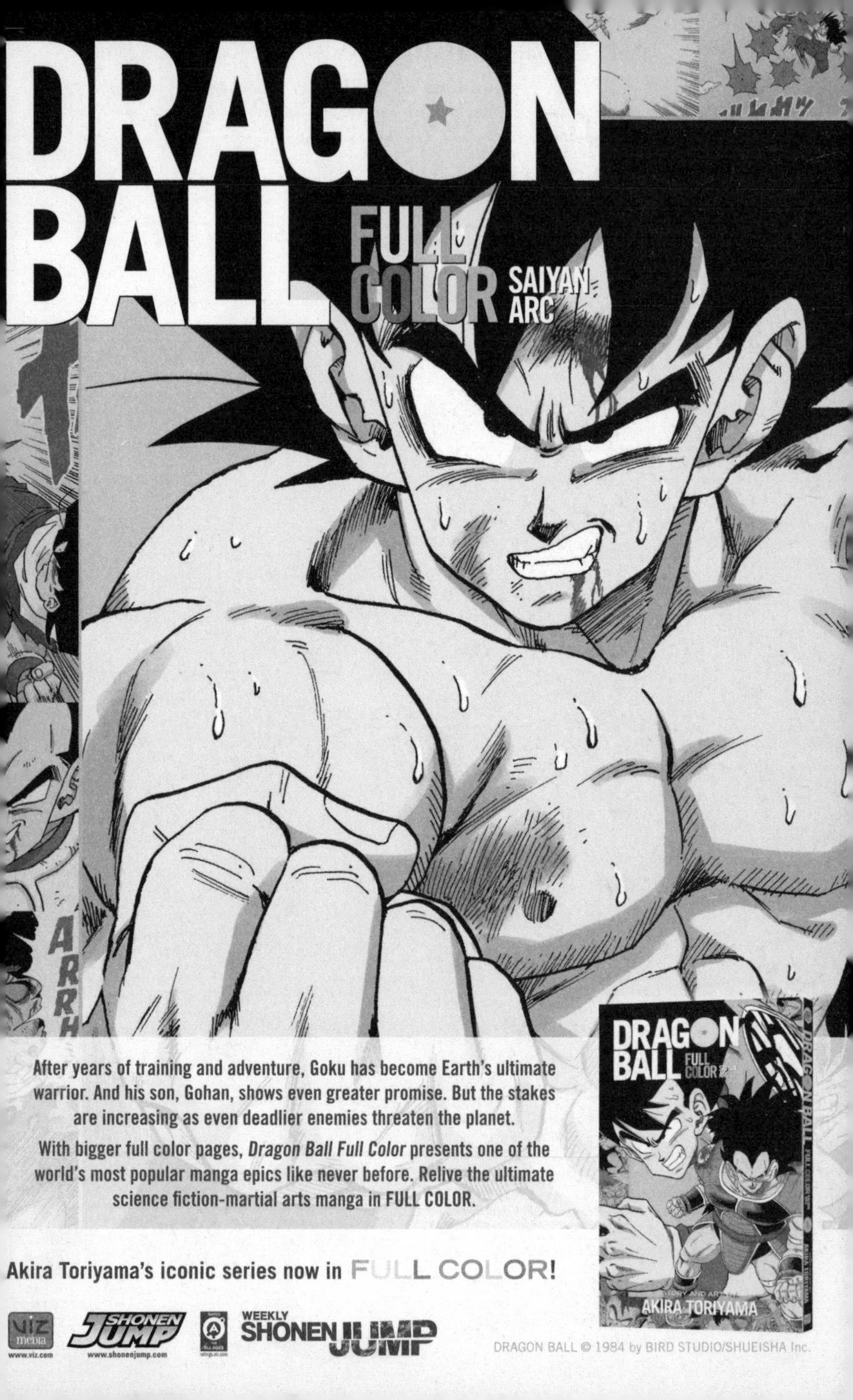
DRAGON BALL
FULL COLOR SAIYAN ARC
ARRH
After years of training and adventure, Goku has become Earth's ultimate warrior. And his son, Gohan, shows even greater promise. But the stakes are increasing as even deadlier enemies threaten the planet.
With bigger full color pages, *Dragon Ball Full Color* presents one of the world's most popular manga epics like never before. Relive the ultimate science fiction-martial arts manga in FULL COLOR.
DRAGON BALL FULL COLOR SAIYAN ARC
STORY AND ART BY
AKIRA TORIYAMA
Akira Toriyama's iconic series now in FULL COLOR!
VIZ media
www.viz.com
SHONEN JUMP
www.shonenjump.com
WEEKLY SHONEN JUMP
DRAGON BALL © 1984 by BIRD STUDIO/SHUEISHA Inc.

You're Reading in the Wrong Direction!!

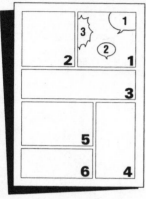

Whoops! Guess what? You're starting at the wrong end of the comic!

...It's true! In keeping with the original Japanese format, **Toriko** is meant to be read from right to left, starting in the upper-right corner.

Unlike English, which is read from left to right, Japanese is read from right to left, meaning that action, sound effects and word-balloon order are completely reversed... something which can make readers unfamiliar with Japanese feel pretty backwards themselves. For this reason, manga or Japanese comics published in the U.S. in English have sometimes been published "flopped"— that is, printed in exact reverse order, as though seen from the other side of a mirror.

By flopping pages, U.S. publishers can avoid confusing readers, but the compromise is not without its downside. For one thing, a character in a flopped manga series who once wore in the original Japanese version a T-shirt emblazoned with "M A Y" (as in "the merry month of") now wears one which reads "Y A M"! Additionally, many manga creators in Japan are themselves unhappy with the process, as some feel the mirror-imaging of their art skews their original intentions.

We are proud to bring you Mitsutoshi Shimabukuro's **Toriko** in the original unflopped format. For now, though, turn to the other side of the book and let the adventure begin...!

—Editor

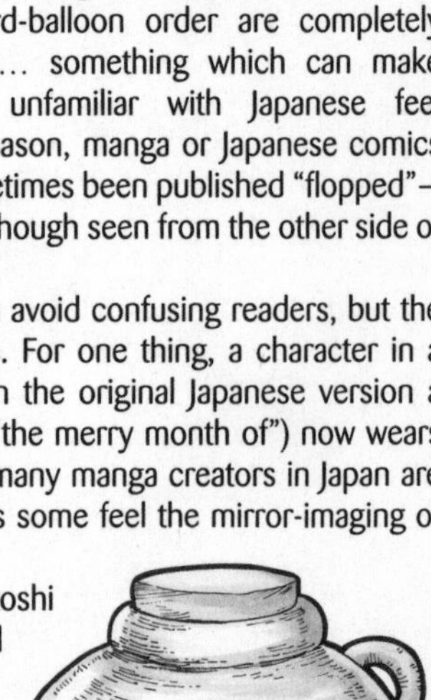